Why

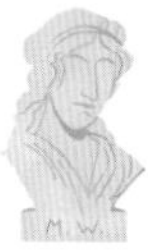
M. W.

She

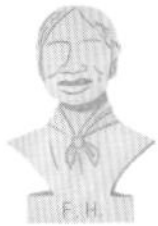
F. H.

Wrote

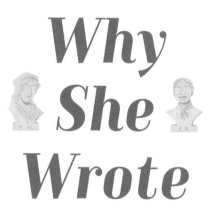

Why She Wrote

A Graphic History of the Lives,
Inspiration, and Influence Behind the
Pens of Classic Women Writers

By Hannah K. Chapman and Lauren Burke
Illustrated by Kaley Bales

CHRONICLE BOOKS
680 SECOND STREET
SAN FRANCISCO, CA 94107

For the writers, the readers, and the listeners.

Library of Congress Cataloging-in-Publication Data
Names: Chapman, Hannah K., author. | Burke, Lauren, author. | Bales, Kaley, illustrator.
Title: Why she wrote : a graphic history of the lives, inspiration, and
influence behind the pens of classic women writers / by Hannah K.
Chapman and Lauren Burke ; illustrated by Kaley Bales.
Description: San Francisco : Chronicle Books, 2021. | Includes bibliographical references.
Identifiers: LCCN 2020047673 | ISBN 9781797202099 (hardcover)
Subjects: LCSH: Women authors--Biography--Comic books, strips, etc. | Women
authors--Biography--Juvenile literature. | LCGFT: Biographies. | Graphic novels.
Classification: LCC PN471 .C45 2021 | DDC 809/.89287 [B]--dc23
LC record available at https://lccn.loc.gov/2020047673

Manufactured in China.

Design by Maggie Edelman.

10 9 8 7 6 5 4 3 2

Chronicle books and gifts are available at special quantity
discounts to corporations, professional associations, literacy
programs, and other organizations. For details and discount
information, please contact our premiums department at
corporatesales@chroniclebooks.com or at 1-800-759-0190.

Chronicle Books LLC
680 Second Street
San Francisco, California 94107
www.chroniclebooks.com

CONTENTS:

INTRODUCTION

It began as a casual conversation between two friends. Now that we were out of college, we didn't have the time for classic literature. We were entering new stages of adulthood, and our days were dominated by an endless train of work: emails and spreadsheets, cocktail mixing and floor mopping. We never got to talk about stories anymore.

A debate ensued over drinks: Who was the Queen of British literature—Jane Austen or Charlotte Brontë? Neither of us had read the entire canon, but we argued anyway. We talked about the ways their books made us feel when we were young women, how they made us want to become writers. We wondered if they would still spark a fire within us, now that we were older and a tiny bit wiser.

For fun, we decided to start a podcast: *Austen vs. Brontë: Bonnets at Dawn*. Just twelve episodes were planned, including "Northanger Abbey vs. Jane Eyre," "Bath vs. Brussels," and "Heathcliff vs. Darcy." We thought that comparing and contrasting the lives and work of these classic women writers would give us fresh insights into their writing, and we were right. While discussing the lives of Jane Austen and Charlotte Brontë, we were struck by their similarities. Both were encouraged to learn and read by their minister fathers; both shared a deep bond with their siblings; both faced frequent economic uncertainties. Both Austen and Brontë received proposals from the brothers of their best friends that they refused. They chose writing over security, each knowing that no husband would encourage, or support, their work. Having committed to their careers, they faced multiple rejections and the challenge of hiding their identities to protect their reputations. Their writing may have been different, but their struggle was the same.

The more we talked about Austen and Brontë, the more other female authors crept into the conversation. Inspired by Austen, Elizabeth Gaskell changed the entire show: Gaskell's own book, *The Life of Charlotte Brontë*, was a major influence on a young writer named Louisa May Alcott, who would, in turn, inspire Beatrix Potter. The more we investigated these connections, the more we realized that our education in women's literature was sorely lacking. We dropped *Austen vs. Brontë* from our title, and the show became a space for biographers and scholars who specialized in women's history and writing to discuss their favorite authors. *Bonnets at Dawn* was now a deep dive into the lives and work of women writers from the eighteenth, nineteenth, and twentieth centuries.

No longer confined by *Austen vs. Brontë*, we were able to expand our reading list to include diarists, activists, poets, and journalists. Once again, patterns emerged. For example, both Frances Hodgson Burnett and Louisa May Alcott wrote for younger audiences as a means of supporting their families, and they were two of the highest earning authors of their time, yet today are dismissed as "just" children's authors. Historically speaking, women's art has rarely been seen as deliberate. Women writers are presented as hobbyists, anomalies, or accidental geniuses. Their authorship is challenged, and their content dismissed. To combat those stereotypes head-on, we wanted to show these women at work.

We narrowed our focus to just eighteen authors: eighteen women whose experiences with publishing were at once relatable and remarkable, and whose stories still resonate today. They were chosen for the stories told about them and what they can tell us about ourselves. Hundreds of years may pass, but we're having the same conversations, facing the same stigmas, and defying the same insecurities.

Each dramatized biography, from Mary Shelley to Louisa May Alcott, focuses on a pivotal moment when their writing became their legacy. These women were daughters, wives, activists, pioneers, and business people. They inspired each other. They supported each other. In a time when women were second-class citizens, each of them was audacious enough to put pen to paper and write. These stories will tell you who she was, what she wanted, and why she wrote.

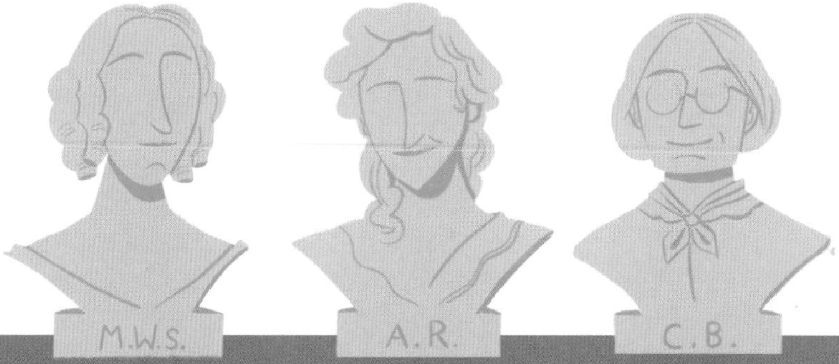
M.W.S.
A.R.
C.B.

The Horror of the Everyday

CHAPTER ONE

"Oh! I am quite delighted with the book! I should like to spend my whole life in reading it," Catherine Morland, the heroine of Jane Austen's *Northanger Abbey*, declares. A fan of "horrid" novels, Catherine is gushing over *The Mysteries of Udolpho* by Ann Radcliffe, which features all of the hallmarks of a classic Gothic text—gloomy atmosphere, wild landscapes, castle ruins, and supernatural twists and turns. When asked why she doesn't read serious and respectable histories, Catherine complains about the lack of female representation. Histories were written by men, while women had found their voice in Gothic novels.

Horace Walpole may have invented the Gothic genre with his novel *The Castle of Otranto* in 1764, but Ann Radcliffe made it her own starting in 1789. She is known as the mother of the Gothic novel, and her influence is palpable in the subsequent work of Jane Austen, Mary Shelley, and the Brontë sisters. Radcliffe's brand of Gothic novel was female-centric. Her stories were told through the eyes of the damsel in distress, who suffered at the hands of a villainous patriarch but prevailed in the end.

Radcliffe also played tricks on her readers. While her novels promised lurid tales of ghosts and monsters, ultimately, the strange phenomenon is always explained. As Sir Walter Scott said of Radcliffe's writing, "All circumstances of her narrative, however mysterious and apparently superhuman, were to be accounted for on natural principles at the winding up of the story." Emily St. Aubert in *The Mysteries of Udolpho* would find that the creature lurking beneath the black veil was nothing more than (spoiler alert) a wax figure. The supernatural served as a misdirect, while the true horror in *The Mysteries of Udolpho,* Emily's abuse and imprisonment at the hands of her uncle, is never concealed.

Radcliffe's heroines found themselves caught up in what Charlotte Brontë would describe in her own Gothic novel *Villette* as a "homely web of truth." Brontë employed Radcliffe's "supernatural explained" device most famously in *Jane Eyre*, when it is revealed that Thornfield Hall is haunted not by a ghost, but rather by the imprisoned wife of the novel's romantic interest, Mr. Rochester. Radcliffe's reveals were rational, but Brontë's were like a loaded gun. In their book *Madwoman in the Attic*, feminist scholars Sandra Gilbert and Susan Gubar assert that Mrs. Rochester serves as the "truest and darkest double" for the titular Jane, a physical manifestation of her repressed rage and anxiety. Through her characters and locked-room imagery, Brontë vents her own feelings and frustrations at the position of women in society.

In the summer of 1816, Mary Shelley was reading Gothic novels, looking for inspiration for her own ghost story. Like Radcliffe, Shelley promised the reader an otherworldly tale in *Frankenstein*: the story of a monster run amok. But the creature's origins are scientific, not supernatural. His pathos, violence, and motivations are revealed. Much like Radcliffe's damsels in distress, he is born and at the mercy of the patriarchal Dr. Frankenstein, a man who dares to take creation into his own hands but abandons his responsibility. Shelley asks the question: Who is the monster, the creature or the man who created his own dark double?

Gothic literature was often referred to as the trash of circulating libraries. Critics of Brontë and Shelley labeled them as coarse, antireligious works and demanded to know what sort of women would write such horrid books. But a better question to ask is: Why they were writing about monsters that weren't monsters, or ghosts that weren't ghosts? The supernatural masked serious conversations Radcliffe, Shelley, and Brontë were exploring about the female condition. Beneath their wild plot lines and shocking reveals, these Gothic novels reflect women trying to make sense of their lives.

Mary Wollstonecraft Shelley

1797–1851

"Invention, it must be humbly admitted, does not consist
in creating out of void, but out of chaos..."

Introduction from the revised edition of *Frankenstein*, 1831

Mary Shelley is a legend. A woman so goth, she carried around her dead husband's calcified heart until the day she died; she made a monster and a whole new literary genre. It's not just *Frankenstein*, it's Mary Shelley's *Frankenstein*.

But before she was a brand, she was a budding writer living in the shadow of her famous parents, Mary Wollstonecraft and William Godwin. Young Mary lost her mother in childbirth, but found her between the pages of her books, and it was said that she learned to read by tracing the letters on her mother's gravestone. Later, she would learn to write by using Wollstonecraft's work as her inspiration.

Mary was raised by her father and stepmother in a busy household that included a mix of half- and stepsiblings. While Mary had no formal education, she was tutored by her father, who was impressed by his daughter's passion and aptitude for learning. Money was tight for the esteemed philosopher, and so in addition to his bookshop and publishing company, he took on students to earn extra funds.

In 1812, Godwin began mentoring the poet Percy Bysshe Shelley. Shelley was an aristocrat who fancied himself a political radical. He hero-worshipped William Godwin, and fell madly in love with sixteen-year-old Mary. Mary adored Shelley and felt that their union echoed the working and romantic relationship of her parents Mary Wollstonecraft and William Godwin. To her surprise, her father was unsupportive of the match; Shelley was a married man, with a child on the way. In 1814, Shelley abandoned his family to start a new life with Mary and her stepsister Claire Clairmont. The three toured the Continent and made plans to start a free-love utopia, but they were ultimately deterred by a lack of funds. Upon her return to London, Mary gave birth to a baby girl, who would die just a few weeks later.

In May 1816, the trio traveled to Geneva, Switzerland, to spend the summer with the infamous poet Lord Byron. Described as "mad, bad, and dangerous to know" by his lover Lady Caroline Lamb, the literary celebrity was in exile following a scandalous divorce. Percy was in awe, Claire was in love, and Mary was lost. Still recovering from the death of her daughter and estranged from her beloved father, she struggled to find her place in the group. While Percy and Byron produced poem after poem, Mary remained silent—but a volcanic eruption would help her find her voice.

The year 1816 was known as the year without a summer. Ash from the 1815 explosion of Mount Tambora in Indonesia billowed into the atmosphere and blotted out the sun, causing severe weather conditions throughout Europe. The violent storms that confined Mary indoors would also enable her to pour her grief and anger into a book that would in turn propel her to literary infamy.

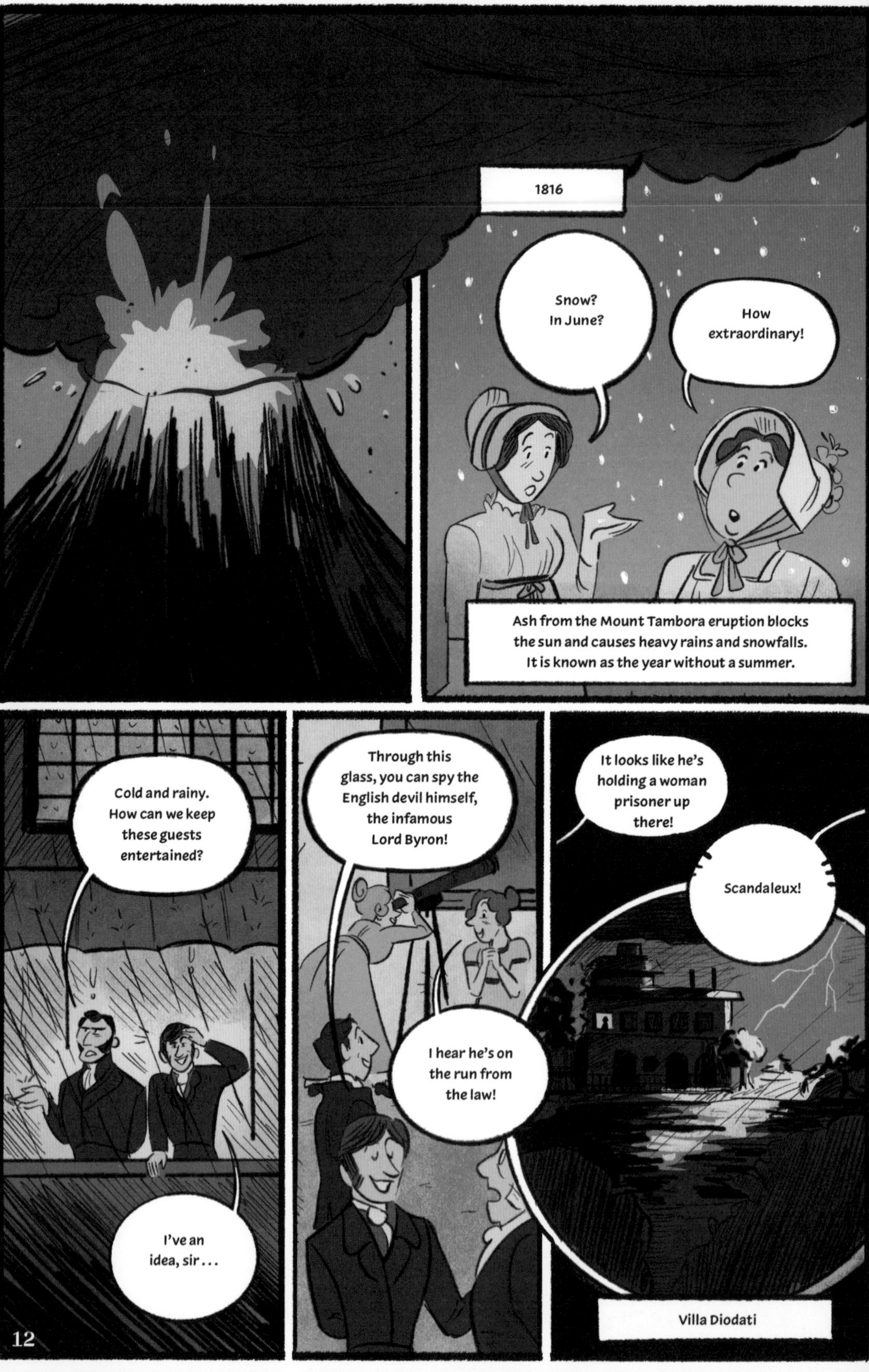
1816
Snow? In June?
How extraordinary!
Ash from the Mount Tambora eruption blocks the sun and causes heavy rains and snowfalls. It is known as the year without a summer.
Cold and rainy. How can we keep these guests entertained?
I've an idea, sir . . .
Through this glass, you can spy the English devil himself, the infamous Lord Byron!
I hear he's on the run from the law!
It looks like he's holding a woman prisoner up there!
Scandaleux!
Villa Diodati

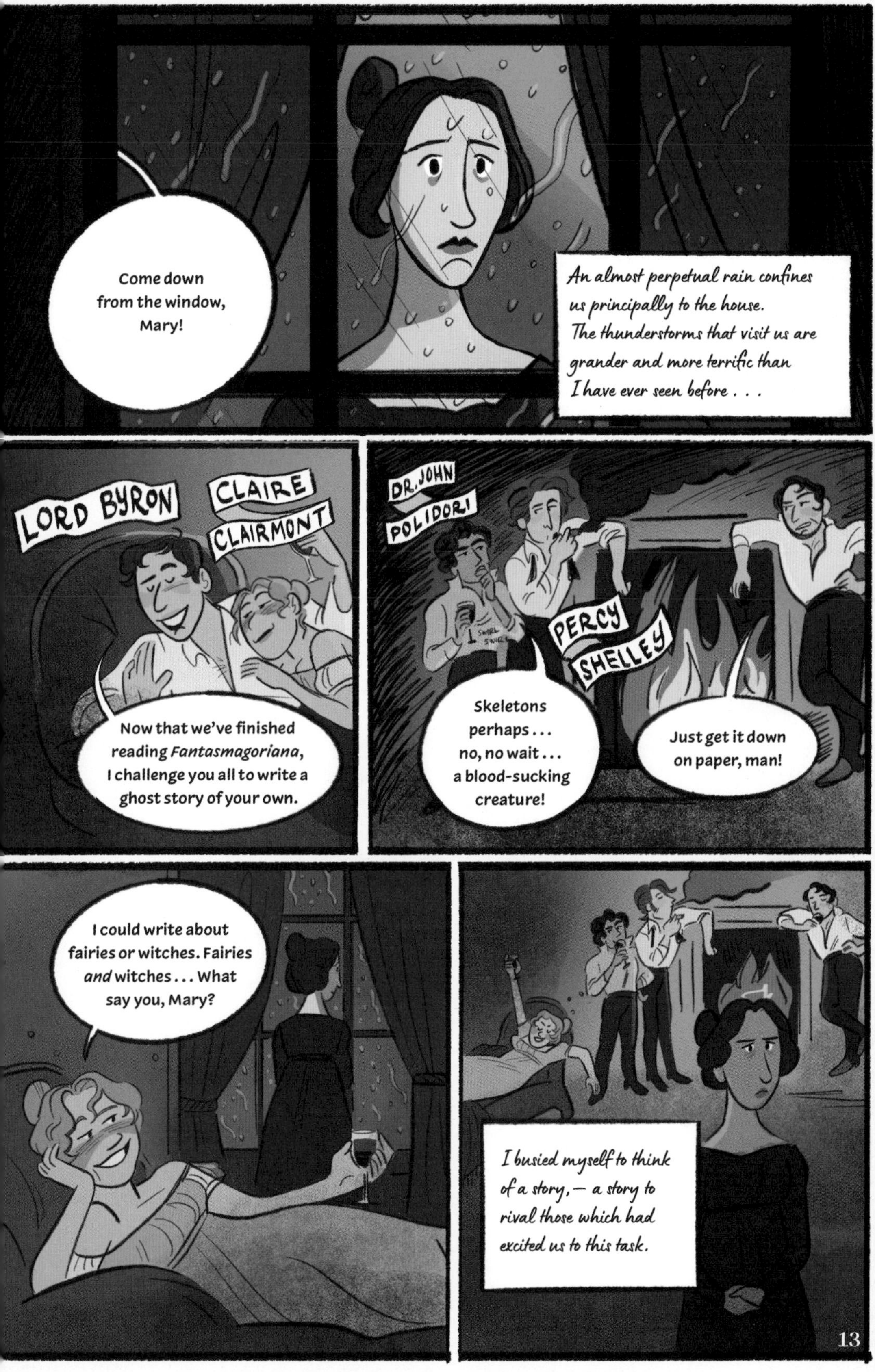
Come down from the window, Mary!
An almost perpetual rain confines us principally to the house. The thunderstorms that visit us are grander and more terrific than I have ever seen before . . .
LORD BYRON
CLAIRE CLAIRMONT
Now that we've finished reading *Fantasmagoriana*, I challenge you all to write a ghost story of your own.
DR. JOHN POLIDORI
PERCY SHELLEY
SWIRL SWIRL
Skeletons perhaps . . . no, no wait . . . a blood-sucking creature!
Just get it down on paper, man!
I could write about fairies or witches. Fairies *and* witches . . . What say you, Mary?
I busied myself to think of a story, — a story to rival those which had excited us to this task.

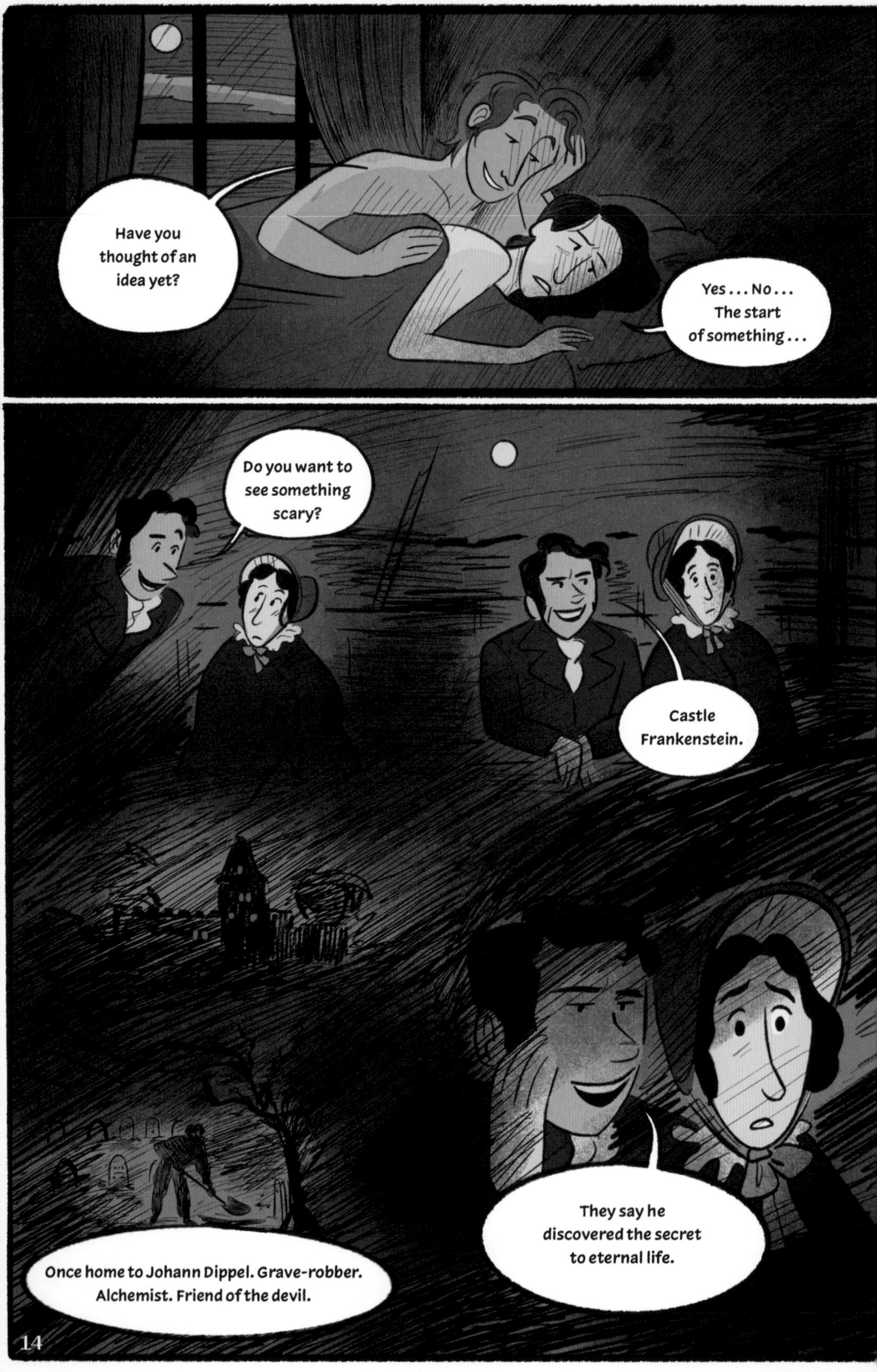
Have you thought of an idea yet?
Yes . . . No . . . The start of something . . .
Do you want to see something scary?
Castle Frankenstein.
Once home to Johann Dippel. Grave-robber. Alchemist. Friend of the devil.
They say he discovered the secret to eternal life.

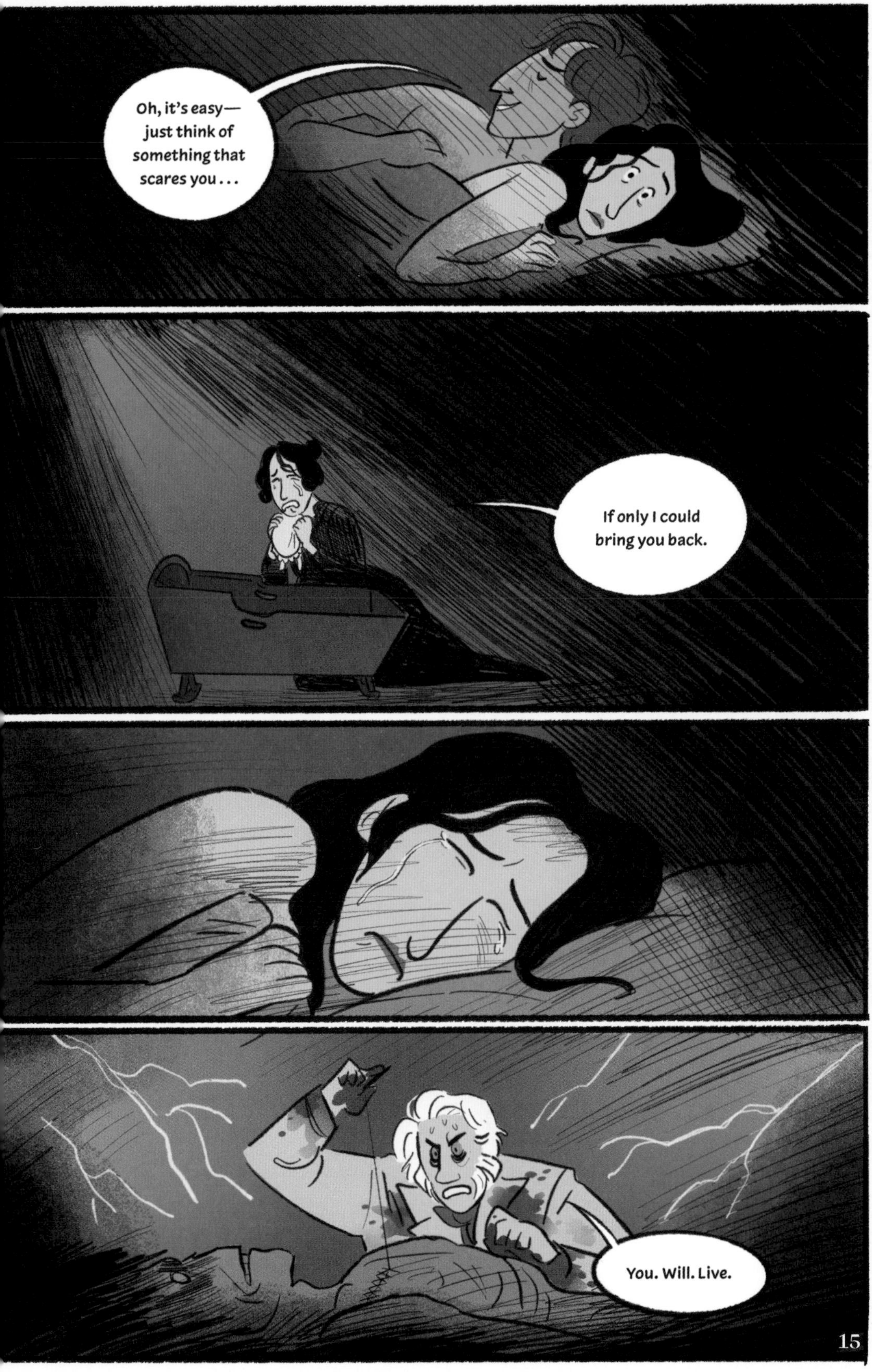
Oh, it's easy—just think of something that scares you . . .
If only I could bring you back.
You. Will. Live.

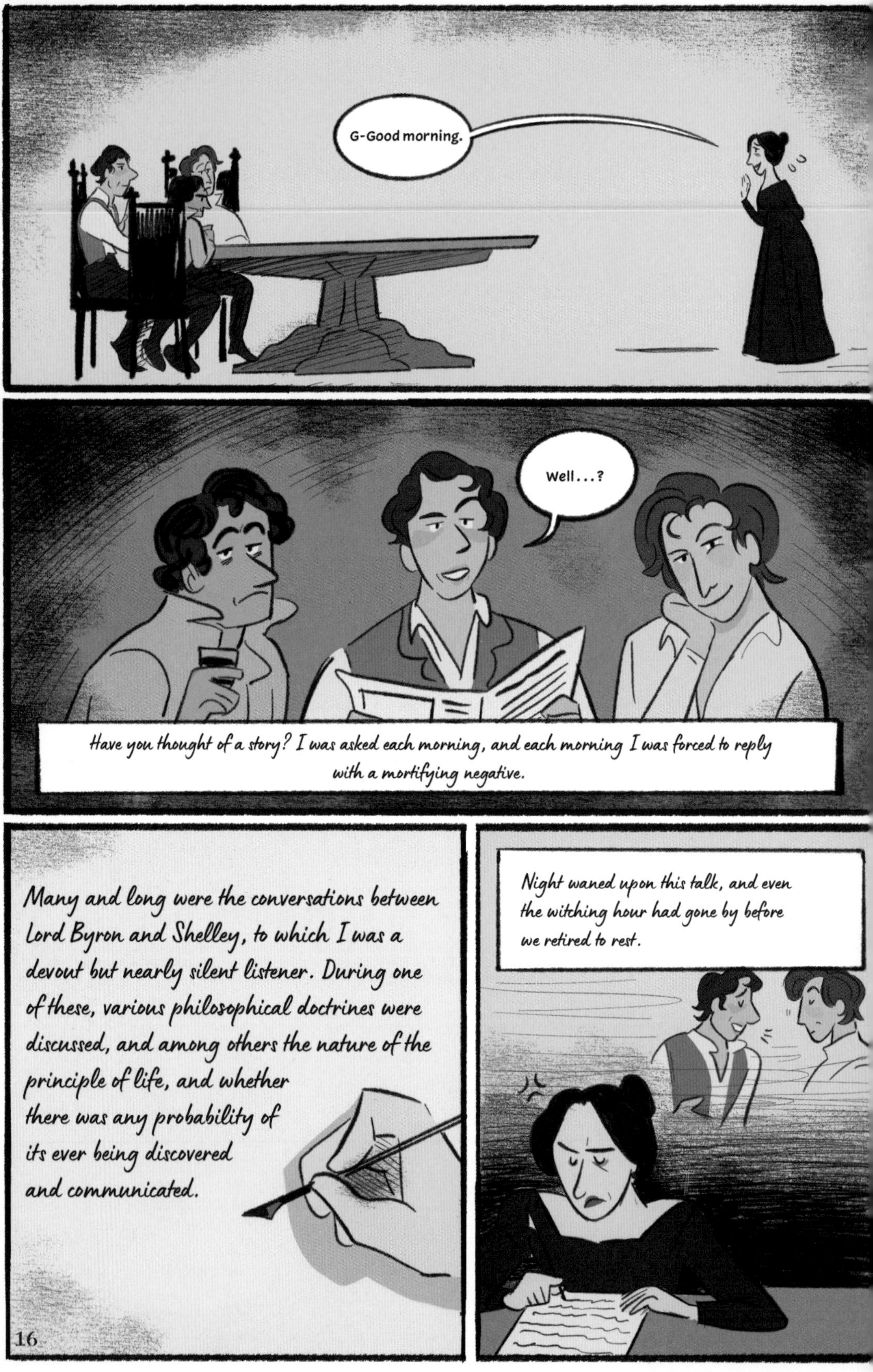
G-Good morning.
Well...?
Have you thought of a story? I was asked each morning, and each morning I was forced to reply with a mortifying negative.
Many and long were the conversations between Lord Byron and Shelley, to which I was a devout but nearly silent listener. During one of these, various philosophical doctrines were discussed, and among others the nature of the principle of life, and whether there was any probability of its ever being discovered and communicated.
Night waned upon this talk, and even the witching hour had gone by before we retired to rest.

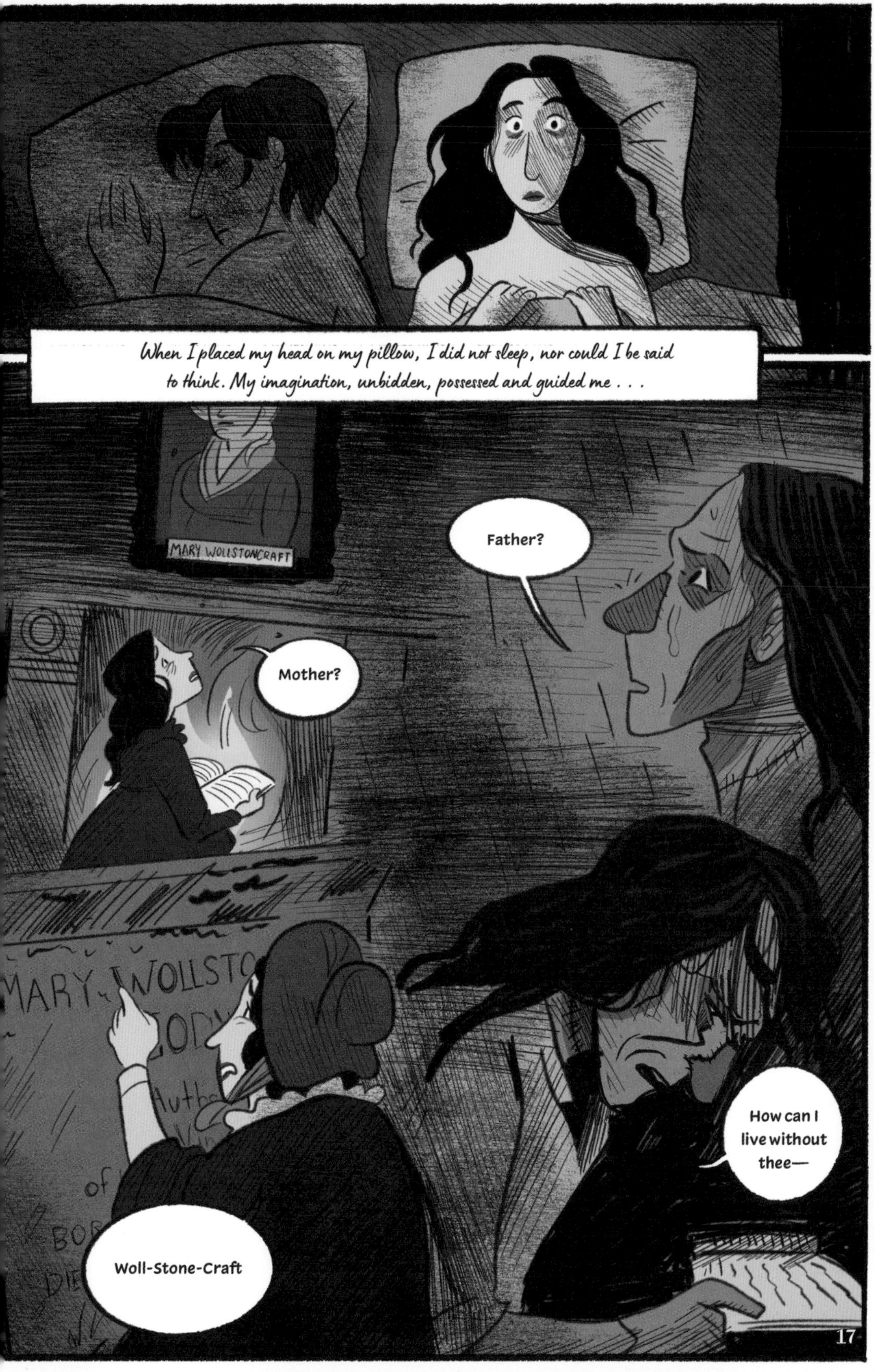
When I placed my head on my pillow, I did not sleep, nor could I be said to think. My imagination, unbidden, possessed and guided me . . .
MARY WOLLSTONECRAFT
Father?
Mother?
How can I live without thee—
Woll-Stone-Craft

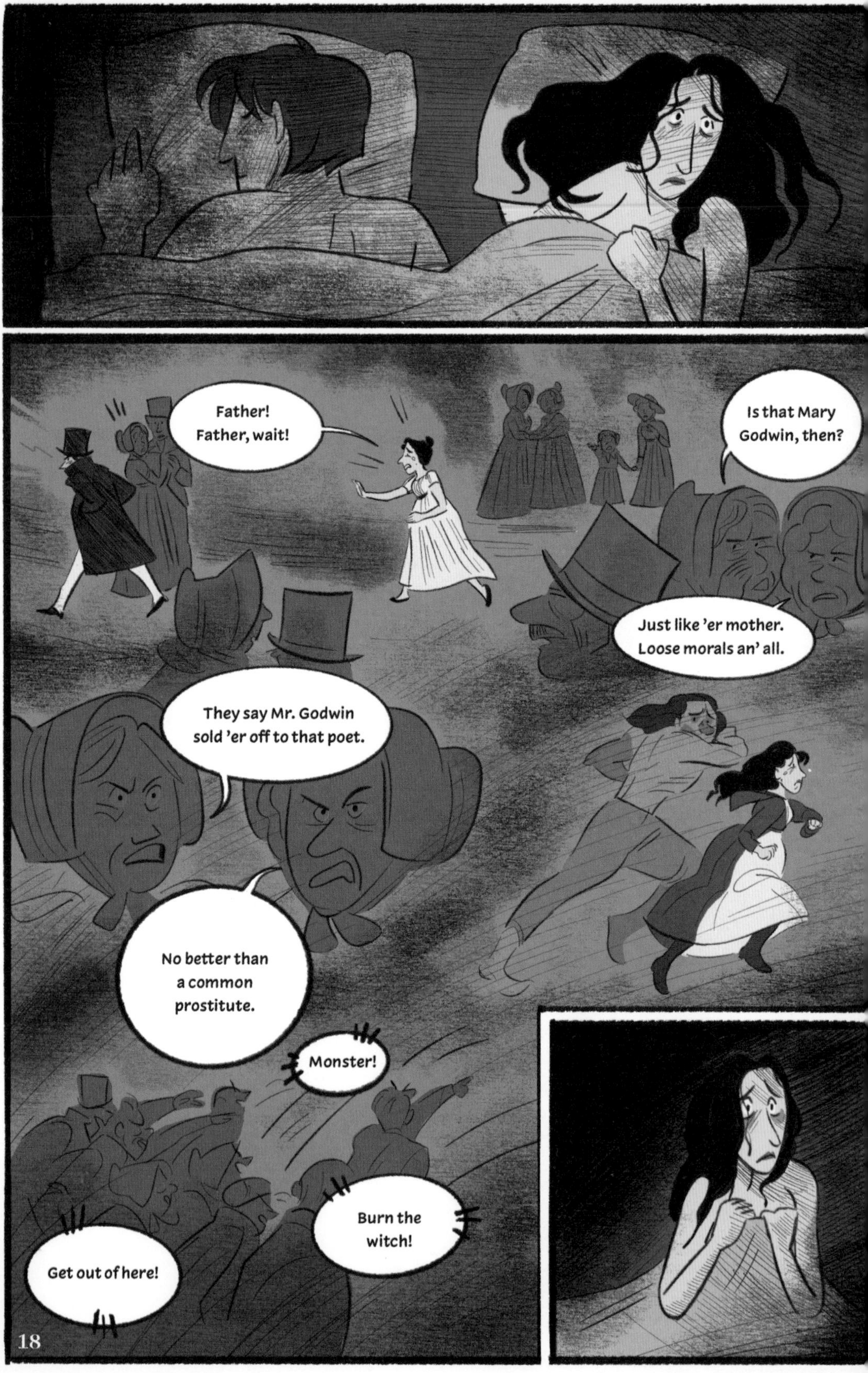
Father!
Father, wait!
Is that Mary Godwin, then?
Just like 'er mother. Loose morals an' all.
They say Mr. Godwin sold 'er off to that poet.
No better than a common prostitute.
Monster!
Burn the witch!
Get out of here!

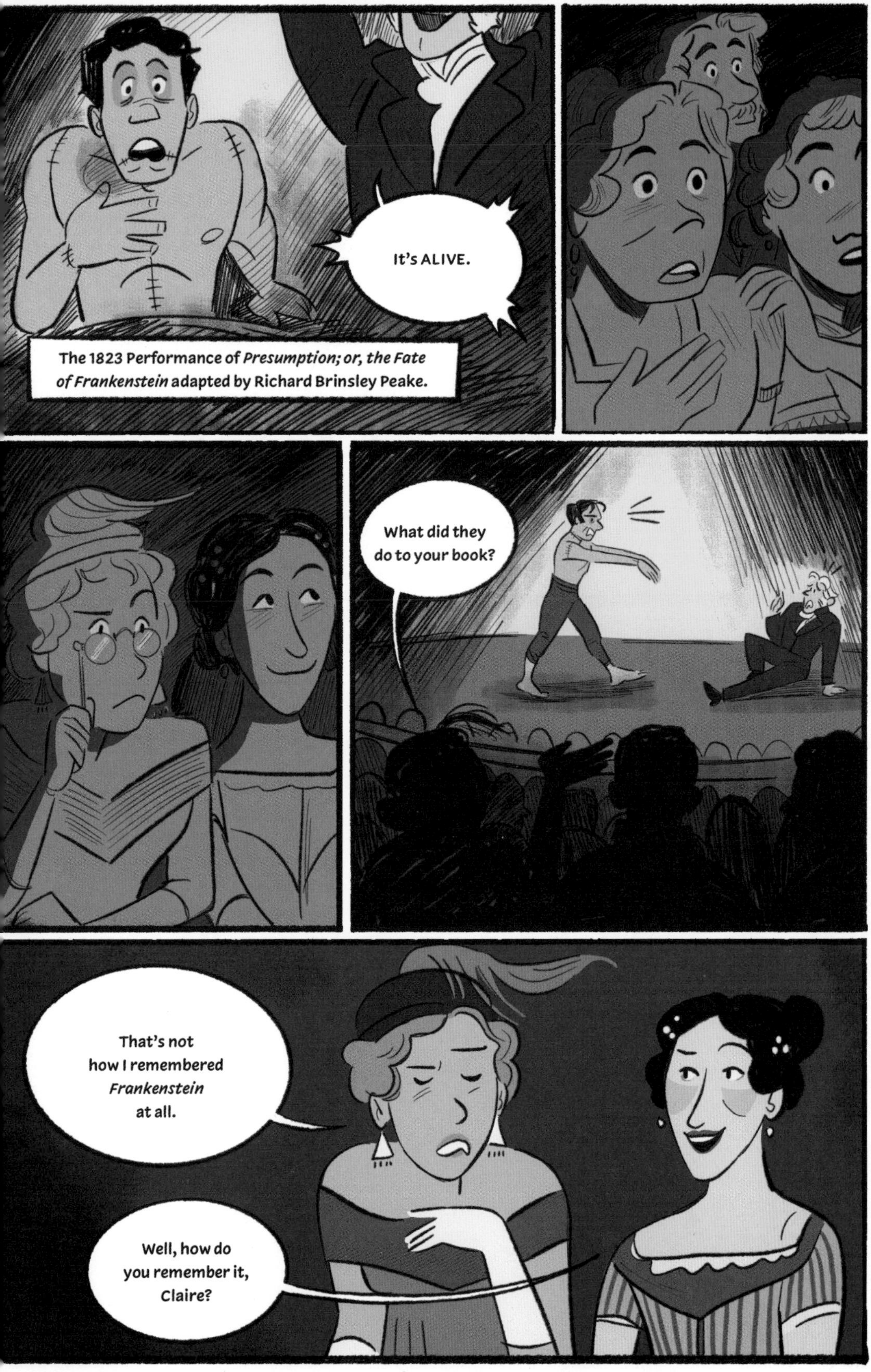

It's ALIVE.
The 1823 Performance of *Presumption; or, the Fate of Frankenstein* adapted by Richard Brinsley Peake.
What did they do to your book?
That's not how I remembered *Frankenstein* at all.
Well, how do you remember it, Claire?

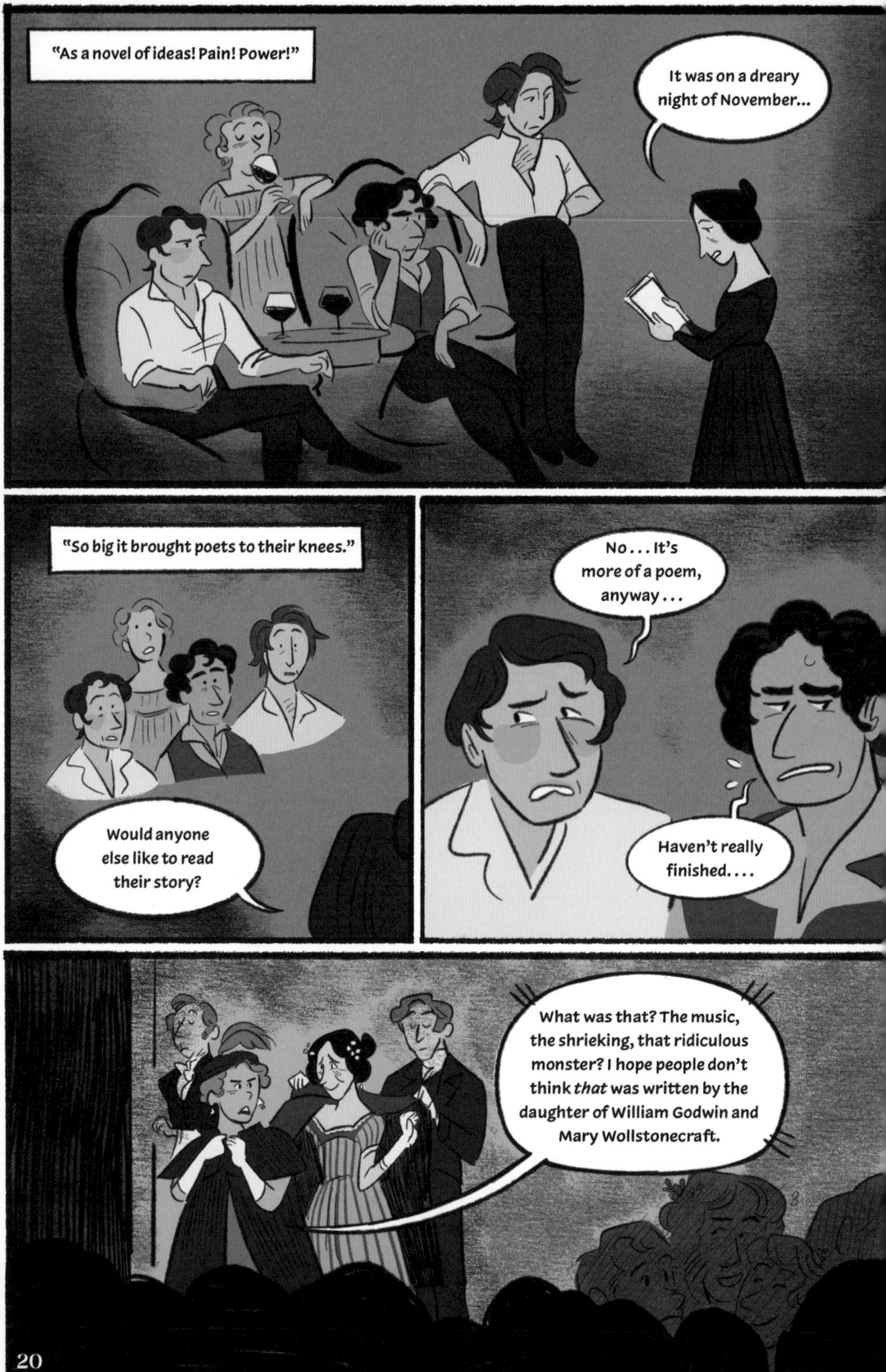
"As a novel of ideas! Pain! Power!"
It was on a dreary night of November...
"So big it brought poets to their knees."
Would anyone else like to read their story?
No . . . It's more of a poem, anyway . . .
Haven't really finished. . . .
What was that? The music, the shrieking, that ridiculous monster? I hope people don't think *that* was written by the daughter of William Godwin and Mary Wollstonecraft.

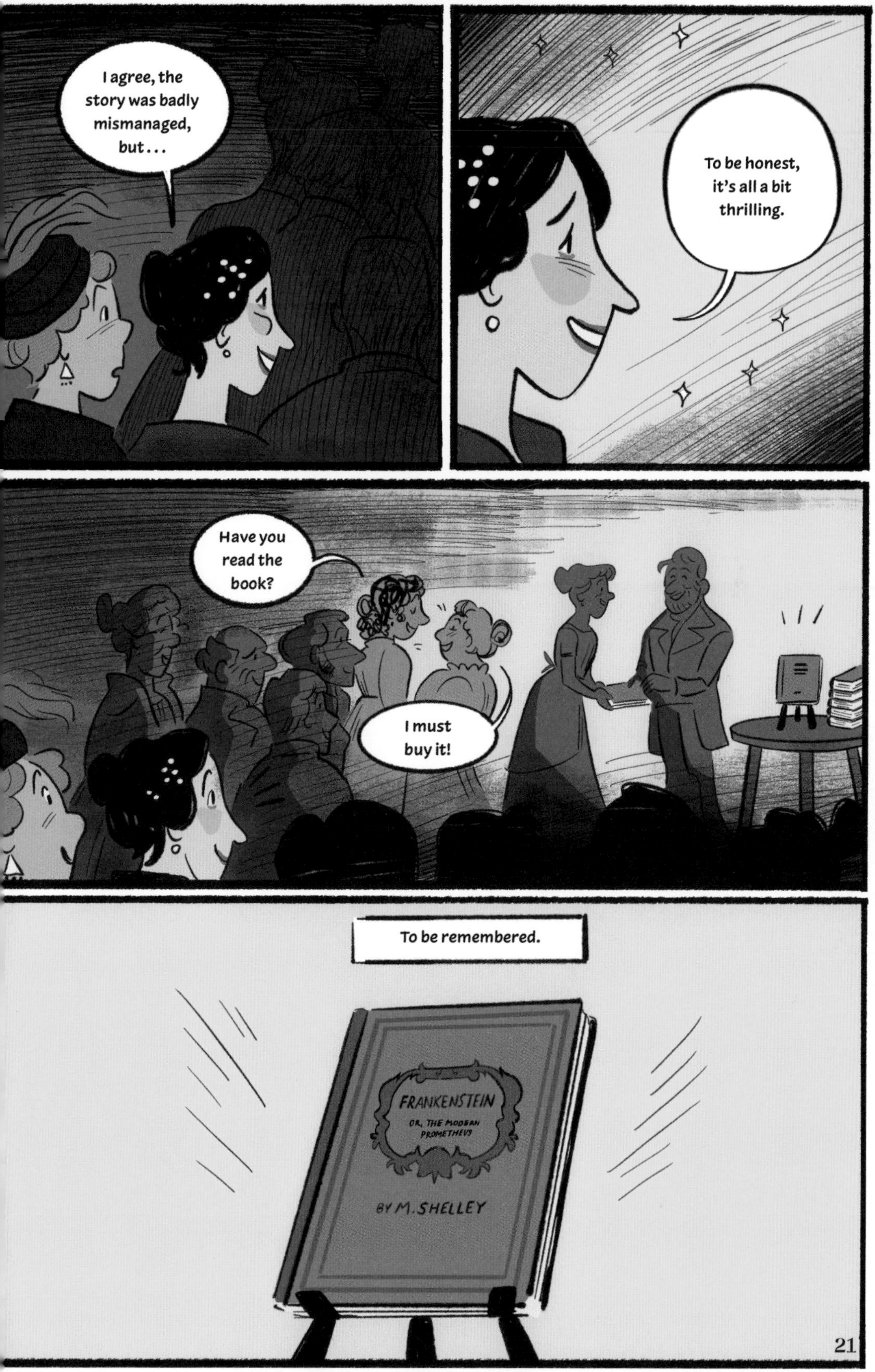
I agree, the story was badly mismanaged, but . . .
To be honest, it's all a bit thrilling.
Have you read the book?
I must buy it!
To be remembered.
FRANKENSTEIN
OR, THE MODERN PROMETHEUS
BY M. SHELLEY

Frankenstein's monster through the ages:

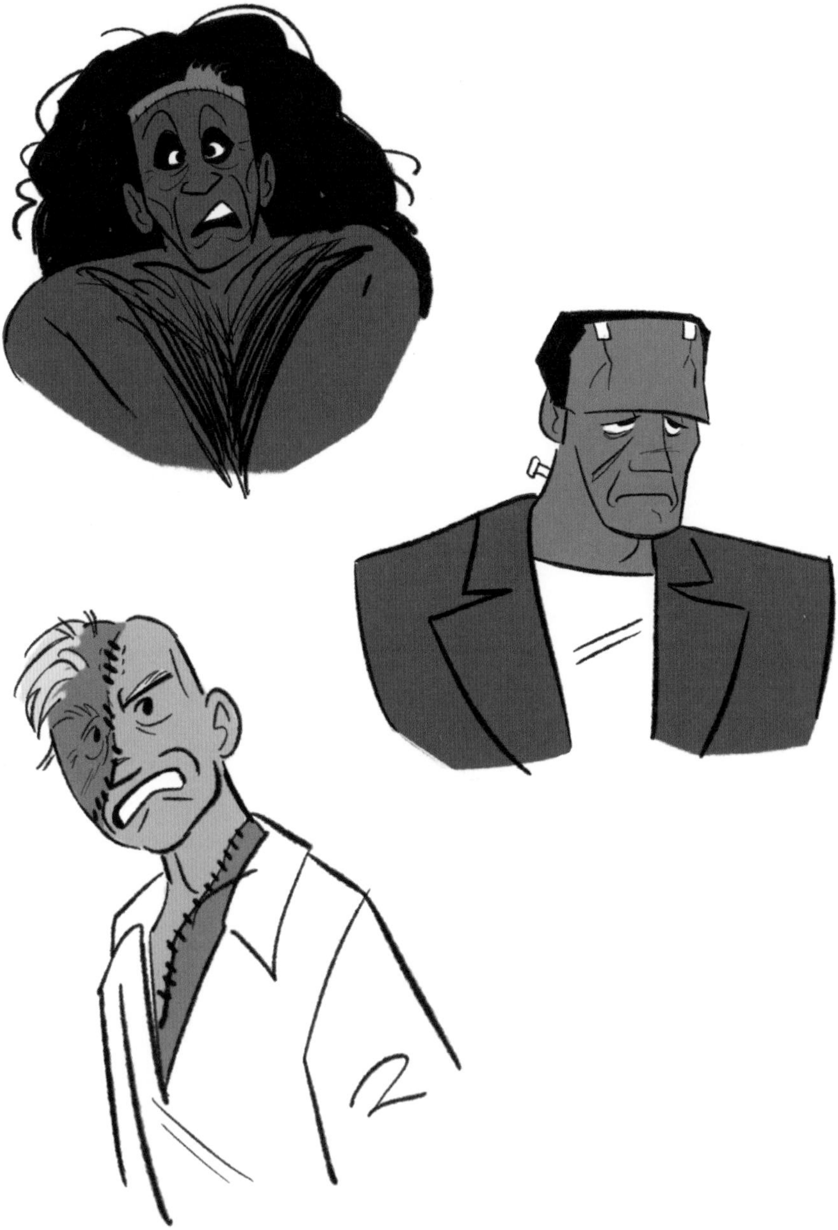

Mary Shelley modeled the first draft of her Gothic novella *Mathilda* after "The Cave of Fancy," a short story written by her mother, Mary Wollstonecraft.

Diarist Anne Lister often wrote book reviews in her journals, and with her interests in human anatomy and sciences, it's no wonder that she enjoyed *Frankenstein*. She called it a "strangely odd, genius-like cleverly written thing."

SELECTED WORKS:

TRAVELOGUES

1817: *History of a Six Weeks' Tour through a Part of France, Switzerland, Germany, and Holland: With Letters Descriptive of a Sail Round the Lake of Geneva, and of the Glaciers of Chamouni*
1844: *Rambles in Germany and Italy, in 1840, 1842, and 1843*

NOVELS

1818: *Frankenstein: Or, The Modern Prometheus*
1823: *Valperga: Or, the Life and Adventures of Castruccio, Prince of Lucca*
1826: *The Last Man*
1830: *The Fortunes of Perkin Warbeck: A Romance*
1835: *Lodore*
1837: *Falkner*
1959: *Mathilda* [published posthumously]

Ann Radcliffe

1764–1823

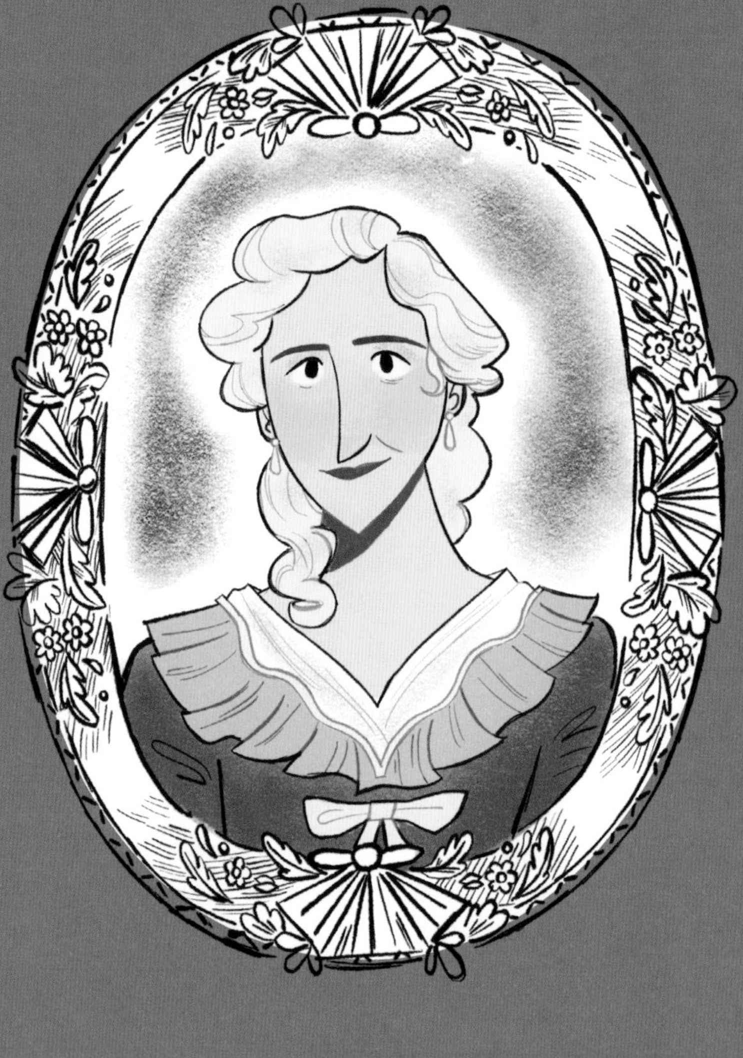

"You speak like a heroine . . .
We shall see whether you can suffer like one."

—*Mysteries of Udolpho*, 1794

In 1883, the poet Christina Rossetti set out to write the biography of one of her greatest literary influences. Shortly after she began researching the woman known as the Great Enchantress, Rossetti wrote to her editor, "I despair and withdraw." She found it impossible to piece together the life of Ann Radcliffe. There simply wasn't enough information.

While the facts are few and far between, it is known that she was born Ann Ward on July 9, 1764. Just a few years later, her family moved from London to Bath, where her father managed a china shop. In 1787, the middle-class, well-read, well-educated Ann married Oxford graduate William Radcliffe. William worked late into the night as an editor and part-owner of the newspaper *The English Chronicle*, and to pass her time alone, Ann wrote poetry, romance, and Gothic fiction, which she would read to him when he returned home. Her first novel, *The Castles of Athlin and Dunbayne*, a romance set in the Scottish Highlands, was published in 1789 to moderate success. It was her third book, *The Romance of the Forest*, in 1791, that propelled her to fame.

A naturally shy person, Ann Radcliffe didn't relish the celebrity. Upon her death, *The Edinburgh Review* wrote that "she never appeared in public, nor mingled in private society, but kept herself apart, like the sweet bird that sings its solitary notes, shrouded and unseen." But Ann Radcliffe was no homebody. Radcliffe frequently attended the opera and theater, but preferred the cheap seats where she wouldn't be recognized. More than anything, she loved to travel with her husband, William. They toured England from north to south. They went abroad to Germany and Holland. Like her own Gothic heroines, she found an escape in the natural world, far from her everyday life.

By the time she was thirty-three, Ann Radcliffe had published five novels and was one of the highest paid and most critically acclaimed authors of her day. Her readers went into a frenzy when she abruptly disappeared from the literary scene in 1797. There was rampant speculation as to her whereabouts. Some theorized that Ann had ended up in a French dungeon. Others believed that she had been driven mad by her own writing, and was institutionalized during the last years of her life. The rumors were so persistent that, following her death, her husband made it clear that his wife had never been to an asylum and had actually died from complications of asthma.

We'll never know what caused Ann to leave the literary scene altogether, but we do know that she continued writing. Ann's final novel, *Gaston de Blondeville*, was published posthumously in 1826 and solidified her reputation as the Shakespeare of Romantic fiction. Her writing and impact on the genre would long outlive her.

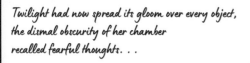
Twilight had now spread its gloom over every object,
the dismal obscurity of her chamber
recalled fearful thoughts...

Darkness, indeed, in the present state of her spirits, made
silence and solitude terrible to her...

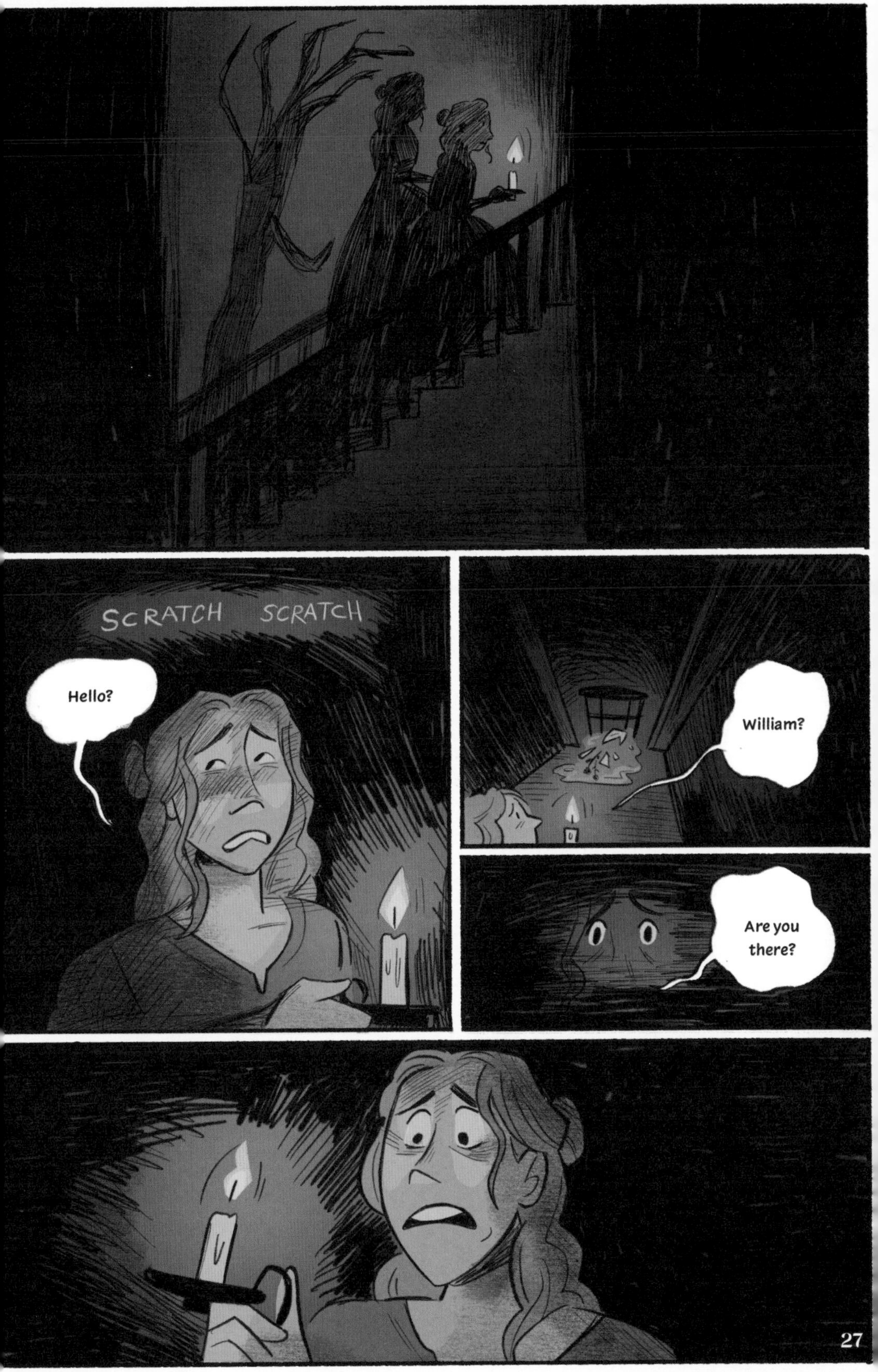
SCRATCH SCRATCH
Hello?
William?
Are you there?

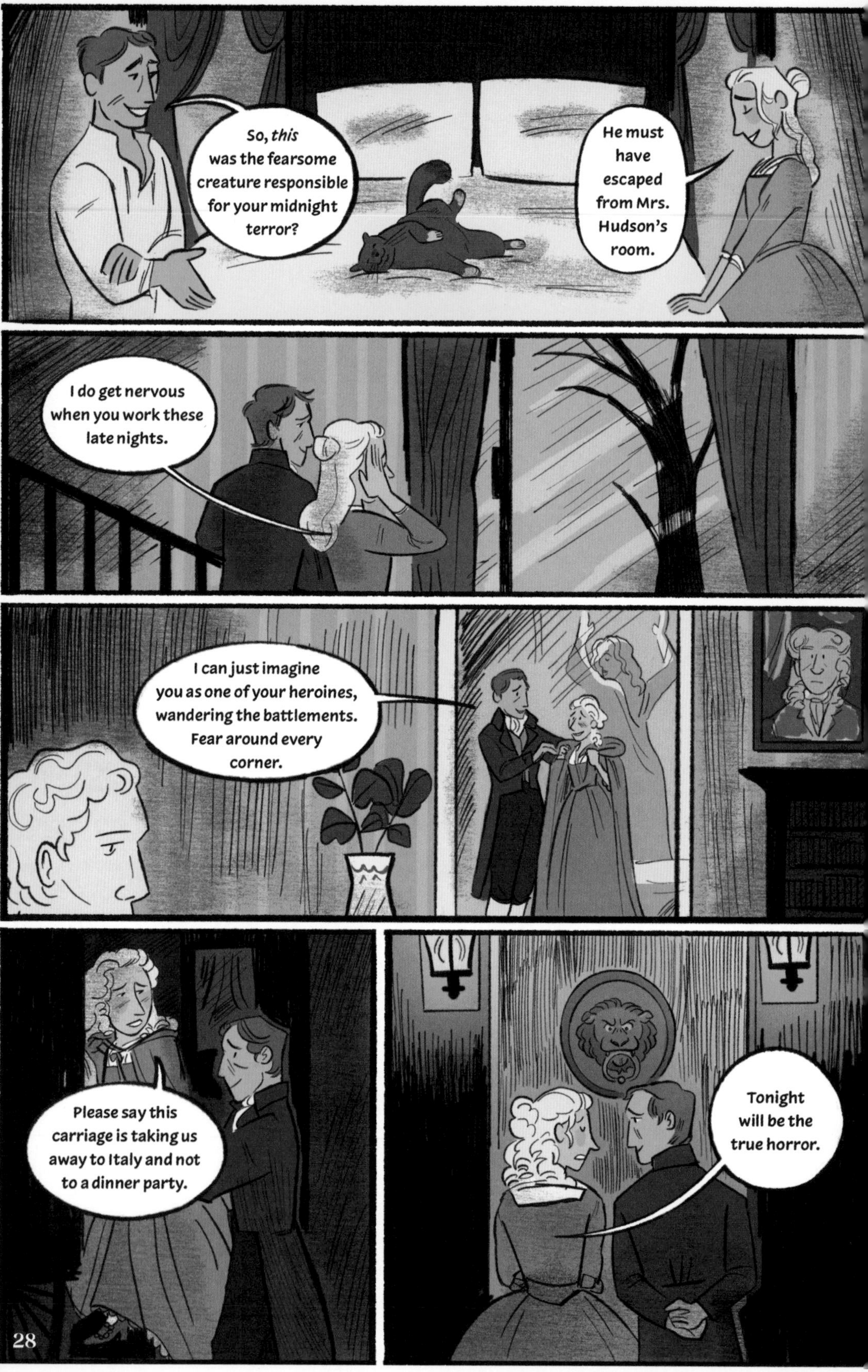
So, *this* was the fearsome creature responsible for your midnight terror?
He must have escaped from Mrs. Hudson's room.
I do get nervous when you work these late nights.
I can just imagine you as one of your heroines, wandering the battlements. Fear around every corner.
Please say this carriage is taking us away to Italy and not to a dinner party.
Tonight will be the true horror.

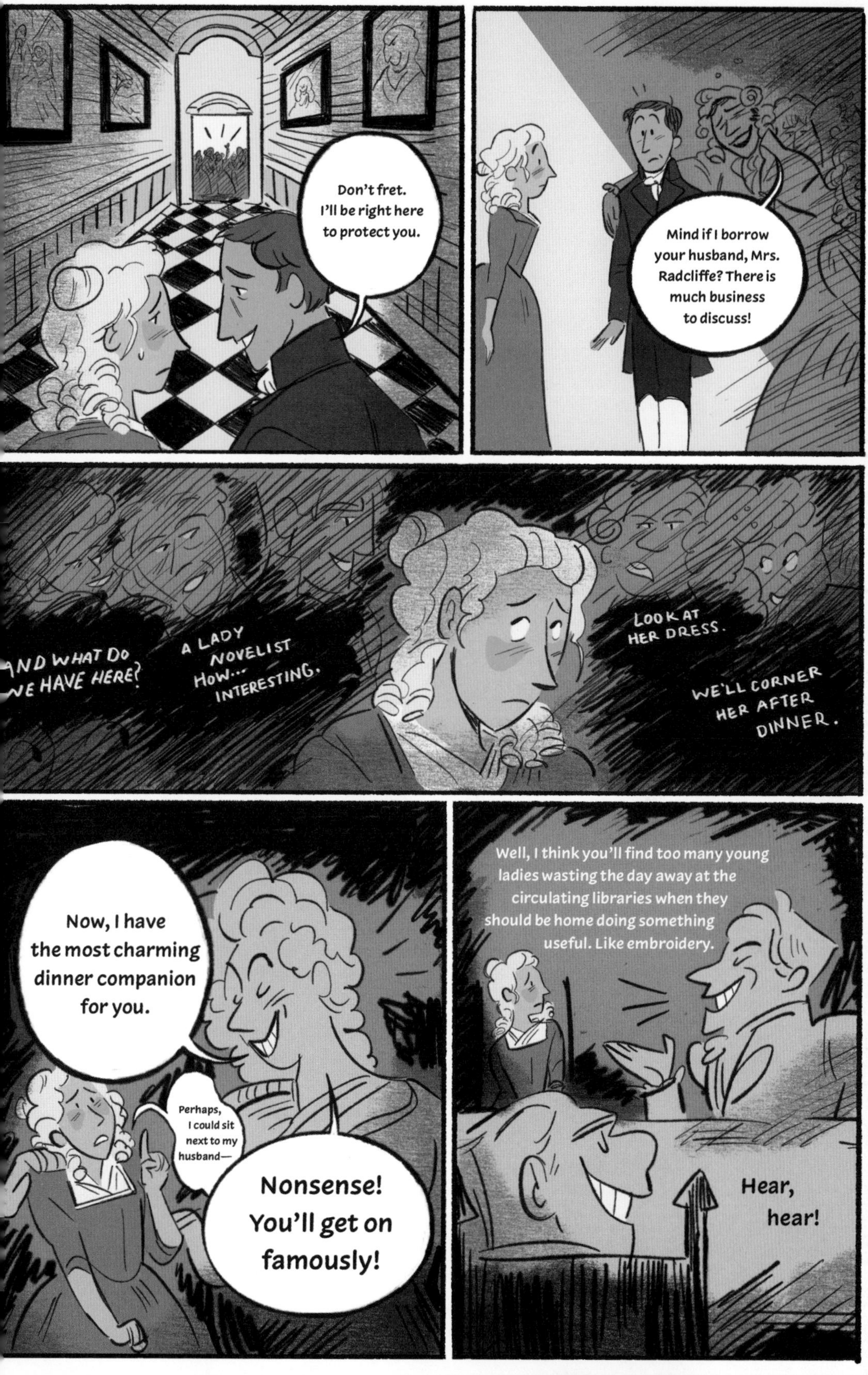
Don't fret. I'll be right here to protect you.
Mind if I borrow your husband, Mrs. Radcliffe? There is much business to discuss!
AND WHAT DO WE HAVE HERE?
A LADY NOVELIST HOW... INTERESTING.
LOOK AT HER DRESS.
WE'LL CORNER HER AFTER DINNER.
Now, I have the most charming dinner companion for you.
Perhaps, I could sit next to my husband—
Nonsense! You'll get on famously!
Well, I think you'll find too many young ladies wasting the day away at the circulating libraries when they should be home doing something useful. Like embroidery.
Hear, hear!

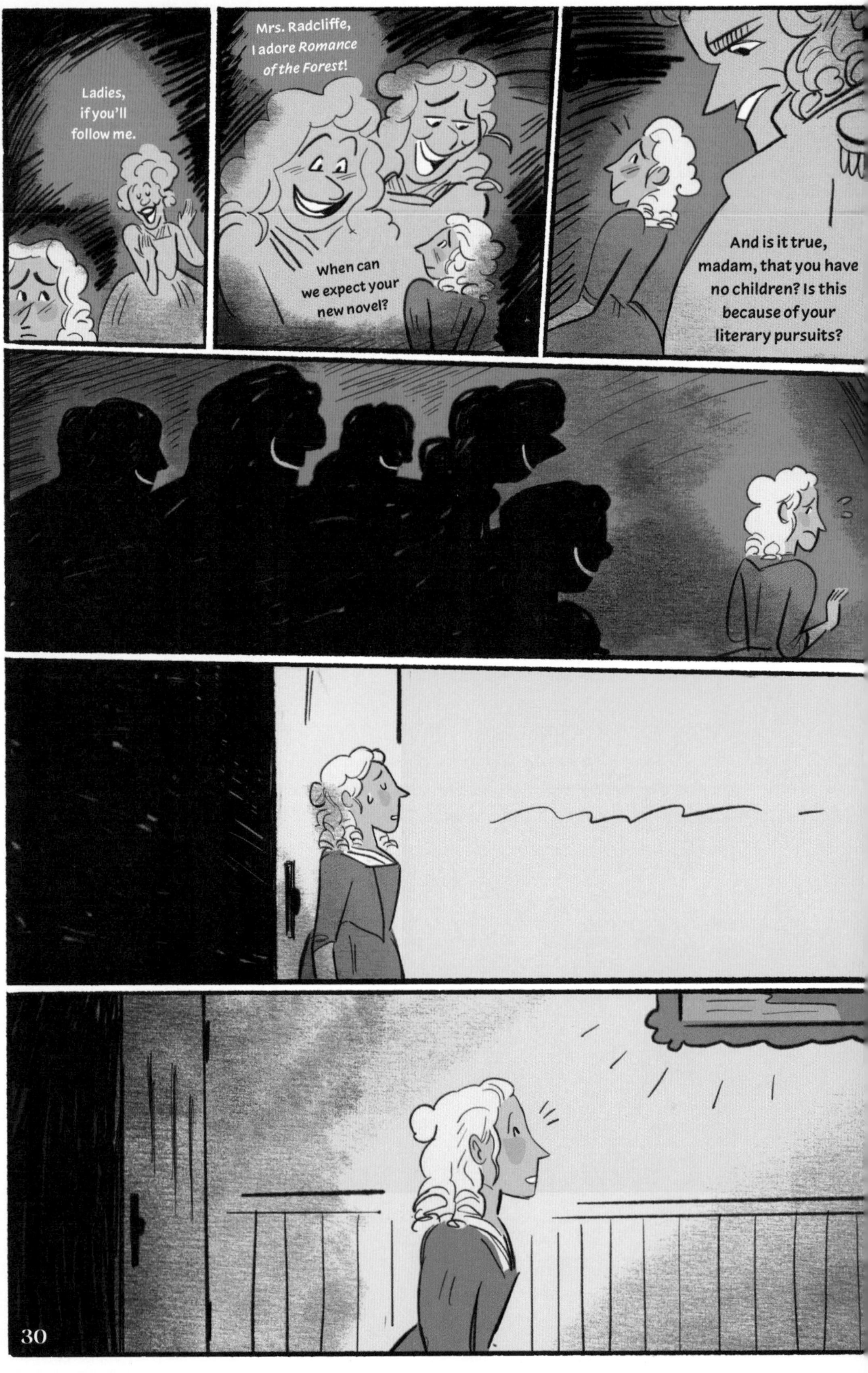
Ladies, if you'll follow me.
Mrs. Radcliffe, I adore *Romance of the Forest*!
When can we expect your new novel?
And is it true, madam, that you have no children? Is this because of your literary pursuits?

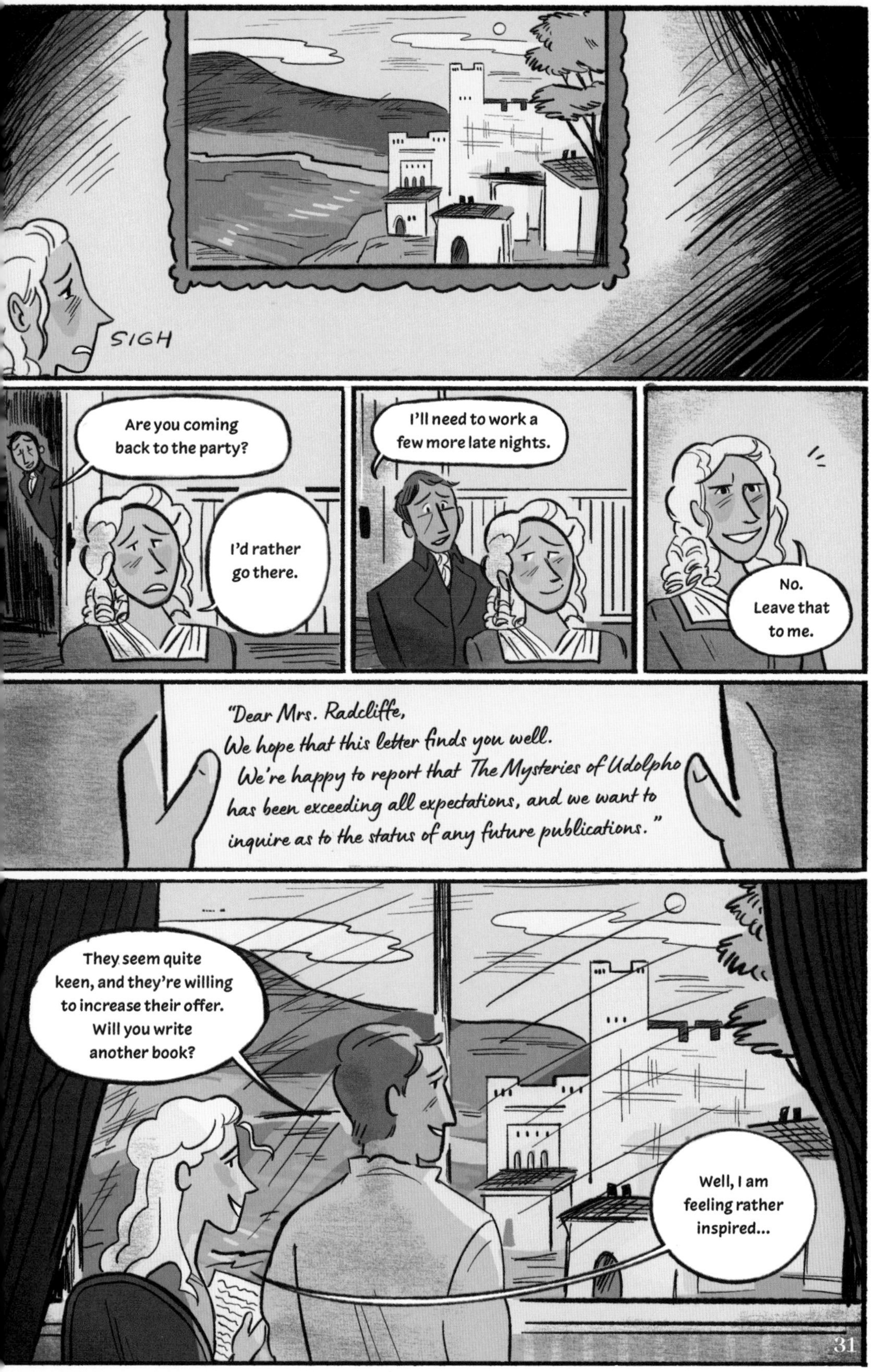
SIGH
Are you coming back to the party?
I'd rather go there.
I'll need to work a few more late nights.
No. Leave that to me.
"Dear Mrs. Radcliffe,
We hope that this letter finds you well.
We're happy to report that The Mysteries of Udolpho has been exceeding all expectations, and we want to inquire as to the status of any future publications."
They seem quite keen, and they're willing to increase their offer. Will you write another book?
Well, I am feeling rather inspired...

Modern readers may be familiar with Ann Radcliffe via the work of Jane Austen. Allusions to Radcliffe and her novels can be found in many of Austen's books, most notably *Northanger Abbey*, which is a gentle parody of *The Mysteries of Udolpho*. The 2007 film *Becoming Jane* imagines a world where Radcliffe not only met Austen, but encouraged her to write— a lovely but unlikely fiction.

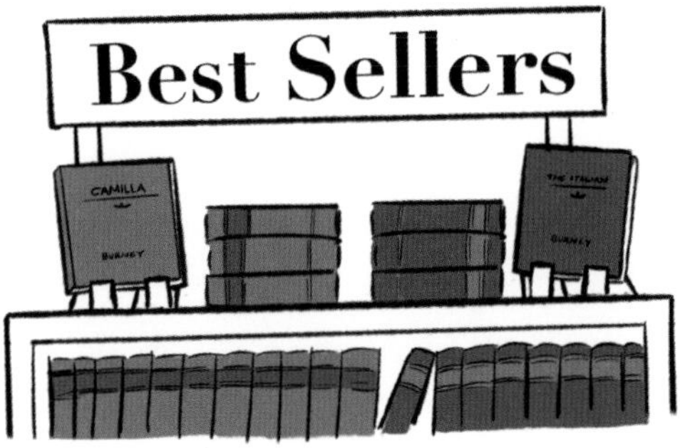
Best Sellers
CAMILLA
BURNEY
BURNEY

Ann Radcliffe was one of the highest paid authors of her day. She earned 500 pounds for the copyright to *The Mysteries of Udolpho* and a whopping 800 pounds for *The Italian*. Combined, that is nearly 175,000 pounds (or 214,000 U.S. dollars) by today's standards. The only female novelist to out-earn her was her contemporary, Frances Burney, who was paid 1,000 pounds for the copyright to *Camilla*.

SELECTED WORKS:

NOVELS

1789: *The Castles of Athlin and Dunbayne: A Highland Story*
1790: *A Sicilian Romance*
1791: *The Romance of the Forest*
1794: *The Mysteries of Udolpho: A Romance*
1797: *The Italian*
1826: *Gaston de Blondeville* [published posthumously]

TRAVELOGUES

1795: *A Journey made in the Summer of 1794: Through Holland and the Western Frontier of Germany, with a Return down the Rhine: to which are Added Observations during a Tour to the Lakes of Lancashire, Westmoreland and Cumberland*

POETRY

1816: *Poems of Ann Radcliffe*, an unauthorized reprint of poems from her novels [published posthumously]

Charlotte Brontë

1816–1855

"I am no bird; and no net ensnares me;
I am a free human being with an independent will..."

—*Jane Eyre*, 1847

Today, Charlotte Brontë is best known as the author of the classic *Jane Eyre,* but in 1849, she was Currer Bell, a mysterious and unknown author with a shocking debut novel, whom the London literati was dying to meet. In November, Currer Bell asked to call on social theorist and writer Harriet Martineau. Martineau eagerly agreed and wondered "whether a tall mustached man six feet high or an aged female, or a girl, or—altogether a ghost, a hoax or a swindler!" would appear at her doorstep.

Instead, she met Charlotte Brontë, a thirty-three-year-old woman from Haworth, Yorkshire. Tiny and bespectacled, she was a fierce presence on the page, but shy in person. No stranger to grief, Charlotte had lost her mother at the tender age of five and her two eldest sisters just four years later. In November 1849, the woman that Harriet Martineau would describe as "a very little sprite of a creature" was privately reeling from the recent loss of her siblings Branwell, Emily, and Anne.

Charlotte was the third of six children born to Maria and the Reverend Patrick Brontë. As a child, she shared a close bond with Branwell, Emily, and Anne that was rooted in their mutual love of storytelling, and together they penned elaborate tales inspired by Branwell's toy soldiers. Charlotte and Branwell labored over their tiny magazines full of ghost stories, political dramas, poems, and reviews. But as the pair grew older, their paths diverged. Charlotte carried on with her writing, while the talented but troubled Branwell dabbled with art and occasional employment, but was ultimately lost to addiction and alcoholism.

Charlotte was a respectable but financially challenged young woman. As the daughter of a curate, she knew that her home would revert back to ownership by the church following the death of her father. To survive, she would need to make her own money. She tried teaching, but ultimately chose writing. In 1837, Brontë sent her best work to the poet laureate Robert Southey, hoping that he would provide her with some career advice. Southey famously responded, "Literature cannot be the business of a woman's life, and it ought not to be."

Charlotte's first attempts at publishing met with disaster. Her debut collaboration with her sisters, *Poems by Currer, Ellis, and Acton Bell*, only sold two copies while her manuscript floundered. *The Professor,* a quiet and understated novel about a teacher named William Crimsworth, was rejected by nearly every publisher in London.

In 1846, Charlotte began drafting the manuscript for *Jane Eyre* while helping her father recover from surgery. She knew that her next attempt at publishing had to be bold. This time she created a protagonist in her own image—a penniless governess struggling for autonomy against all odds. Realism combined with Gothic conventions and tinged with fairytales proved to be a winning combination. *Jane Eyre* has never been out of print since its original publication in 1847.

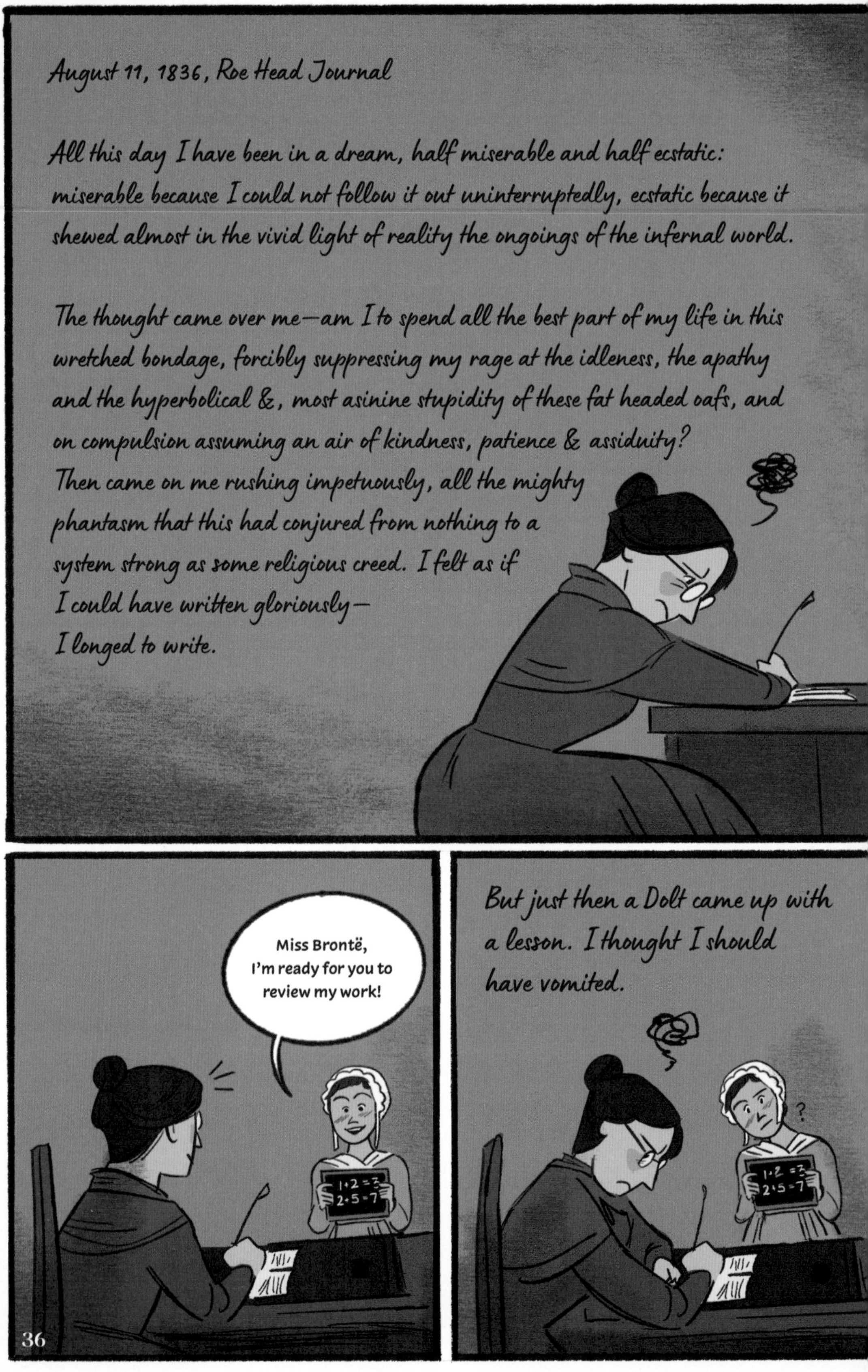
August 11, 1836, Roe Head Journal
All this day I have been in a dream, half miserable and half ecstatic: miserable because I could not follow it out uninterruptedly, ecstatic because it shewed almost in the vivid light of reality the ongoings of the infernal world.
The thought came over me—am I to spend all the best part of my life in this wretched bondage, forcibly suppressing my rage at the idleness, the apathy and the hyperbolical &, most asinine stupidity of these fat headed oafs, and on compulsion assuming an air of kindness, patience & assiduity?
Then came on me rushing impetuously, all the mighty phantasm that this had conjured from nothing to a system strong as some religious creed. I felt as if I could have written gloriously—I longed to write.
Miss Brontë, I'm ready for you to review my work!
1+2=3
2+5=7
But just then a Dolt came up with a lesson. I thought I should have vomited.
?

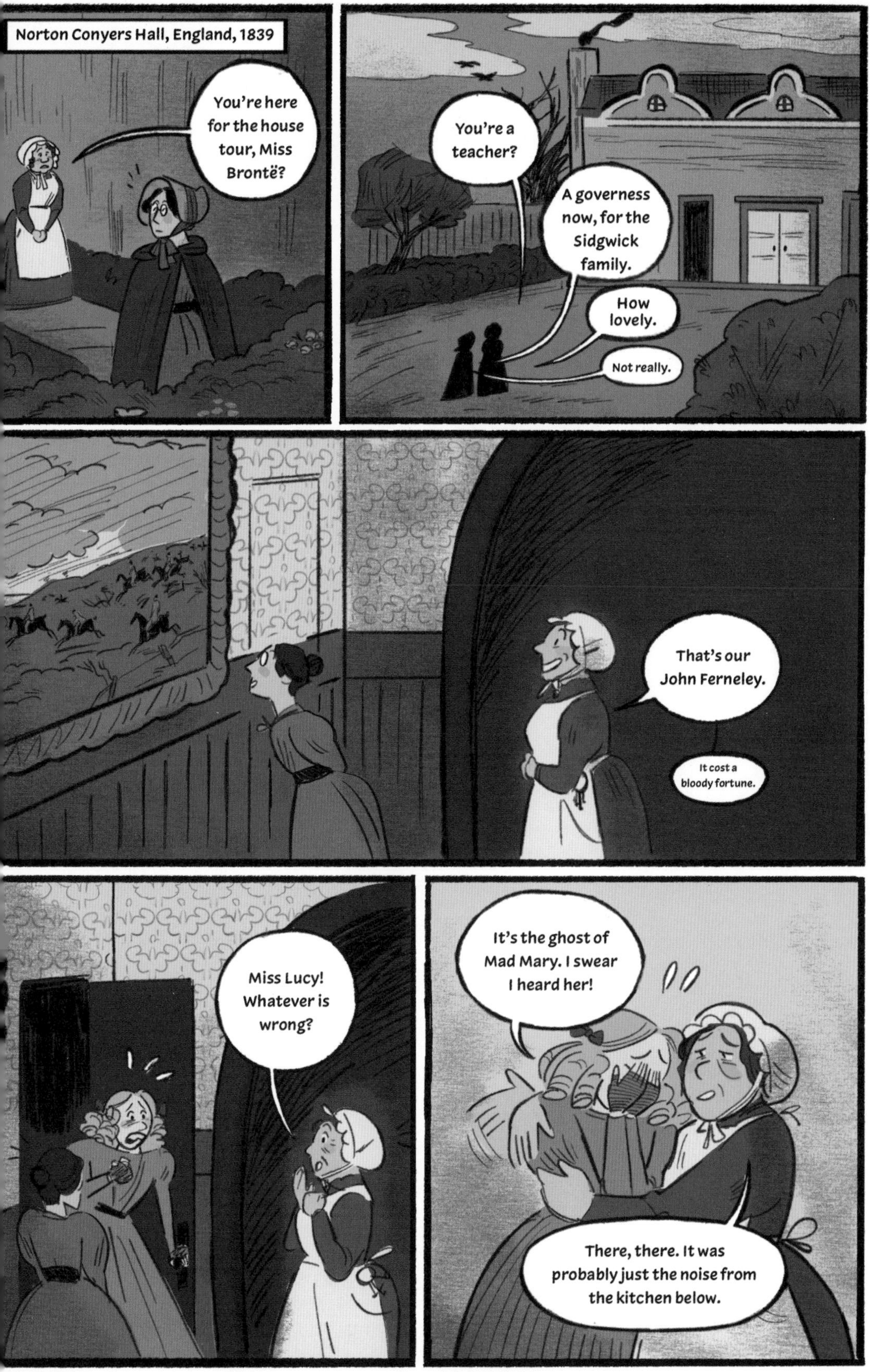

Norton Conyers Hall, England, 1839
You're here for the house tour, Miss Brontë?
You're a teacher?
A governess now, for the Sidgwick family.
How lovely.
Not really.
That's our John Ferneley.
It cost a bloody fortune.
Miss Lucy! Whatever is wrong?
It's the ghost of Mad Mary. I swear I heard her!
There, there. It was probably just the noise from the kitchen below.

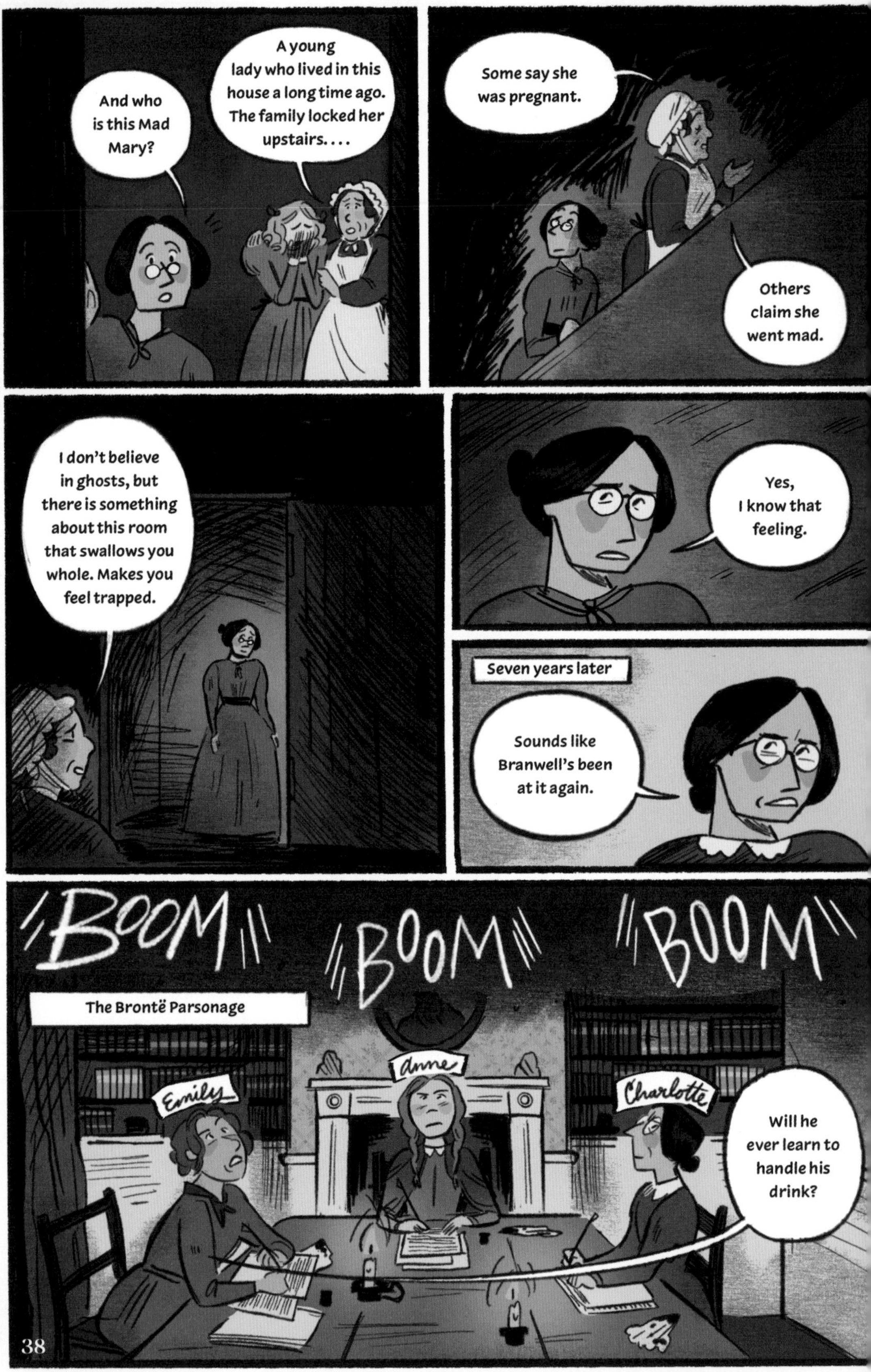

And who is this Mad Mary?
A young lady who lived in this house a long time ago. The family locked her upstairs. . . .
Some say she was pregnant.
Others claim she went mad.
I don't believe in ghosts, but there is something about this room that swallows you whole. Makes you feel trapped.
Yes, I know that feeling.
Seven years later
Sounds like Branwell's been at it again.
BOOM
BOOM
BOOM
The Brontë Parsonage
Emily
Anne
Charlotte
Will he ever learn to handle his drink?

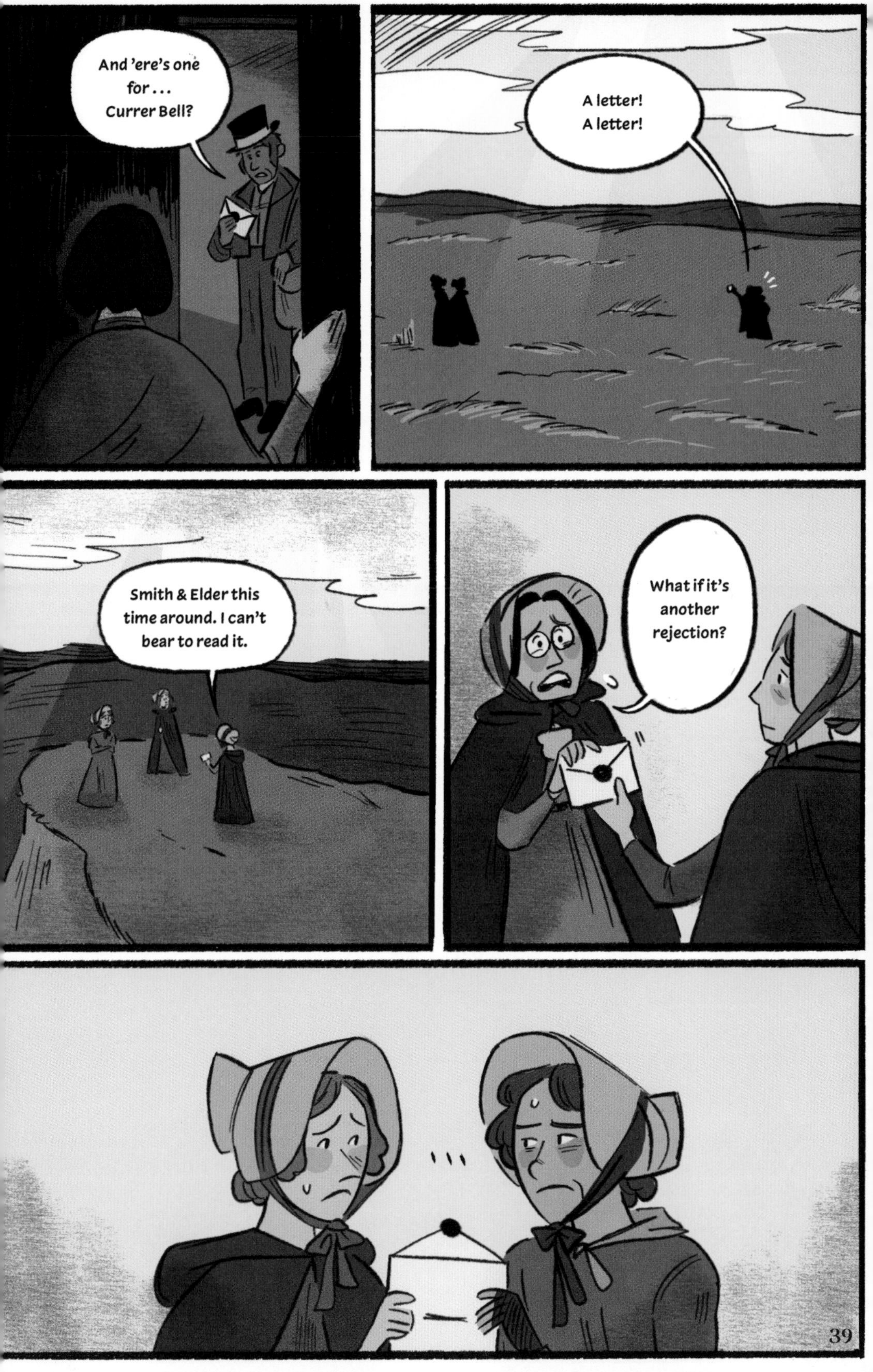

And 'ere's one for . . . Currer Bell?
A letter! A letter!
Smith & Elder this time around. I can't bear to read it.
What if it's another rejection?
. . .

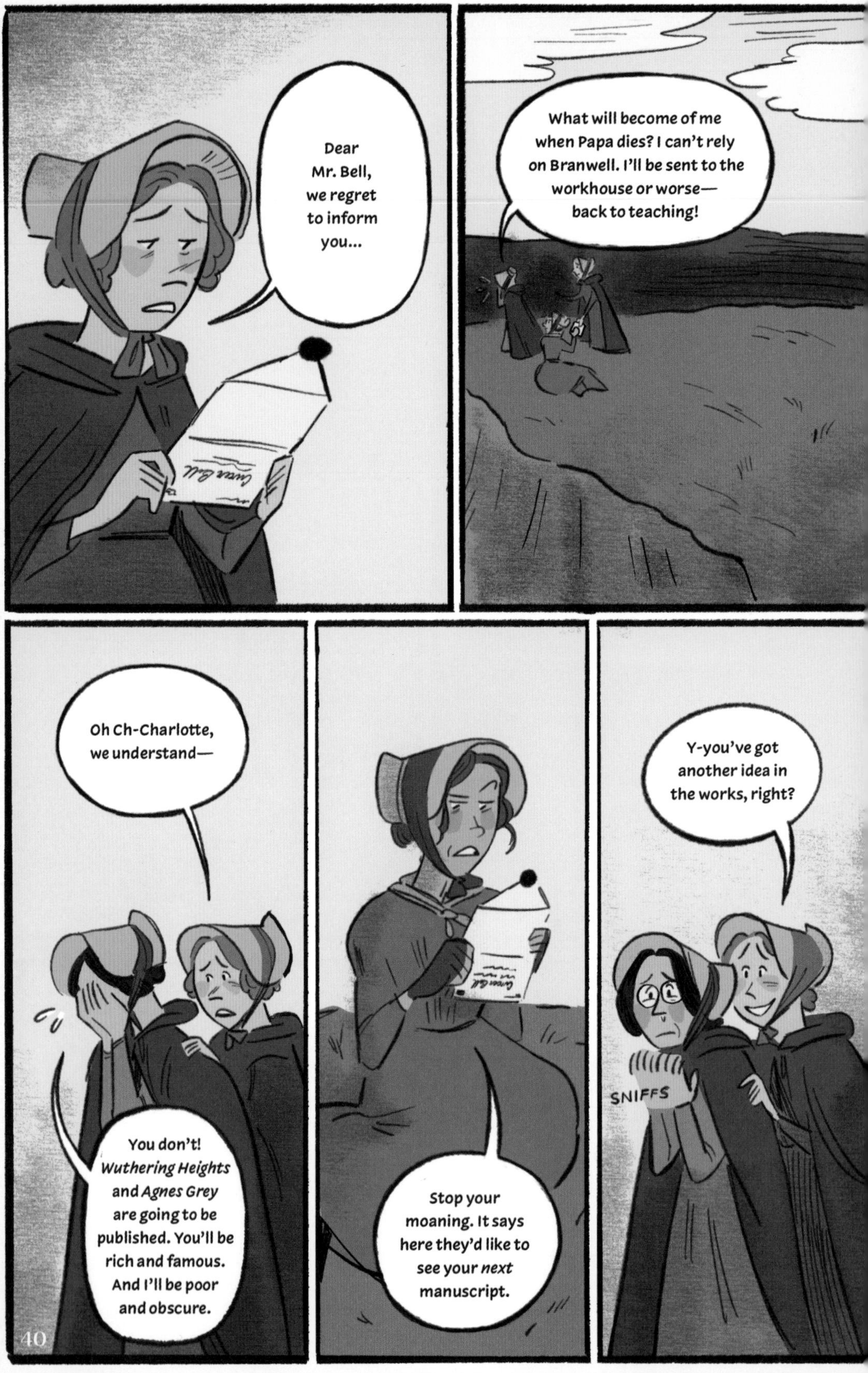
Dear Mr. Bell, we regret to inform you...
What will become of me when Papa dies? I can't rely on Branwell. I'll be sent to the workhouse or worse— back to teaching!
Oh Ch-Charlotte, we understand—
You don't! *Wuthering Heights* and *Agnes Grey* are going to be published. You'll be rich and famous. And I'll be poor and obscure.
Stop your moaning. It says here they'd like to see your *next* manuscript.
Y-you've got another idea in the works, right?
SNIFFS

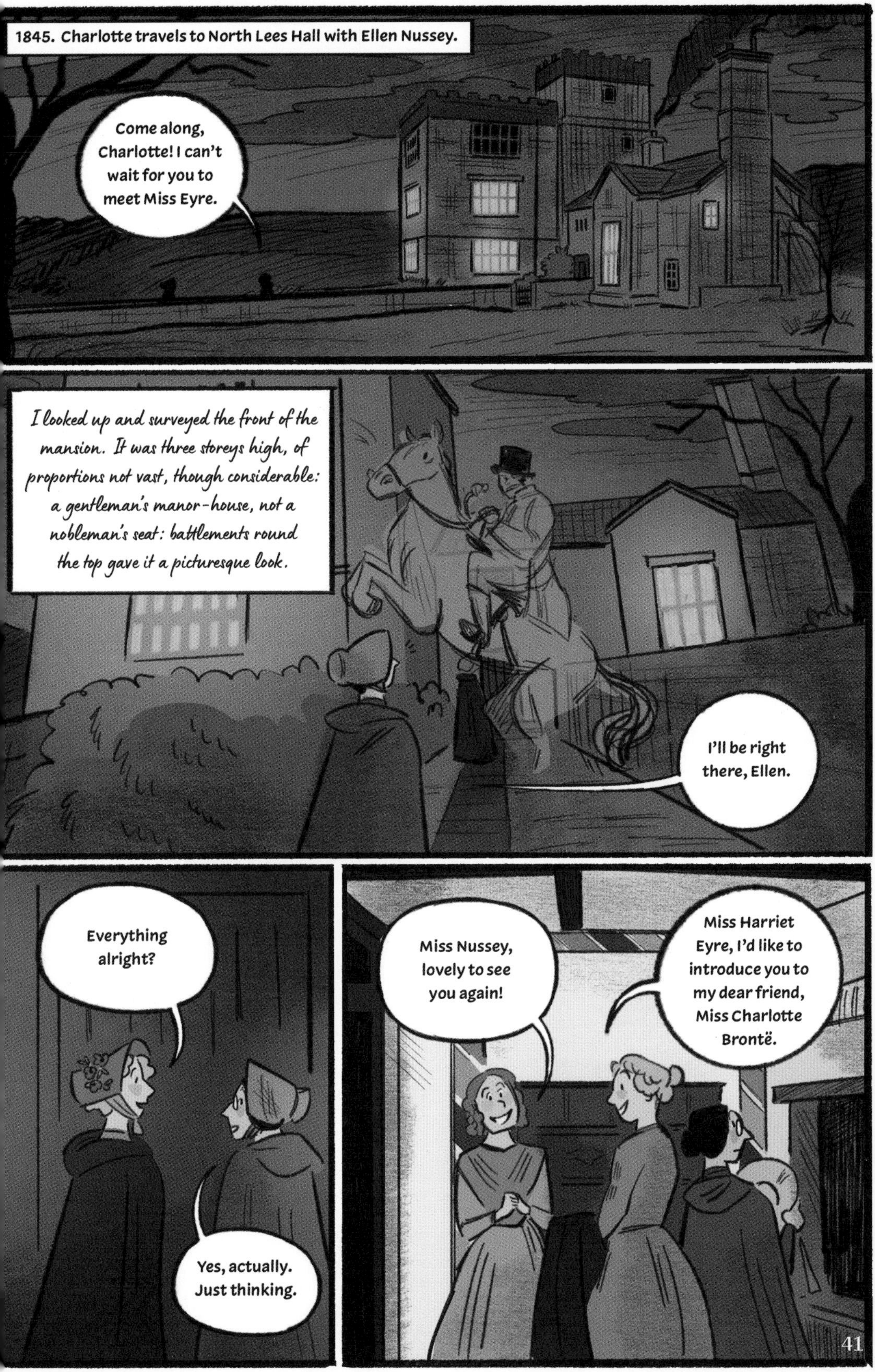
1845. Charlotte travels to North Lees Hall with Ellen Nussey.
Come along, Charlotte! I can't wait for you to meet Miss Eyre.
I looked up and surveyed the front of the mansion. It was three storeys high, of proportions not vast, though considerable: a gentleman's manor-house, not a nobleman's seat: battlements round the top gave it a picturesque look.
I'll be right there, Ellen.
Everything alright?
Yes, actually. Just thinking.
Miss Nussey, lovely to see you again!
Miss Harriet Eyre, I'd like to introduce you to my dear friend, Miss Charlotte Brontë.

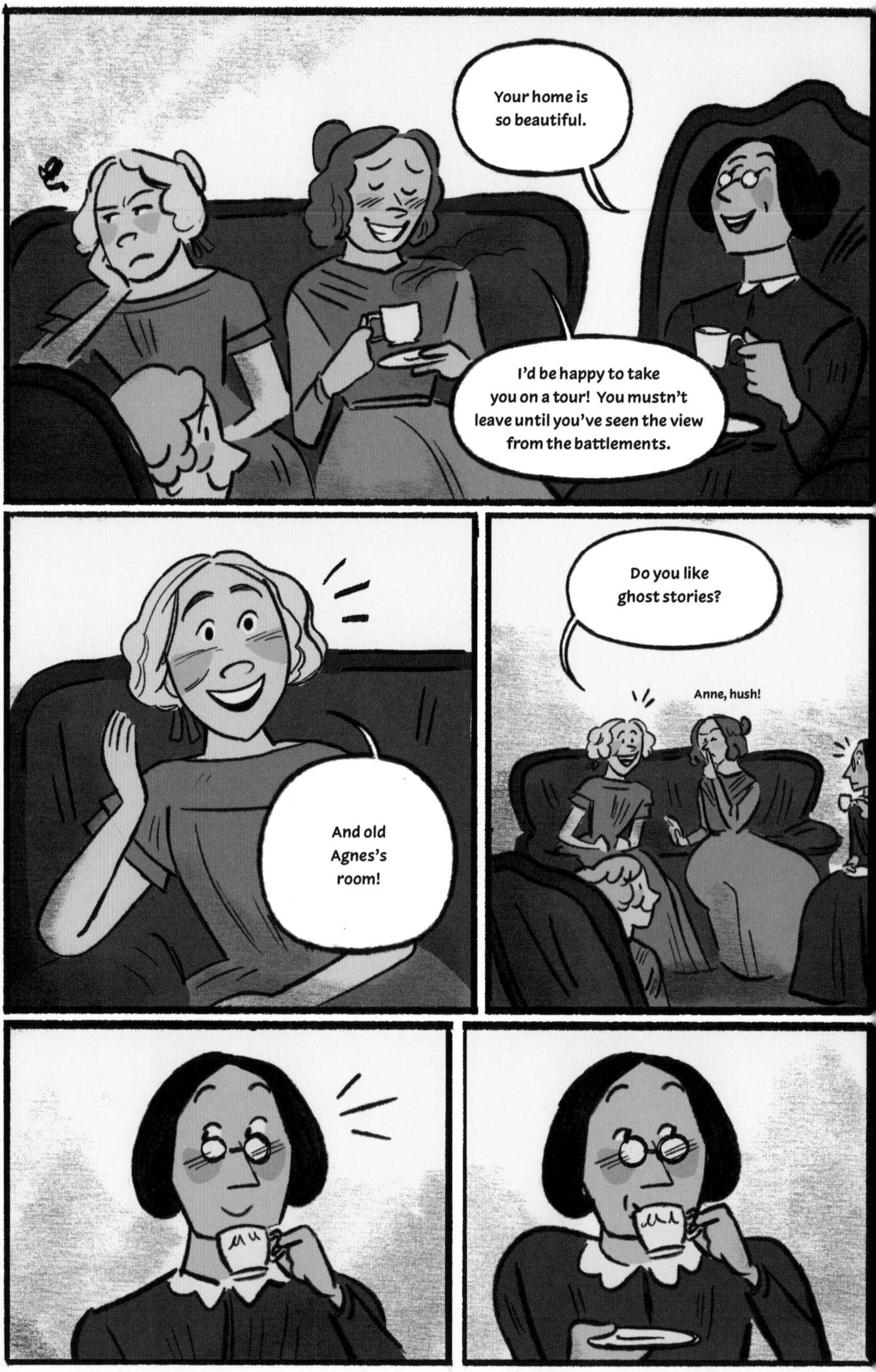
Your home is so beautiful.
I'd be happy to take you on a tour! You mustn't leave until you've seen the view from the battlements.
And old Agnes's room!
Do you like ghost stories?
Anne, hush!

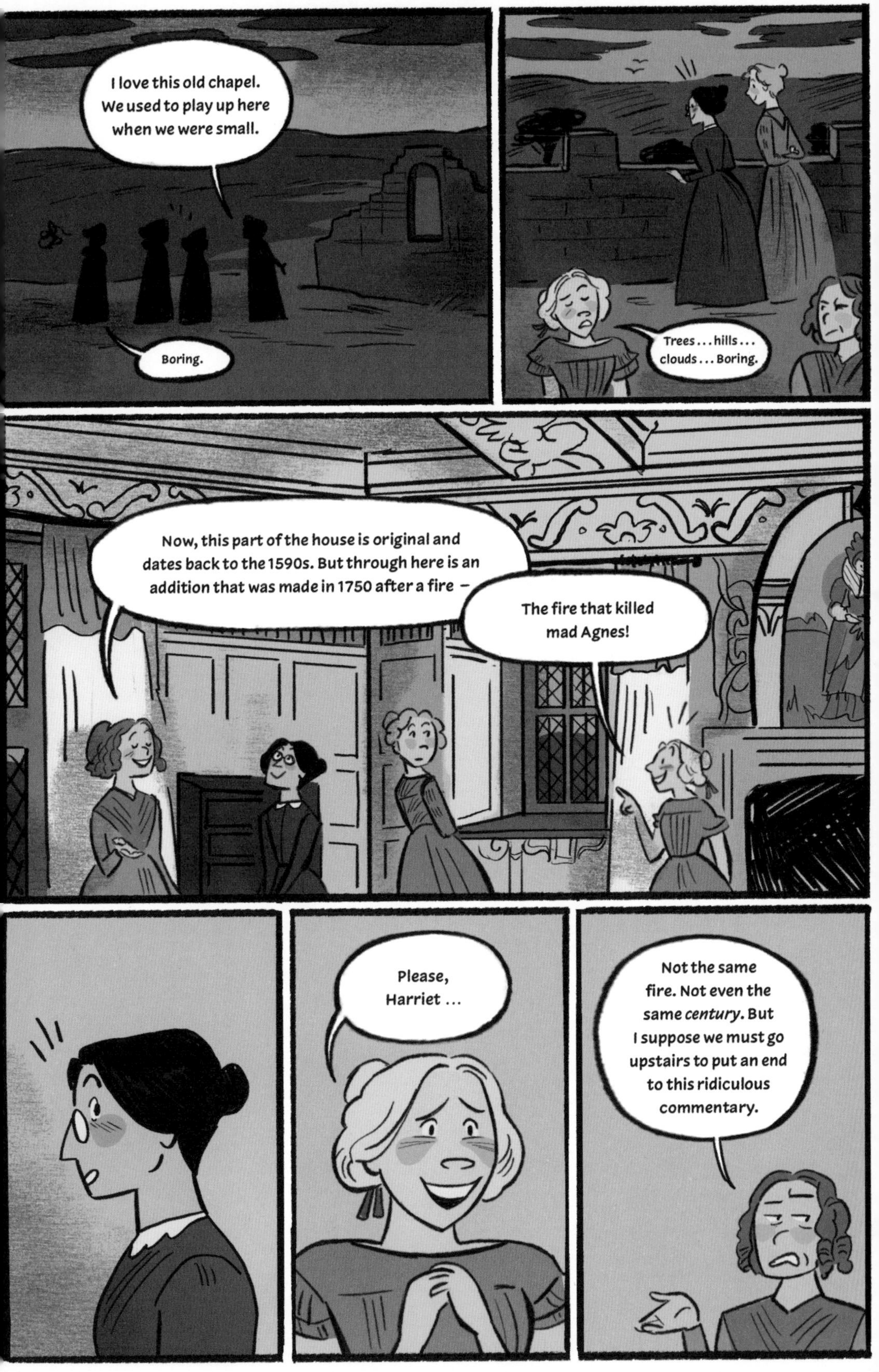
I love this old chapel. We used to play up here when we were small.
Boring.
Trees . . . hills . . . clouds . . . Boring.
Now, this part of the house is original and dates back to the 1590s. But through here is an addition that was made in 1750 after a fire –
The fire that killed mad Agnes!
Please, Harriet . . .
Not the same fire. Not even the same *century*. But I suppose we must go upstairs to put an end to this ridiculous commentary.

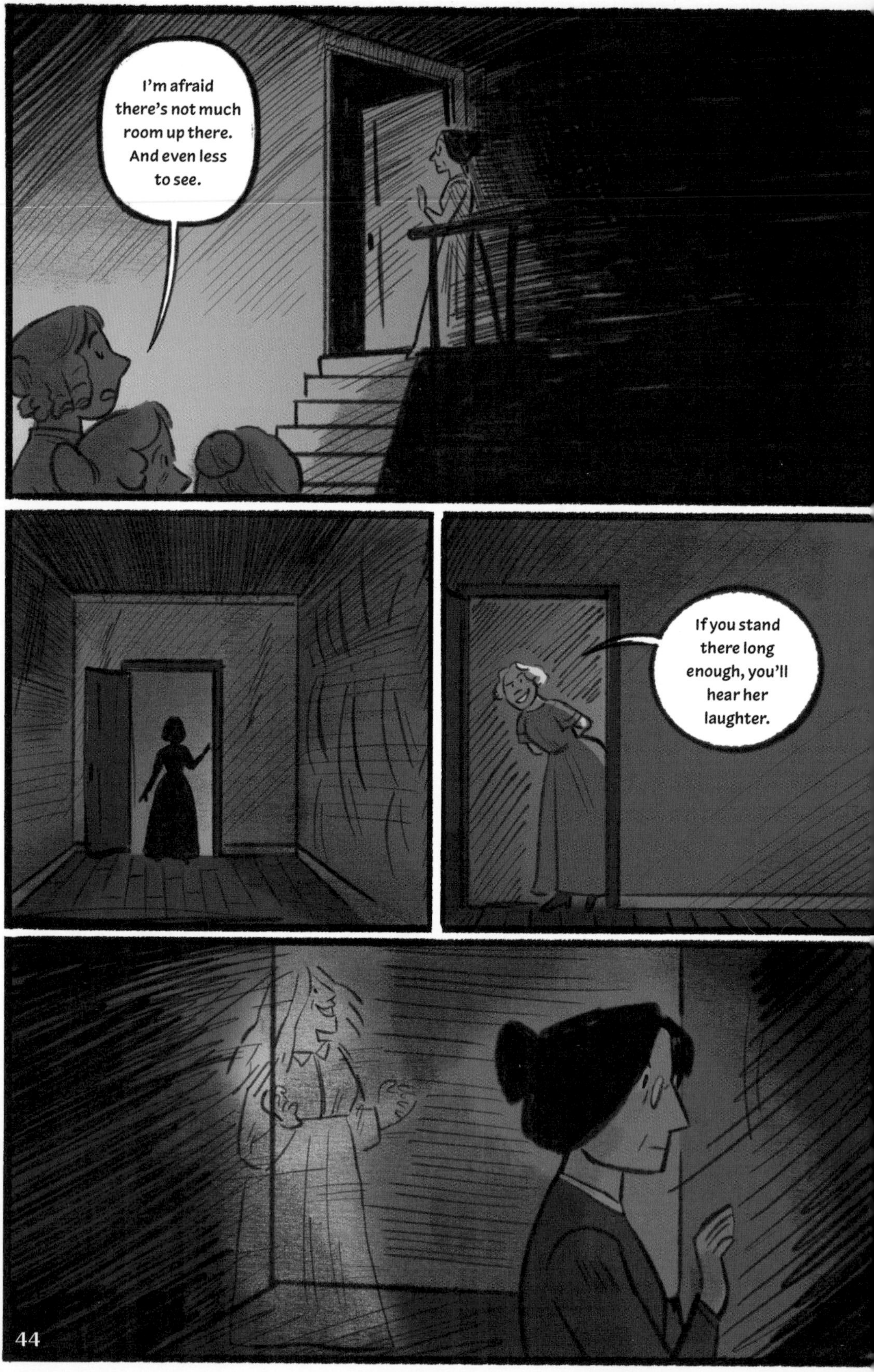
I'm afraid there's not much room up there. And even less to see.
If you stand there long enough, you'll hear her laughter.

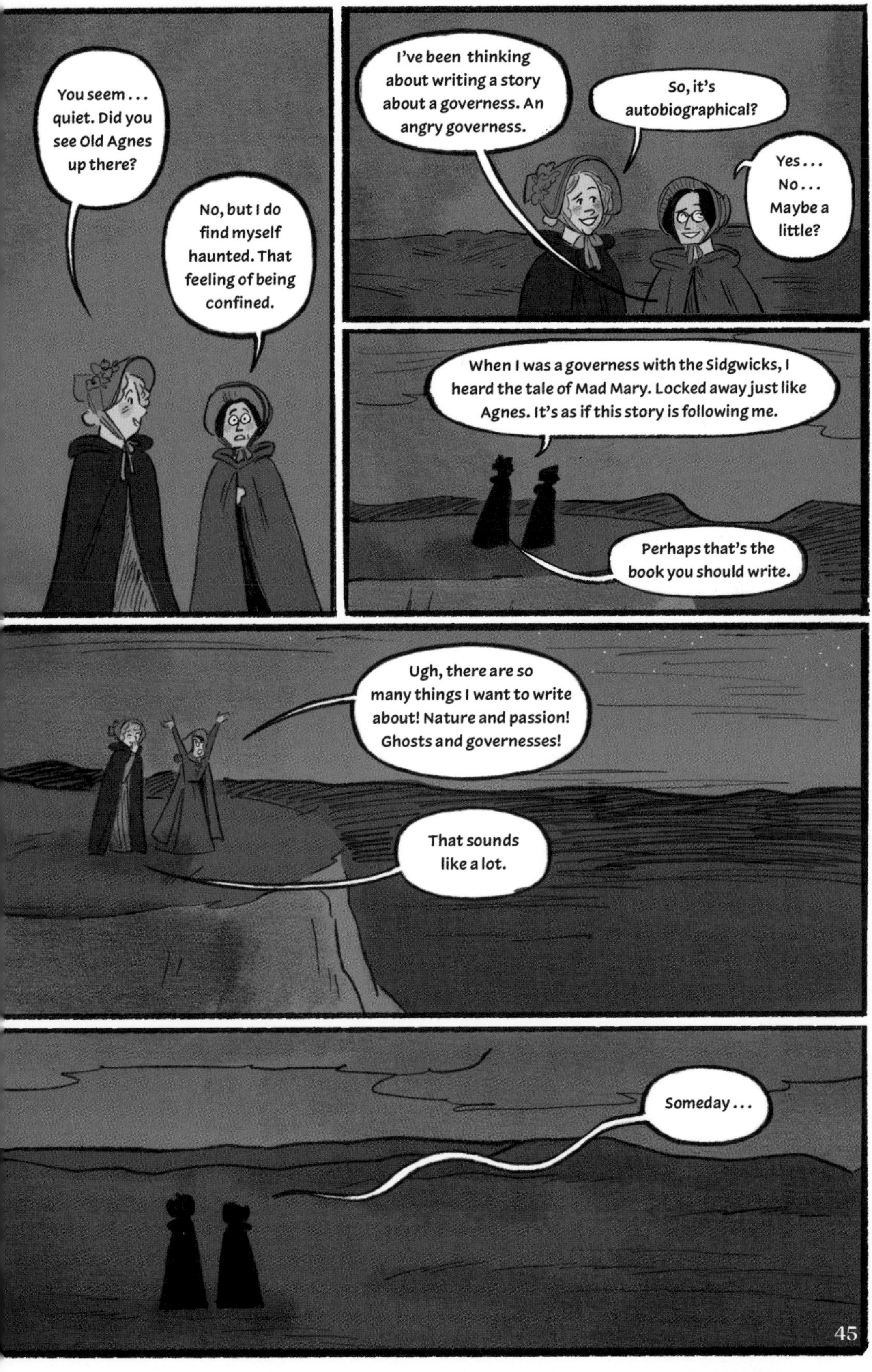
You seem . . . quiet. Did you see Old Agnes up there?
No, but I do find myself haunted. That feeling of being confined.
I've been thinking about writing a story about a governess. An angry governess.
So, it's autobiographical?
Yes . . . No . . . Maybe a little?
When I was a governess with the Sidgwicks, I heard the tale of Mad Mary. Locked away just like Agnes. It's as if this story is following me.
Perhaps that's the book you should write.
Ugh, there are so many things I want to write about! Nature and passion! Ghosts and governesses!
That sounds like a lot.
Someday . . .

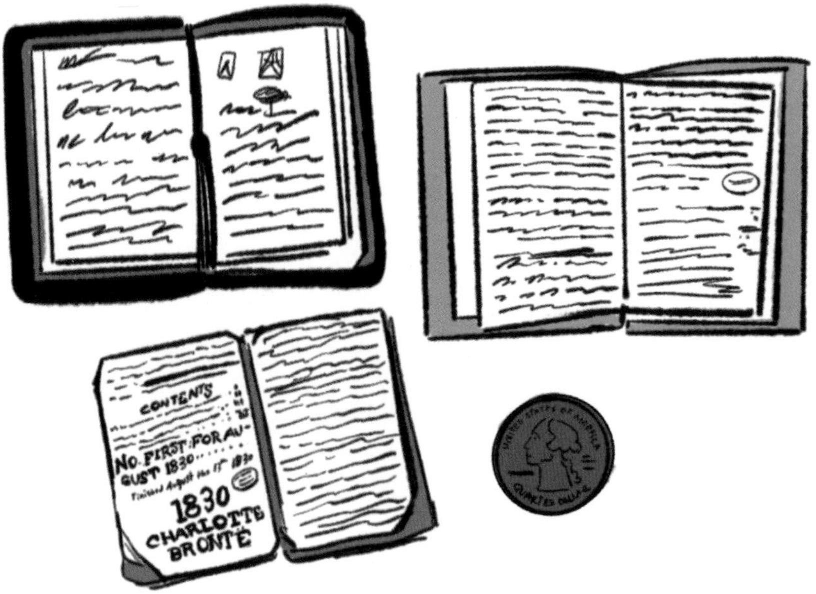
CONTENTS
No. FIRST FOR AU-
GUST 1830
1830
CHARLOTTE
BRONTË

The Brontë siblings famously made teeny-tiny hand-stitched books to house their juvenilia. These books, composed from scraps of paper, measured less than 1 inch by 2 inches. In 2015, a lost manuscript containing a short story and a poem by Charlotte was discovered in a book belonging to her mother. It was published by the Brontë Society in 2018.

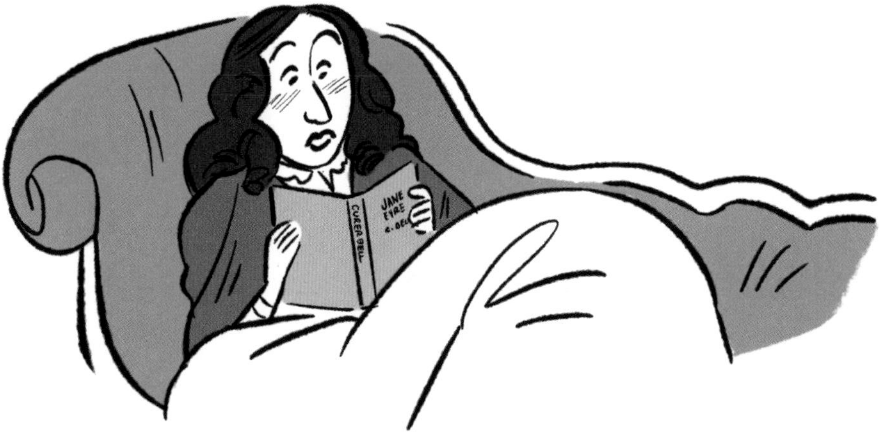
JANE EYRE
CURRER BELL

Charlotte dedicated the second edition of *Jane Eyre* to the novelist William Thackeray, causing a stir in literary London. Unbeknownst to Charlotte, Thackeray's wife had been institutionalized. Those in the know speculated that Currer Bell must have been Thackeray's real-life governess. Elizabeth Barrett Browning, however, did not agree. "I certainly don't think that the qualities, half savage and & half freethinking, expressed in 'Jane Eyre,' are likely to suit a model governess," she wrote to friend Mary Mitford.

SELECTED WORKS:

POETRY

1846: *Poems by Currer, Ellis, and Acton Bell*

FICTION

1847: *Jane Eyre*
1849: *Shirley*
1853: *Villette*
1857: *The Professor*
1860: *Emma** [published posthumously]
*Before she died, Charlotte started work on a novel entitled *Emma*. Sadly, she only completed twenty pages. It was published posthumously in 1860 in William Thackeray's *Cornhill Magazine*, and it is believed to be the inspiration for Frances Hodgson Burnett's novel *The Little Princess.*

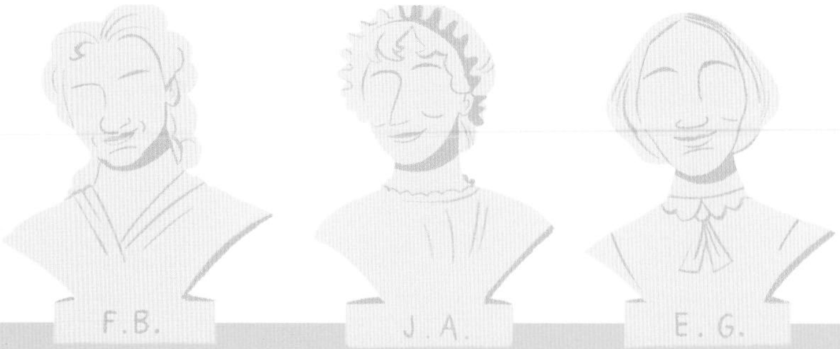
F.B.
J.A.
E.G.

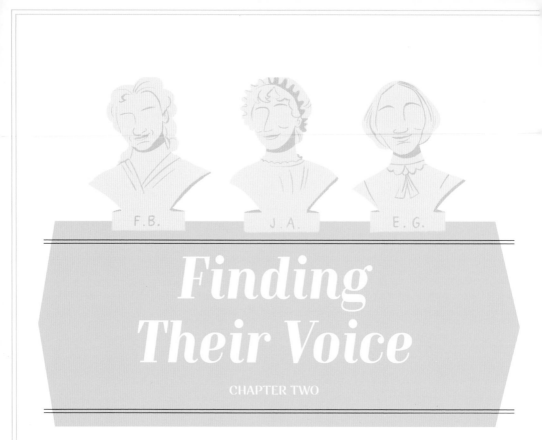

Finding Their Voice

CHAPTER TWO

Close your eyes and imagine, for a moment, time passing you by. Hours. Hours and hours and hours. Cheeks aching from the faces you make as you write, hands cramping from holding your pen, back stiff from sitting upright for hours on end. Consider the cost of paper; having no place to write that is wholly your own; the scornful way in which novelists are spoken of; the lack of a formal education; the pressure to marry; the hundred and one responsibilities of running a household and caring for children; ill health; war. . . .

If Frances Burney, Jane Austen, and Elizabeth Gaskell can tell us anything, it is that the road to publication requires perseverance. These authors not only recorded the hardest trials of their lives, but by committing their experiences to paper, they framed how they would be remembered. They lived and re-lived and, more importantly, they wrote and rewrote.

When Frances Burney fell ill in late 1810, trapped in Paris and cut off from her home and family by an army blockade, writing was the only way to validate and share her experience. In a letter to her sister Esther, to which she sewed an annotated copy of her medical report, Burney detailed an experience many women, before and after, silently endured: a mastectomy for possible breast cancer.

For young Jane Austen, who would go on to great success, publication seemed far out of reach in 1803. While living in Bath, she found herself—possibly for the first time—unequal to the task of writing. The first novel she sold was never released, forgotten by the publisher; and the next novel she started was never completed, forgotten by Jane herself. Rather than give up, she doubled down, returning to earlier works with fresh eyes and a sense of renewed purpose.

And even after writing, after being published, when the reviews come rolling in—what then? For Elizabeth Gaskell, who endured waves of criticism and complaints after publishing *The Life of Charlotte Brontë* in 1857, the work was not over. She would spend months cutting and expanding her work to placate those whom her biography had accused or offended.

Though writing came easily to these women, they still faced many obstacles—intense physical discomfort, self-doubt, and the criticisms of others—which at the time seemed insurmountable. But however painful the process, all three persisted. Their stories were pored over, edited, hacked apart, and perfected, works of precision rather than accident. They chose their words carefully. And their voices were heard.

Frances Burney

1752–1840

"You must learn not only to judge but to act for yourself."

—*Evelina*, 1778

Who is Frances Burney? Virginia Woolf called her "the mother of English fiction" and Jane Austen admired her so much that she plucked the name of her most enduring novel, *Pride and Prejudice,* from the pages of Burney's novel *Cecilia.* Why then, if Burney was held in such high regard by her contemporaries and peers, is she relegated to the footnotes of literary history?

Born in 1752, Burney was the daughter of the prominent music historian Charles Burney and his wife, Esther Sleepe Burney. Despite her father's academic credentials, Burney's education was sadly neglected. Her mother's long-term illness and death when Frances was young meant attention was focused elsewhere; and, at the age of eight, she did not know the alphabet. By the age of ten, however, she had taught herself to write through extensive reading in her father's library, and entertained herself by writing in her journal. By fifteen, Burney had completed her first novel, *Caroline Evelyn,* but within the year she burned the manuscript and other writings of her childhood.

Though popular, novels were not respected by the wider public; at best, they were considered an inferior form of writing and at worst, dangerous, exposing their readers to radical ideas. No novelist could be respectable, and a lady novelist even less so. For Burney, this lack of respectability was distressing. Her resolve to quit writing was short-lived, however, and by 1768 she had begun a new journal, addressing it to "Nobody." Through writing Burney was able to express herself and "reveal every thought, every wish of my heart, with the most unlimited confidence, the most unremitting sincerity to the end of my life!" In later years Burney would turn to her journals for inspiration for her novels.

In 1778 when Burney, aged 27, published her first novel, *Evelina,* she did so anonymously. Her early concerns about respectability still plagued her. The book proved a success, however, and within two years, four editions had been printed. By the time Burney's third novel, *Camilla,* was published in 1796, her identity was an open secret. Now forty-four, with a husband and young son, Burney used her earnings to provide for her family. Her husband, General Alexandre D'Arblay, was penniless, having left France under the shadow of the French Revolution, and he looked to Burney for financial support. In 1802, D'Arblay decided to return to France to attempt to reclaim his lands and fortune, and Burney agreed to follow him, little knowing that what was intended as a short visit would turn into exile.

For the next ten years, while the Napoleonic Wars raged on, Burney and her husband and son, on the wrong side of a military blockade, were unable to leave France. It was one of the most trying experiences of Burney's life. Just as she had at fifteen, Burney turned to writing to share, with "unremitting sincerity," a personal and very rare account of surgery in the nineteenth century.

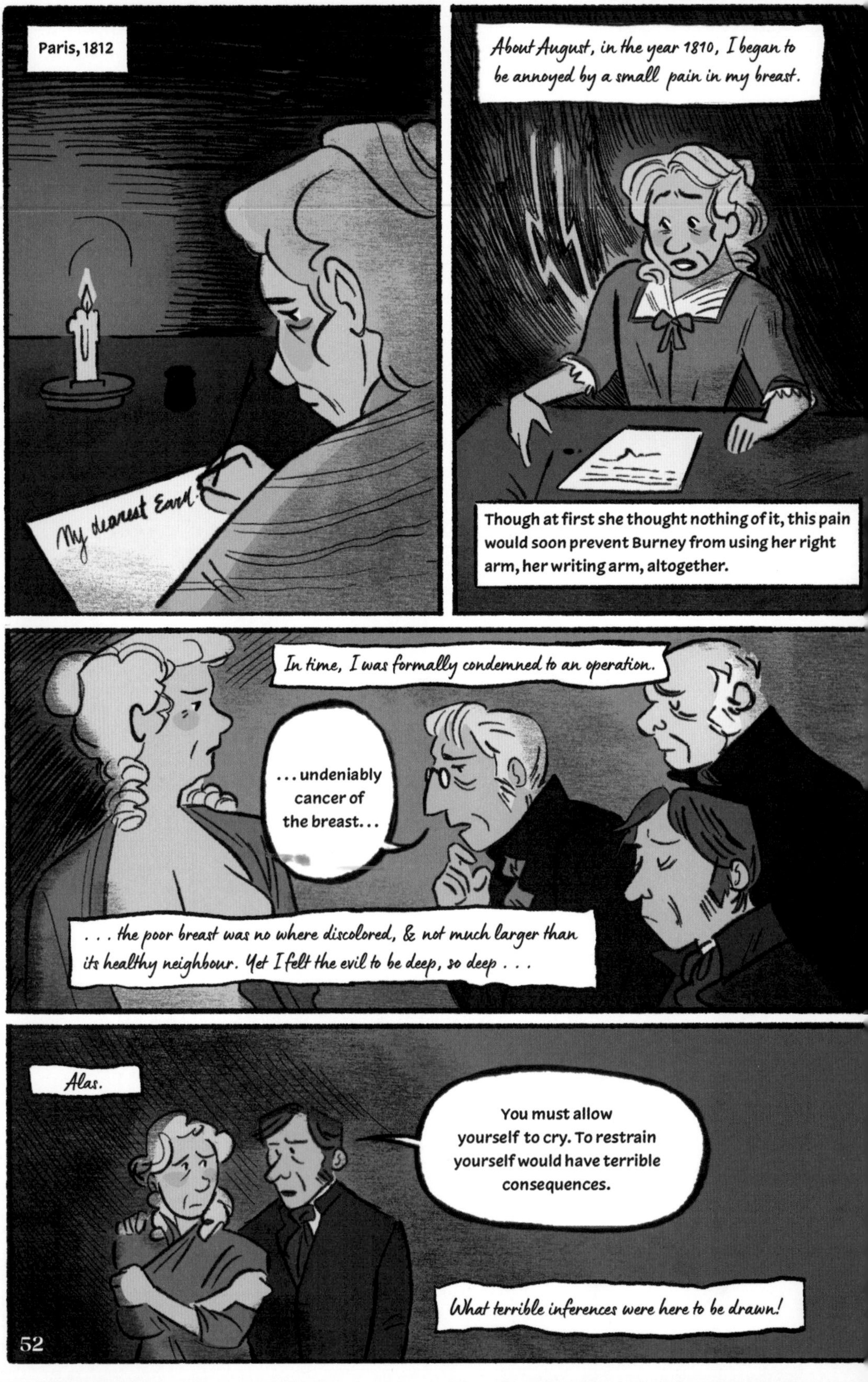
Paris, 1812
My dearest Esm
About August, in the year 1810, I began to be annoyed by a small pain in my breast.
Though at first she thought nothing of it, this pain would soon prevent Burney from using her right arm, her writing arm, altogether.
In time, I was formally condemned to an operation.
. . . undeniably cancer of the breast. . .
. . . the poor breast was no where discolored, & not much larger than its healthy neighbour. Yet I felt the evil to be deep, so deep . . .
Alas.
You must allow yourself to cry. To restrain yourself would have terrible consequences.
What terrible inferences were here to be drawn!

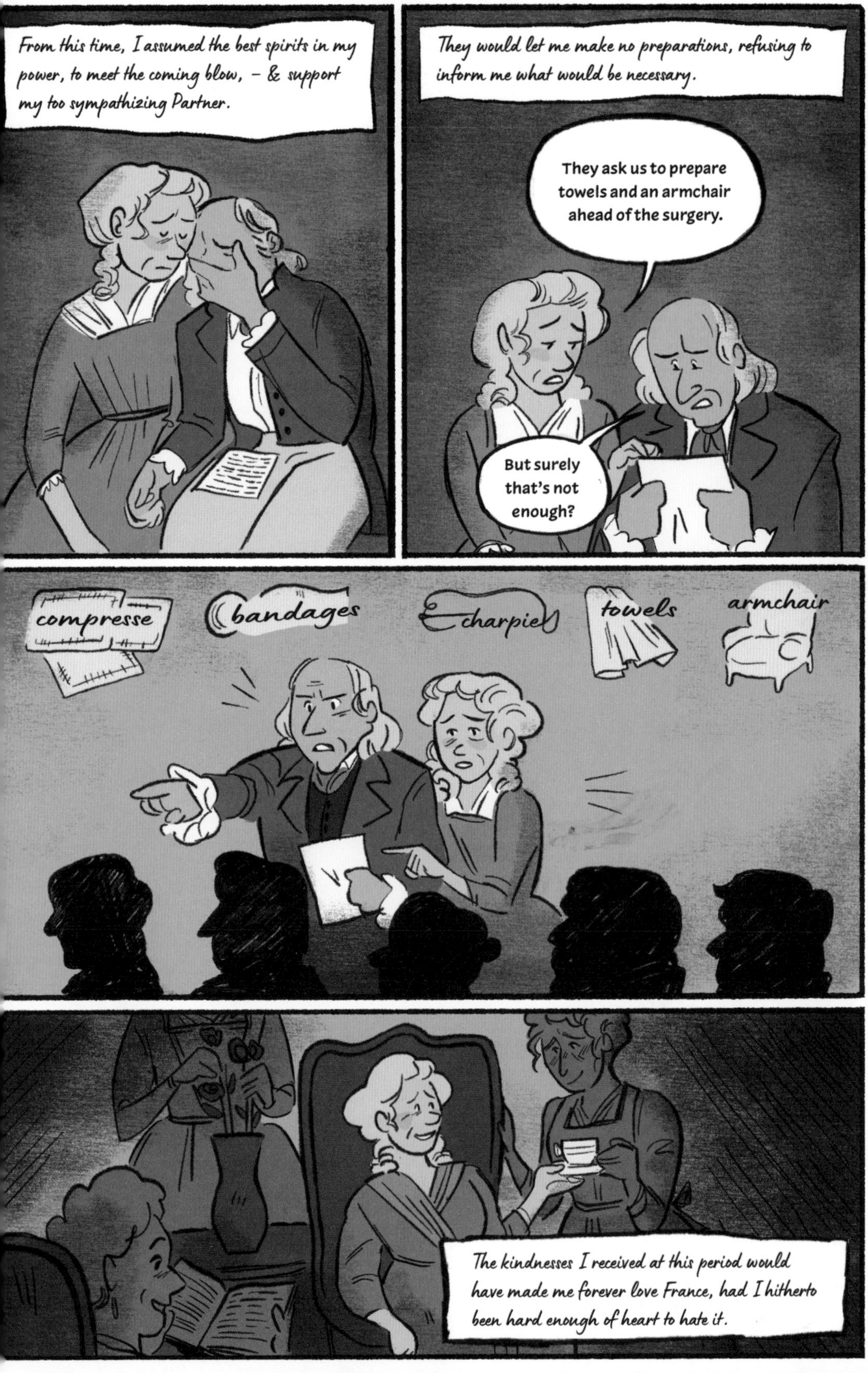
From this time, I assumed the best spirits in my power, to meet the coming blow, – & support my too sympathizing Partner.
They would let me make no preparations, refusing to inform me what would be necessary.
They ask us to prepare towels and an armchair ahead of the surgery.
But surely that's not enough?
compresse
bandages
charpie
towels
armchair
The kindnesses I received at this period would have made me forever love France, had I hitherto been hard enough of heart to hate it.

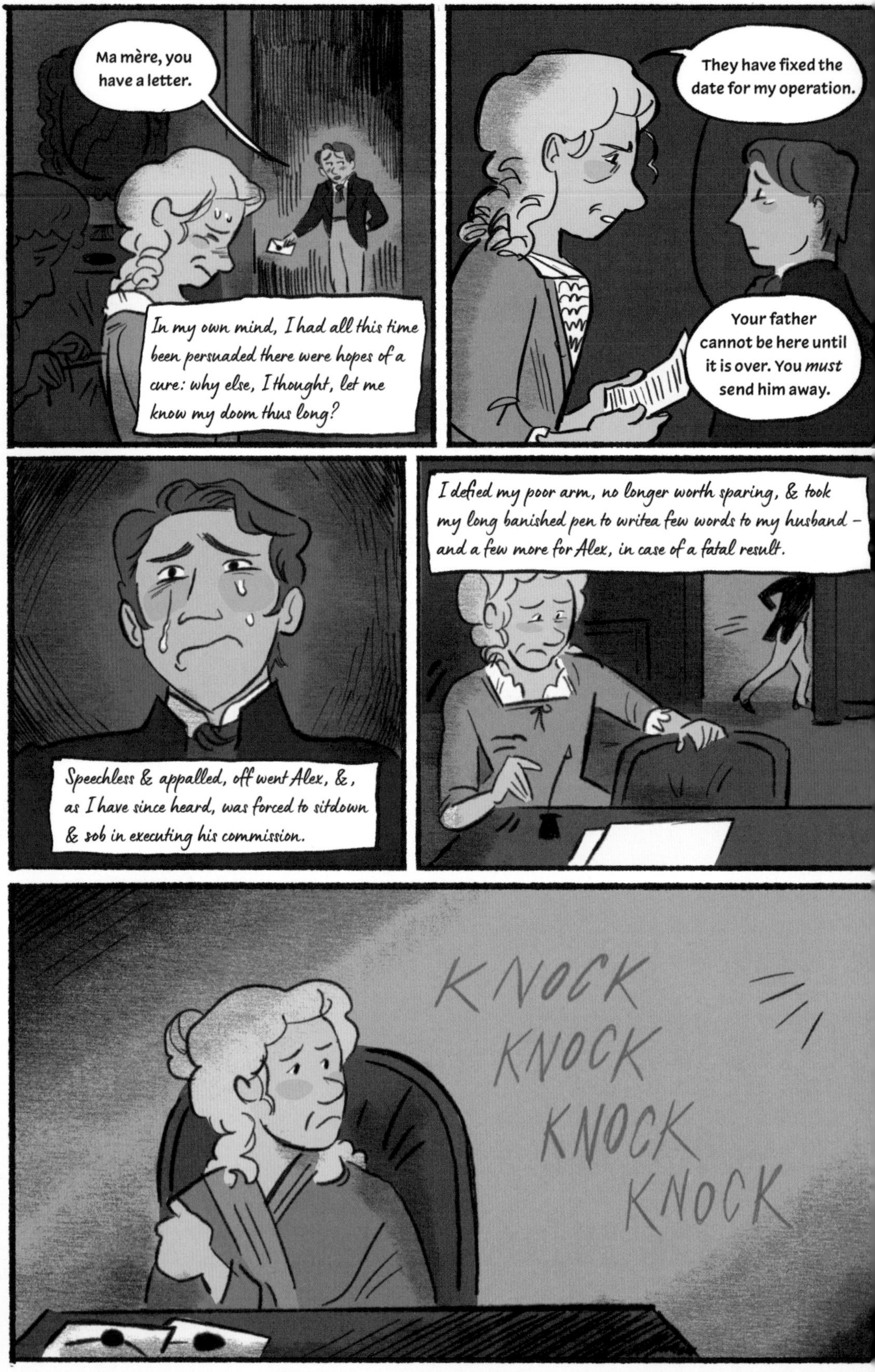
Ma mère, you have a letter.
In my own mind, I had all this time been persuaded there were hopes of a cure: why else, I thought, let me know my doom thus long?
They have fixed the date for my operation.
Your father cannot be here until it is over. You *must* send him away.
Speechless & appalled, off went Alex, &, as I have since heard, was forced to sitdown & sob in executing his commission.
I defied my poor arm, no longer worth sparing, & took my long banished pen to writea few words to my husband – and a few more for Alex, in case of a fatal result.
KNOCK
KNOCK
KNOCK
KNOCK

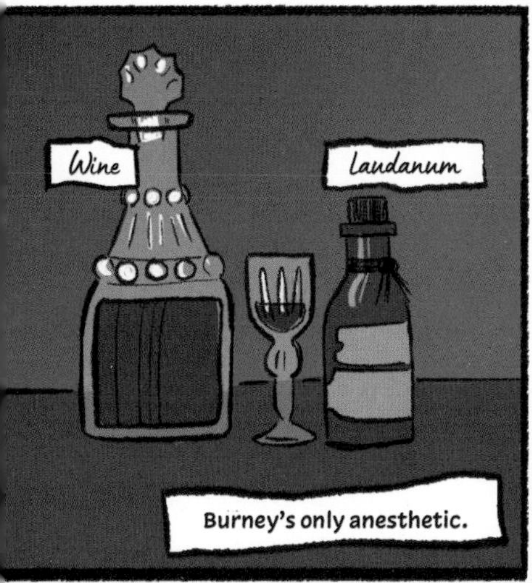
Wine
Laudanum
Burney's only anesthetic.

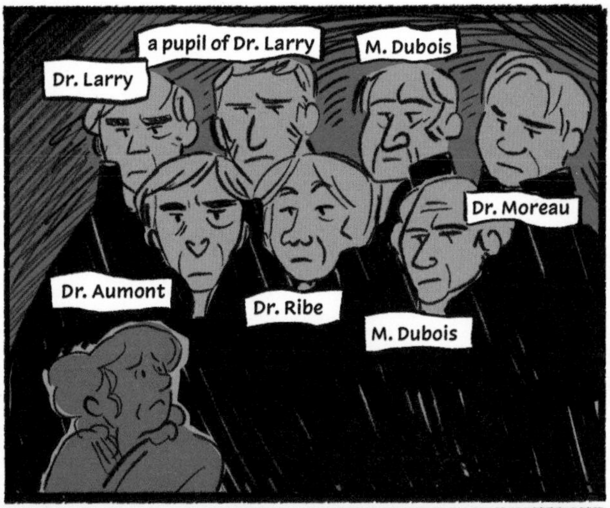
a pupil of Dr. Larry
M. Dubois
Dr. Larry
Dr. Moreau
Dr. Aumont
Dr. Ribe
M. Dubois

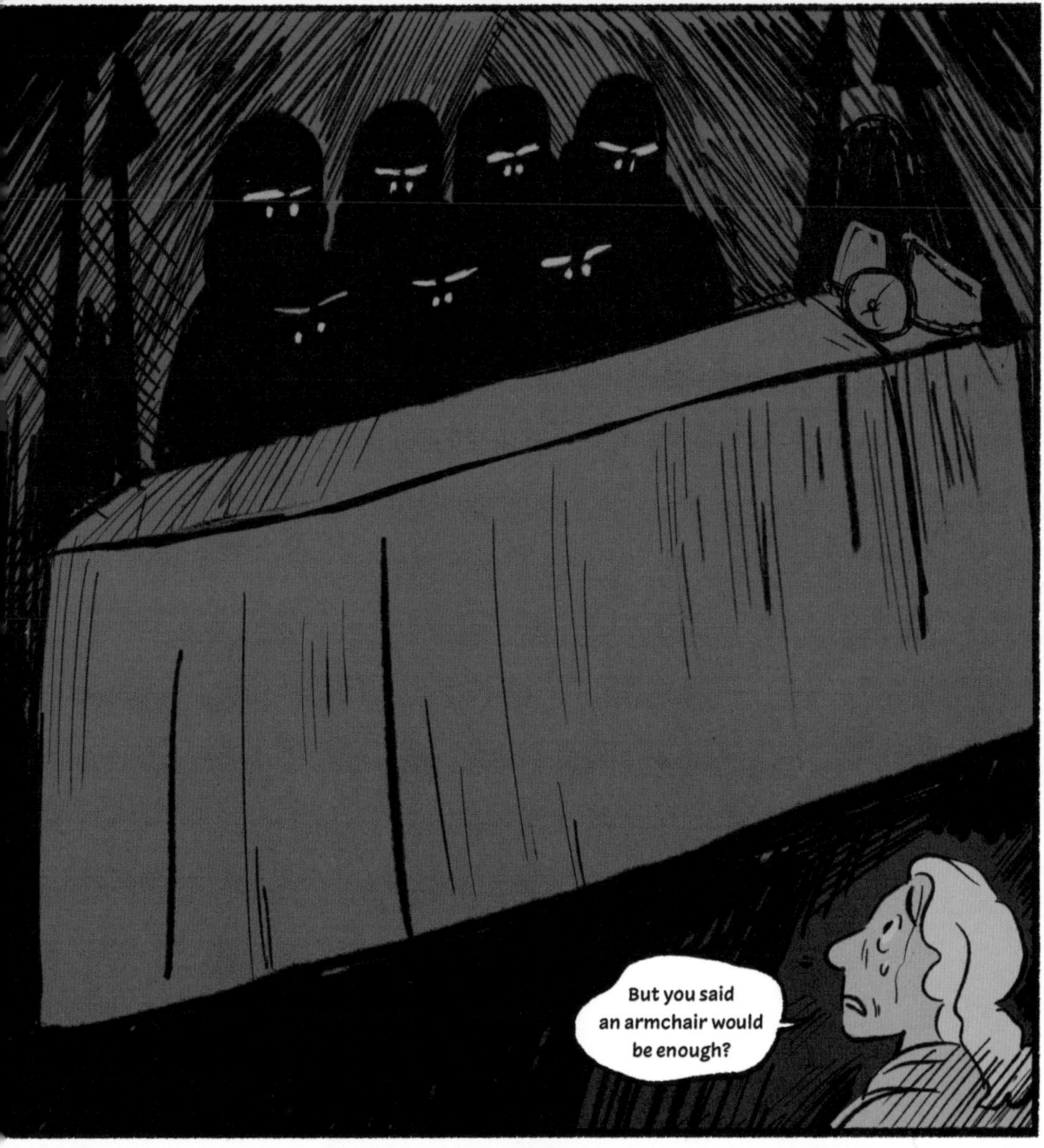
But you said an armchair would be enough?

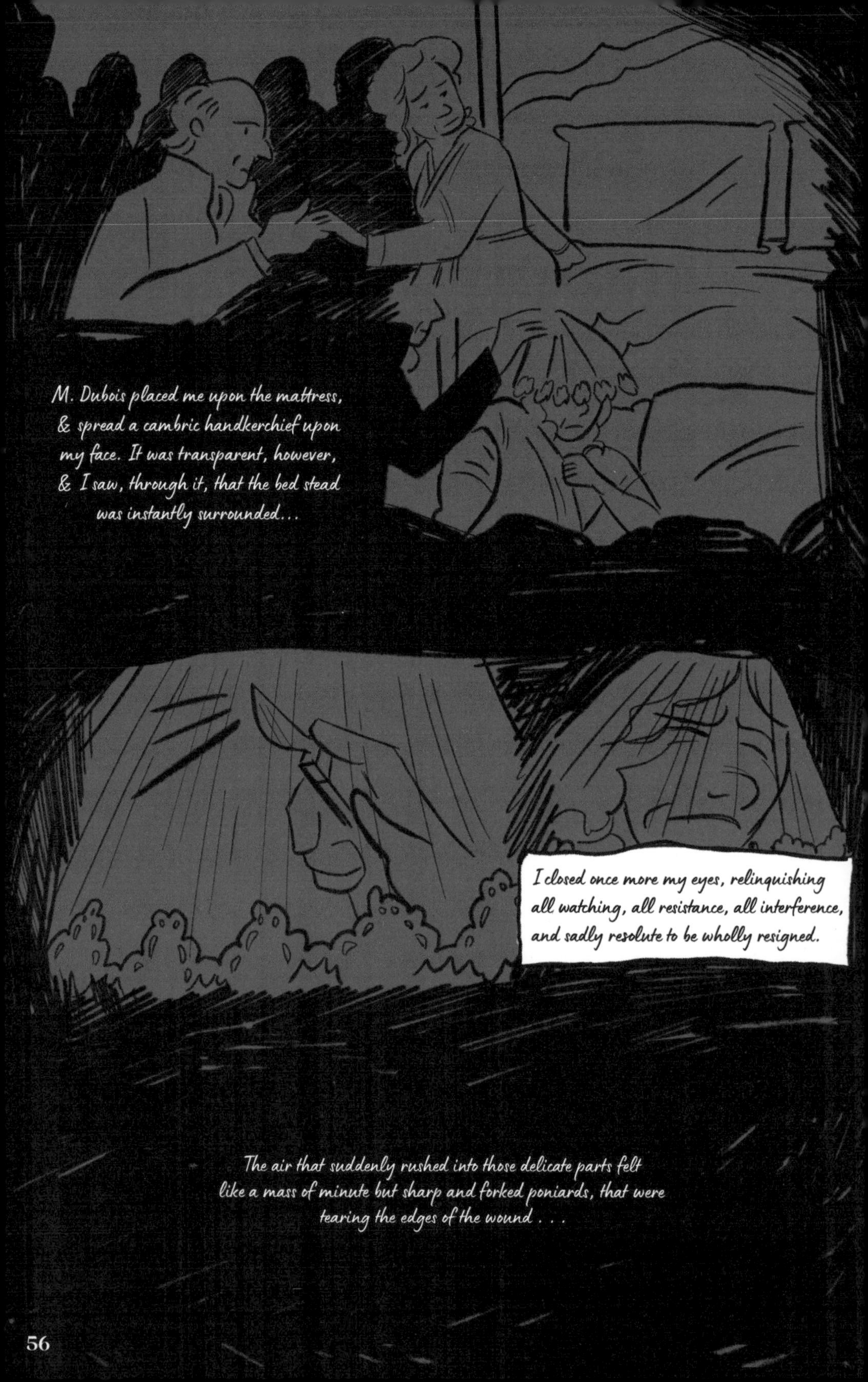
M. Dubois placed me upon the mattress, & spread a cambric handkerchief upon my face. It was transparent, however, & I saw, through it, that the bed stead was instantly surrounded...
I closed once more my eyes, relinquishing all watching, all resistance, all interference, and sadly resolute to be wholly resigned.
The air that suddenly rushed into those delicate parts felt like a mass of minute but sharp and forked poniards, that were tearing the edges of the wound . . .

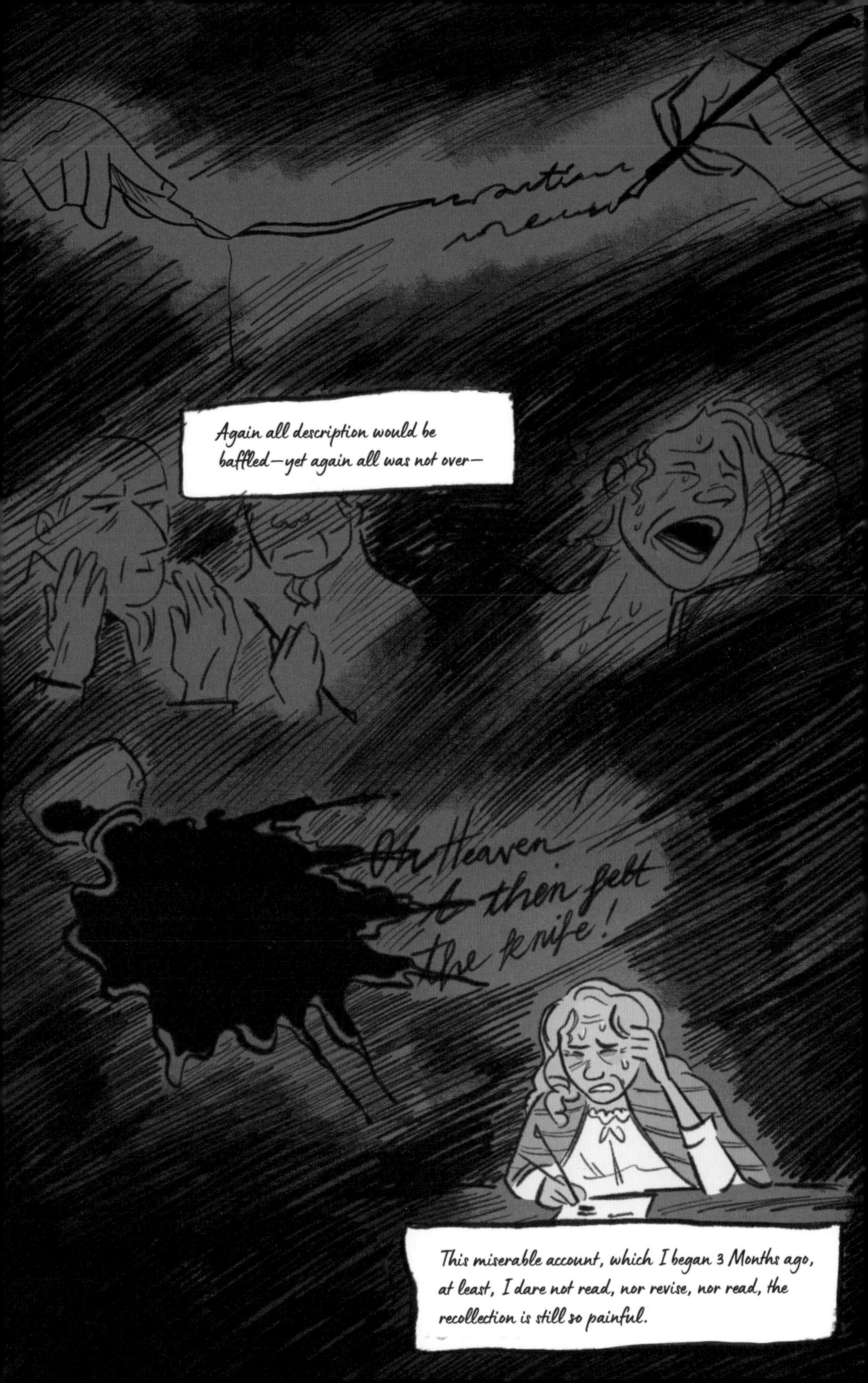
Again all description would be baffled—yet again all was not over—
Oh Heaven
I then felt
the knife!
This miserable account, which I began 3 Months ago, at least, I dare not read, nor revise, nor read, the recollection is still so painful.

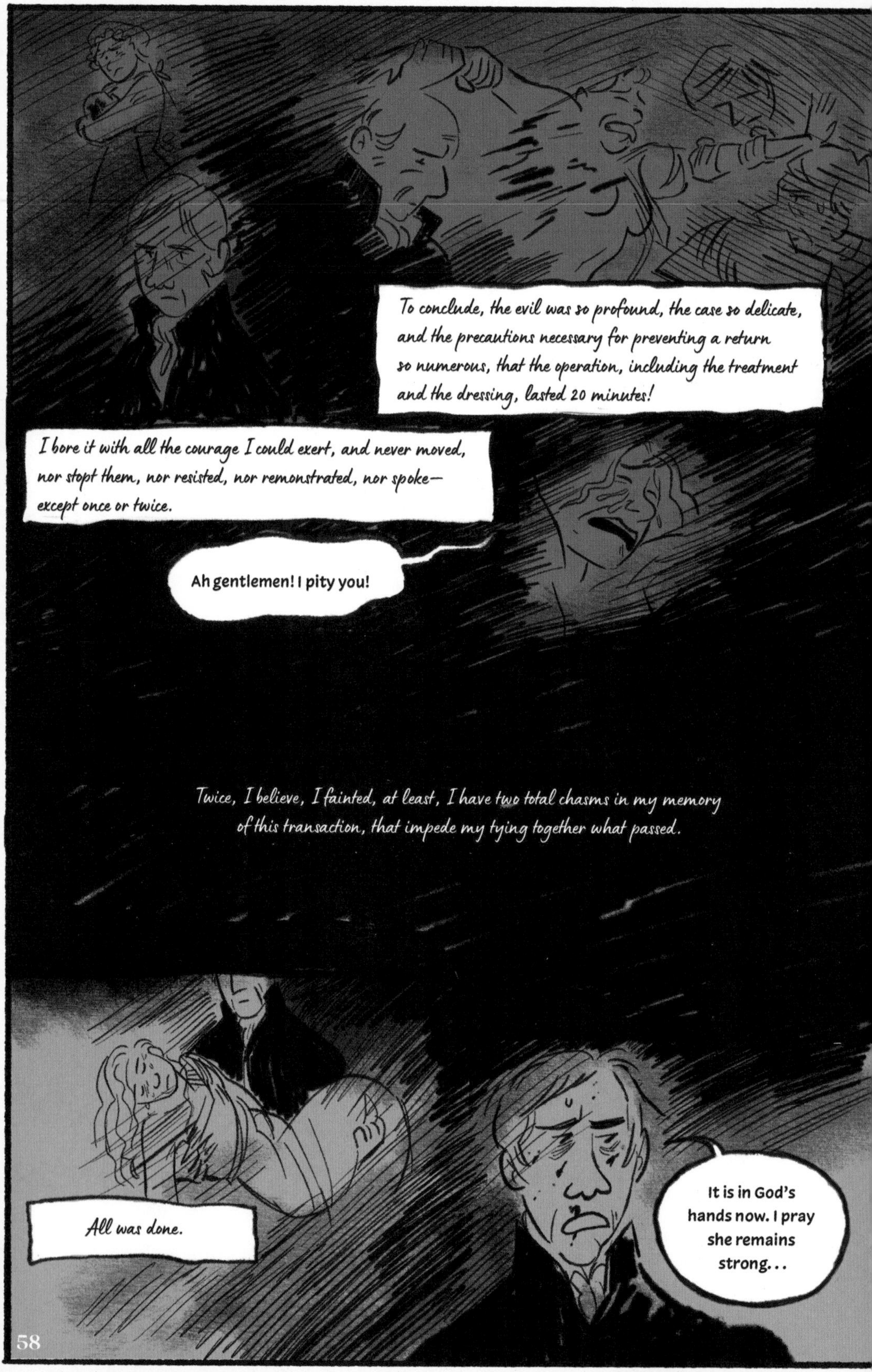
To conclude, the evil was so profound, the case so delicate, and the precautions necessary for preventing a return so numerous, that the operation, including the treatment and the dressing, lasted 20 minutes!
I bore it with all the courage I could exert, and never moved, nor stopt them, nor resisted, nor remonstrated, nor spoke— except once or twice.
Ah gentlemen! I pity you!
Twice, I believe, I fainted, at least, I have two total chasms in my memory of this transaction, that impede my tying together what passed.
All was done.
It is in God's hands now. I pray she remains strong...

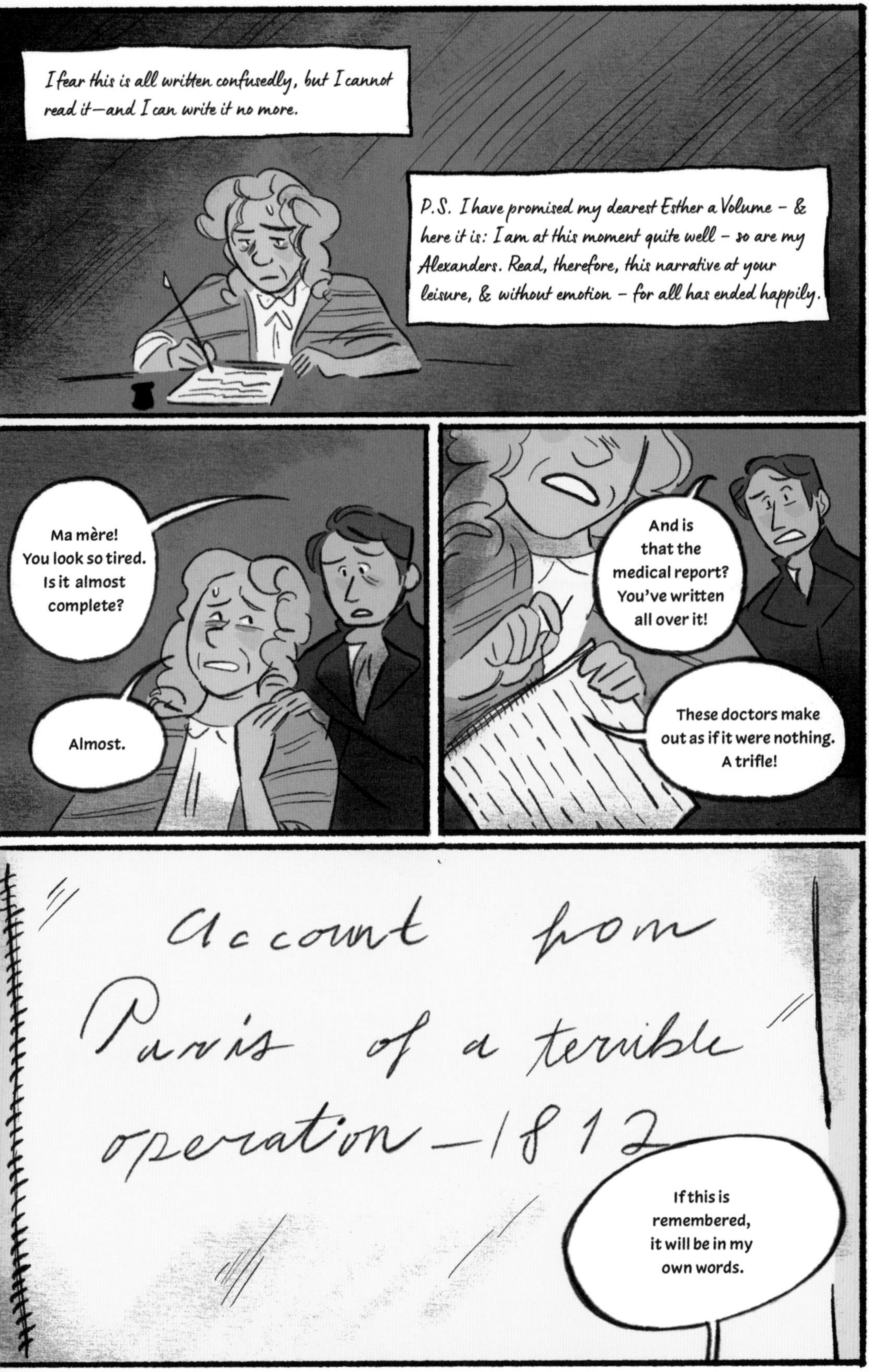
I fear this is all written confusedly, but I cannot read it—and I can write it no more.
P.S. I have promised my dearest Esther a Volume – & here it is: I am at this moment quite well – so are my Alexanders. Read, therefore, this narrative at your leisure, & without emotion – for all has ended happily.
Ma mère! You look so tired. Is it almost complete?
Almost.
And is that the medical report? You've written all over it!
These doctors make out as if it were nothing. A trifle!
Account from Paris of a terrible operation—1812
If this is remembered, it will be in my own words.

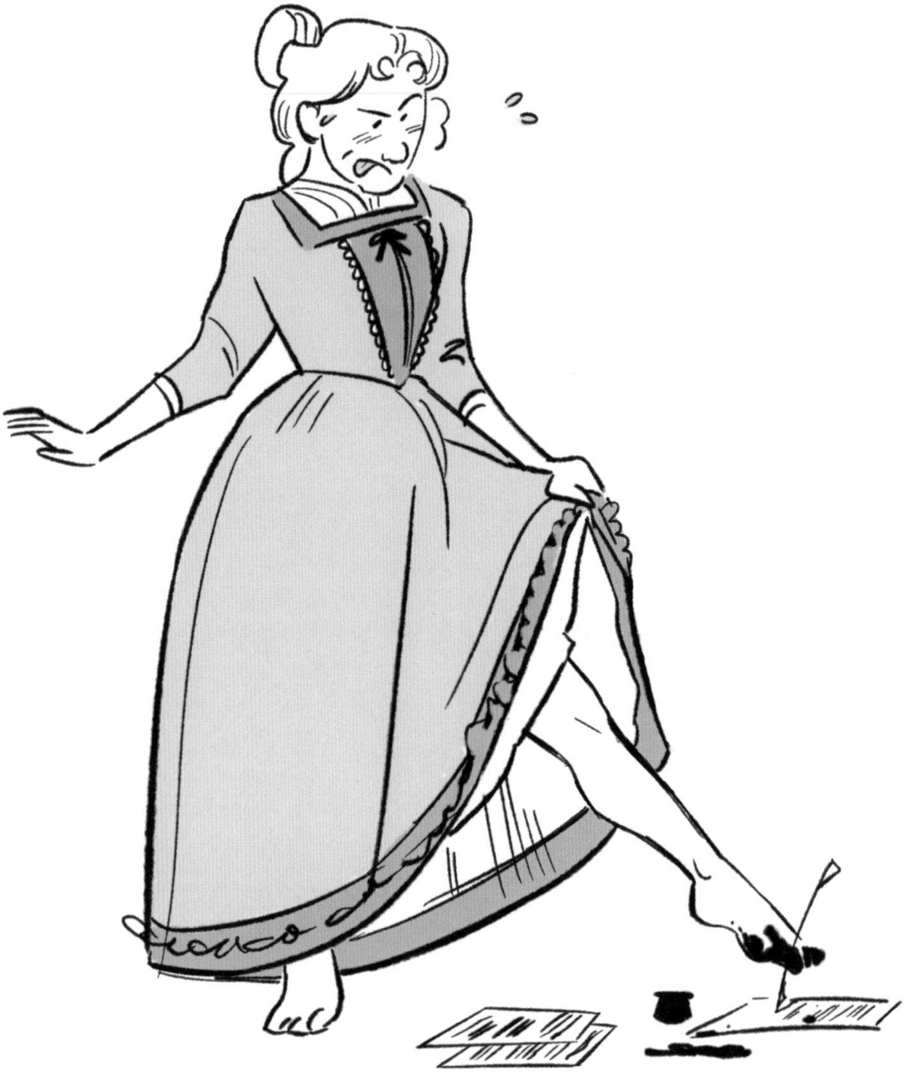

When Burney sent *Evelina* to publishers in London, she disguised her handwriting. She had been making fair (clean) copies of her father's books for years and was worried her penmanship would be recognized.

The house that books built. When Burney sold her third novel, *Camilla*, she built a home for her family with the money she had earned.

SELECTED WORKS:

NOVELS

1778: *Evelina*
1782: *Cecilia*
1796: *Camilla*
1814: *The Wanderer; or Female Difficulties*

NONFICTION

1793: *Brief Reflections relative to the Emigrant French Clergy; earnestly submitted to the humane consideration of the Ladies of Great Britain*
1832: *Memoirs of Doctor Burney, Arranged from his own manuscripts, from family papers and from personal recollections by his daughter, Madame d'Arblay*
1842: *Diary and Letters of Madame D'Arblay* [Edited by her niece Charlotte Barrett]

PLAYS:

1779: *The Witlings*
1788-1795: *Edwy and Elgiva*
1790-97: *Hubert de Vere*
1790-91: *The Siege of Pevensey*
1791: *Elberta*
1798-1800: *Love and Fashion*
1801-02: *A Busy Day*
1801-02: *The Woman-Hater*

Jane Austen

1775–1817

"I am not at all in a humour for writing; I must write on until I am."

—Jane Austen in a letter to Cassandra Austen, October 26, 1813

Though Jane Austen completed just six novels and saw only four of them published in her lifetime, it is undeniable that the cultural impact of *Sense and Sensibility, Pride and Prejudice, Emma, Mansfield Park, Northanger Abbey,* and *Persuasion* far outweighs their number. And though the light and comedic hand with which she wrote suggests a life of genteel solitude, the pain and uncertainty that plagued much of her adult life does not completely disappear behind her stories of matchmaking, balls, and bonnets.

In 1801 Jane Austen's father, George, a retired clergyman, moved his wife and two unmarried daughters to the fashionable yet faded resort city of Bath. All but one of their six sons had already left the family home to pursue careers in the Church, the navy, and the militia. Jane was pursuing a career of her own in writing, and she had already completed three novels—*Elinor and Marianne, First Impressions,* and *Susan*—which would later be titled *Sense and Sensibility, Pride and Prejudice,* and *Northanger Abbey.* Jane's brother Henry was busy trying to sell *Susan* on her behalf, but while Jane waited anxiously for news of her book, her parents harbored other hopes for her future.

The Austen parents, George and Cassandra, had fallen in love and married in Bath forty years earlier, and it was here, perhaps, that they hoped to find husbands for their daughters, Cassandra and Jane, twenty-seven and twenty-six, respectively. According to legend, Jane was so distressed when told of the move that she fainted on the spot. Bath had once been a desirable city, but with the rise of seaside resort towns like Brighton, its reputation was in decline. However, despite its dated appeal and aging residents, it still offered a great many distractions and a complete change of pace from their country upbringing in Steventon. There were balls at the Assembly Rooms, new plays to see at the Theatre Royal, new dresses to order, and a seemingly endless stream of social calls. Even within this sociable chaos, Jane was unable to escape the uncertainty of her future. Though comfortably middle class, the Austens were not wealthy, and more than once they found themselves on the hunt for cheaper accommodation.

Easy then to imagine Austen's writing desk packed away, unused and unthought-of. Certainly, the lack of novels completed in this time suggests that the five years she lived in Bath were so miserable that even the sparkling and lively Jane Austen could not make light of them. But though her time there was often an unhappy one, the Bath of Austen's novels is a catalyst for self-reflection, for taking charge of one's life, and for opportunity.

It may seem hard to imagine Austen, the woman to whom writing came so naturally, neglecting her pen, but all those distractions, the worry and uncertainty of her years in Bath, are part of what made her later works so successful. Tucked into the pages of *Pride and Prejudice, Sense and Sensibility, Persuasion,* and the rest, are glimpses of this time when she could not write.

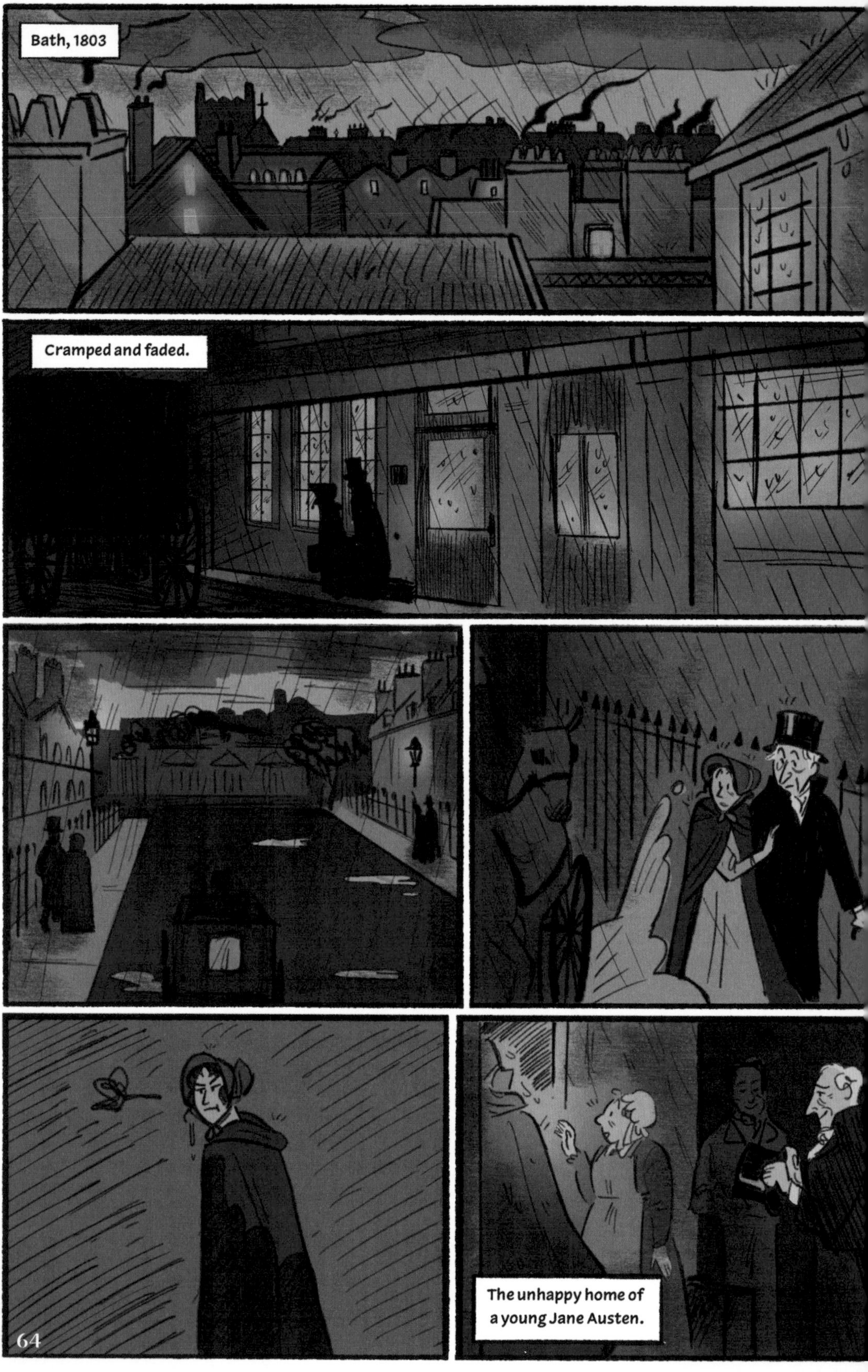
Bath, 1803
Cramped and faded.
The unhappy home of
a young Jane Austen.

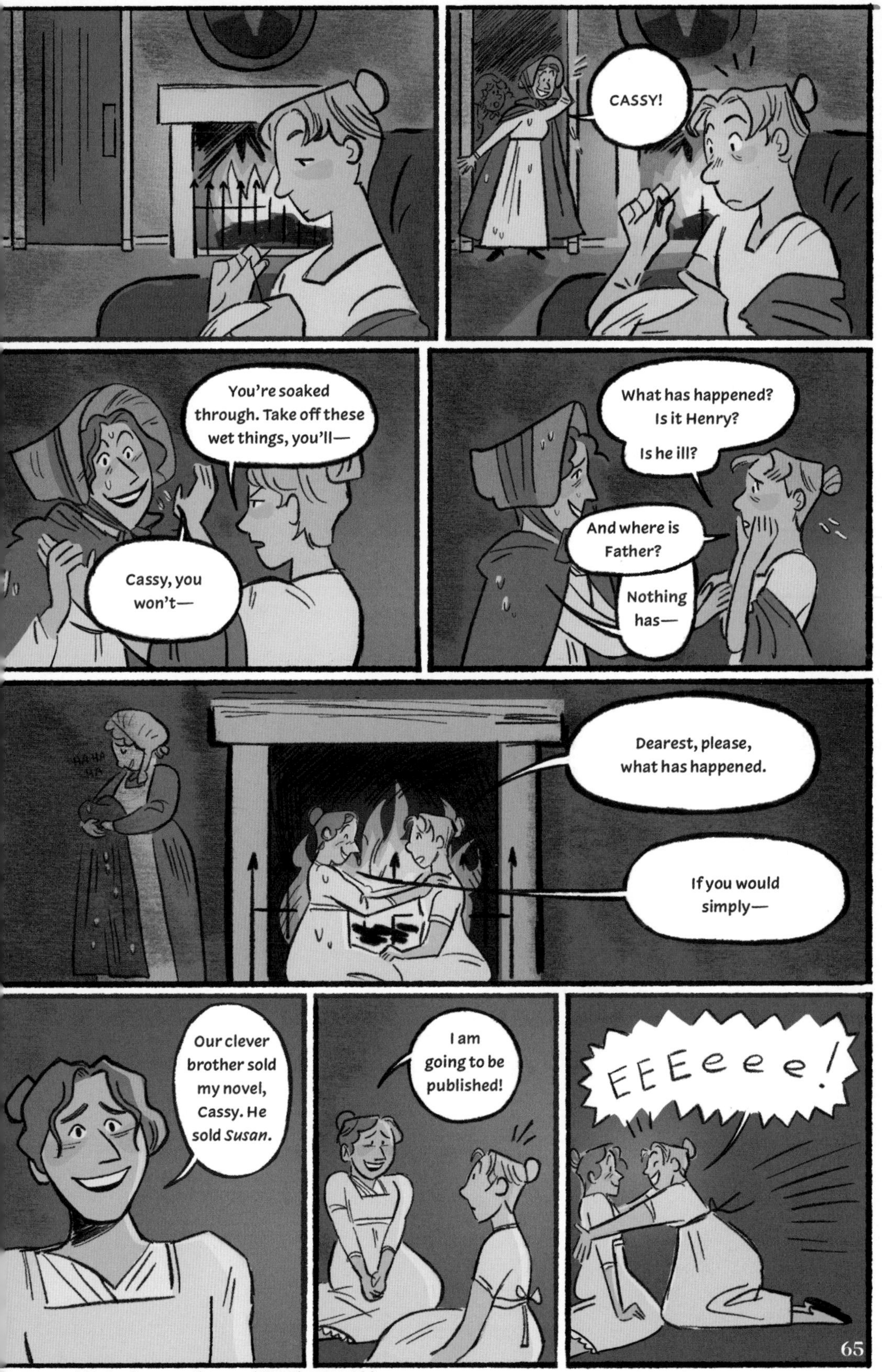
CASSY!
You're soaked through. Take off these wet things, you'll—
Cassy, you won't—
What has happened? Is it Henry?
Is he ill?
And where is Father?
Nothing has—
Dearest, please, what has happened.
If you would simply—
Our clever brother sold my novel, Cassy. He sold *Susan*.
I am going to be published!
EEEeeee!

usan would later become the novel *Northanger Abbey*.

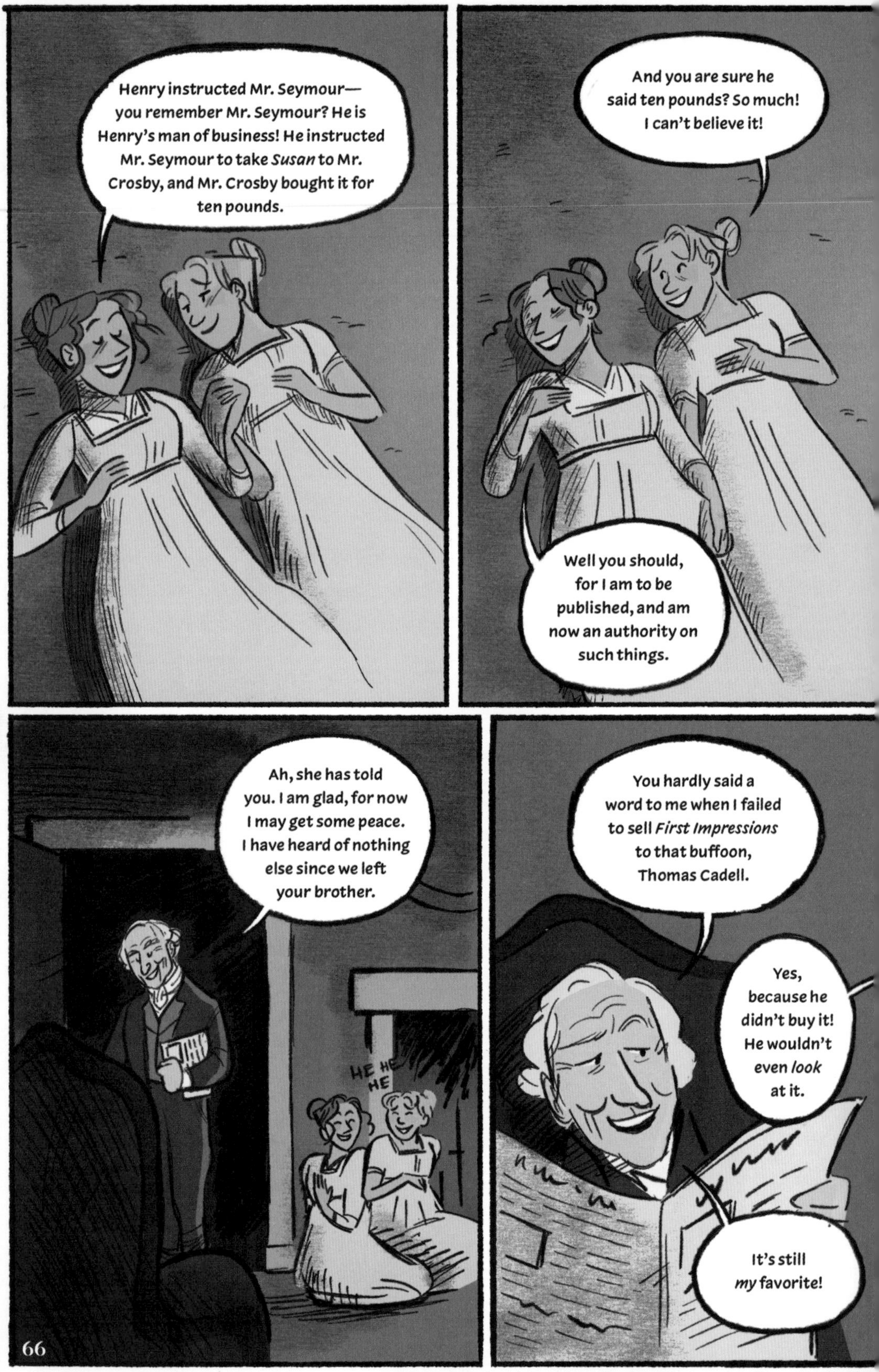

Henry instructed Mr. Seymour— you remember Mr. Seymour? He is Henry's man of business! He instructed Mr. Seymour to take *Susan* to Mr. Crosby, and Mr. Crosby bought it for ten pounds.
And you are sure he said ten pounds? So much! I can't believe it!
Well you should, for I am to be published, and am now an authority on such things.
Ah, she has told you. I am glad, for now I may get some peace. I have heard of nothing else since we left your brother.
HE HE HE
You hardly said a word to me when I failed to sell *First Impressions* to that buffoon, Thomas Cadell.
Yes, because he didn't buy it! He wouldn't even *look* at it.
It's still *my* favorite!

First Impressions would later become the novel *Pride and Prejudice*.

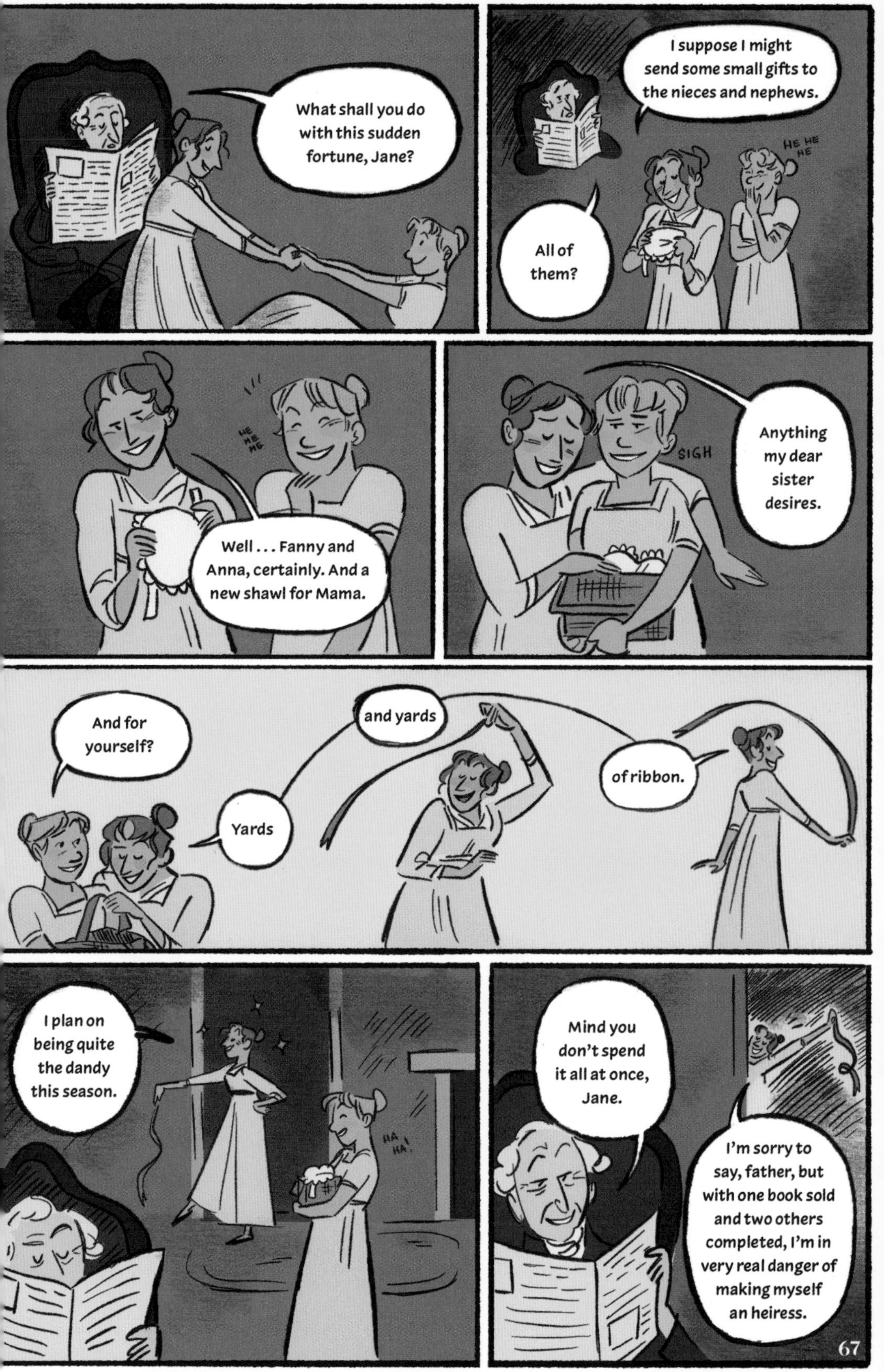
What shall you do with this sudden fortune, Jane?
I suppose I might send some small gifts to the nieces and nephews.
HE HE HE
All of them?
HE HE HE
Well . . . Fanny and Anna, certainly. And a new shawl for Mama.
Anything my dear sister desires.
SIGH
And for yourself?
Yards
and yards
of ribbon.
I plan on being quite the dandy this season.
HA HA!
Mind you don't spend it all at once, Jane.
I'm sorry to say, father, but with one book sold and two others completed, I'm in very real danger of making myself an heiress.

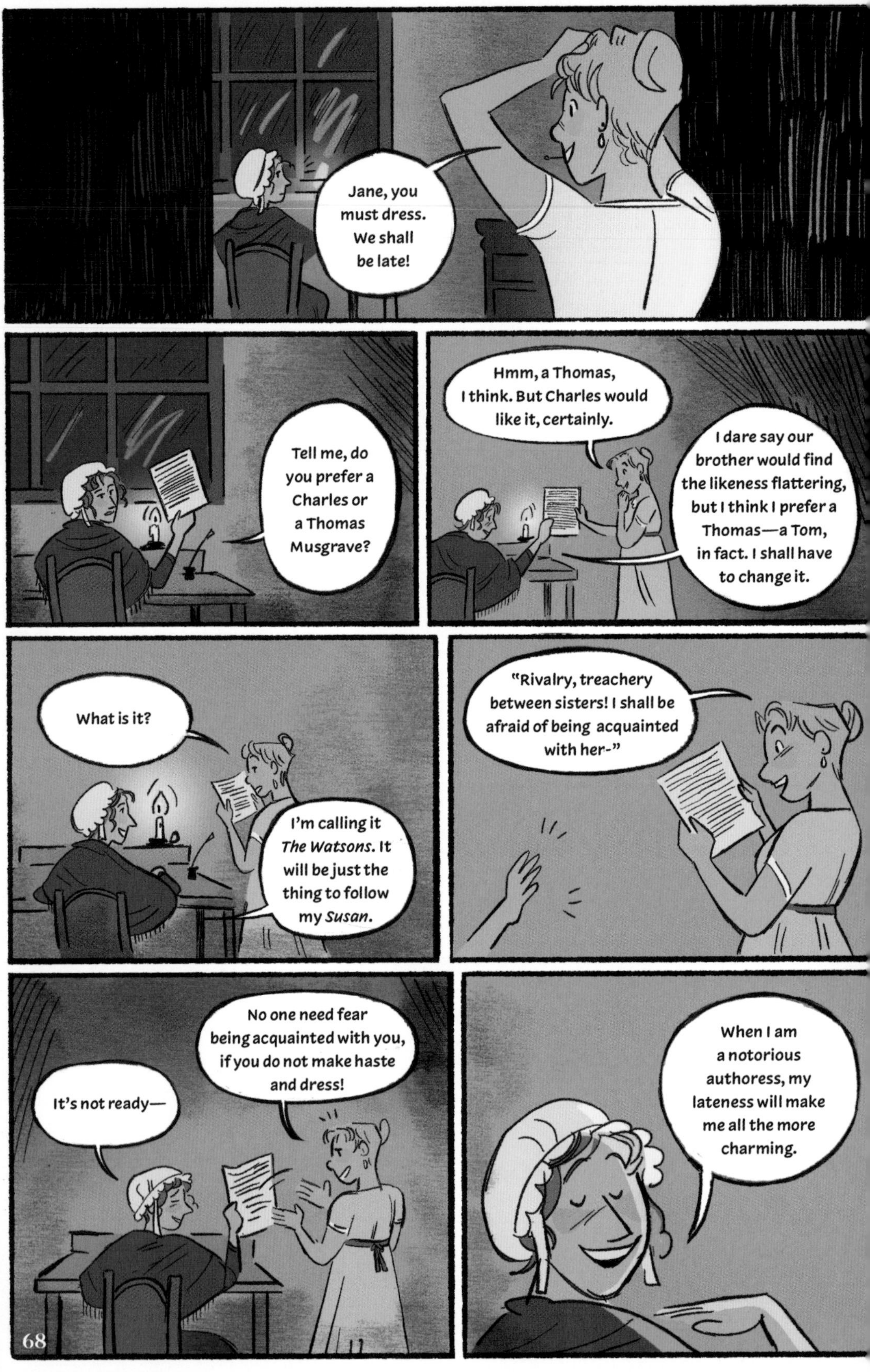
Jane, you must dress. We shall be late!
Tell me, do you prefer a Charles or a Thomas Musgrave?
Hmm, a Thomas, I think. But Charles would like it, certainly.
I dare say our brother would find the likeness flattering, but I think I prefer a Thomas—a Tom, in fact. I shall have to change it.
What is it?
I'm calling it *The Watsons*. It will be just the thing to follow my *Susan*.
"Rivalry, treachery between sisters! I shall be afraid of being acquainted with her-"
It's not ready—
No one need fear being acquainted with you, if you do not make haste and dress!
When I am a notorious authoress, my lateness will make me all the more charming.

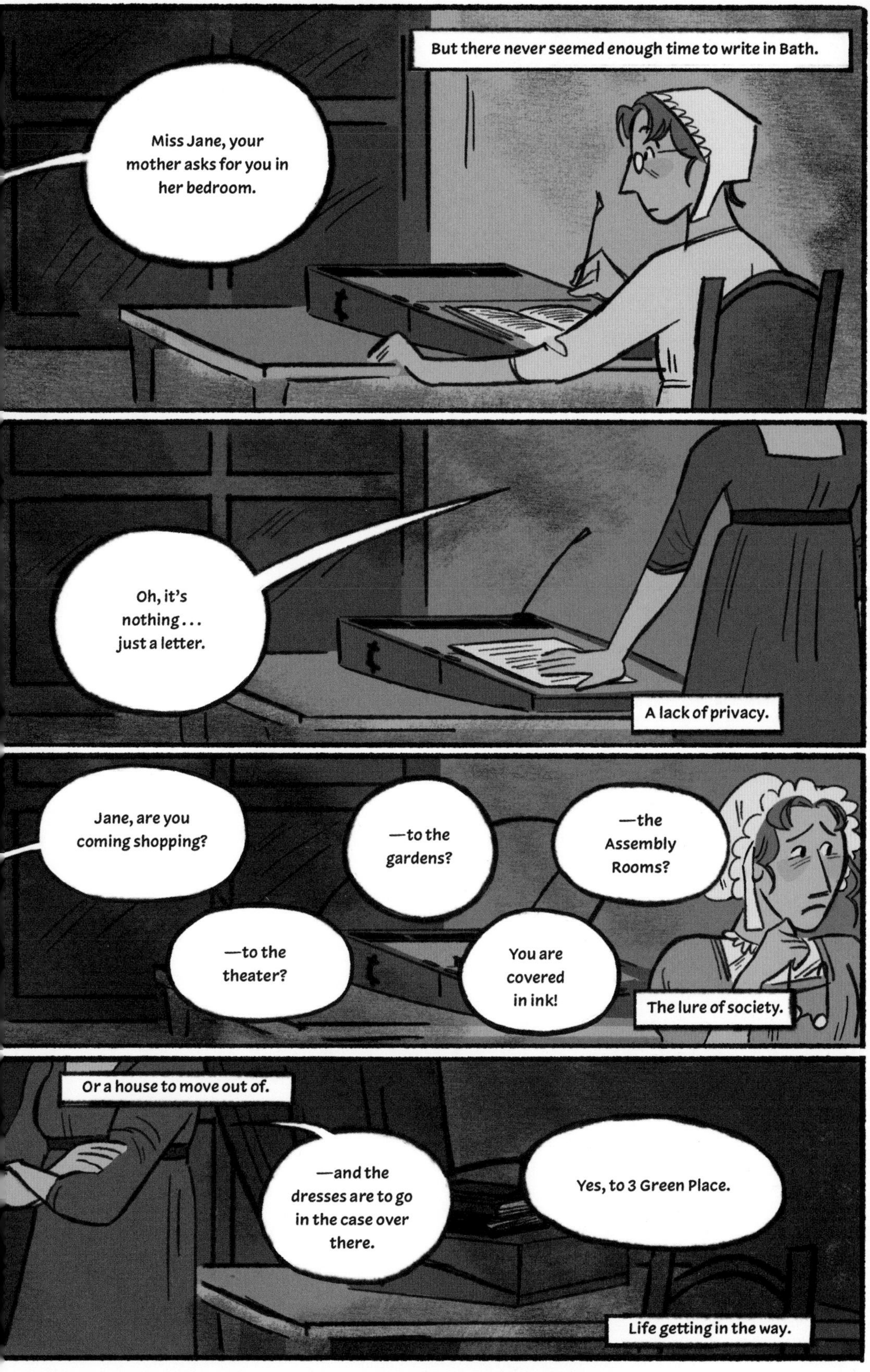
But there never seemed enough time to write in Bath.
Miss Jane, your mother asks for you in her bedroom.
Oh, it's nothing... just a letter.
A lack of privacy.
Jane, are you coming shopping?
—to the gardens?
—the Assembly Rooms?
—to the theater?
You are covered in ink!
The lure of society.
Or a house to move out of.
—and the dresses are to go in the case over there.
Yes, to 3 Green Place.
Life getting in the way.

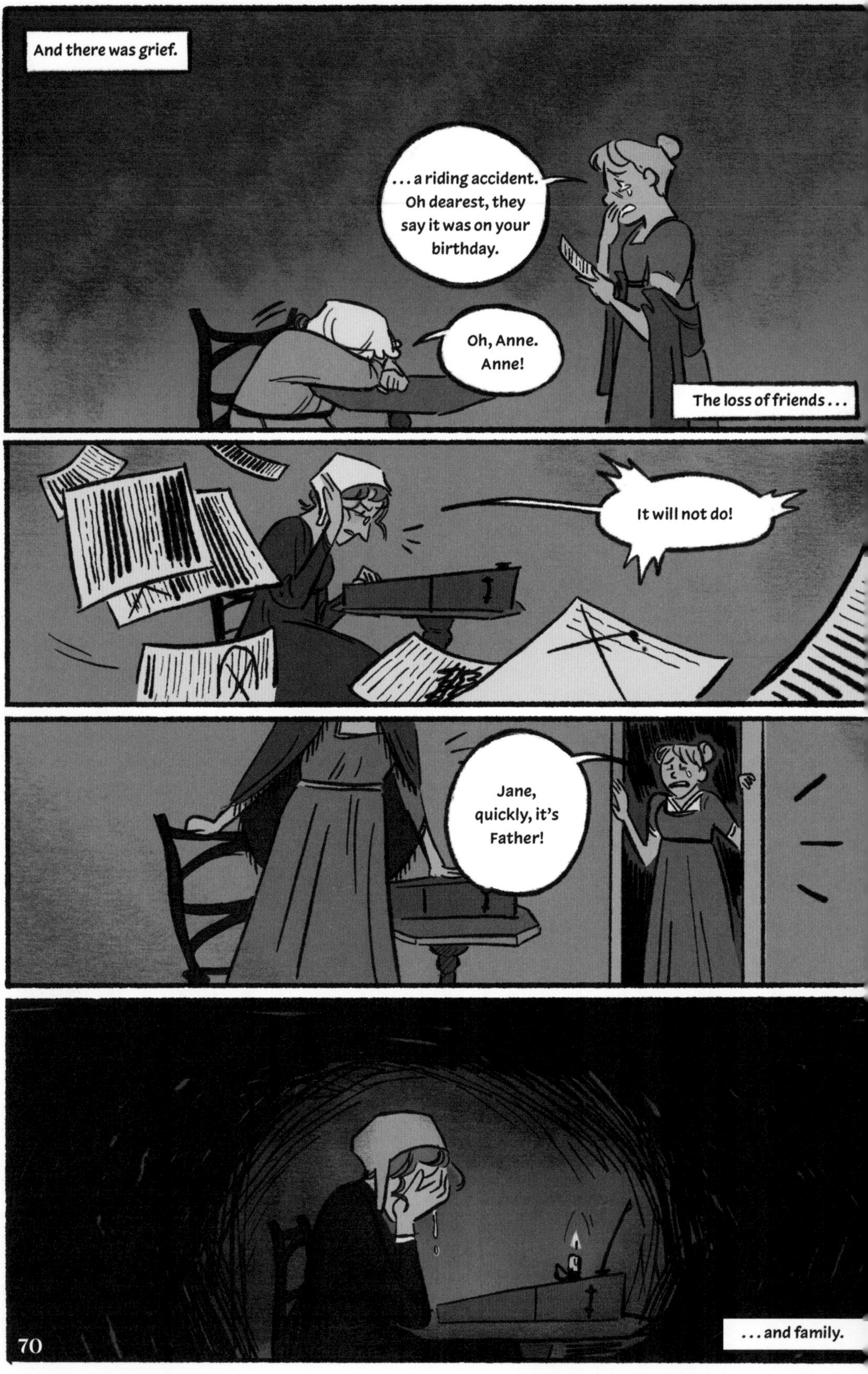
And there was grief.
. . . a riding accident. Oh dearest, they say it was on your birthday.
Oh, Anne. Anne!
The loss of friends . . .
It will not do!
Jane, quickly, it's Father!
. . . and family.

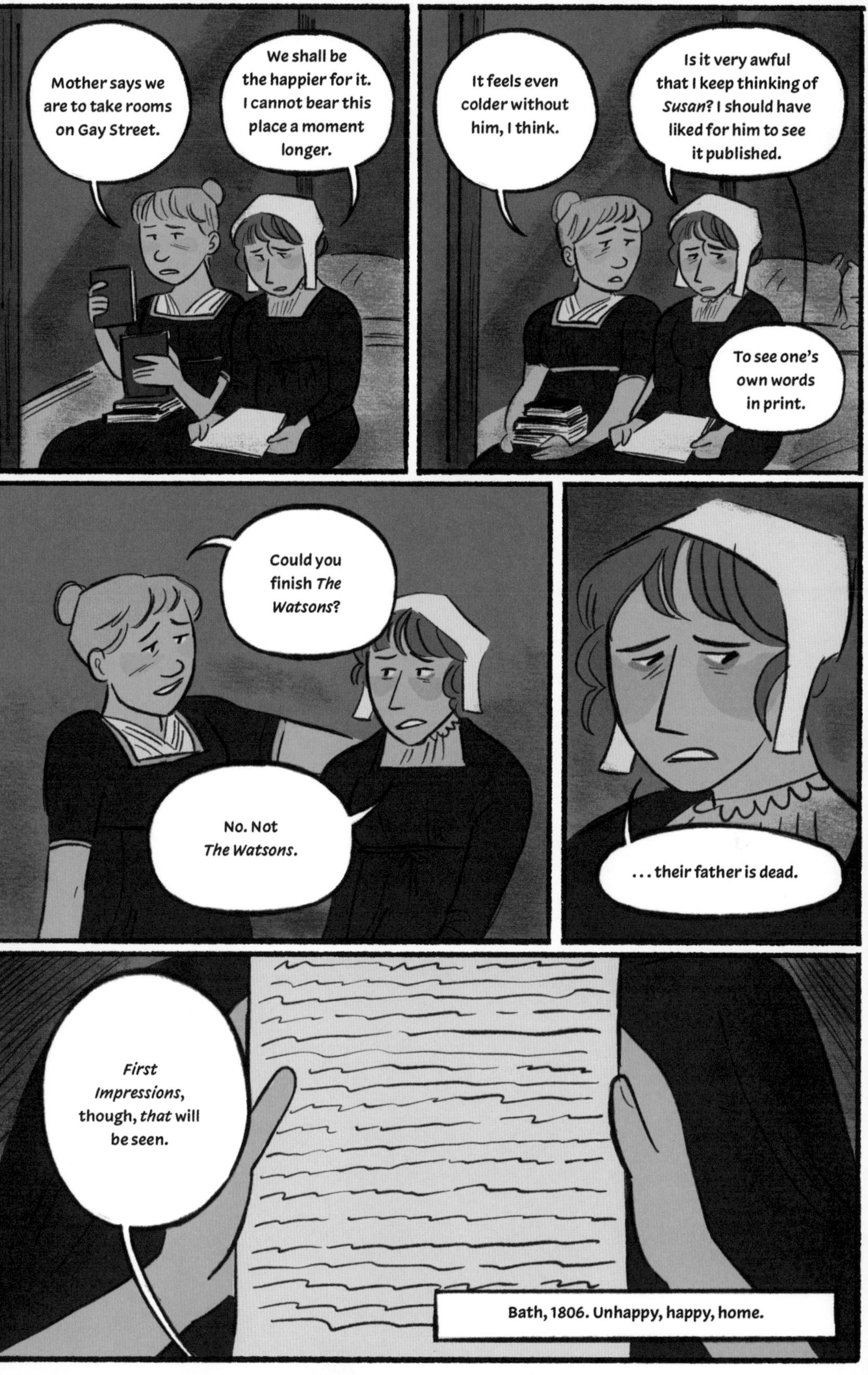
Mother says we are to take rooms on Gay Street.
We shall be the happier for it. I cannot bear this place a moment longer.
It feels even colder without him, I think.
Is it very awful that I keep thinking of *Susan*? I should have liked for him to see it published.
To see one's own words in print.
Could you finish *The Watsons*?
No. Not *The Watsons*.
. . . their father is dead.
First Impressions, though, *that* will be seen.
Bath, 1806. Unhappy, happy, home.

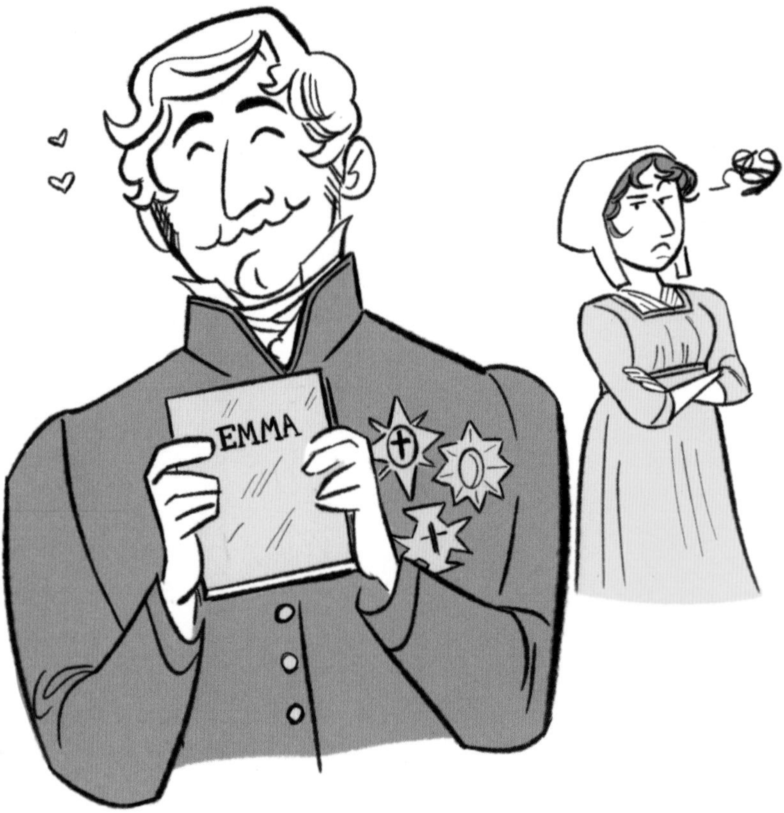
EMMA

The Prince Regent was such a fan of Austen's work that he bought a copy of *Sense and Sensibility* before it went on sale and requested that *Emma* be dedicated to him. The feeling was not mutual.

CECILIA
CECILIA
BURNEY
PRIDE AND PREJUDICE
JANE AUSTEN

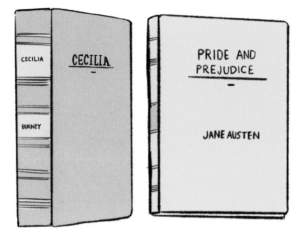

When Austen needed a new name for *First Impressions,* she turned to Frances Burney for inspiration. The phrase "pride and prejudice" appears no less than three times in the final paragraph of Burney's novel *Cecilia,* which Austen described as a "work in which the greatest powers of the mind are displayed."

SELECTED WORKS:

NOVELS

1811: *Sense and Sensibility*
1813: *Pride and Prejudice*
1814: *Mansfield Park*
1815: *Emma*
1818: *Northanger Abbey* [published posthumously]
1818: *Persuasion* [published posthumously]
1825: *Sanditon* [unfinished in 1817, published posthumously]
1871: *The Watsons* [unfinished in 1804, published posthumously]
1871: *Lady Susan* [published posthumously]

Elizabeth Gaskell

1810–1865

"I'll not listen to reason . . . reason always means
what someone else has got to say."

—*Cranford*, 1853

Elizabeth Cleghorn Gaskell was one of the most widely read and also most divisive authors of the Victorian age. She lived in Manchester with her Unitarian minister husband, William, and their four daughters: Marianne, Meta, Flossie, and Julia. Their home was busy and sociable and the family often hosted famous friends, including Charles Dickens and Harriet Beecher Stowe.

Gaskell had risen to fame with the publication of her first novel, *Mary Barton* (1848), a deeply personal book that drew much from Gaskell's own experience of losing a child. But it would be looking to the life of another that shaped Gaskell's legacy and infamy. In 1857, *The Life of Charlotte Brontë* made its way into the world and Gaskell made her way to Europe.

Two years before, in 1855, Gaskell was returning to Manchester from Paris. She had fled the critical reviews of her recently completed *North and South* (1855) and did not know if she would write again. She came home to distressing news: Her once close friend and long-time correspondent, Charlotte Brontë, was dead.

It was a letter from Patrick Brontë that persuaded her to write about his daughter's life. He had suffered through weeks of inaccurate tributes and attacks on his daughter's character and decided a response was needed. Perhaps Gaskell, who had known Charlotte so well and for so long, would be the person to answer them. In a letter to Brontë's publisher, George Smith, Gaskell explained that she wanted the world to "honour the woman as much as they have admired the writer."

The bulk of Gaskell's research was undertaken by collecting personal anecdotes from those who had known Charlotte, and through reading the author's correspondence. While the letters did, as Gaskell wished, paint a vivid and sympathetic portrait of a remarkable and often tragic life, it also threw the actions of many whom Charlotte had encountered into question. There was the school, Cowan Bridge, where Charlotte and many other children had suffered from neglect; Charlotte's brother Branwell and his former employer, Lady Scott, with whom he had had an affair; the publisher, Thomas Newby, who had used Charlotte's anonymity to sell books written by her sister Anne, and the unrequited love Charlotte herself had harbored for a Belgian schoolmaster. What to include and what to gloss over was up to Gaskell, and she knew, even before the manuscript was finished, that people would not be happy.

The book was completed in 1857, almost two full years after Gaskell received news of Brontë's death. Gaskell had never written a biography before; the very task of collecting, copying, and reading the letters, separating fact from fiction, and expressing it all as truthfully as possible was "a most difficult thing for a writer of fiction."

Just as with the publication of *North and South*, Gaskell was determined to get away from the reviewers. This time she fled England for Rome with her two eldest daughters, Meta and Marianne, leaving her husband William to handle the fallout.

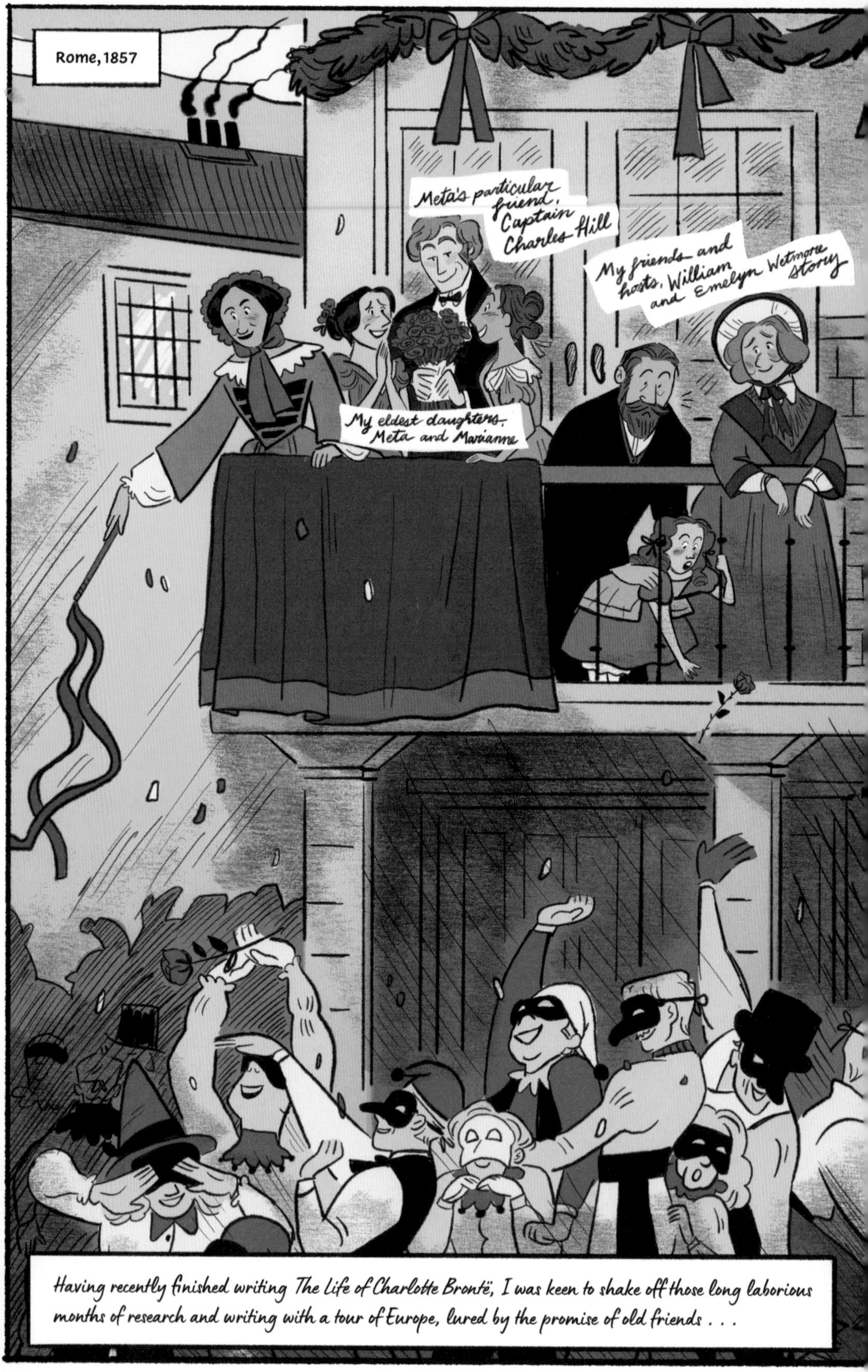
Rome, 1857
Meta's particular friend, Captain Charles Hill
My friends and hosts, William and Emelyn Wetmore Story
My eldest daughters, Meta and Marianne
Having recently finished writing The Life of Charlotte Brontë, I was keen to shake off those long laborious months of research and writing with a tour of Europe, lured by the promise of old friends . . .

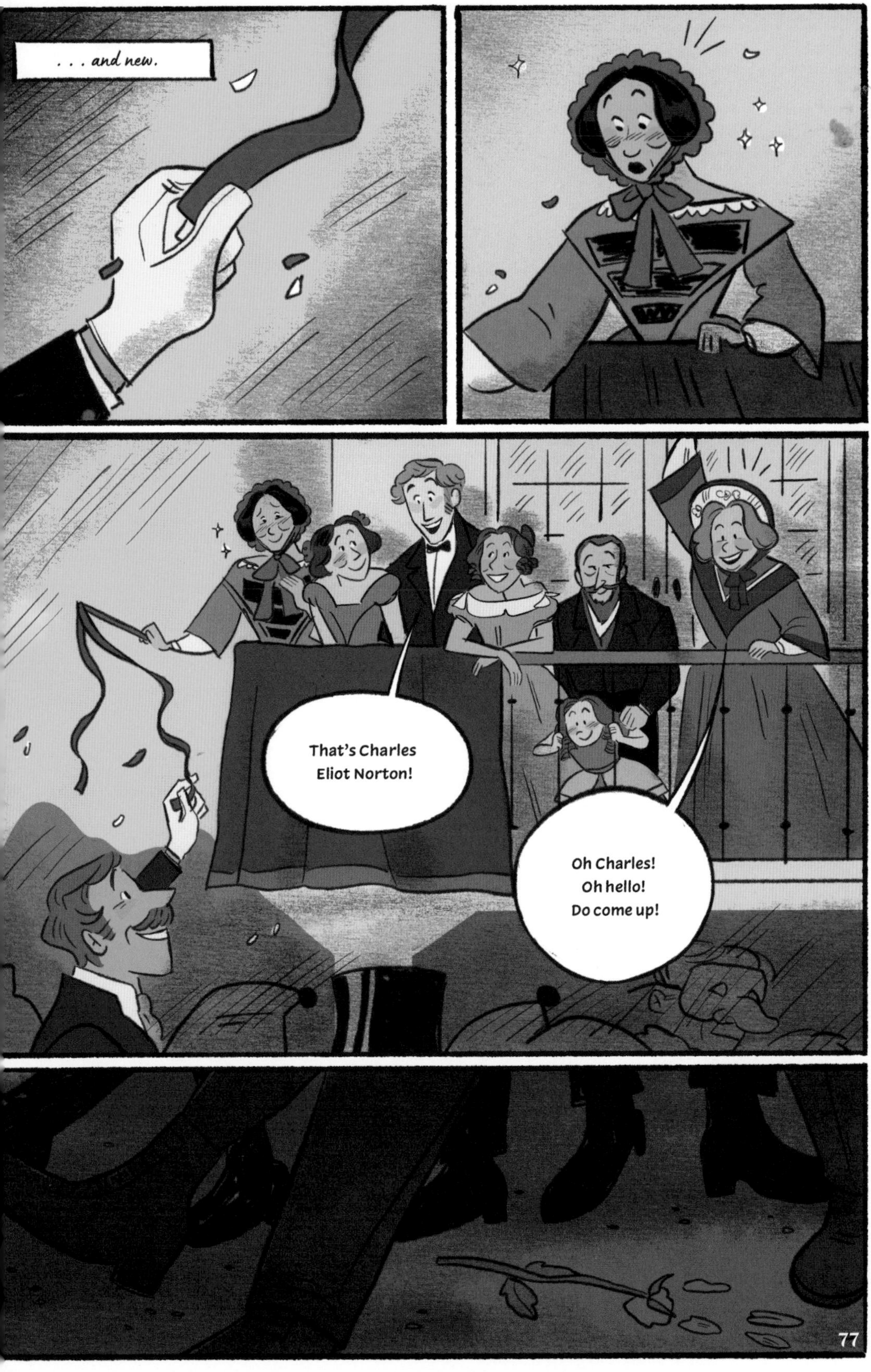
. . . and new.
That's Charles Eliot Norton!
Oh Charles! Oh hello! Do come up!

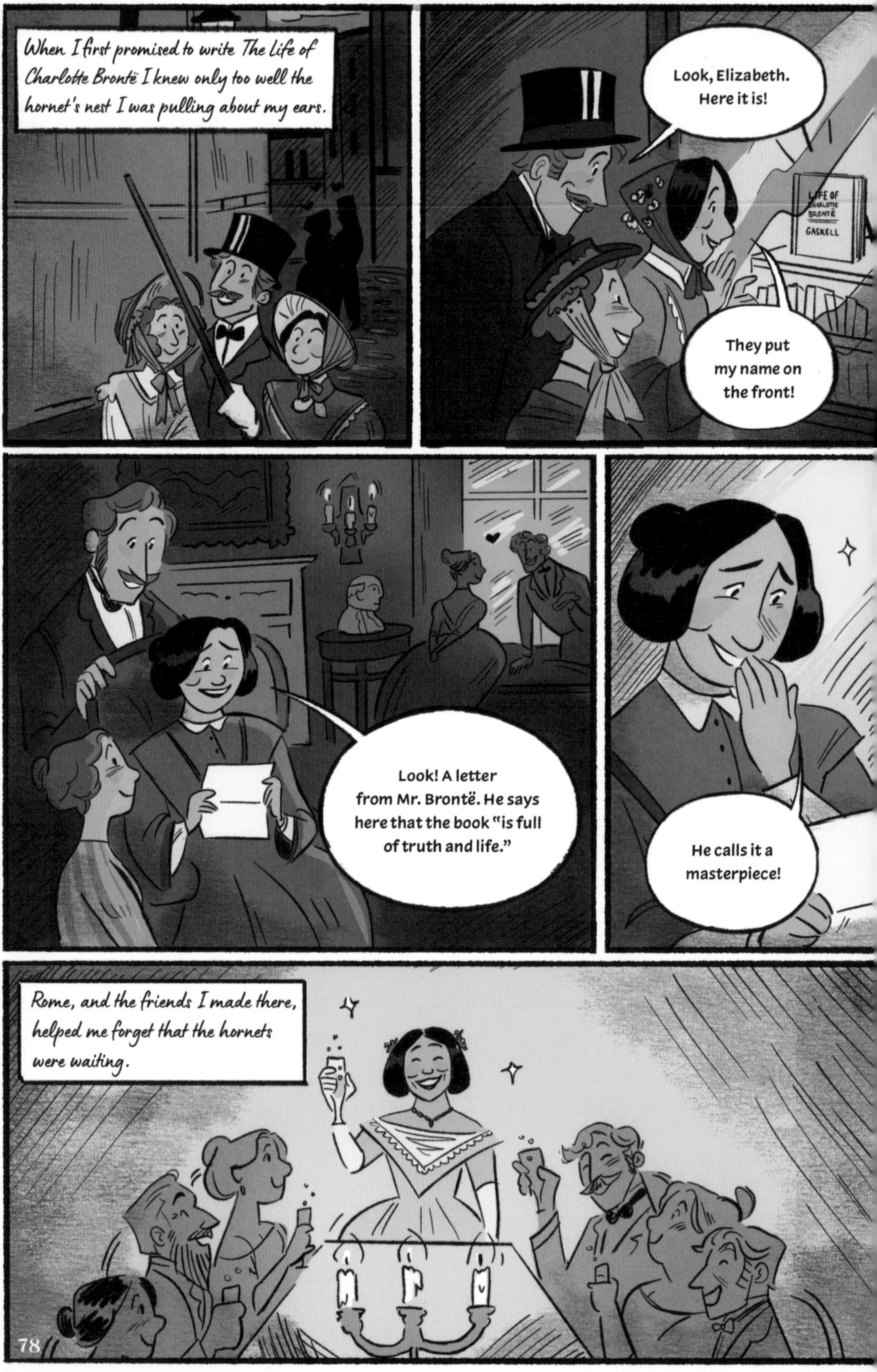
When I first promised to write The Life of Charlotte Brontë I knew only too well the hornet's nest I was pulling about my ears.
Look, Elizabeth. Here it is!
LIFE OF CHARLOTTE BRONTË GASKELL
They put my name on the front!
Look! A letter from Mr. Brontë. He says here that the book "is full of truth and life."
He calls it a masterpiece!
Rome, and the friends I made there, helped me forget that the hornets were waiting.

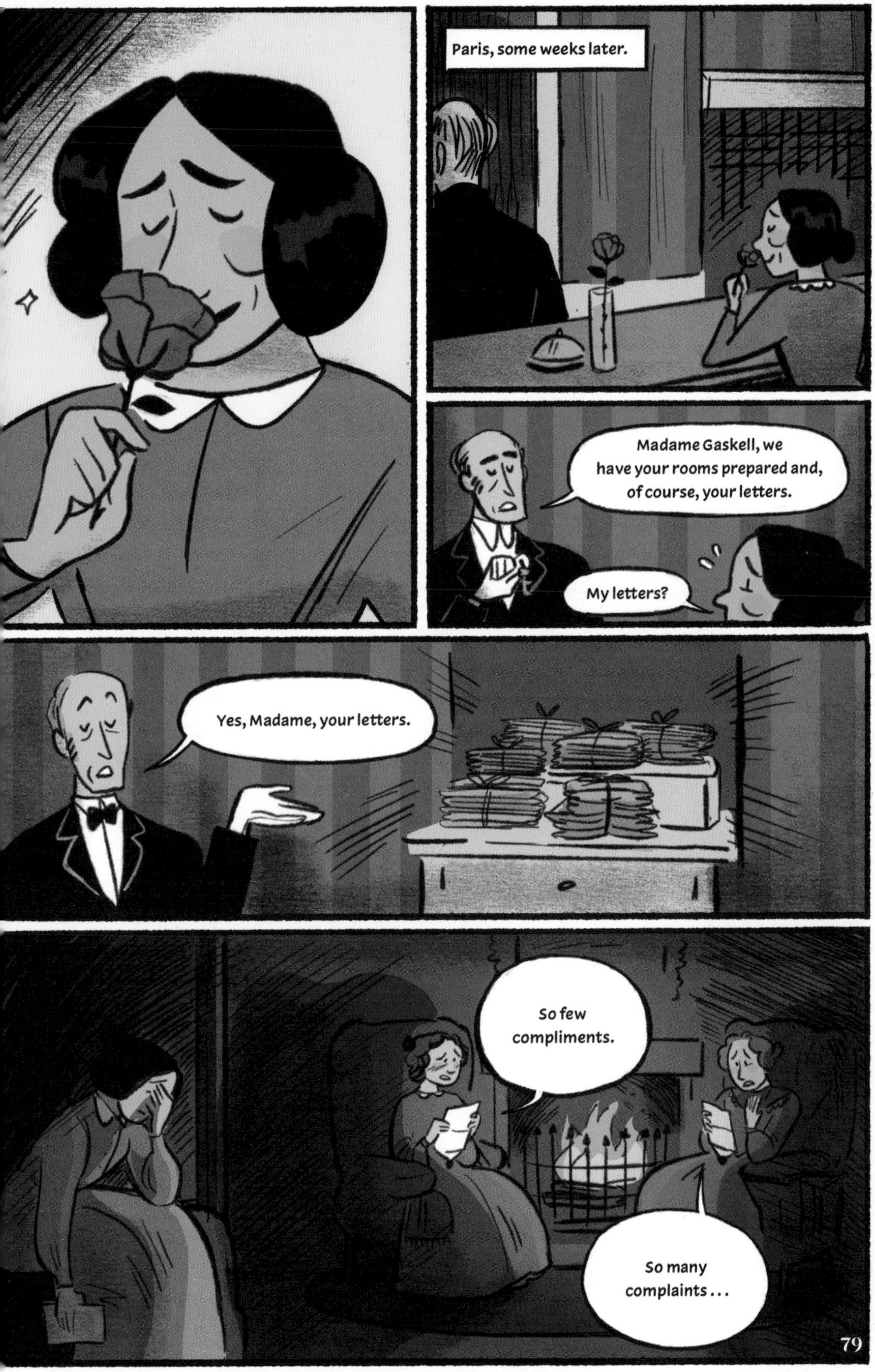
Paris, some weeks later.
Madame Gaskell, we have your rooms prepared and, of course, your letters.
My letters?
Yes, Madame, your letters.
So few compliments.
So many complaints . . .

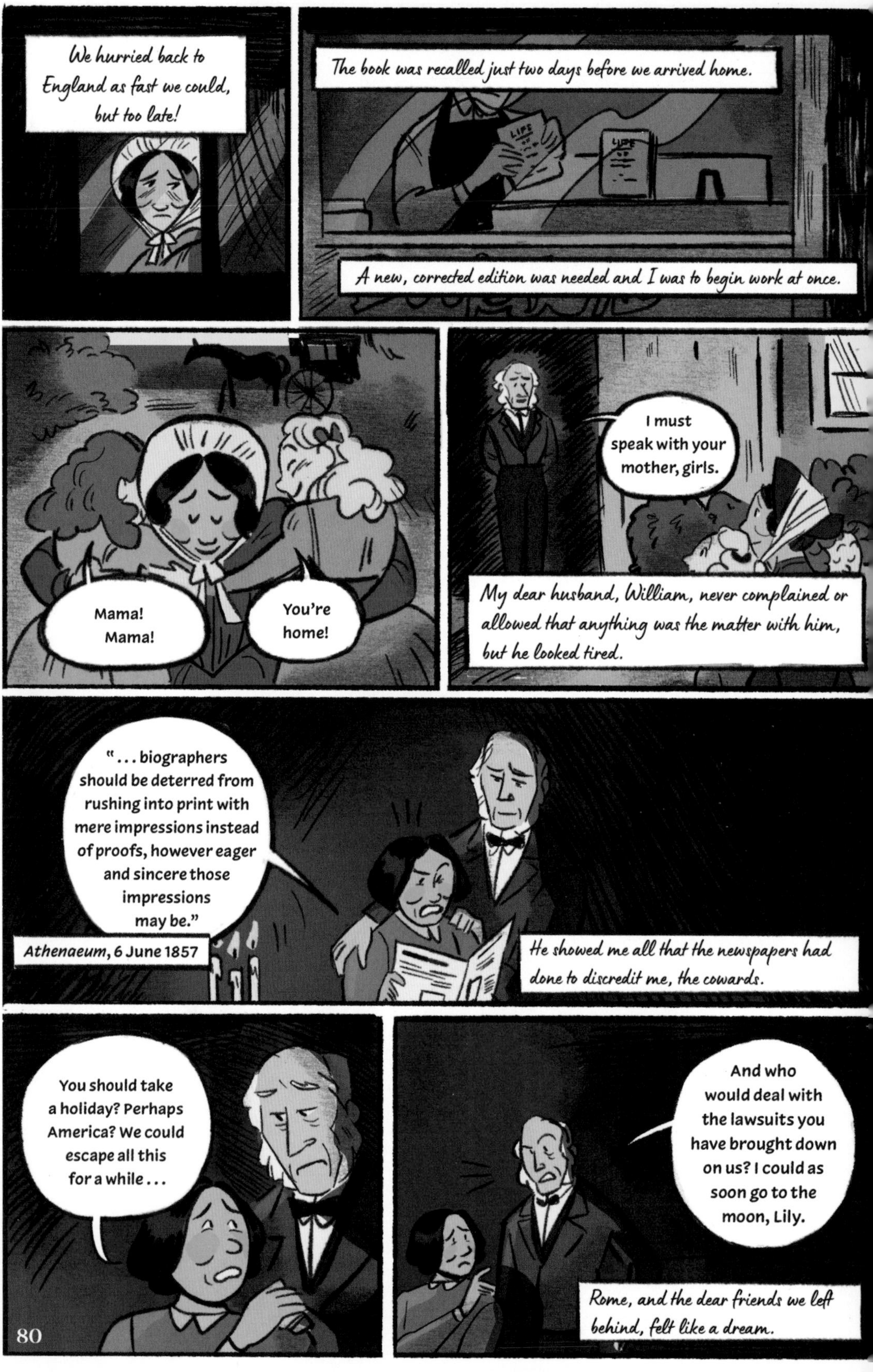
We hurried back to England as fast we could, but too late!
The book was recalled just two days before we arrived home.
A new, corrected edition was needed and I was to begin work at once.
Mama! Mama!
You're home!
I must speak with your mother, girls.
My dear husband, William, never complained or allowed that anything was the matter with him, but he looked tired.
". . . biographers should be deterred from rushing into print with mere impressions instead of proofs, however eager and sincere those impressions may be."
Athenaeum, 6 June 1857
He showed me all that the newspapers had done to discredit me, the cowards.
You should take a holiday? Perhaps America? We could escape all this for a while . . .
And who would deal with the lawsuits you have brought down on us? I could as soon go to the moon, Lily.
Rome, and the dear friends we left behind, felt like a dream.

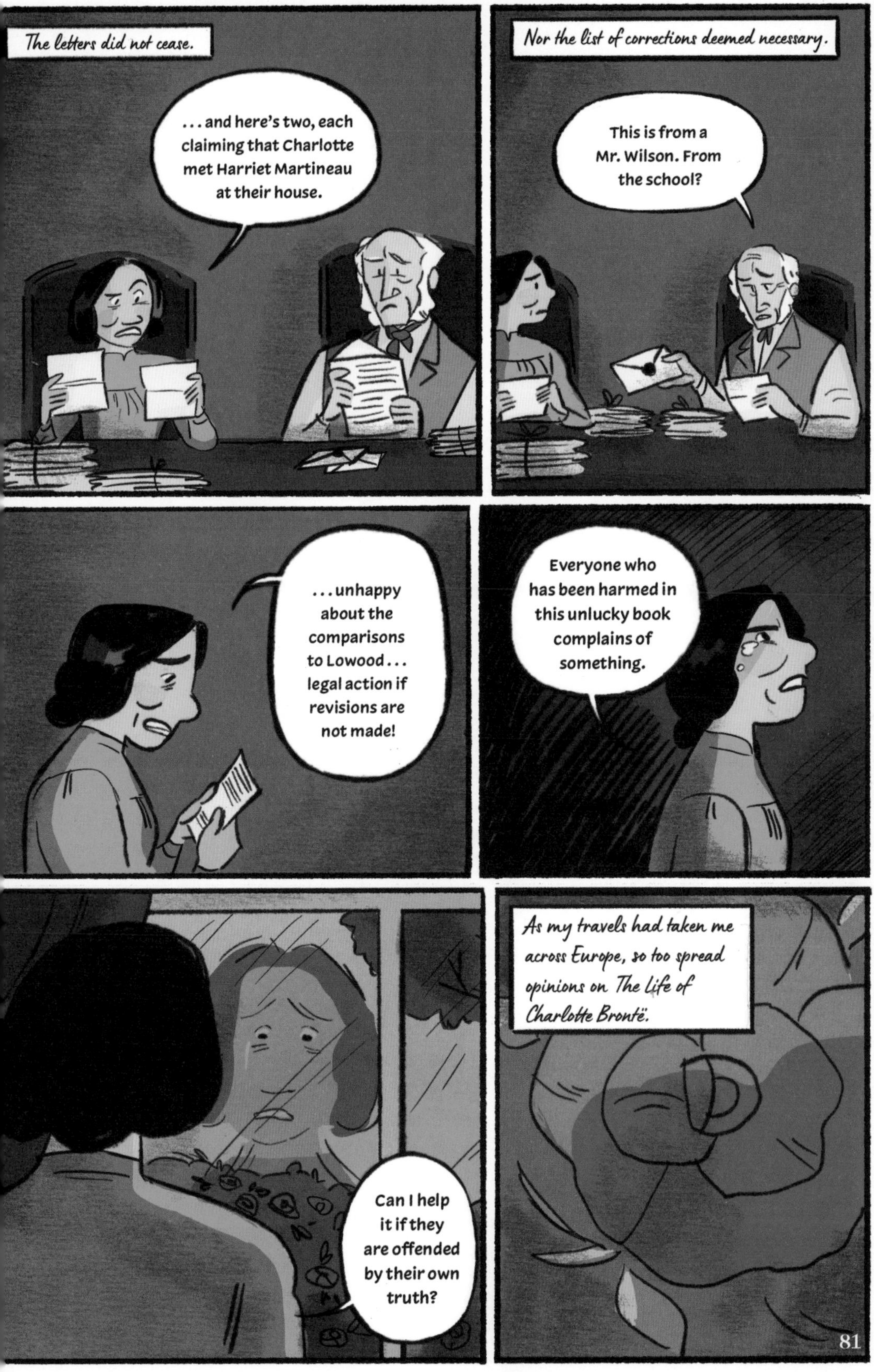
The letters did not cease.
. . . and here's two, each claiming that Charlotte met Harriet Martineau at their house.
Nor the list of corrections deemed necessary.
This is from a Mr. Wilson. From the school?
. . . unhappy about the comparisons to Lowood . . . legal action if revisions are not made!
Everyone who has been harmed in this unlucky book complains of something.
Can I help it if they are offended by their own truth?
As my travels had taken me across Europe, so too spread opinions on The Life of Charlotte Brontë.

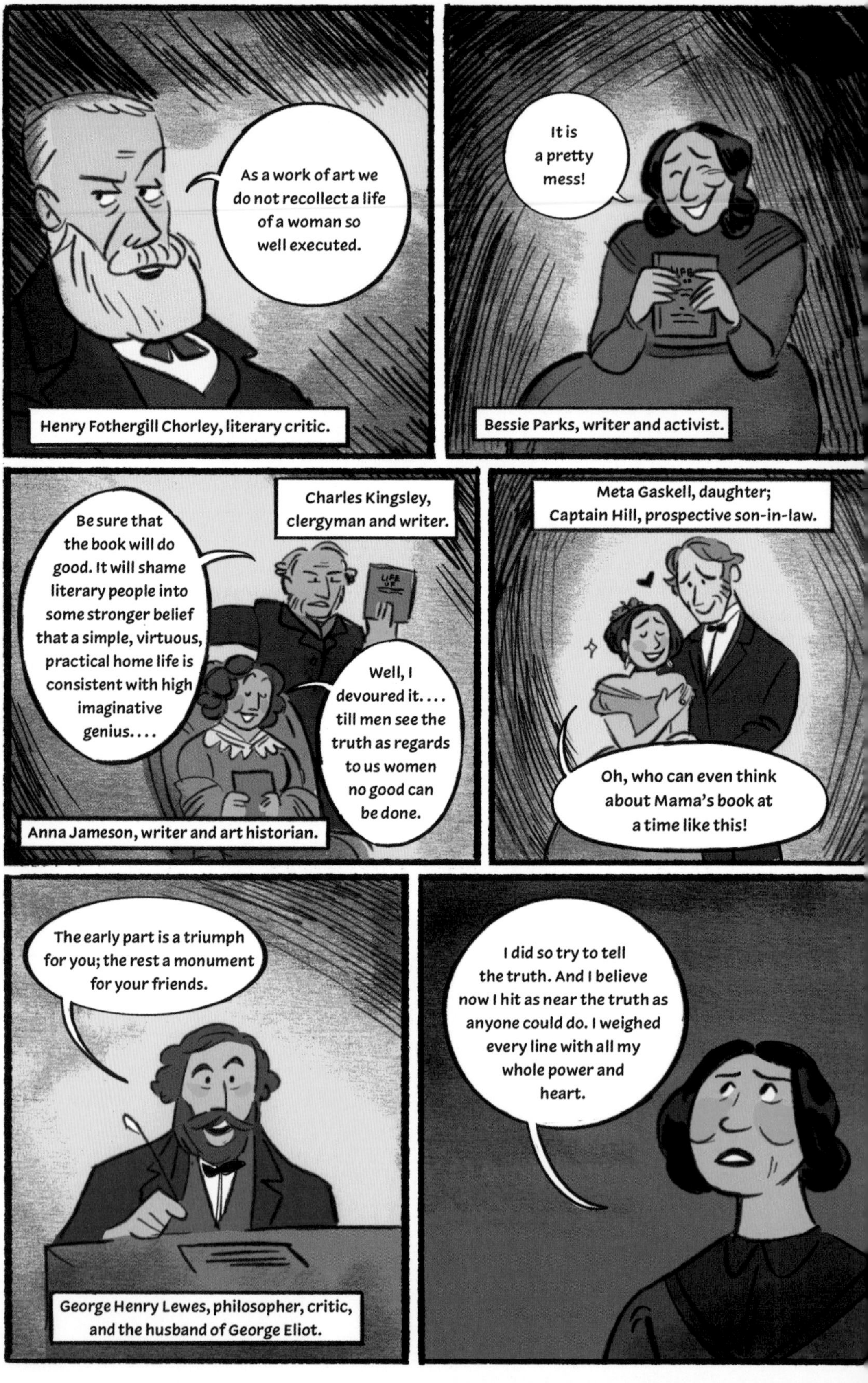
As a work of art we do not recollect a life of a woman so well executed.
Henry Fothergill Chorley, literary critic.
It is a pretty mess!
Bessie Parks, writer and activist.
Charles Kingsley, clergyman and writer.
Be sure that the book will do good. It will shame literary people into some stronger belief that a simple, virtuous, practical home life is consistent with high imaginative genius. . . .
Well, I devoured it. . . . till men see the truth as regards to us women no good can be done.
Anna Jameson, writer and art historian.
Meta Gaskell, daughter; Captain Hill, prospective son-in-law.
Oh, who can even think about Mama's book at a time like this!
The early part is a triumph for you; the rest a monument for your friends.
George Henry Lewes, philosopher, critic, and the husband of George Eliot.
I did so try to tell the truth. And I believe now I hit as near the truth as anyone could do. I weighed every line with all my whole power and heart.

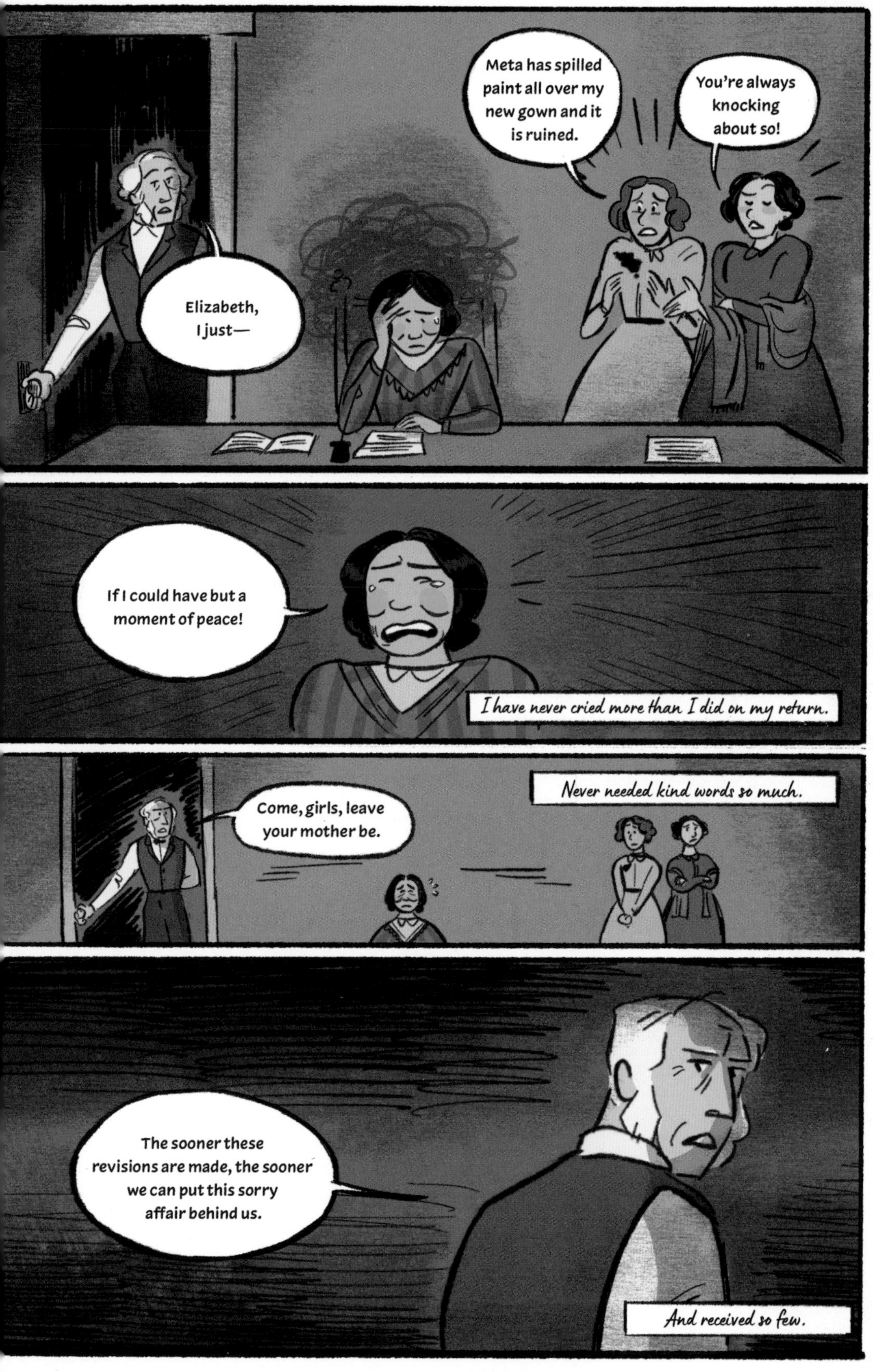
Meta has spilled paint all over my new gown and it is ruined.
You're always knocking about so!
Elizabeth, I just—
If I could have but a moment of peace!
I have never cried more than I did on my return.
Never needed kind words so much.
Come, girls, leave your mother be.
The sooner these revisions are made, the sooner we can put this sorry affair behind us.
And received so few.

By night, at least, I had the house and my thoughts to myself.
Elizabeth, it's very late. You must come to bed.
It's finished. I don't think these edits will make anybody truly happy, but it is finished.
"If anybody is displeased with any statement or words in the following pages, I beg leave to with-draw it, and express my deep regret for having offered so expensive an article as truth to the Public."
I might put that in the new preface. Isn't it funny?
None of this is very funny, Lily.
I am sorry, William. For all the fuss and for leaving you behind while I—
I know.
People are so quick to cast judgment, William, and on women especially! She was a good woman, but the *things* they wrote about her . . . so little of it fair or true.
I only wanted for my friend to be known and valued.

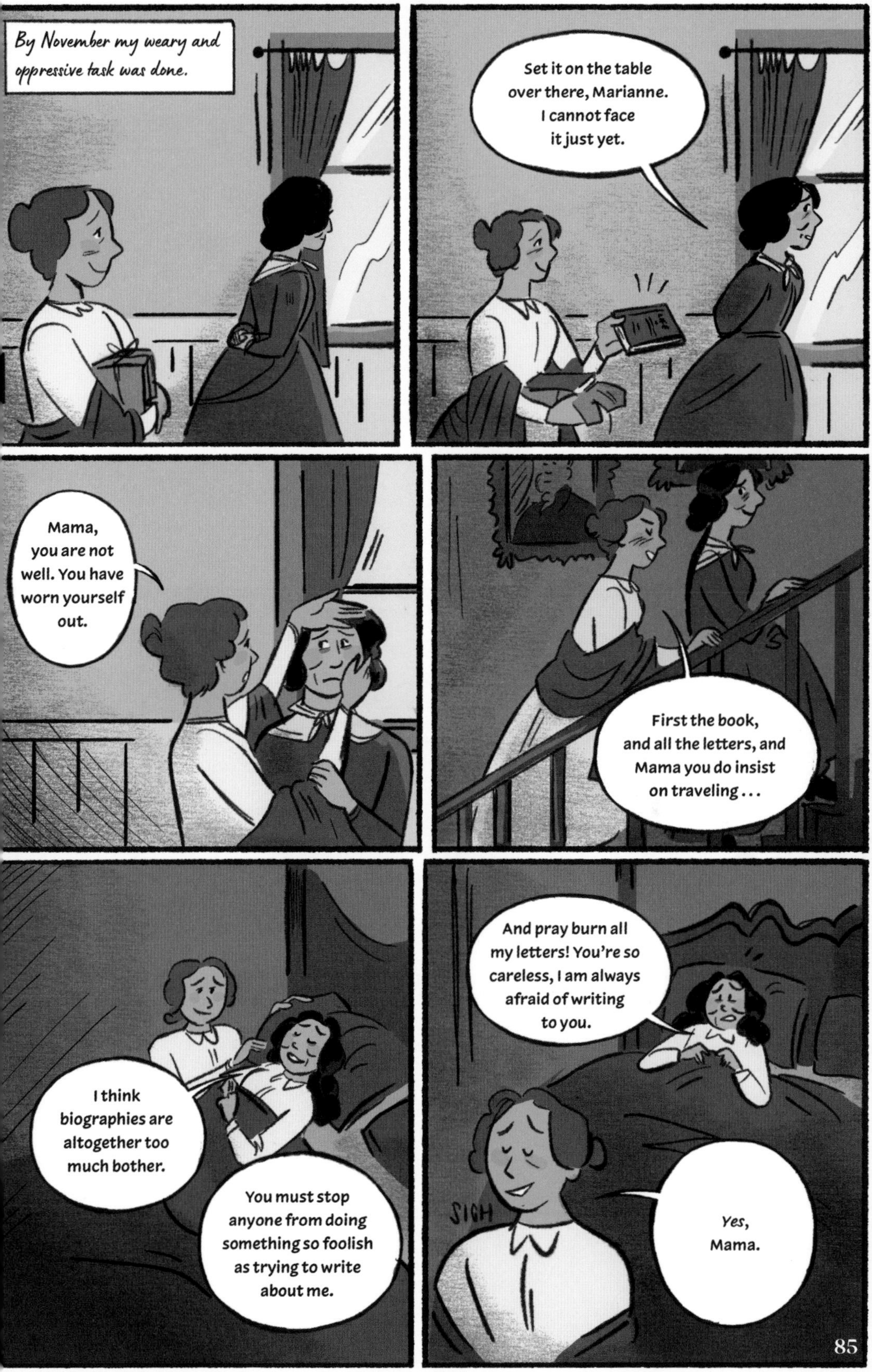
By November my weary and oppressive task was done.
Set it on the table over there, Marianne. I cannot face it just yet.
Mama, you are not well. You have worn yourself out.
First the book, and all the letters, and Mama you do insist on traveling . . .
I think biographies are altogether too much bother.
You must stop anyone from doing something so foolish as trying to write about me.
And pray burn all my letters! You're so careless, I am always afraid of writing to you.
SIGH
Yes, Mama.

While staying with the Gaskells in 1853, Charlotte Brontë was so overcome by nerves when another visitor came to meet her that she hid behind a curtain in the drawing room and only came out when the coast was clear.

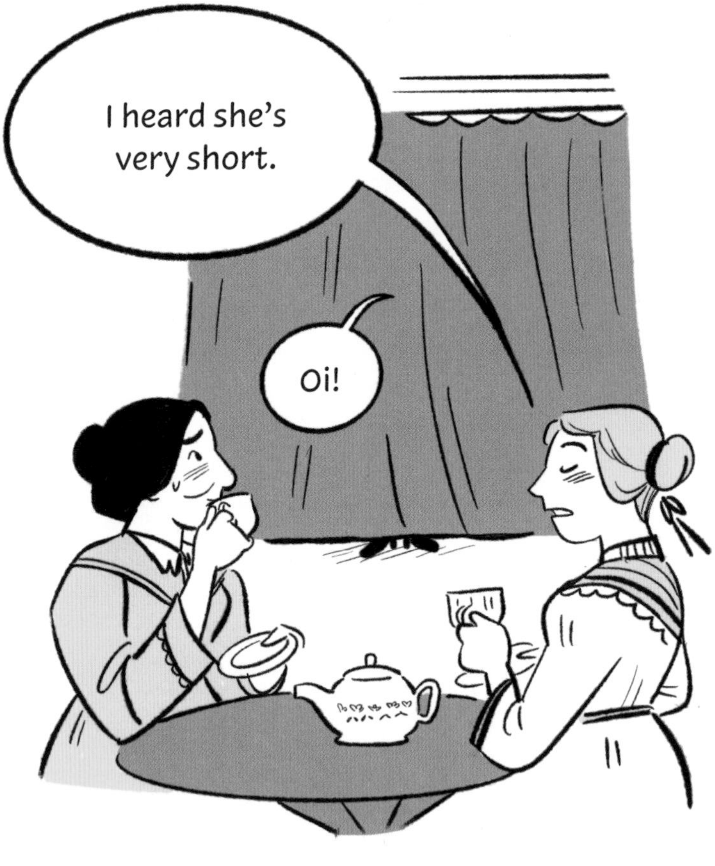
I heard she's very short.
Oi!

Charles Dickens was such a fan of Gaskell that he called her "darling Scheherazade" after the storyteller from the *One Thousand and One Nights*.

SELECTED WORKS:

NOVELS

1848: *Mary Barton*
1850: *The Moorland Cottage*
1853: *Ruth*
1853: *Cranford*
1855: *North and South*
1858 *My Lady Ludlow*
1863: *Sylvia's Lovers*
1863: *A Dark Night's Work*
1864: *Cousin Phillis*
1866: *Wives and Daughters* [unfinished]

NONFICTION

1837: *Sketches Among the Poor* [co-written with William Gaskell]
1857: *The Life of Charlotte Brontë*

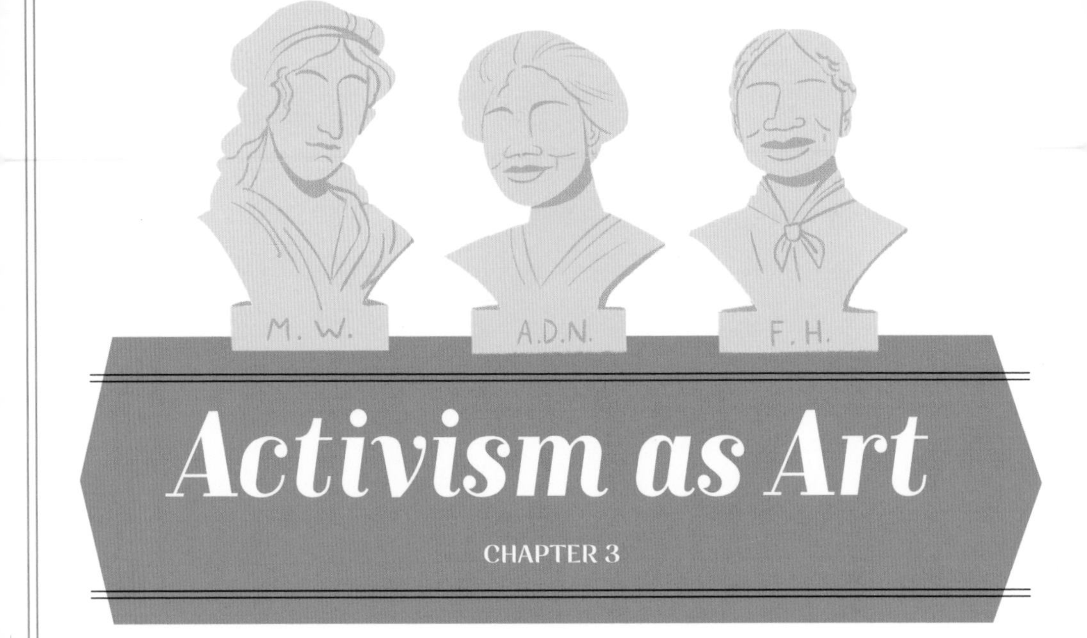
M. W.
A.D.N.
F. H.

Activism as Art

CHAPTER 3

Respectable women weren't supposed to behave like Mary Wollstonecraft, Frances E. W. Harper, or Alice Dunbar Nelson. They weren't supposed to ask questions or pursue an education, let alone a career in the public sphere. They couldn't vote, inherit property, or obtain a divorce. Respectable women were quiet, married well, and hoped for the best, but Wollstonecraft, Harper, and Dunbar Nelson couldn't sit still. They dedicated their lives to tackling injustice.

Wollstonecraft's groundbreaking pamphlet *A Vindication of the Rights of Woman* lit the fire. She argued that, contrary to popular belief, women are not naturally inferior to men, but lack the same opportunities. *Vindication* notoriously called for equal legal, social, and economic rights for women. What qualifies as common sense now was classified as radical thought in Georgian England. Mary Wollstonecraft was a renegade made even more dangerous by her support of the French Revolution. She was such a believer in the ideals of the revolution that she was not content to observe from a distance. She had to live it to write it.

Mary Wollstonecraft wasn't the only one who lived dangerously. At twenty-eight, Frances E. W. Harper gave up her career as a teacher to become a full-time abolitionist. Emboldened by her work with the Underground Railroad, she joined the American Anti-Slavery Society as a traveling speaker for the cause. It was rare for women to join the circuit, as the working conditions were less than ideal. Pay was low, workdays were long, and safety was not guaranteed. Harper delivered up to three speeches a day, never knowing how the audience might receive her. While some welcomed her message, others heckled and spewed racist insults.

At times, violence ensued. The constant travel and stress took a toll on her health. Harper was often ill and often lonely, but she had no regrets. She continued to lecture for the rest of her life.

After slavery was abolished, Harper devoted her time and energy to voting rights, anti-lynching campaigns, and supporting African American women. Following her talks, she made a point to meet privately with newly freed women. "Part of my lectures are given privately to women, and for them I never make any charge, or take up any collection . . . [I] talk with them about their daughters, and about the things connected with the welfare of the race. Now is the time for our women to begin to try and lift up their heads and plant the roots of progress under hearthstone."

Alice Dunbar Nelson was part of a generation of African American women who would do just that. She began her activist career as a charter member of the Phillis Wheatley Club in 1895. Named for the poet, these clubs formed a network of Black women committed to improving their communities by raising money and awareness for various social causes. Some clubs focused on suffrage, while other tackled homelessness. Dunbar Nelson worked with her branch to found a teaching hospital for Black doctors and nurses in 1896.

In many ways, Dunbar Nelson's later career picked up right where Harper's left off. She was a teacher and traveling speaker who took leadership roles in suffrage and anti-lynching campaigns. She was the first Black woman to serve on the State Republican Committee of Delaware and was also the publisher of the progressive Black newspaper *The Wilmington Advocate.*

Wollstonecraft, Harper, and Dunbar Nelson were fighters as well as writers. Despite numerous setbacks, their commitment to equal rights never wavered. They knew the world could be changed by their words, even if they wouldn't experience it firsthand.

Mary Wollstonecraft

1759–1797

"Virtue can only flourish amongst equals."

—*A Vindication of the Rights of Men*, 1790

Mary Wollstonecraft had many professions in her thirty-eight years of life. She was a teacher, writer, translator, philosopher, and, most memorably, an advocate for women's rights. Today she is often referred to as the first modern feminist.

Wollstonecraft was born into a middle-class London family as the second of seven children. Her father was an alcoholic who was prone to fits of violence. At night, a teenage Mary would sleep in front of her mother's door in an effort to protect her from his abuse. When he finally drank his family into poverty, Mary left home and was immediately dismayed by the limited career options available to an intelligent but impoverished gentlewoman. She longed to write, and her time spent as a lady's companion, teacher, and governess served as valuable inspiration for her first publication, *Thoughts on the Education of Daughters* in 1787. One chapter title, "Unfortunate Situation of Females, Fashionably Educated and Left Without Fortune" reads like the opening line to an Austen novel.

In 1787, Wollstonecraft wrote to her sister that she planned to become the "first of a new genus" of women to support themselves by writing full-time. She moved to London and found steady employment with progressive publisher Joseph Johnson as an editor, critic, and translator. Johnson welcomed Wollstonecraft into his circle of literary radicals that included the likes of Thomas Paine and William Godwin, Wollstonecraft's future husband. The pair first met at a dinner party hosted by Johnson, but it wasn't love at first sight; Godwin remarked that he heard too much of Wollstonecraft and very little of everyone else.

Wollstonecraft, Paine, and Godwin would soon find themselves in the middle of a political pamphlet war with conservative politician Edmund Burke during the French Revolution. In 1789, the overtaxed and starving citizens of France overthrew their monarchy with the goal of establishing a republic. The following year, Burke would write *Reflections on the Revolution in France* to voice his sympathy for the last queen of France, Marie Antoinette. As a staunch supporter of the aristocracy and believer in the divine right of kings, Burke vehemently opposed the revolution. Wollstonecraft crafted a response entitled *A Vindication of the Rights of Men* that argued for a free and just society and attacked hereditary privilege. It was an instant success, and her follow-up, *A Vindication of the Rights of Woman*, would further cement her legacy as an advocate for equal rights. Emboldened by her recent success as a political writer, Wollstonecraft decided to travel to France in 1792 to write a firsthand account of the revolution.

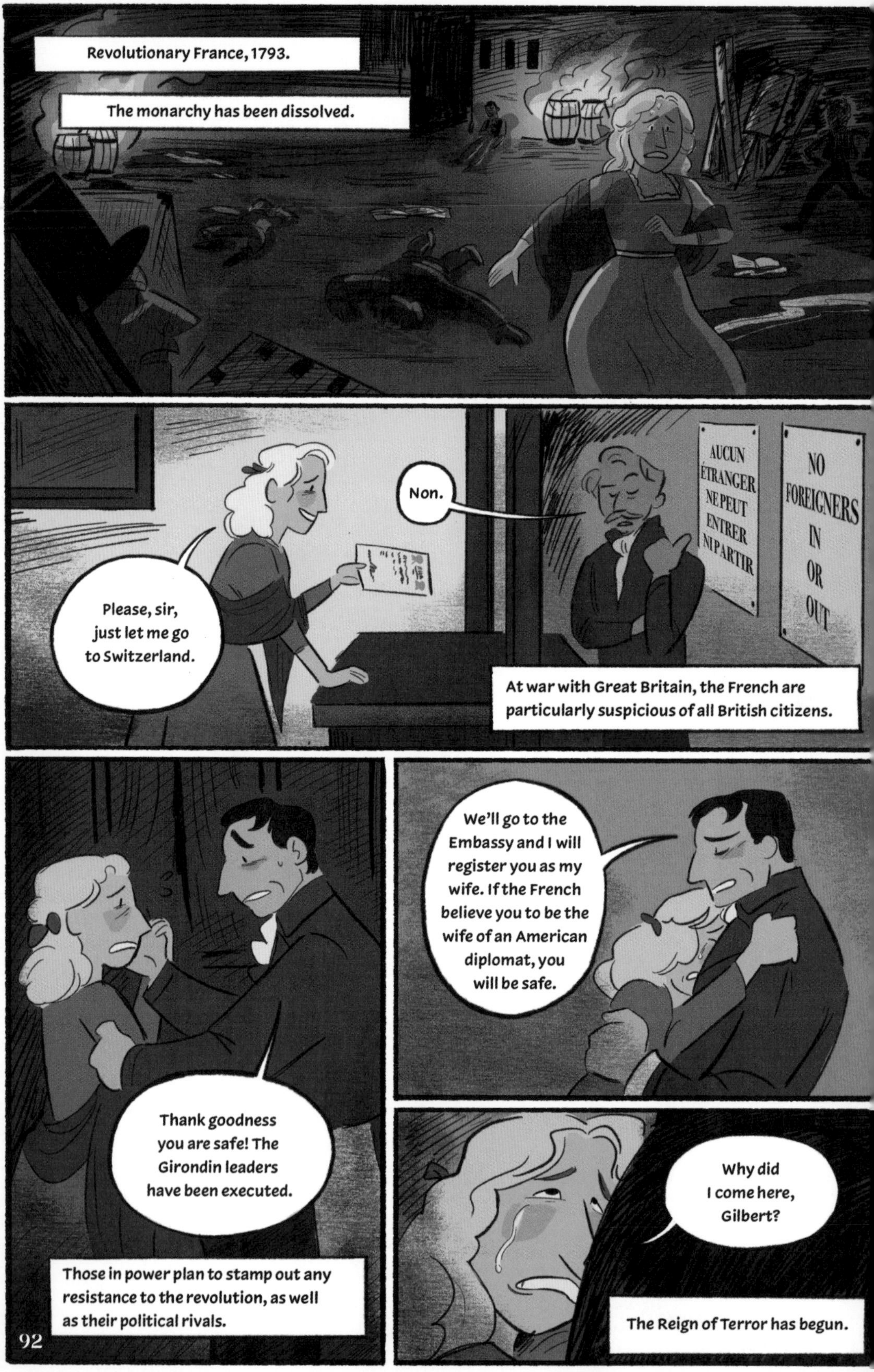
Revolutionary France, 1793.
The monarchy has been dissolved.
Please, sir, just let me go to Switzerland.
Non.
AUCUN ÉTRANGER NE PEUT ENTRER NI PARTIR
NO FOREIGNERS IN OR OUT
At war with Great Britain, the French are particularly suspicious of all British citizens.
Thank goodness you are safe! The Girondin leaders have been executed.
Those in power plan to stamp out any resistance to the revolution, as well as their political rivals.
We'll go to the Embassy and I will register you as my wife. If the French believe you to be the wife of an American diplomat, you will be safe.
Why did I come here, Gilbert?
The Reign of Terror has begun.

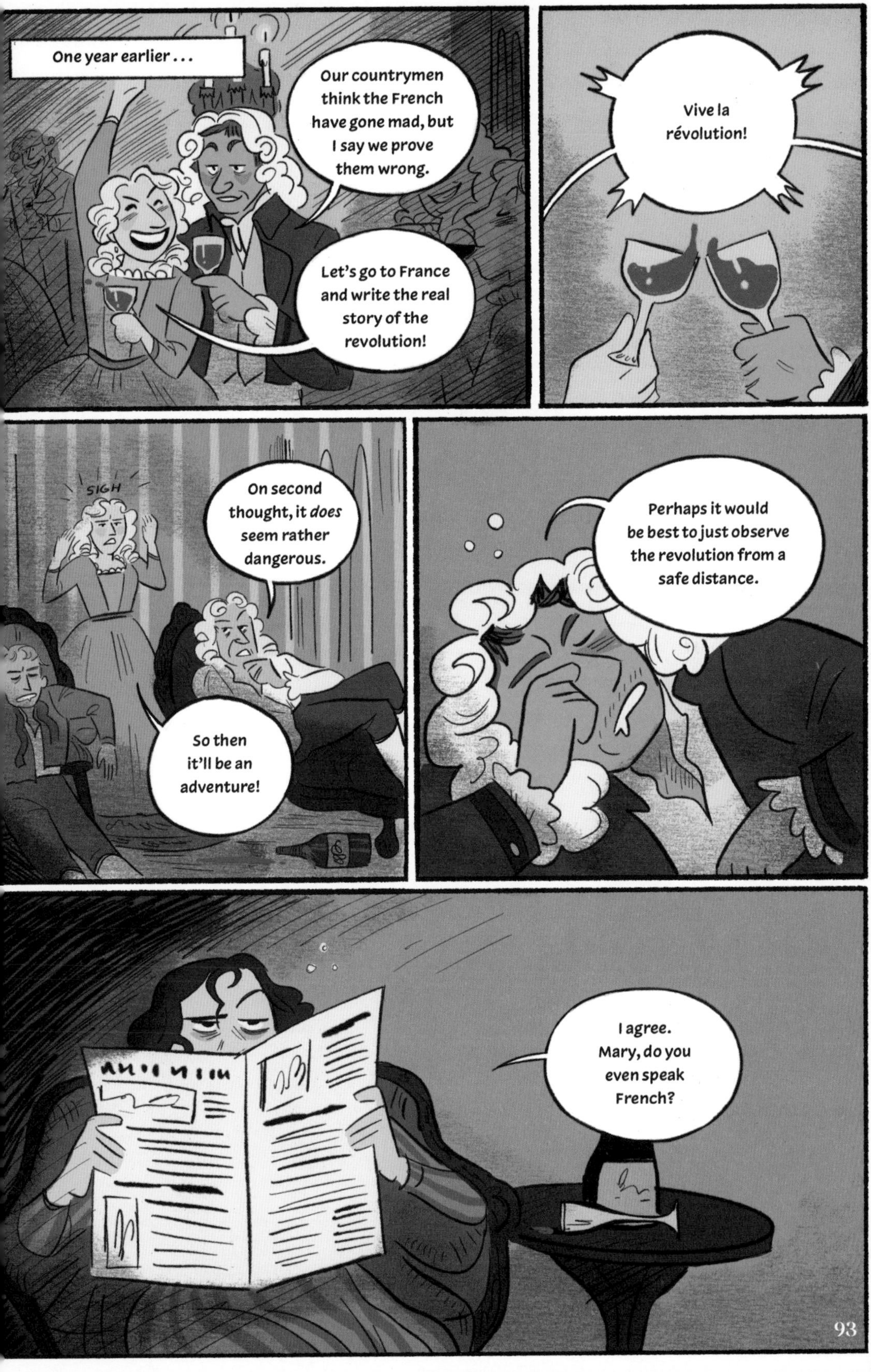

One year earlier . . .
Our countrymen think the French have gone mad, but I say we prove them wrong.
Let's go to France and write the real story of the revolution!
Vive la révolution!
SIGH
On second thought, it *does* seem rather dangerous.
So then it'll be an adventure!
Perhaps it would be best to just observe the revolution from a safe distance.
I agree. Mary, do you even speak French?

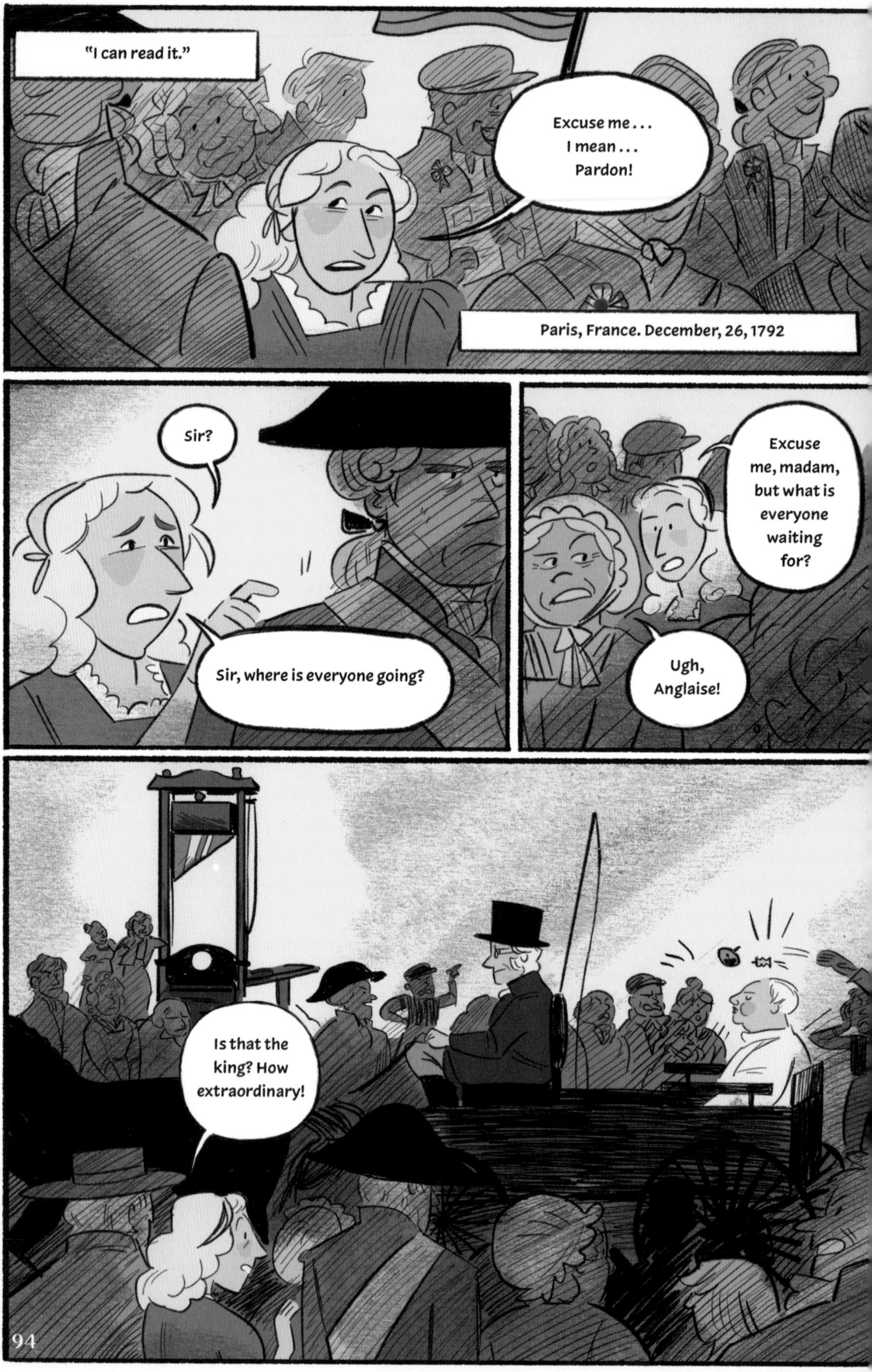
"I can read it."
Excuse me . . . I mean . . . Pardon!
Paris, France. December, 26, 1792
Sir?
Sir, where is everyone going?
Excuse me, madam, but what is everyone waiting for?
Ugh, Anglaise!
Is that the king? How extraordinary!

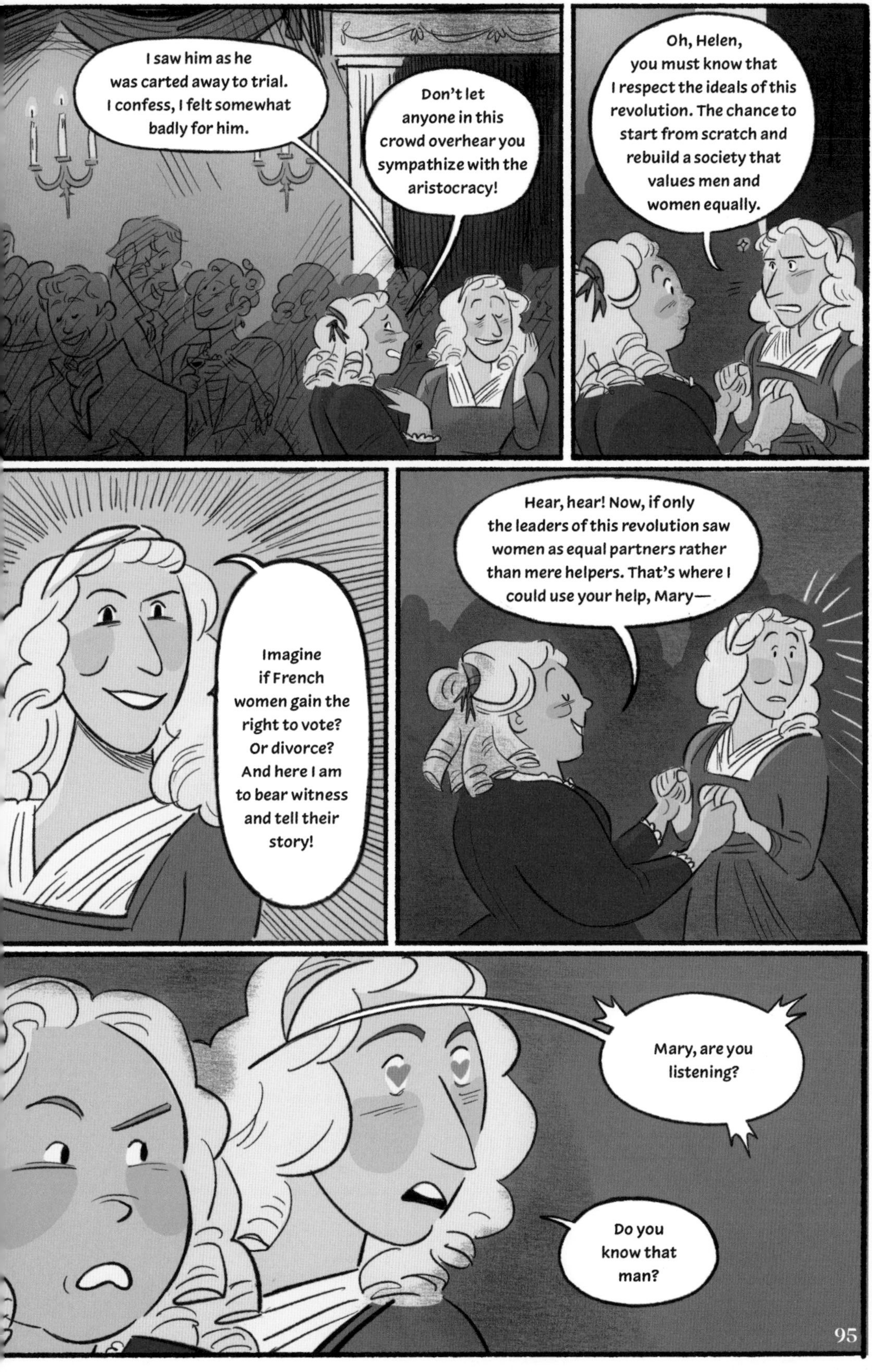
I saw him as he was carted away to trial. I confess, I felt somewhat badly for him.
Don't let anyone in this crowd overhear you sympathize with the aristocracy!
Oh, Helen, you must know that I respect the ideals of this revolution. The chance to start from scratch and rebuild a society that values men and women equally.
Imagine if French women gain the right to vote? Or divorce? And here I am to bear witness and tell their story!
Hear, hear! Now, if only the leaders of this revolution saw women as equal partners rather than mere helpers. That's where I could use your help, Mary—
Mary, are you listening?
Do you know that man?

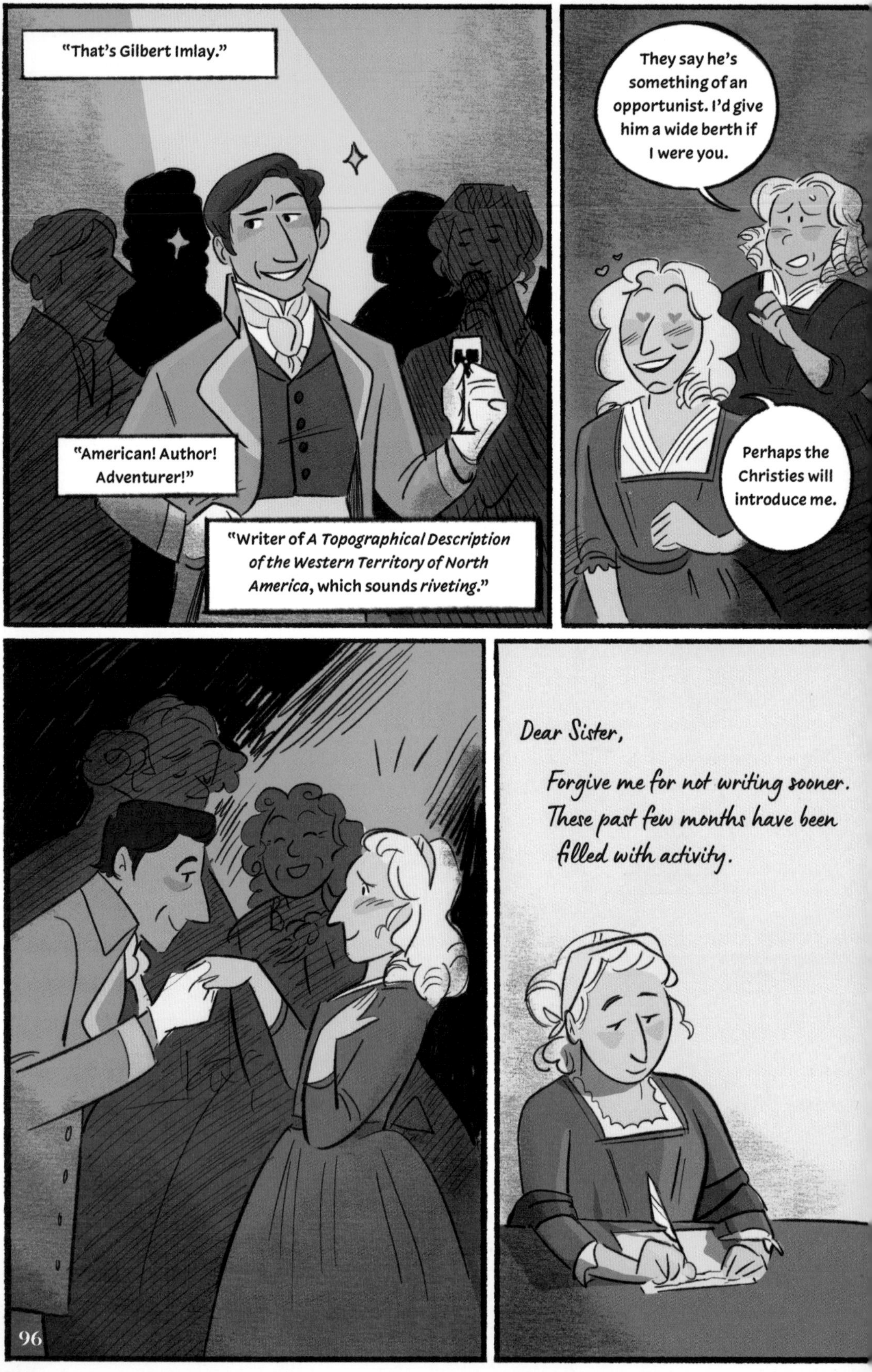
"That's Gilbert Imlay."
"American! Author! Adventurer!"
"Writer of *A Topographical Description of the Western Territory of North America*, which sounds *riveting*."
They say he's something of an opportunist. I'd give him a wide berth if I were you.
Perhaps the Christies will introduce me.
Dear Sister,
Forgive me for not writing sooner. These past few months have been filled with activity.

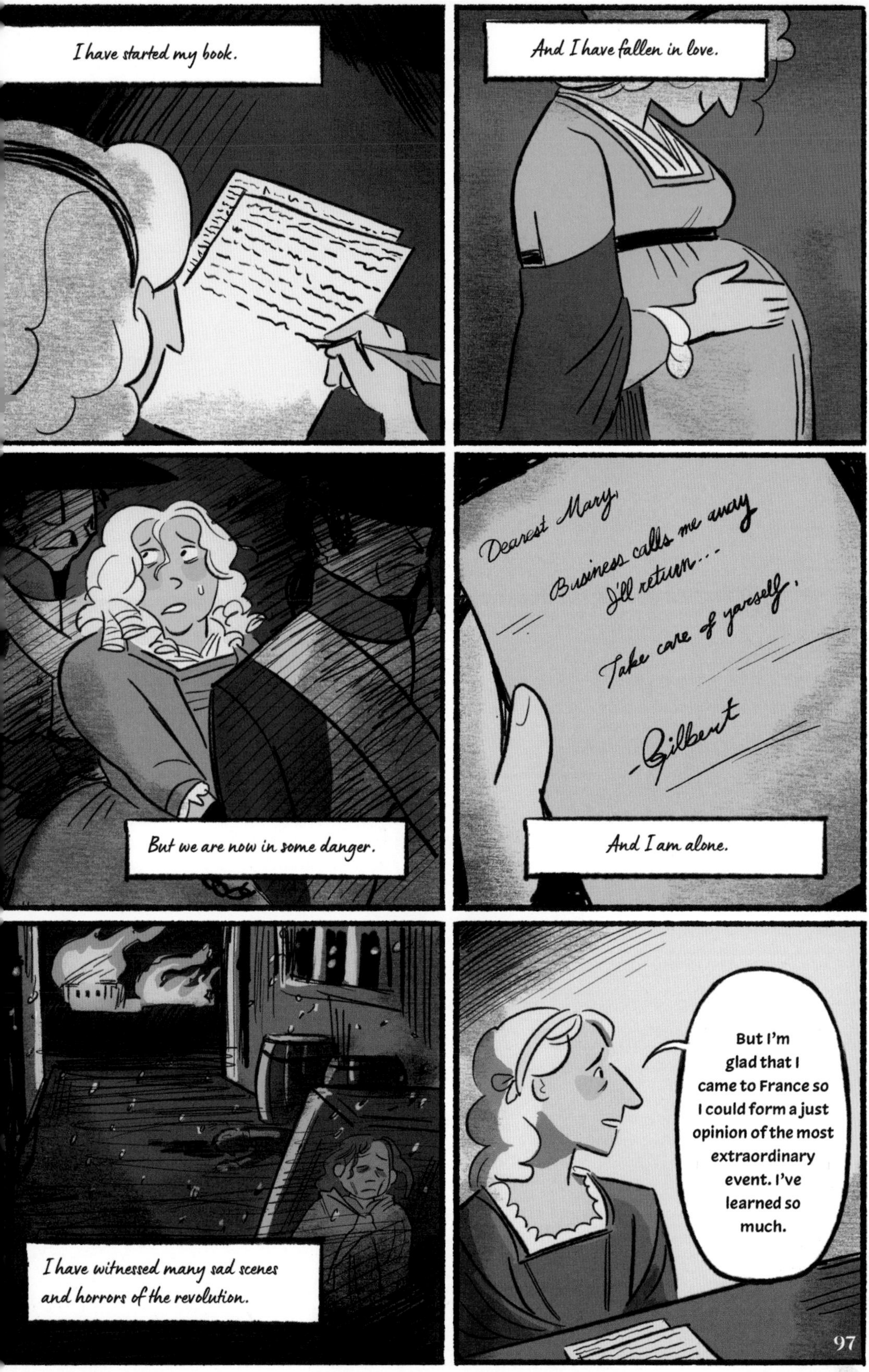
I have started my book.
And I have fallen in love.
But we are now in some danger.
Dearest Mary,
Business calls me away
I'll return...
Take care of yourself.
-Gilbert
And I am alone.
I have witnessed many sad scenes and horrors of the revolution.
But I'm glad that I came to France so I could form a just opinion of the most extraordinary event. I've learned so much.

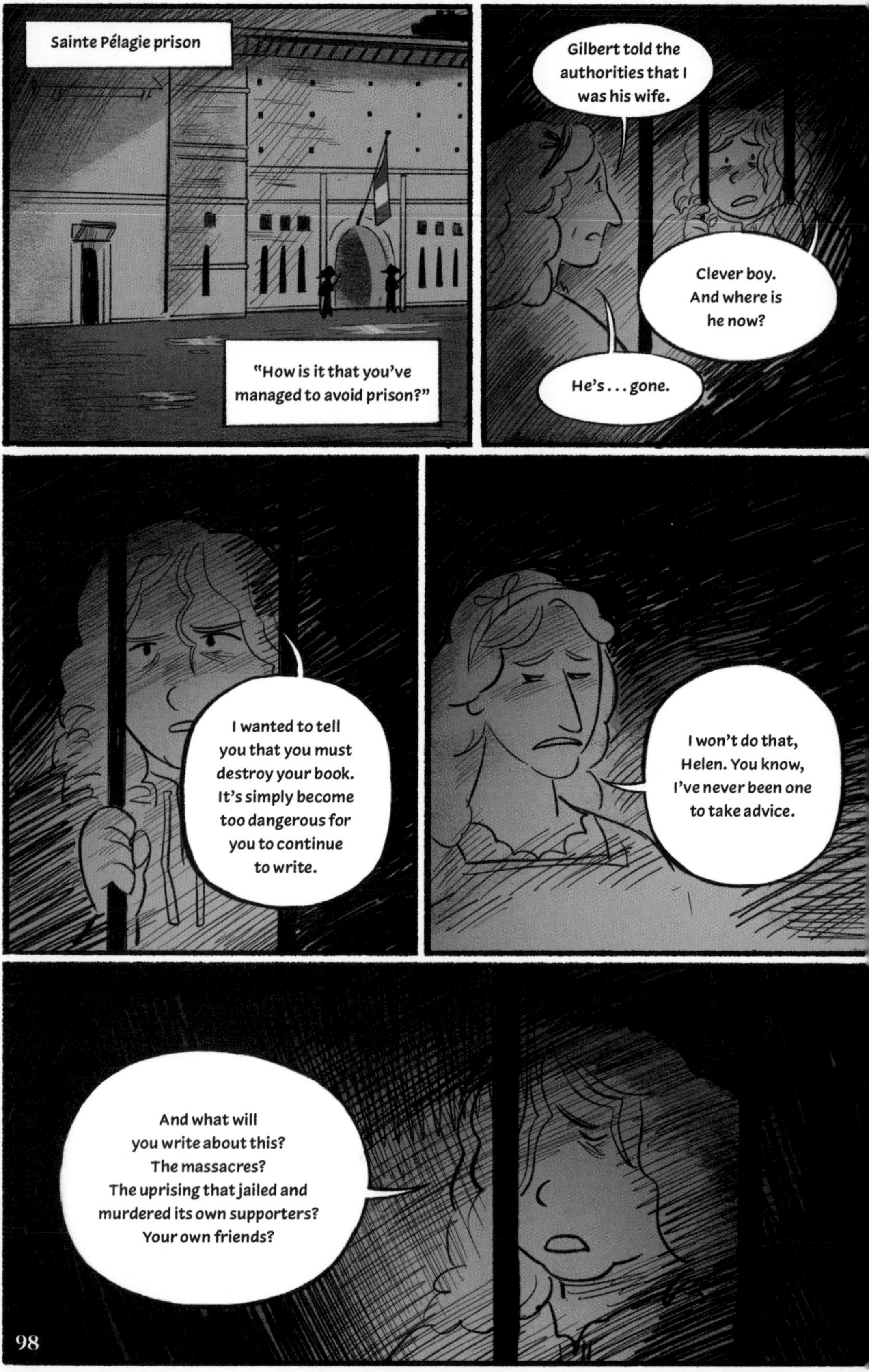
Sainte Pélagie prison
"How is it that you've managed to avoid prison?"
Gilbert told the authorities that I was his wife.
Clever boy. And where is he now?
He's . . . gone.
I wanted to tell you that you must destroy your book. It's simply become too dangerous for you to continue to write.
I won't do that, Helen. You know, I've never been one to take advice.
And what will you write about this? The massacres? The uprising that jailed and murdered its own supporters? Your own friends?

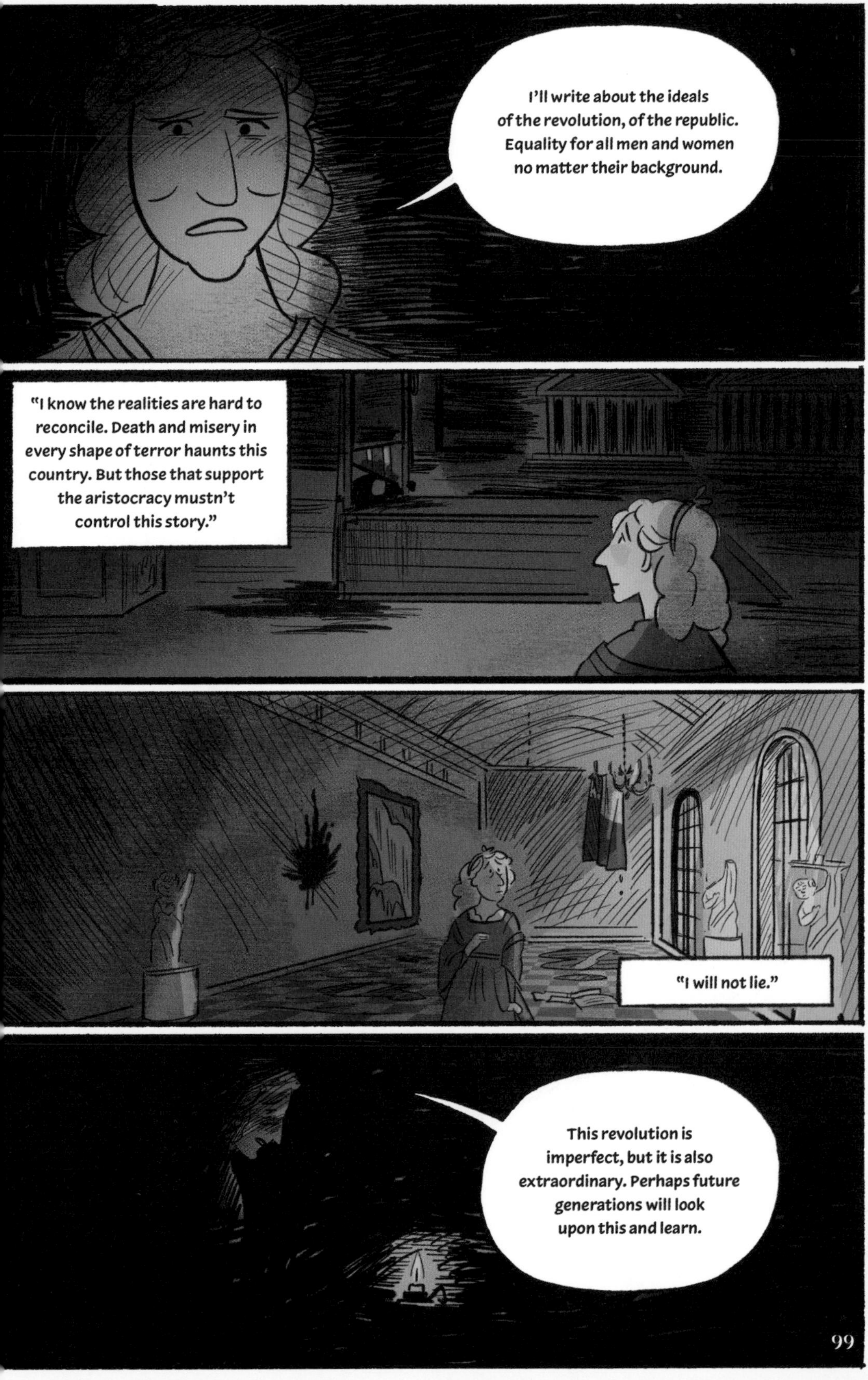
I'll write about the ideals of the revolution, of the republic. Equality for all men and women no matter their background.
"I know the realities are hard to reconcile. Death and misery in every shape of terror haunts this country. But those that support the aristocracy mustn't control this story."
"I will not lie."
This revolution is imperfect, but it is also extraordinary. Perhaps future generations will look upon this and learn.

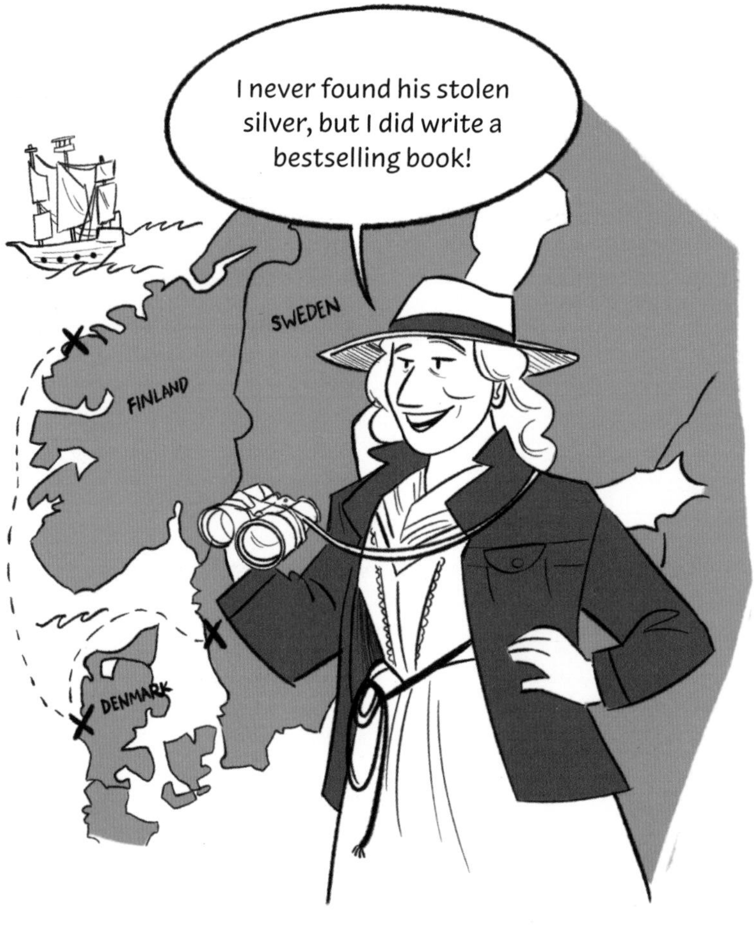
I never found his stolen silver, but I did write a bestselling book!
SWEDEN
FINLAND
DENMARK

Wollstonecraft's *Letters Written during a Short Residence in Sweden, Norway, and Denmark* was enormously popular in the 1790s and served as an inspiration for her daughter Mary Shelley's *History of a Six Weeks' Tour*. Part memoir, part travelogue, the narrative tells the story of Wollstonecraft's search for lost treasure in Scandinavia in a series of letters to an unnamed lover.

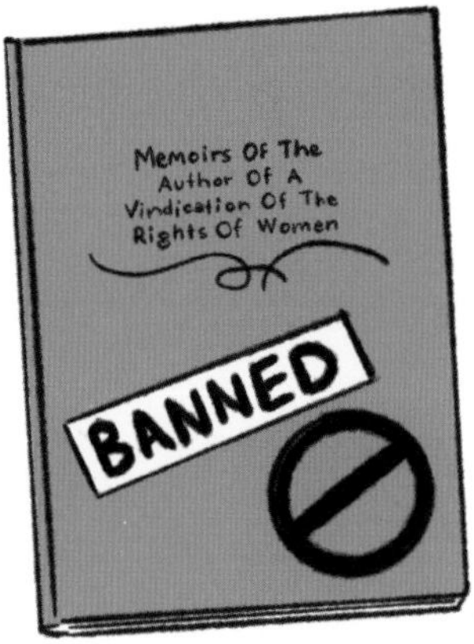
Memoirs Of The Author Of A Vindication Of The Rights Of Women
BANNED

In 1798, William Godwin published *Memoirs of the Author of A Vindication of the Rights of Woman* with the intention of posthumously honoring his wife. The book ended up doing more harm than good, however. Unlike Elizabeth Gaskell, who came under fire for omitting facts in *The Life of Charlotte Brontë*, Godwin was criticized for giving too much detail in his wife's biography. *Memoirs of the Author* exposed the more scandalous details of Wollstonecraft's life, including her premarital relations, suicide attempt, and child born out of wedlock, which shocked her readers and ruined her reputation for some time.

SELECTED WORKS:

NONFICTION

1787: *Thoughts on the Education of Daughters: With Reflections on Female Conduct, in the More Important Duties of Life*
1790: *A Vindication of the Rights of Men, in a Letter to the Right Honourable Edmund Burke*
1792: *A Vindication of the Rights of Woman: with Strictures on Moral and Political Subjects*
1794: *An Historical and Moral View of the Origin and Progress of the French Revolution*

NOVELS

1788: *Mary: A Fiction*
1798: *Maria: Or, The Wrongs of Woman*

TRAVELOGUES

1796: *Letters Written during a Short Residence in Sweden, Norway, and Denmark*

Frances
E. W. Harper

1825–1911

"There is light beyond the darkness,
joy beyond the present pain . . . the shadows bear
a promise of a brighter coming day."

—*Iola Leroy*, 1892

For over one hundred years, it was believed that Frances Harper's first book was lost to time. *Forest Leaves*, a slim volume of poems on nature, love, and religion, was first published in 1845, when Frances was just twenty years old. On a whim, doctoral student Johanna Ortner went in search of the lost book in 2015, and to her surprise, she found a perfect copy in the Maryland Historical Society. Frances Harper's career as an author, lecturer, and social activist spanned over five decades, but like so many authors of color, her legacy has been poorly preserved. The archive didn't realize they were in possession of a lost treasure.

Frances Ellen Watkins Harper was born free in Baltimore, Maryland, in 1825. Following the death of her parents, a three-year-old Frances was sent to live with her maternal aunt and uncle, Henrietta and William Watkins. Reverend Watkins was a renowned abolitionist and speaker who educated his young niece at his Academy for Negro Youth. Under his guidance, she published her first antislavery piece at just fourteen, but she did much more than just write. In 1851, Frances moved to Pennsylvania to help escaped slaves on the Underground Railroad make their way to Canada, and in 1854, she would use the proceeds from her bestselling book, *Poems on Miscellaneous Subjects,* to assist them financially. That same year, she began her career as a lecturer and toured the country giving abolitionist speeches in the years leading up to the Civil War.

In 1860, Frances married Fenton Harper, a widower with three children. The family settled down on an Ohio farm, where Frances gave birth to a daughter, Mary, and continued to write. Their domestic bliss was short-lived, however; just four years later, Frances was a widow and single mother. In need of money, she returned full-time to activism and writing following the Civil War. With the end of slavery, she turned her attention to voting rights.

Frances was troubled to discover that many of her allies in abolition had now become her opponents in suffrage. There was a "great schism" in the women's rights movement caused by a disagreement over who should get the right to vote first—women or African American men. Some suffragettes even marched under banners that read, "Women first, Negro last." Frances's feminism was inter-sectional, and she campaigned for the rights of Black people as well as women. In 1866, she was invited to speak at the Eleventh National Women's Rights Convention, where she would fire back at racist remarks in the movement and deliver one of her most memorable speeches.

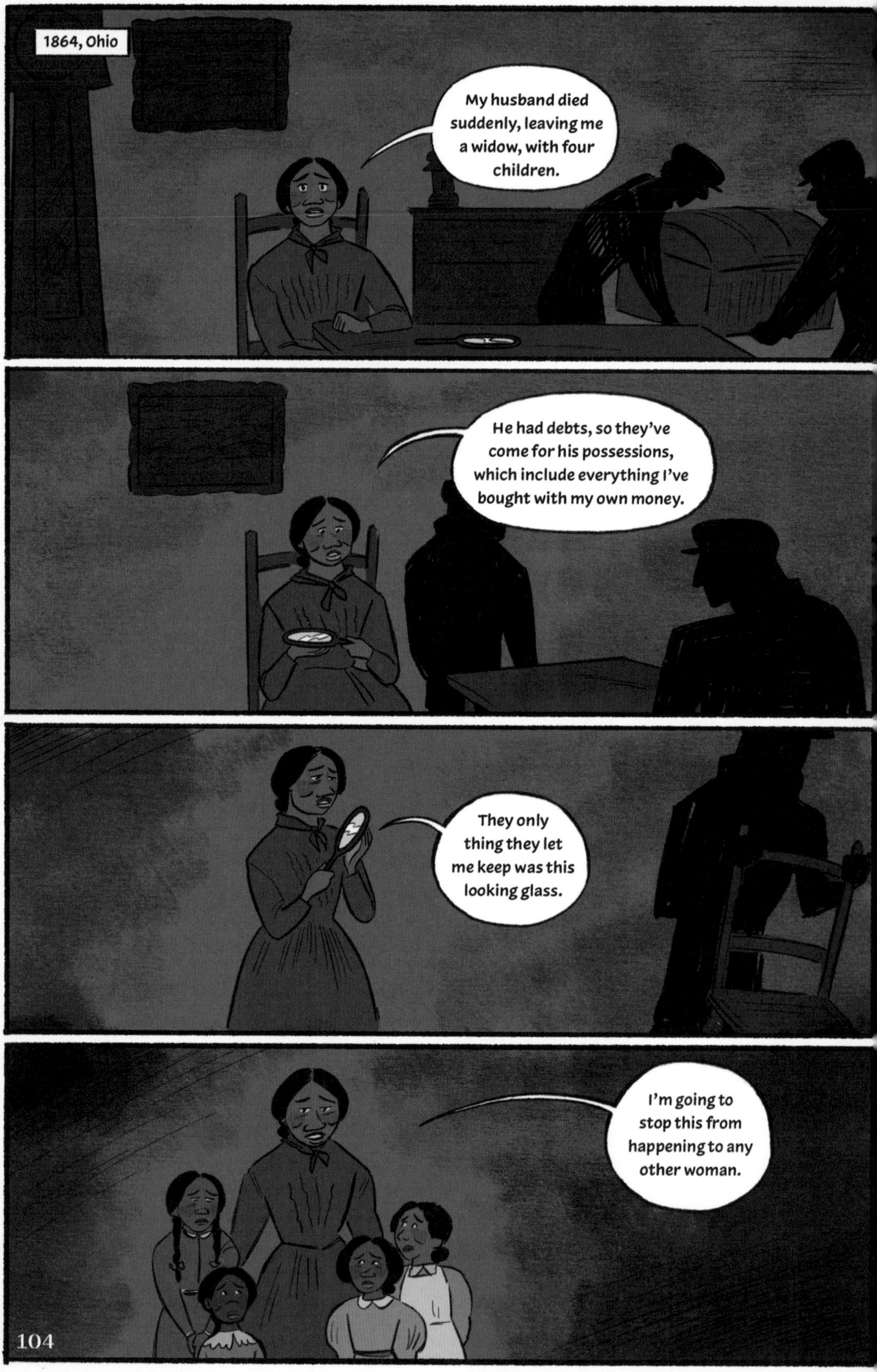
1864, Ohio
My husband died suddenly, leaving me a widow, with four children.
He had debts, so they've come for his possessions, which include everything I've bought with my own money.
They only thing they let me keep was this looking glass.
I'm going to stop this from happening to any other woman.

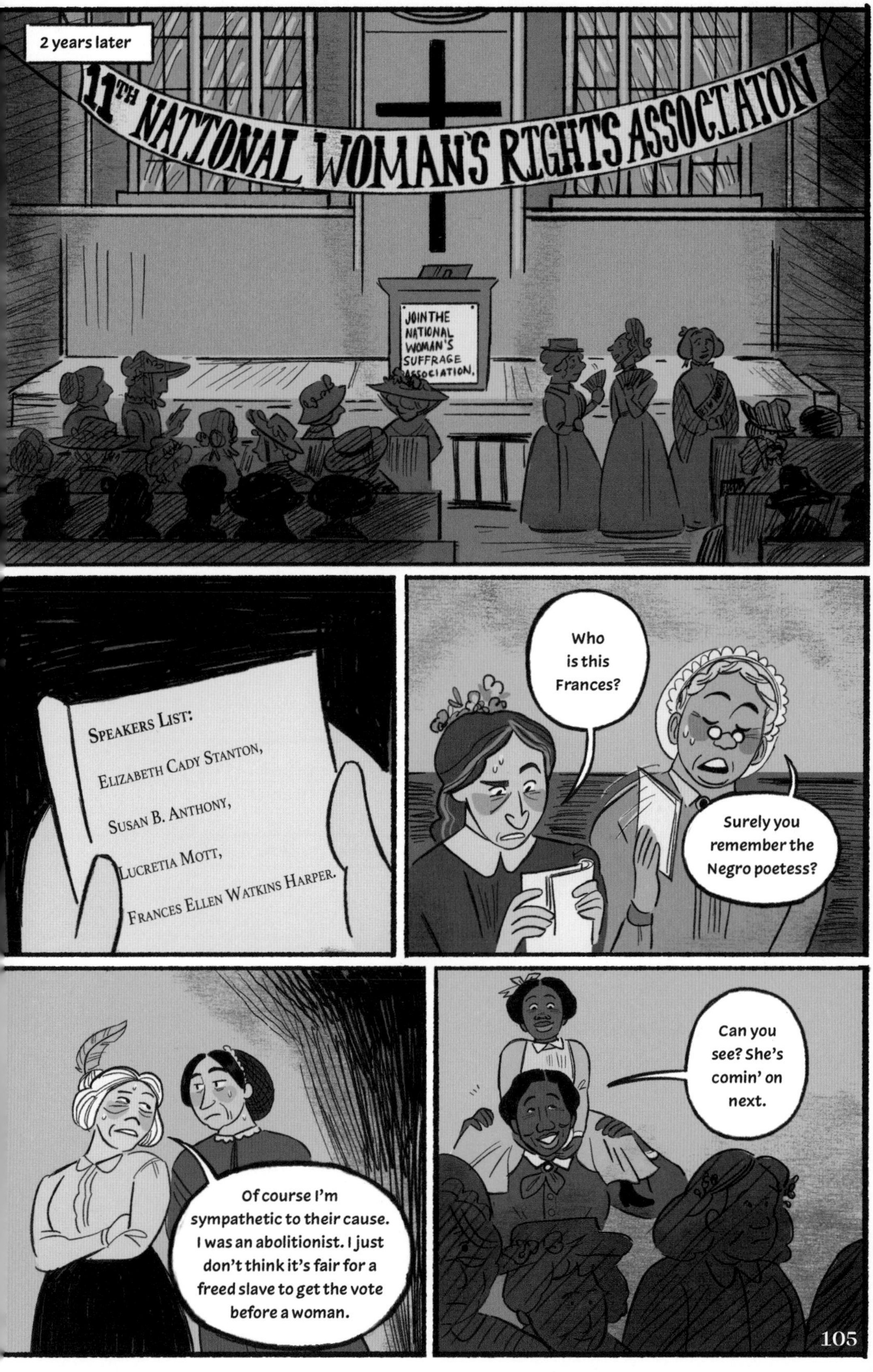
2 years later
11TH NATIONAL WOMAN'S RIGHTS ASSOCIATON
JOIN THE NATIONAL WOMAN'S SUFFRAGE ASSOCIATION.
SPEAKERS LIST:
ELIZABETH CADY STANTON,
SUSAN B. ANTHONY,
LUCRETIA MOTT,
FRANCES ELLEN WATKINS HARPER.
Who is this Frances?
Surely you remember the Negro poetess?
Of course I'm sympathetic to their cause. I was an abolitionist. I just don't think it's fair for a freed slave to get the vote before a woman.
Can you see? She's comin' on next.

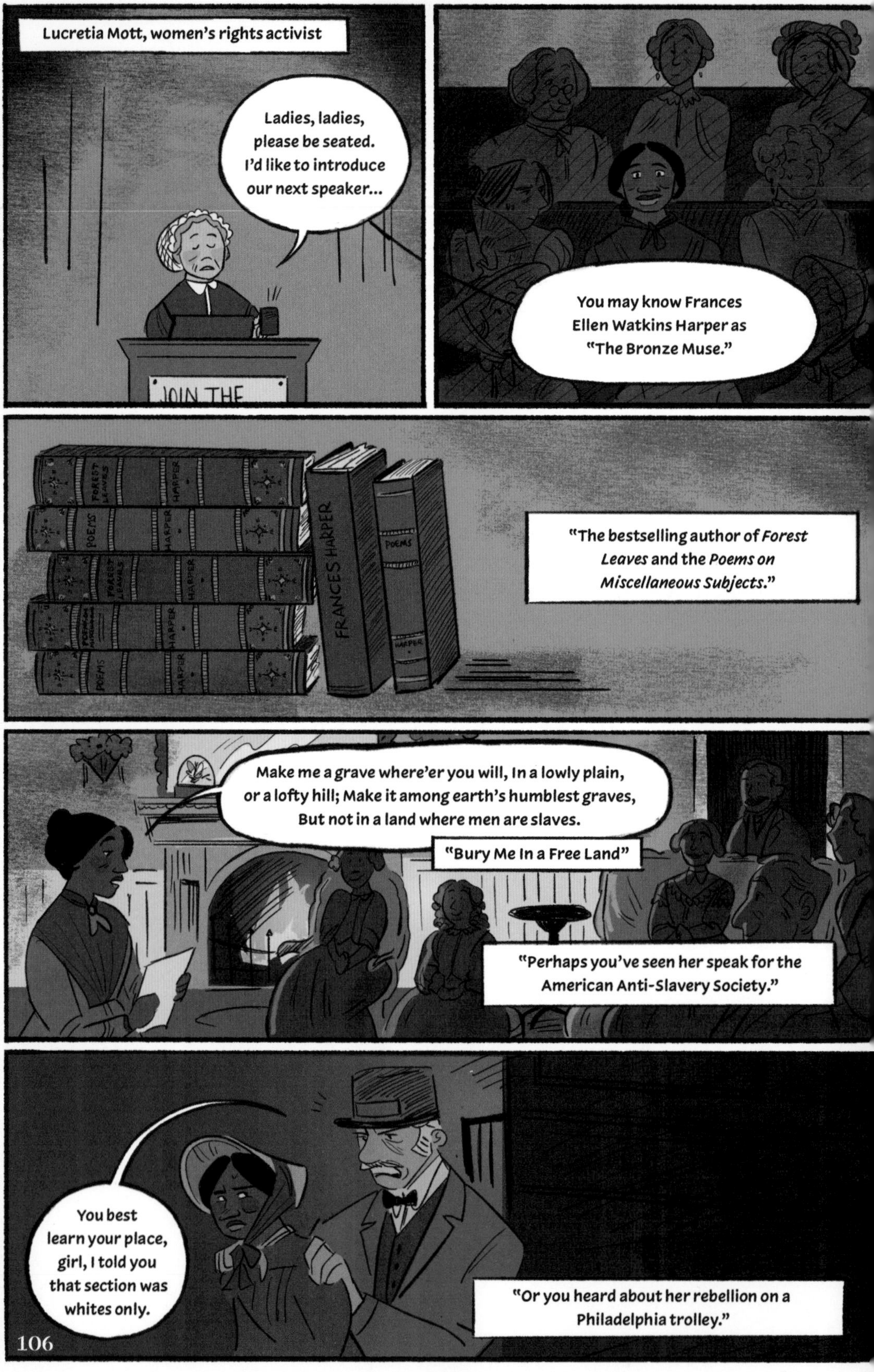
Lucretia Mott, women's rights activist
Ladies, ladies, please be seated. I'd like to introduce our next speaker...
JOIN THE
You may know Frances Ellen Watkins Harper as "The Bronze Muse."
FOREST LEAVES
POEMS
HARPER
FRANCES HARPER
"The bestselling author of *Forest Leaves* and the *Poems on Miscellaneous Subjects*."
Make me a grave where'er you will, In a lowly plain, or a lofty hill; Make it among earth's humblest graves, But not in a land where men are slaves.
"Bury Me In a Free Land"
"Perhaps you've seen her speak for the American Anti-Slavery Society."
You best learn your place, girl, I told you that section was whites only.
"Or you heard about her rebellion on a Philadelphia trolley."

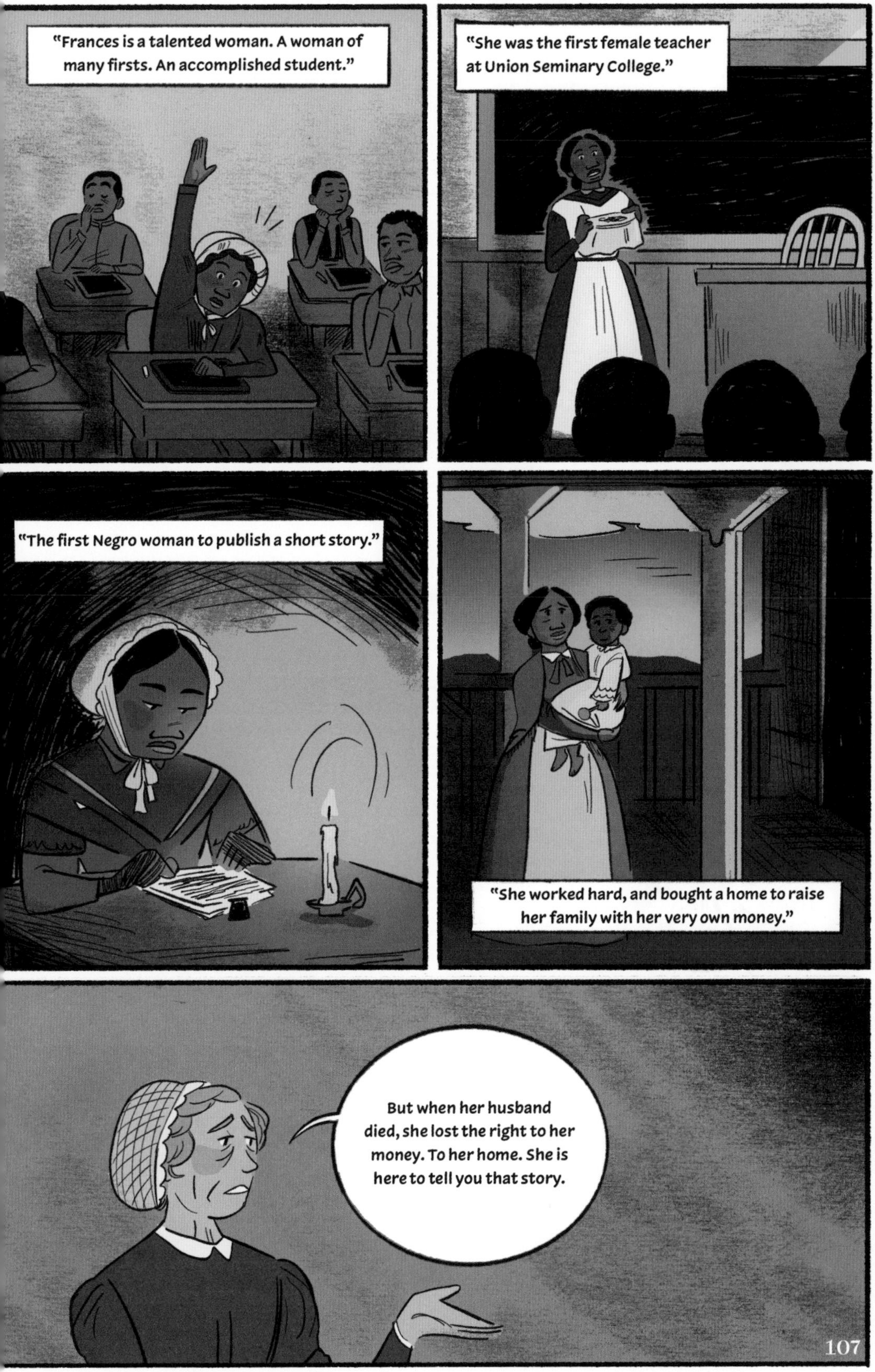
"Frances is a talented woman. A woman of many firsts. An accomplished student."
"She was the first female teacher at Union Seminary College."
"The first Negro woman to publish a short story."
"She worked hard, and bought a home to raise her family with her very own money."
But when her husband died, she lost the right to her money. To her home. She is here to tell you that story.

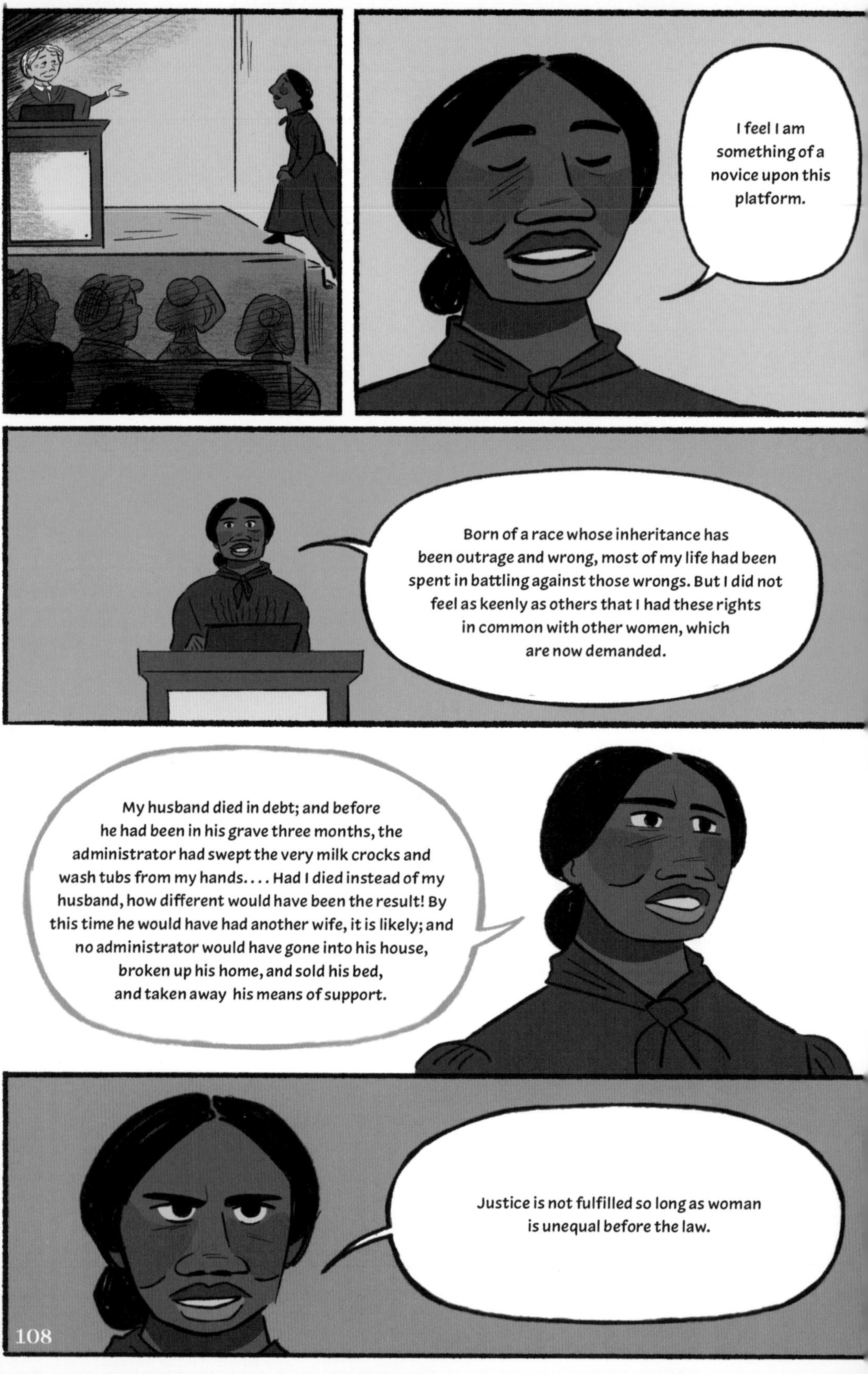
I feel I am something of a novice upon this platform.
Born of a race whose inheritance has been outrage and wrong, most of my life had been spent in battling against those wrongs. But I did not feel as keenly as others that I had these rights in common with other women, which are now demanded.
My husband died in debt; and before he had been in his grave three months, the administrator had swept the very milk crocks and wash tubs from my hands. . . . Had I died instead of my husband, how different would have been the result! By this time he would have had another wife, it is likely; and no administrator would have gone into his house, broken up his home, and sold his bed, and taken away his means of support.
Justice is not fulfilled so long as woman is unequal before the law.

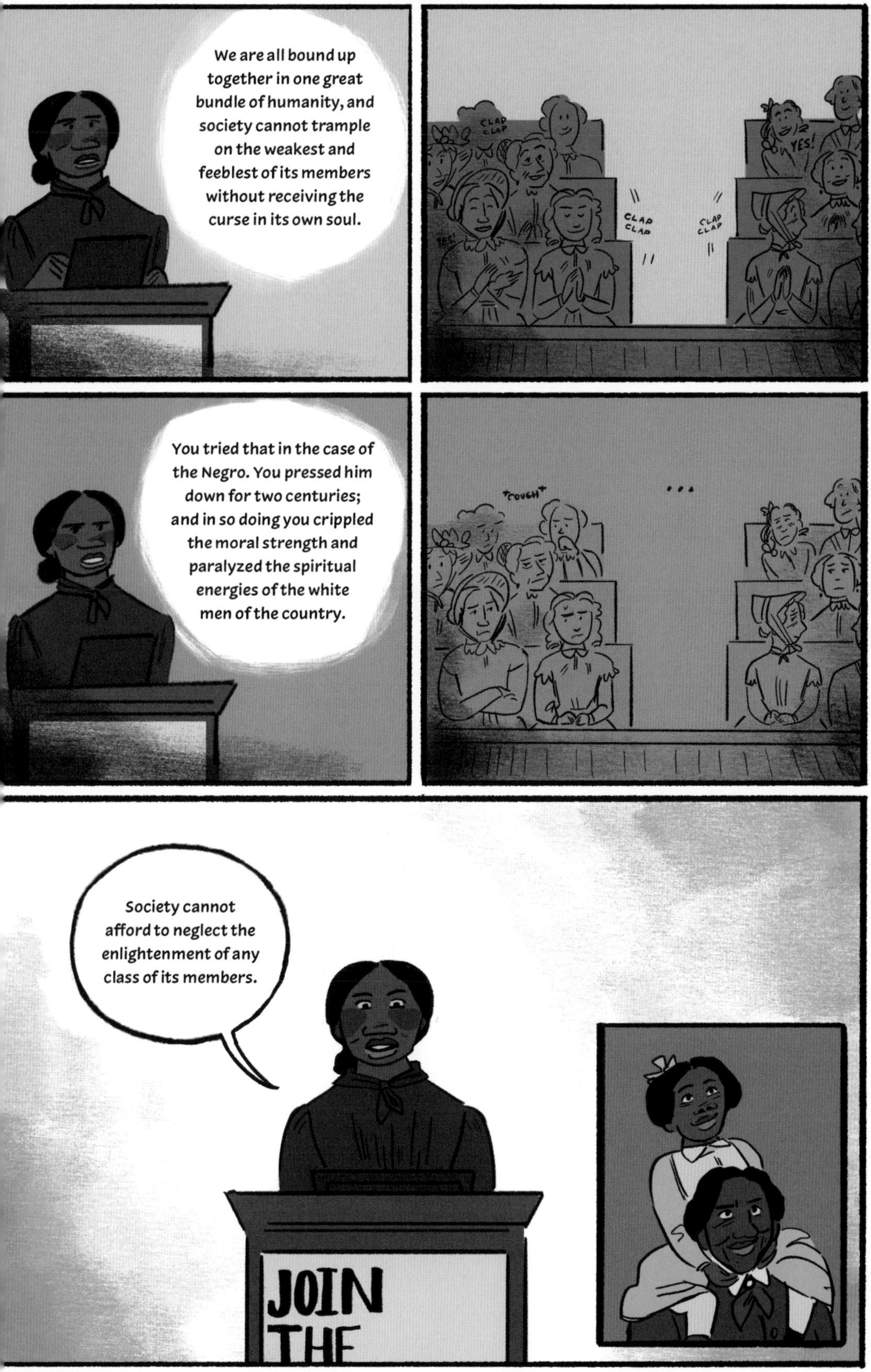
We are all bound up together in one great bundle of humanity, and society cannot trample on the weakest and feeblest of its members without receiving the curse in its own soul.
CLAP CLAP
YES!
CLAP CLAP
CLAP CLAP
YES!
You tried that in the case of the Negro. You pressed him down for two centuries; and in so doing you crippled the moral strength and paralyzed the spiritual energies of the white men of the country.
COUGH
...
Society cannot afford to neglect the enlightenment of any class of its members.
JOIN THE

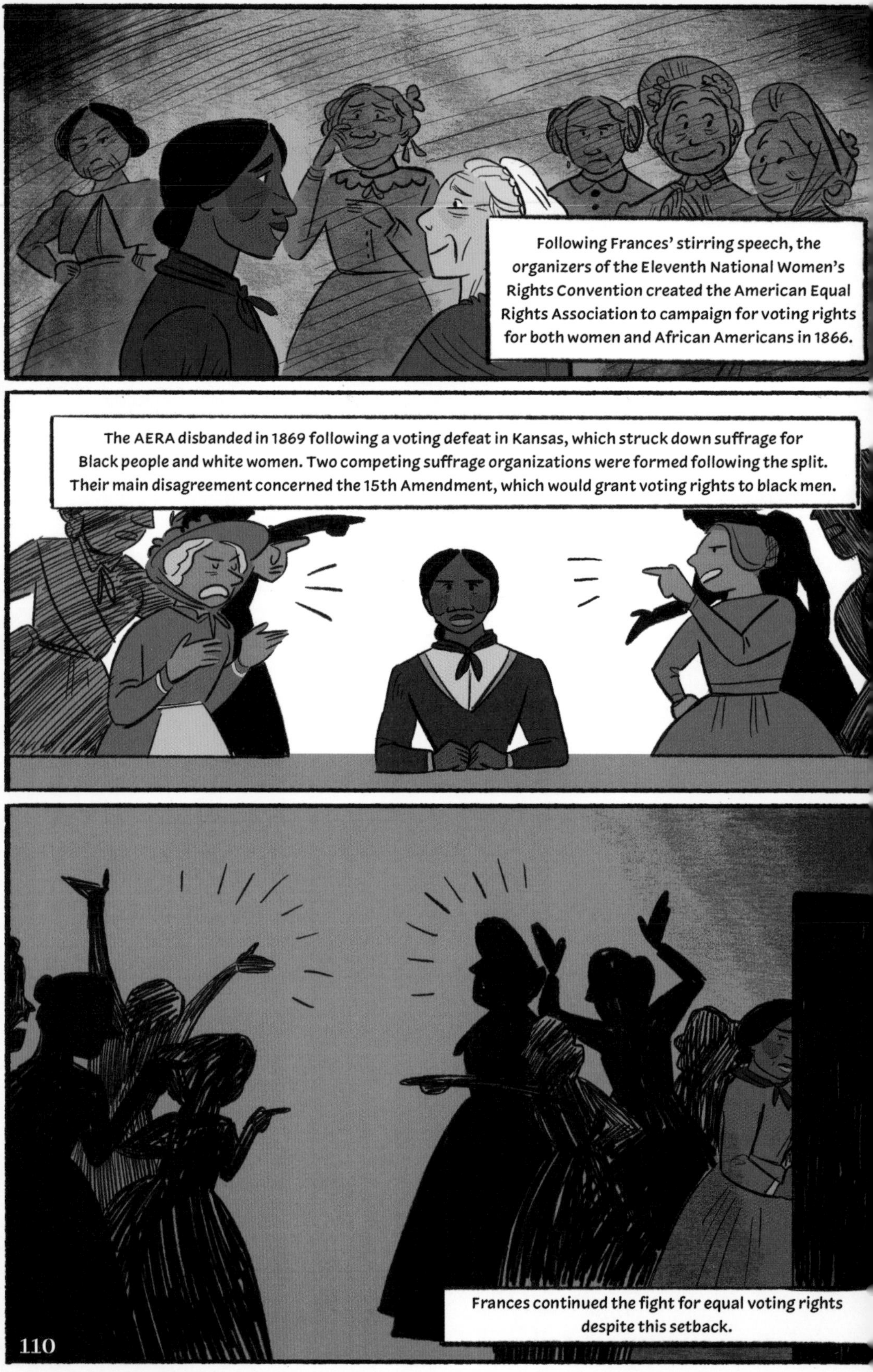
Following Frances' stirring speech, the organizers of the Eleventh National Women's Rights Convention created the American Equal Rights Association to campaign for voting rights for both women and African Americans in 1866.
The AERA disbanded in 1869 following a voting defeat in Kansas, which struck down suffrage for Black people and white women. Two competing suffrage organizations were formed following the split. Their main disagreement concerned the 15th Amendment, which would grant voting rights to black men.
Frances continued the fight for equal voting rights despite this setback.

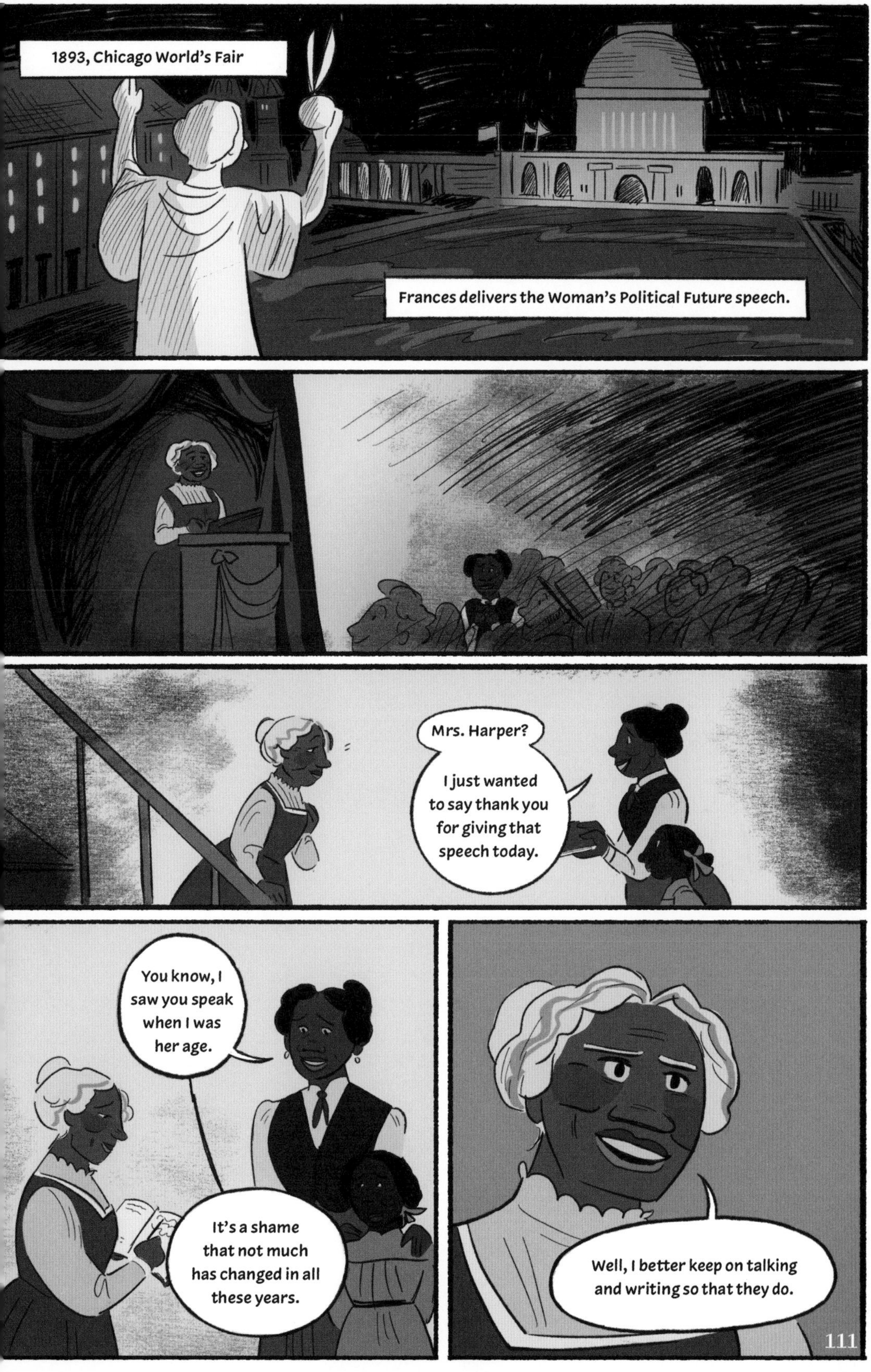
1893, Chicago World's Fair
Frances delivers the Woman's Political Future speech.
Mrs. Harper?
I just wanted to say thank you for giving that speech today.
You know, I saw you speak when I was her age.
It's a shame that not much has changed in all these years.
Well, I better keep on talking and writing so that they do.

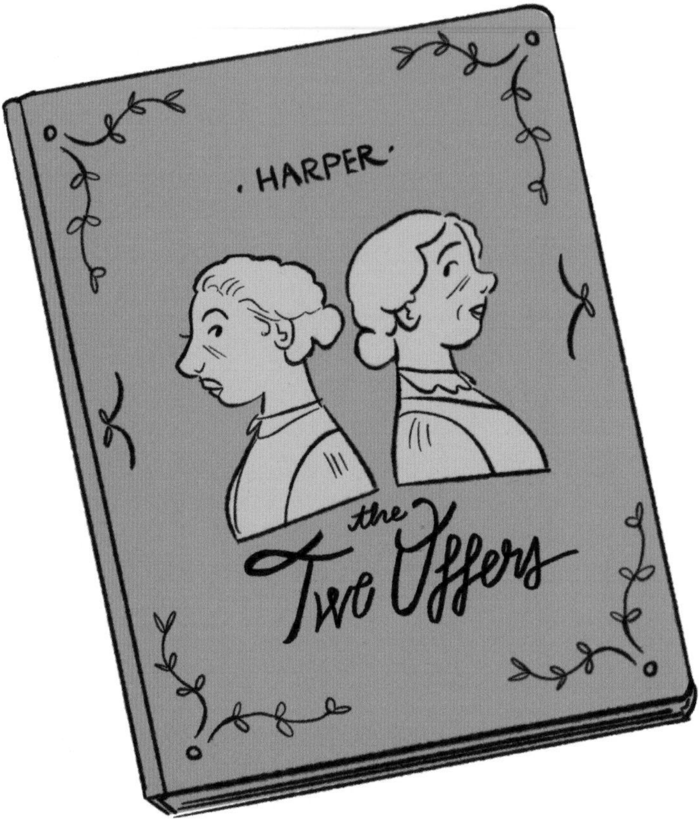
HARPER
the Two Offers

Frances Harper's "The Two Offers" is the first short story published by an African American woman. The story revolves around two cousins with opposing views on marriage. Laura Lagrange is desperate to marry so that she will not become an old maid, while her cousin, Janette Alston, is happy to forgo marriage entirely so that she can focus on her career as a writer. The name Janette Alston is an allusion to Jane Austen.

One hundred years before Rosa Parks, in 1858, Harper refused to give up her seat on a segregated trolley in Philadelphia. This experience served as the inspiration for her popular poem, "Bury Me in a Free Land."

SELECTED WORKS

POETRY COLLECTIONS

1845: *Forest Leaves*
1854: *Poems on Miscellaneous Subjects*
1872: *Sketches of Southern Life*
1890: *Light Beyond the Darkness*
1894: *The Martyr of Alabama and Other Poems*
1901: *Idylls of the Bible*

SHORT STORIES

1859: "The Two Offers"

NOVELS

1869: *Moses: A Story of the Nile*
1876: *Sowing and Reaping: A Temperance Story*
1888: *Minnie's Sacrifice*
1892: *Iola Leroy, or Shadows Uplifted*

Alice Dunbar Nelson

1875–1935

"And now—unwittingly, you've made me dream

Of violets, and my soul's forgotten gleam."

— "Sonnet," 1922

The résumé of Alice Dunbar Nelson is nothing short of awe-inspiring. A well-known figure during the Harlem Renaissance in New York, she was a poet, journalist, and short-story writer. She was also an educator, social activist, and sought-after speaker, who campaigned for the rights of women and African Americans. Unfortunately, this information was missing from the headline on her obituary, which referred to her simply as "wife of poet."

Born in New Orleans in 1875, just ten years after the end of the Civil War, Alice Moore was the daughter of a former slave and a merchant marine. At a time when it was rare for Black Americans to attend college at all, Alice graduated from Straight University, where she trained as a teacher. By twenty, she published her first short story collection, entitled *Violets and Other Tales*, and the following year, she cofounded a school for girls in New York City called the White Rose Mission. It was during this time she began her romance with the man hailed as the Negro Poet Laureate.

After spotting her picture in the paper, Paul Laurence Dunbar couldn't resist the urge to send Alice a letter. Following a two-year epistolary romance, they married in 1898 and became known as a literary power couple. In 1899, Alice released her sophomore collection of short stories entitled *The Goodness of St. Rocque, and Other Stories* alongside Paul's *Poems of Cabin and Field*. Their romance mirrored that of the legendary poets, Elizabeth Barrett Browning and Robert Browning, but it lacked the fairytale ending. Paul was abusive; and Alice left him in 1904. He died two years later.

According to her obituary, Alice's next marriage was to civil rights activist Robert "Bobbo" Nelson in 1916, but Alice was a woman of many secrets. Her diaries, edited and published in 1984 by Gloria T. Hull, revealed a previously undisclosed marriage to Henry Callis in 1910, and numerous relationships with women. Perhaps most significantly, this included her affair with journalist Fay Jackson Robinson, whom she called her "little blue dream of loveliness."

The diaries of Alice Dunbar Nelson tell the story of an ambitious, complex, and deeply unsatisfied woman. Publicly, Alice was seen as a successful and charismatic figure. Privately she sank into frequent bouts of depression, crushed by the weight of her own expectations and straining to financially support her husband, sister, and mother. The loss of her steady teaching job in 1920 nearly broke her. Alice's luck would turn around in 1928, when she was appointed executive secretary of the American Friends Inter-Racial Peace Committee. It was a position that allowed Alice to continue her activism, earn a steady income, and gain peace of mind.

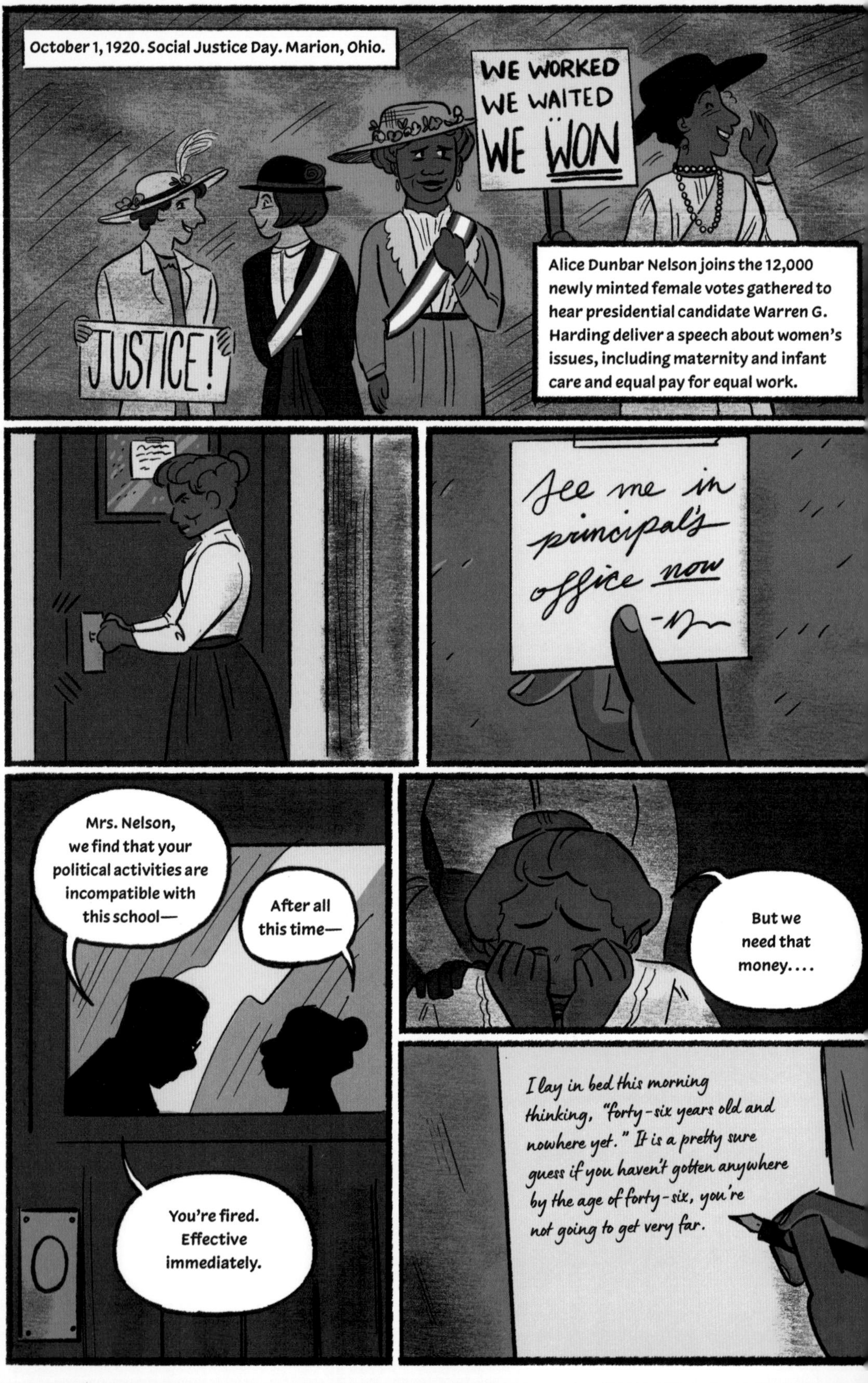
October 1, 1920. Social Justice Day. Marion, Ohio.
WE WORKED WE WAITED WE WON
JUSTICE!
Alice Dunbar Nelson joins the 12,000 newly minted female votes gathered to hear presidential candidate Warren G. Harding deliver a speech about women's issues, including maternity and infant care and equal pay for equal work.
See me in principal's office now
Mrs. Nelson, we find that your political activities are incompatible with this school—
After all this time—
You're fired. Effective immediately.
But we need that money. . . .
I lay in bed this morning thinking, "forty-six years old and nowhere yet." It is a pretty sure guess if you haven't gotten anywhere by the age of forty-six, you're not going to get very far.

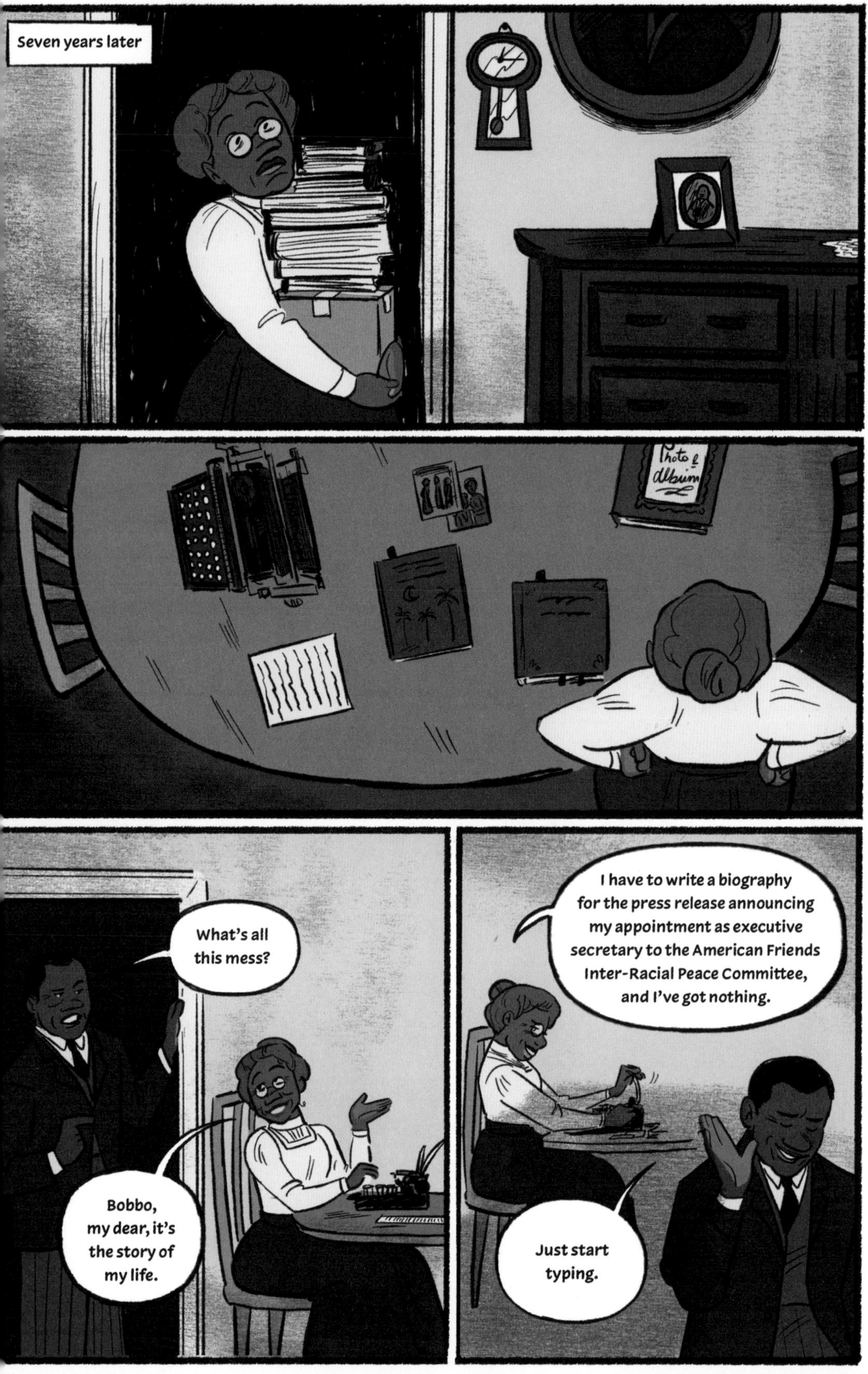
Seven years later
Photo Album
What's all this mess?
Bobbo, my dear, it's the story of my life.
I have to write a biography for the press release announcing my appointment as executive secretary to the American Friends Inter-Racial Peace Committee, and I've got nothing.
Just start typing.

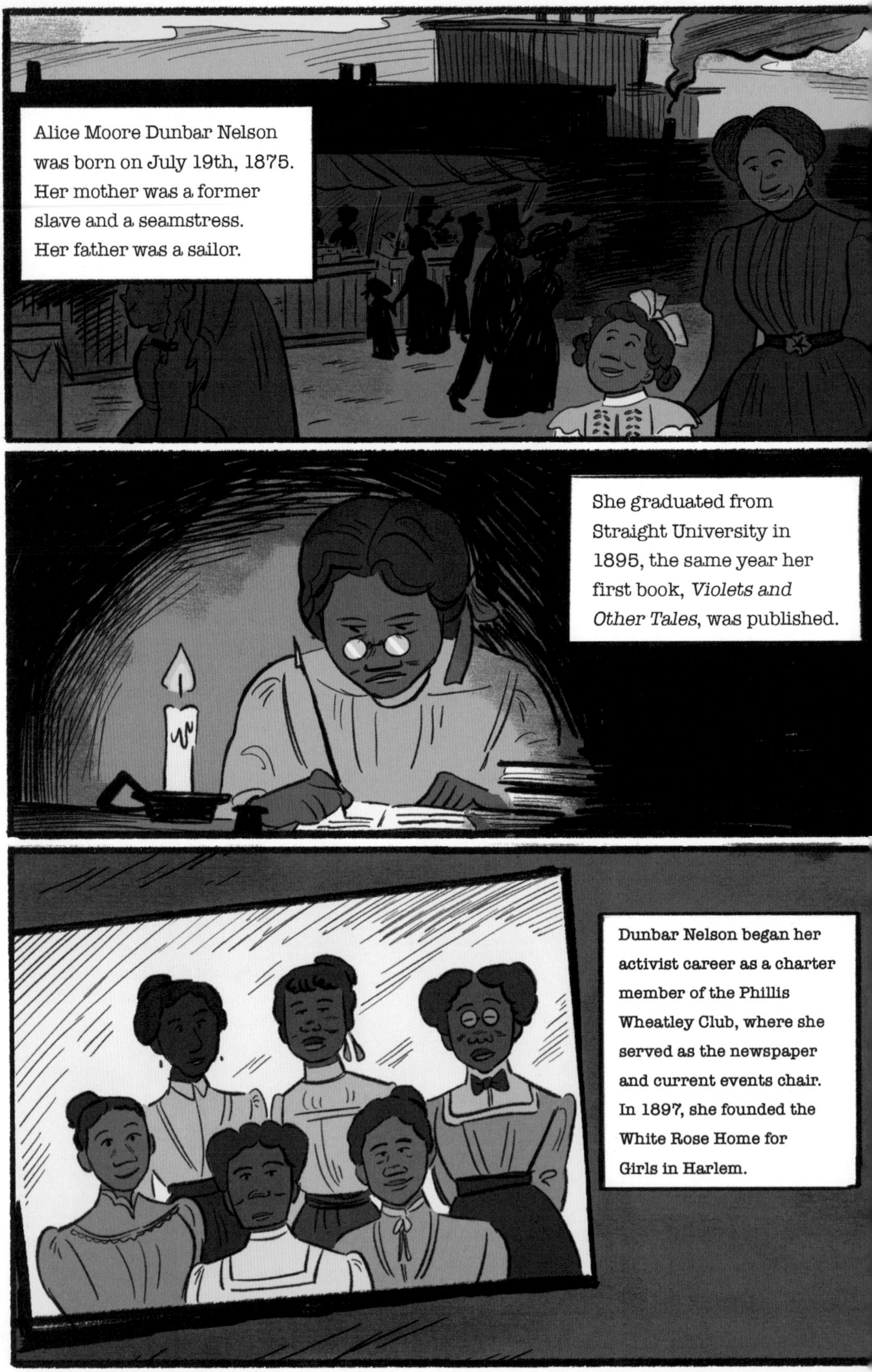
Alice Moore Dunbar Nelson was born on July 19th, 1875. Her mother was a former slave and a seamstress. Her father was a sailor.
She graduated from Straight University in 1895, the same year her first book, *Violets and Other Tales*, was published.
Dunbar Nelson began her activist career as a charter member of the Phillis Wheatley Club, where she served as the newspaper and current events chair. In 1897, she founded the White Rose Home for Girls in Harlem.

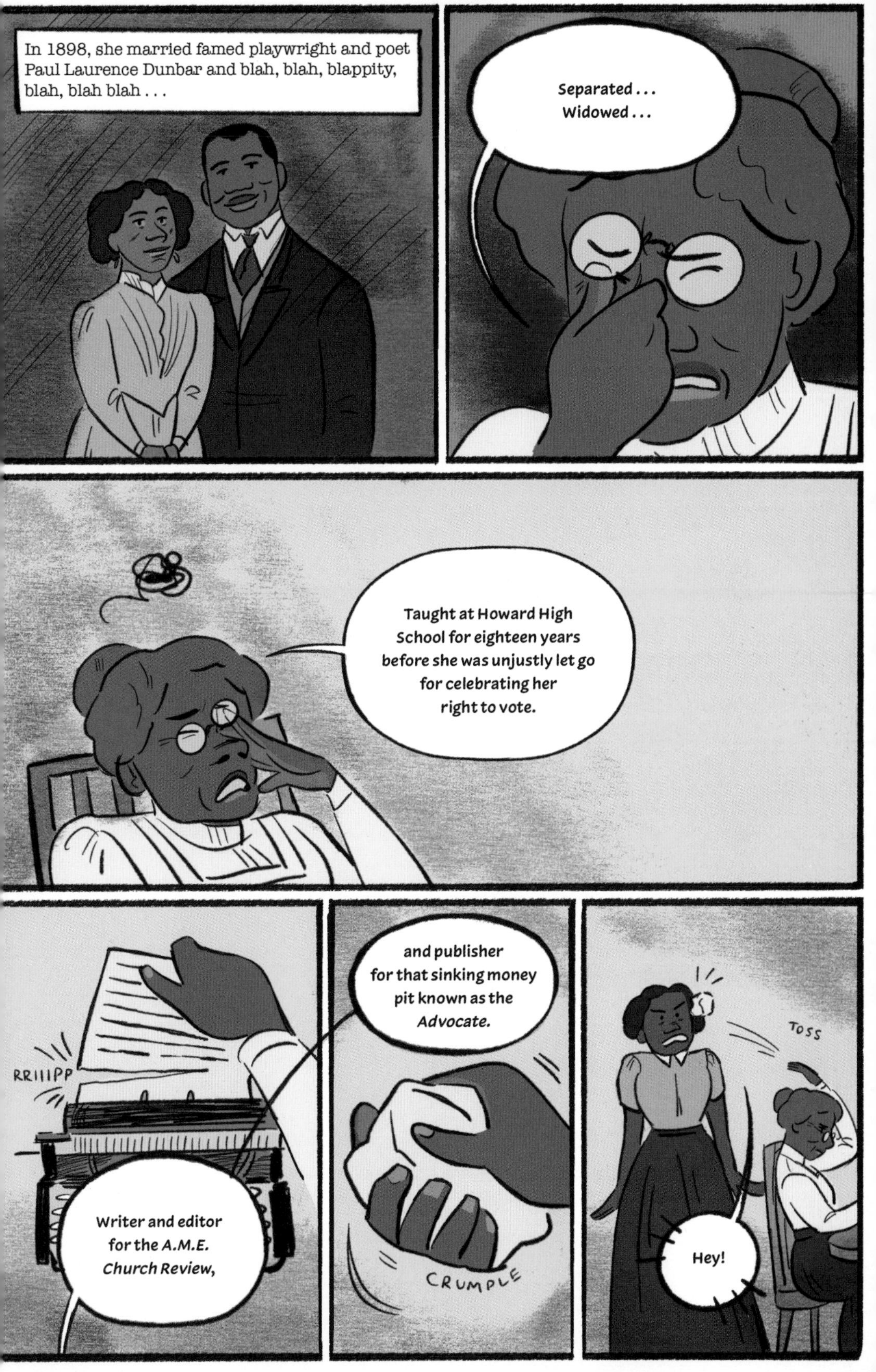
In 1898, she married famed playwright and poet Paul Laurence Dunbar and blah, blah, blappity, blah, blah blah . . .
Separated . . . Widowed . . .
Taught at Howard High School for eighteen years before she was unjustly let go for celebrating her right to vote.
RRIIIPP
Writer and editor for the *A.M.E. Church Review*,
and publisher for that sinking money pit known as the *Advocate*.
CRUMPLE
TOSS
Hey!

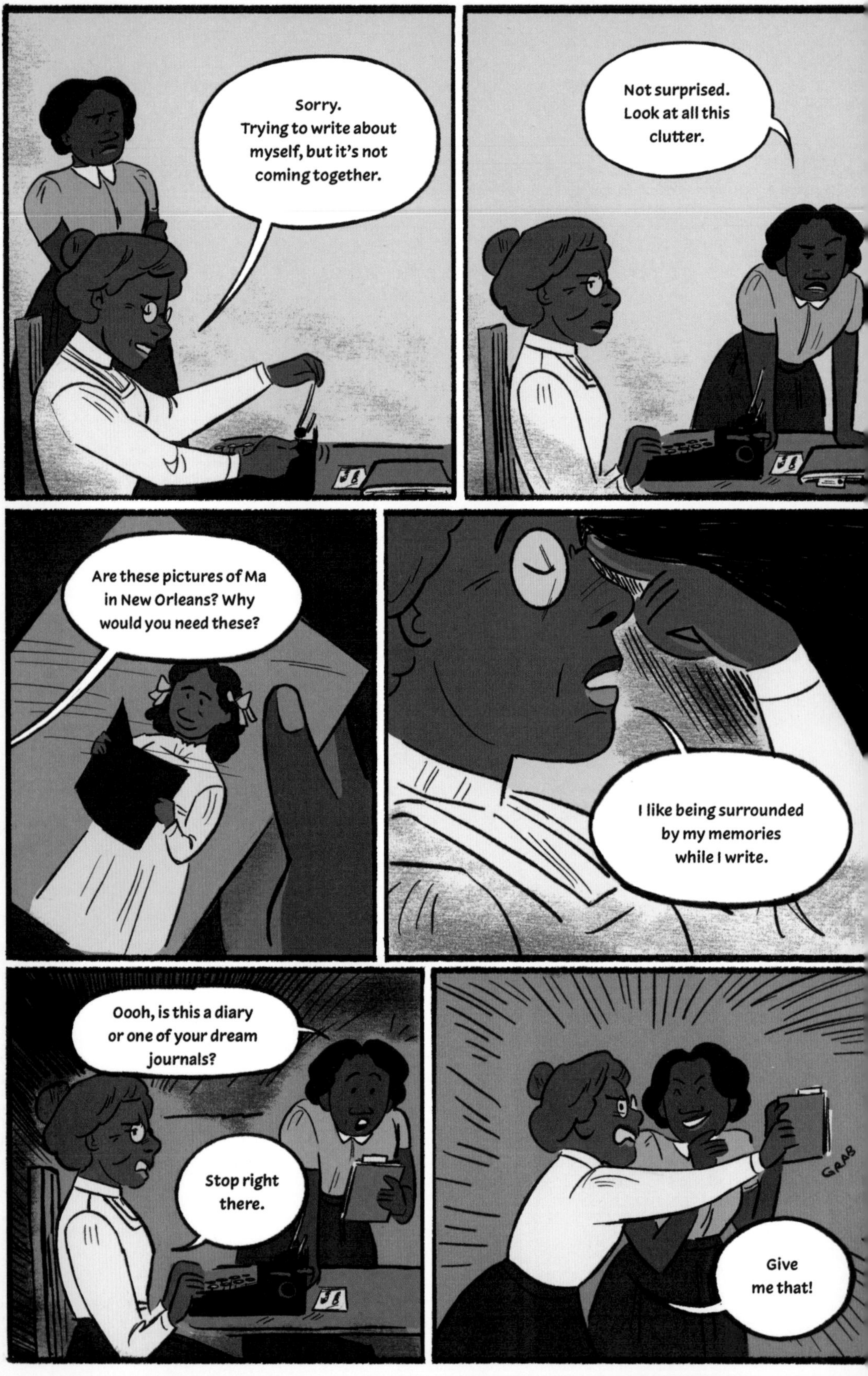
Sorry.
Trying to write about myself, but it's not coming together.
Not surprised. Look at all this clutter.
Are these pictures of Ma in New Orleans? Why would you need these?
I like being surrounded by my memories while I write.
Oooh, is this a diary or one of your dream journals?
Stop right there.
GRAB
Give me that!

Let's see...

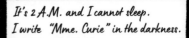

It's 2 A.M. and I cannot sleep. I write "Mme. Curie" in the darkness.

Oft have I thrilled at deeds of high emprise,
And yearned to venture into realms unknown,
Thrice blessed she, I deemed, whom God had shown
How to achieve great deeds in woman's guise.

How's this for my press release, "Times are tough. Money's tight. Debts staggering.... Truth from the diary of Alice Dunbar Nelson."

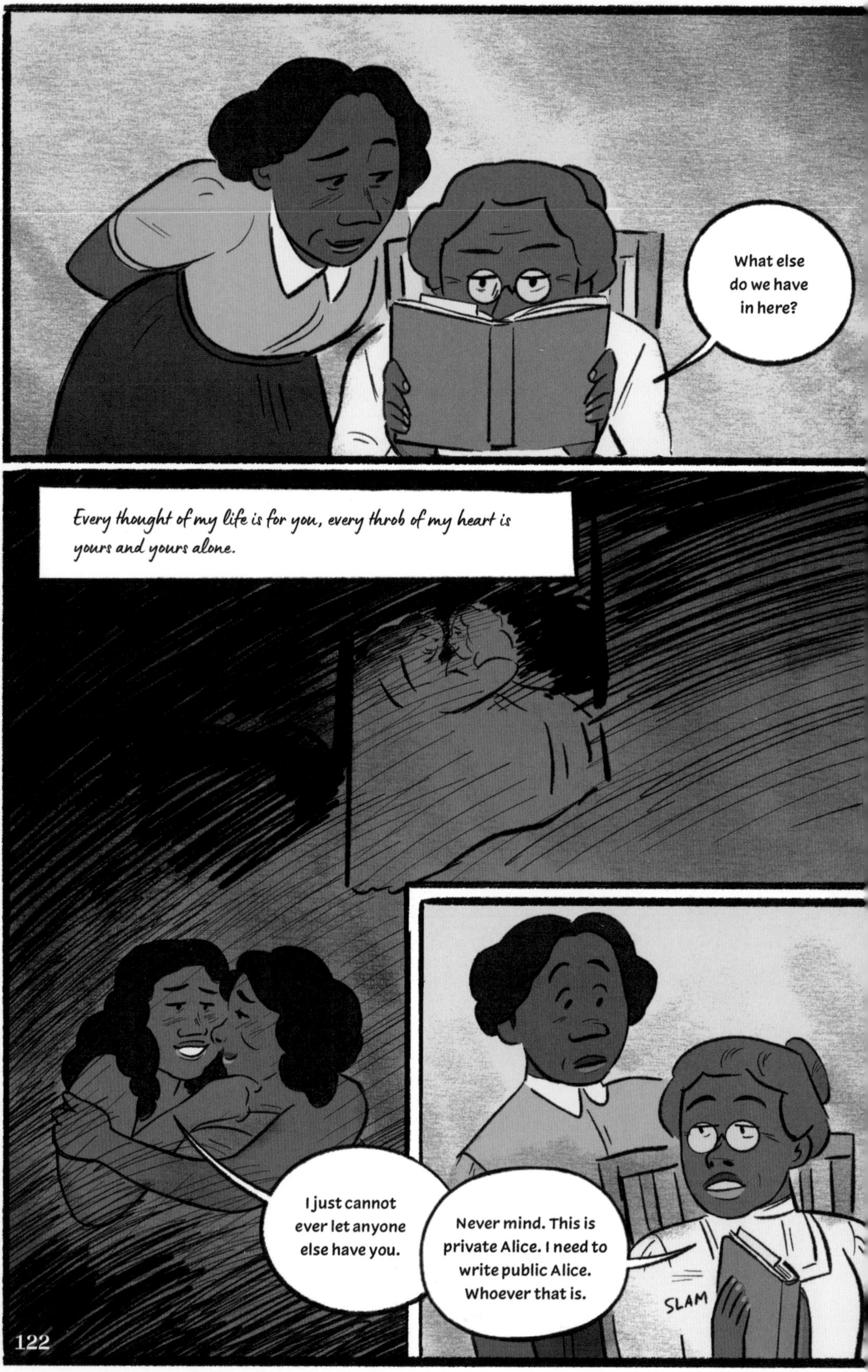
What else do we have in here?
Every thought of my life is for you, every throb of my heart is yours and yours alone.
I just cannot ever let anyone else have you.
Never mind. This is private Alice. I need to write public Alice. Whoever that is.
SLAM

Well, the public Alice Dunbar Nelson was a field organizer for women's suffrage and the head of the Anti-Lynching Crusaders.

For all the good it's done.

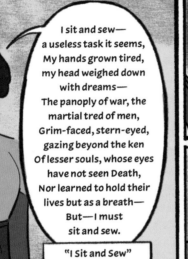

I sit and sew—
a useless task it seems,
My hands grown tired,
my head weighed down
with dreams—
The panoply of war, the
martial tred of men,
Grim-faced, stern-eyed,
gazing beyond the ken
Of lesser souls, whose eyes
have not seen Death,
Nor learned to hold their
lives but as a breath—
But—I must
sit and sew.

"I Sit and Sew"

I've always loved that poem. If memory serves correctly, you struggled with it. But it came together in the end.

You're right.

Now, if you'll excuse me . . .

"I have some writing to do."

TAP TAPTAP

In 1904, Alice Dunbar Nelson attended summer school at Cornell University, where she penned the essay "Why I Like Jane Austen." In it, she declares her love for Austen by saying, "And so, to those who prefer caviare, let us of the plain dinner table, where the family even perchance uses napkin rings, say humbly that because of Jane Austen's simple style, quiet humor, keen irony, sprightly narrative, mischievous poking into our homely, everyday souls, and gentle ending of her stories, we like her and them, though they be the Apotheosis of the Commonplace."

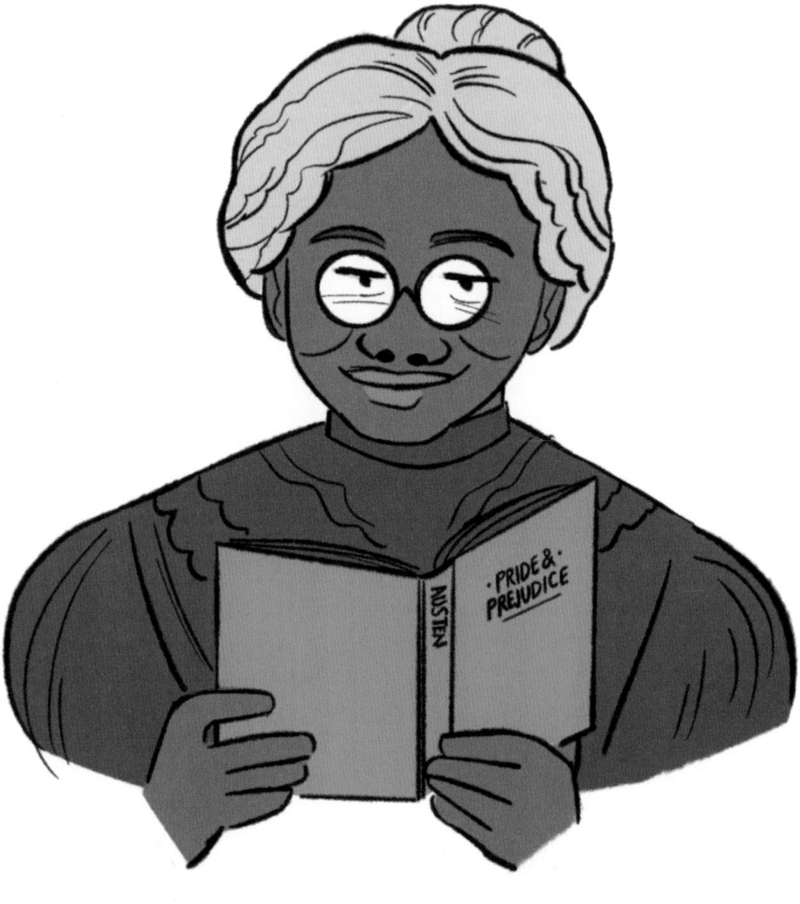
AUSTEN
·PRIDE&·
PREJUDICE

A great lover of music, Alice played the violin, cello, and mandolin. As part of her work for the American Inter-Racial Peace Committee, she organized the National Negro Music Festival in 1929.

SELECTED WORKS

POETRY AND SHORT STORY COLLECTIONS

1895: *Violets and Other Tales*
1899: *The Goodness of St. Rocque and Other Stories*

ESSAYS, ARTICLES AND COLUMNS

1909: *Wordsworth's Use of Milton's Description of the Building of Pandemonium*
1917: *People of Color in Louisiana*
1926: *From a Woman's Point of View*
1926–1930: *As in a Looking Glass*, newspaper column for *Washington Eagle*
1930: *So It Seems to Alice Dunbar Nelson*, newspaper column for the *Pittsburgh Courier*

PLAYS

1918: *Mine Eyes Have Seen*

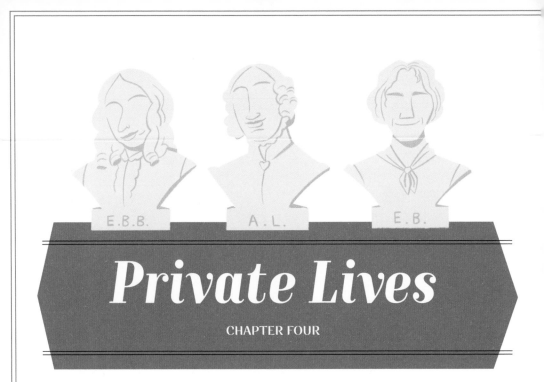

E.B.B.   A.L.   E.B.

Private Lives

CHAPTER FOUR

Publishing isn't always the primary objective. The blank page can also serve as a confidant, allowing the author to express themselves free of judgment. Buried in code, verse, and secret stories, Anne Lister, Emily Brontë, and Elizabeth Barrett Browning unleashed their innermost thoughts in journals that were never intended for publication.

Anne Lister was a compulsive writer. Her teenage diary turned into a daily log documenting the large and small details of her life and times between 1806 and 1840. Her descendant John was her first editor. An avid historian, John Lister felt that Anne's twenty-six journals he had inherited were of the utmost importance. Using her journals, he tracked the social and political history of their hometown and, between 1887 and 1892, he published 200,000 of Anne's words on agriculture, town business, and travel in the *Halifax Guardian*. John was baffled, however, by the numerous coded entries in Anne's journals. He had no way of knowing he was setting out to decode the secret life of the first modern lesbian.

Charlotte Brontë had a habit of interfering with her sisters' writing. Following the death of Emily and Anne, she made edits to their novels and poetry, she blocked Anne's *Tenant of Wildfell Hall* from further publication, and there's even a rumor that she torched Emily's second manuscript.

There is another theory, however. It is possible that Emily destroyed the manuscript herself once she realized that she was dying. Unlike Charlotte, Emily never craved literary fame. The fictional world of Gondal that she created with Anne was like a secret language between the sisters. Her further poetry was for her eyes only. It was Charlotte who insisted on publishing the work after she "discovered" Emily's private notebook. Emily reluctantly agreed to do so, as long as her identity was obscured and the poems were altered.

Elizabeth Barrett lived in a time when poetry was the business of serious men, and it was only proper for women to write romantic, flowery, or religious verses. Instead, she defied conventions with her impressive Greek translations and anti-slavery poetry. Something of a recluse, Elizabeth was not a healthy woman, and spent most of her life bedridden. In 1840, she suffered the loss of her favorite brother, which sent her into a deep depression. The following year, she closed herself off in her bedroom at 50 Wimpole Street.

In 1845, Elizabeth began an epistolary courtship with fellow poet Robert Browning. Immediately following their first meeting, Elizabeth began keeping a journal of verse, which she used as a space to document her feelings about Browning and their secret relationship. Three years after they were wed, she shared the poems with Browning, who encouraged her to publish. At first, Elizabeth was hesitant. Unlike her previous work, these sentimental and emotional verses were deeply private. But a few alterations and a clever title would provide a buffer between Elizabeth's private life and published work.

In a strange twist of fate, these secret works have only added to the allure of Anne Lister, Emily Brontë, and Elizabeth Barrett Browning. The discovery and translation of Lister's diaries has led to several modern reproductions, including a 2019 television series, and a brand new set of fans, even over a hundred years after her death. Unraveling Emily's mysterious poetry and lost novel has been the subject of countless books and scholarly investigations. And Victorians and modern audiences alike found the fairytale nature of the Barrett-Browning courtship and poetry too good to resist: "How do I love thee? Let me count the ways" remains one of the most famous lines of poetry of all time.

Anne Lister

1791–1840

"What a comfort [are] my journals, how I can
write in crypt all as it really is..."

—Anne Lister's diaries, *Nature's Domain: Anne Lister and the
Landscape of Desire*, transcribed by Jill Liddington

Anne Lister was a diarist, landowner, and entrepreneur who was infamous for her masculine style of dress. A striking and charismatic figure, her rumored sexuality and bold business ventures fueled the gossip mill in her hometown of Halifax in West Yorkshire, England. They called her Gentleman Jack.

It was rare for a woman to become a landowner in her own right in the 1800s. Anne Lister was the second of six children born to Jeremy and Rebecca Lister, but all four of her brothers passed away, leaving her the heir to the family estate, Shibden Hall. Although she didn't officially inherit until 1836, her uncle and father were happy to let the bright and motivated Anne take charge of Shibden Hall in 1826. Lister made extensive renovations to the home and gardens, opened a colliery for coal mining, and invested heavily in properties in town. It is unclear whether or not her family was aware of her sexuality, but they seemed rather pleased that Lister had no plans of marrying a man, as they didn't want the estate falling into the hands of an "unscrupulous fortune hunter."

Anne Lister was, however, intent on marrying a woman. On the rebound from a serious relationship with Mariana Belcombe, Lister began pursuing local heiress Ann Walker in 1832. The pair fell in love and married in secret two years later in what is thought to be the first lesbian marriage held in Britain. Ever the world traveler, Lister took her new bride on a honeymoon to France and Switzerland that same year. The pair would set out again for Europe in 1839 for a grand tour of France, Denmark, Sweden, and Russia, during which Lister contracted a fever and died.

In 1836, Anne Lister had drawn a will that bestowed her estate to Ann Walker with the condition that upon Walker's death or remarriage, the estate would then revert back to the Lister family. In 1843, however, Ann Walker's family had her declared legally insane and forcibly removed her from Shibden Hall. With Walker now declared a "lunatic," the Lister family made claim to the estate, and in 1855, a young John Lister would move into Shibden Hall.

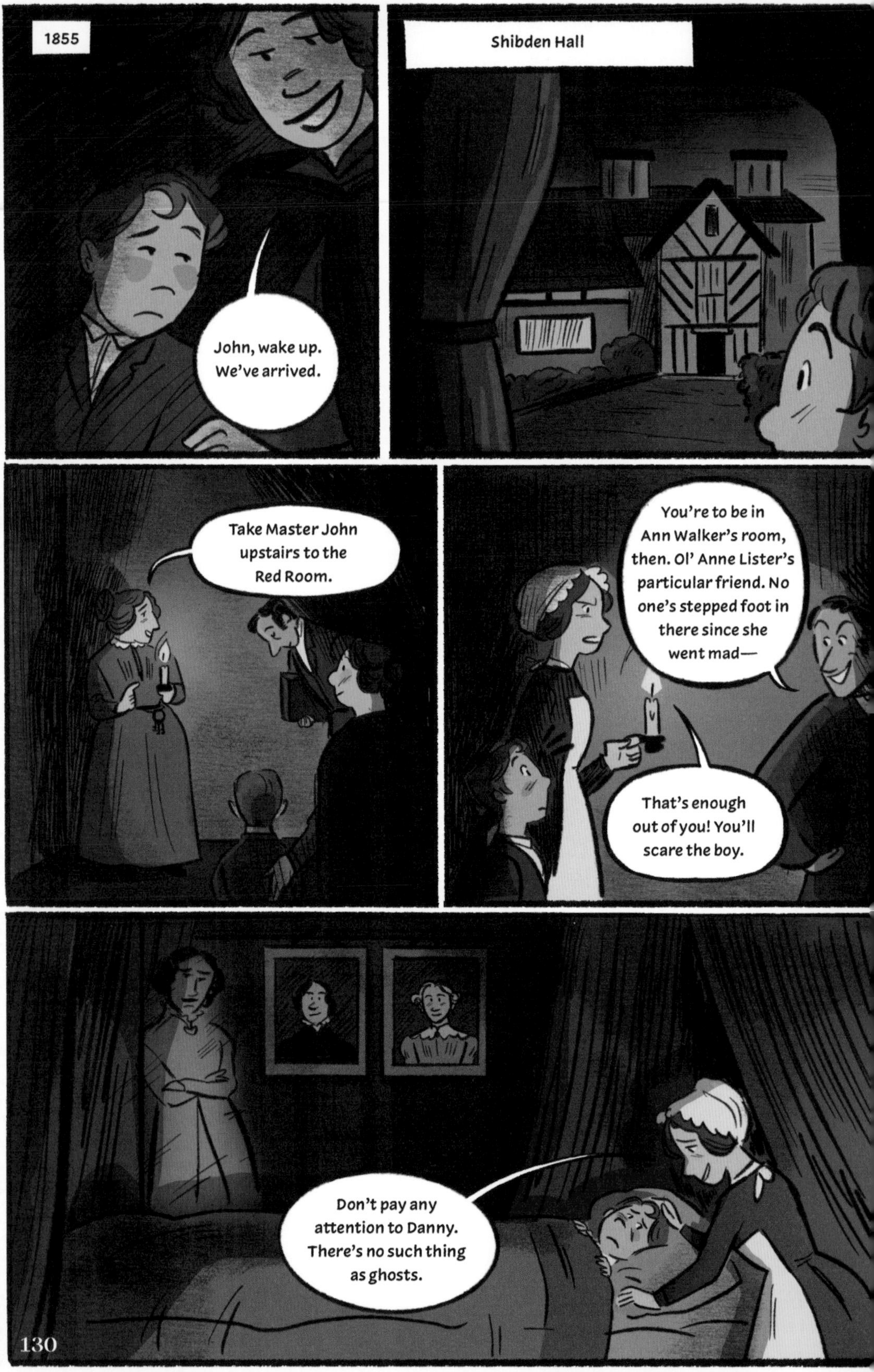
1855
John, wake up. We've arrived.
Shibden Hall
Take Master John upstairs to the Red Room.
You're to be in Ann Walker's room, then. Ol' Anne Lister's particular friend. No one's stepped foot in there since she went mad—
That's enough out of you! You'll scare the boy.
Don't pay any attention to Danny. There's no such thing as ghosts.

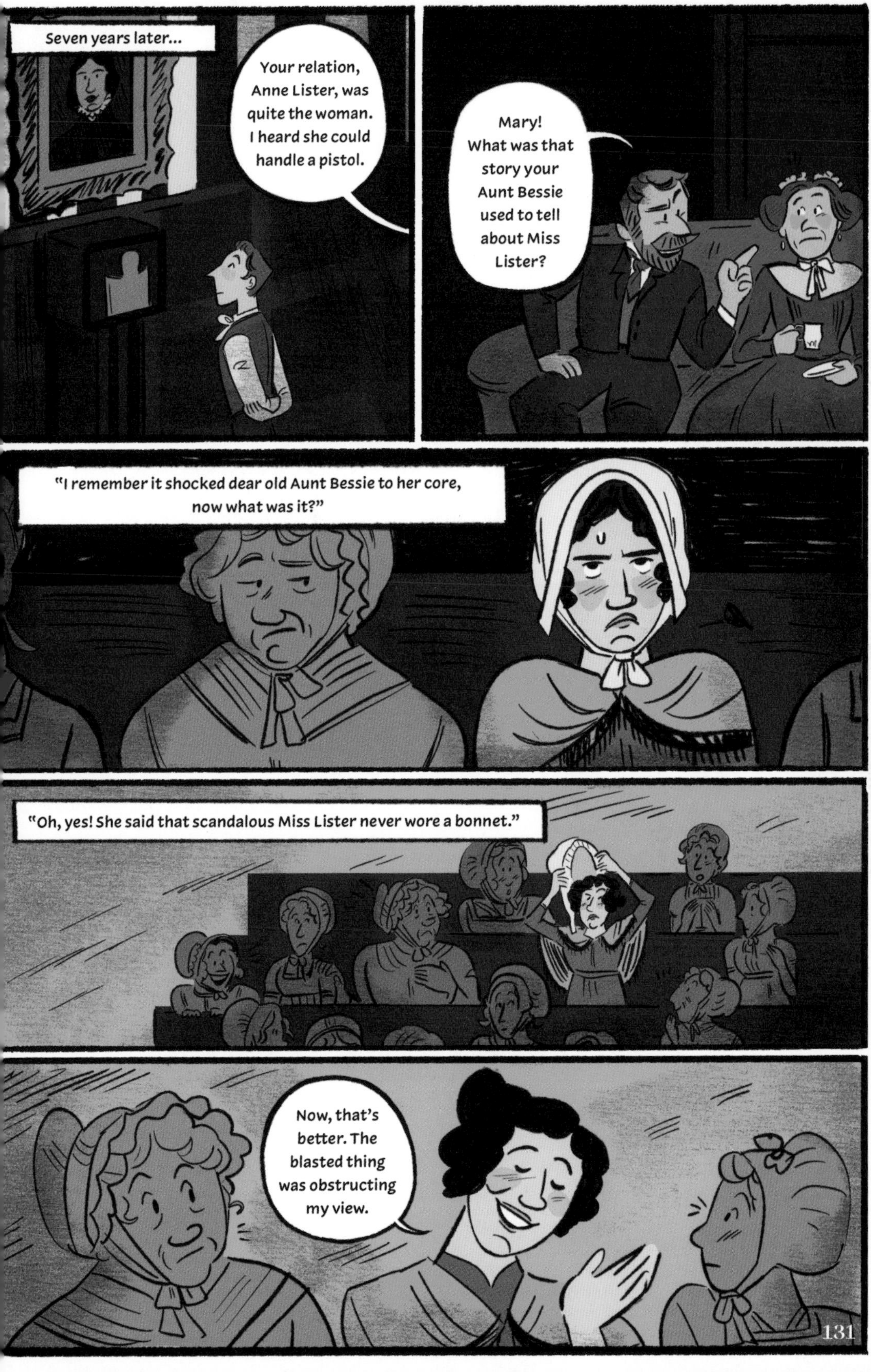
Seven years later...
Your relation, Anne Lister, was quite the woman. I heard she could handle a pistol.
Mary! What was that story your Aunt Bessie used to tell about Miss Lister?
"I remember it shocked dear old Aunt Bessie to her core, now what was it?"
"Oh, yes! She said that scandalous Miss Lister never wore a bonnet."
Now, that's better. The blasted thing was obstructing my view.

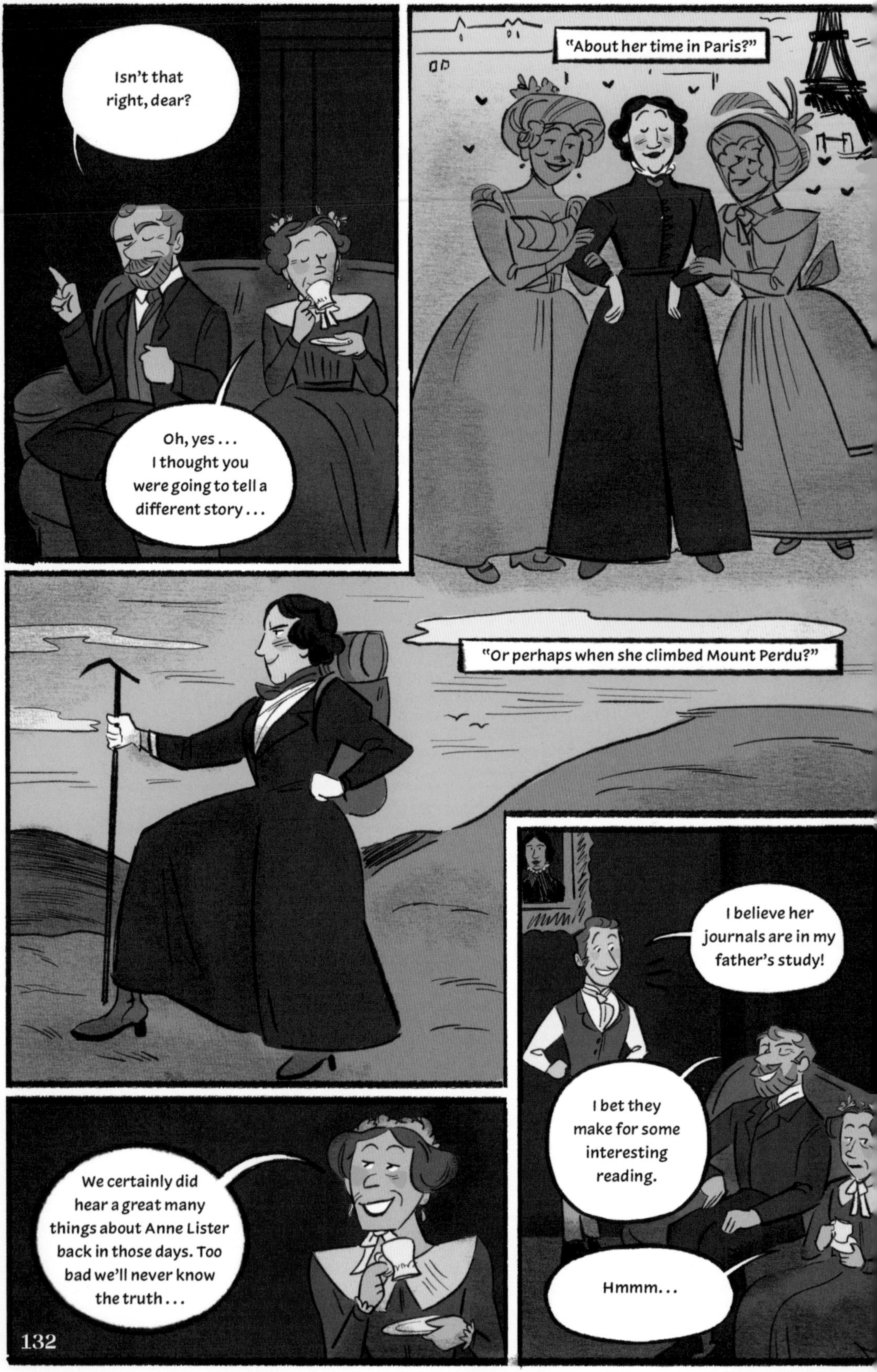
Isn't that right, dear?
Oh, yes . . . I thought you were going to tell a different story . . .
"About her time in Paris?"
"Or perhaps when she climbed Mount Perdu?"
I believe her journals are in my father's study!
I bet they make for some interesting reading.
Hmmm. . .
We certainly did hear a great many things about Anne Lister back in those days. Too bad we'll never know the truth . . .

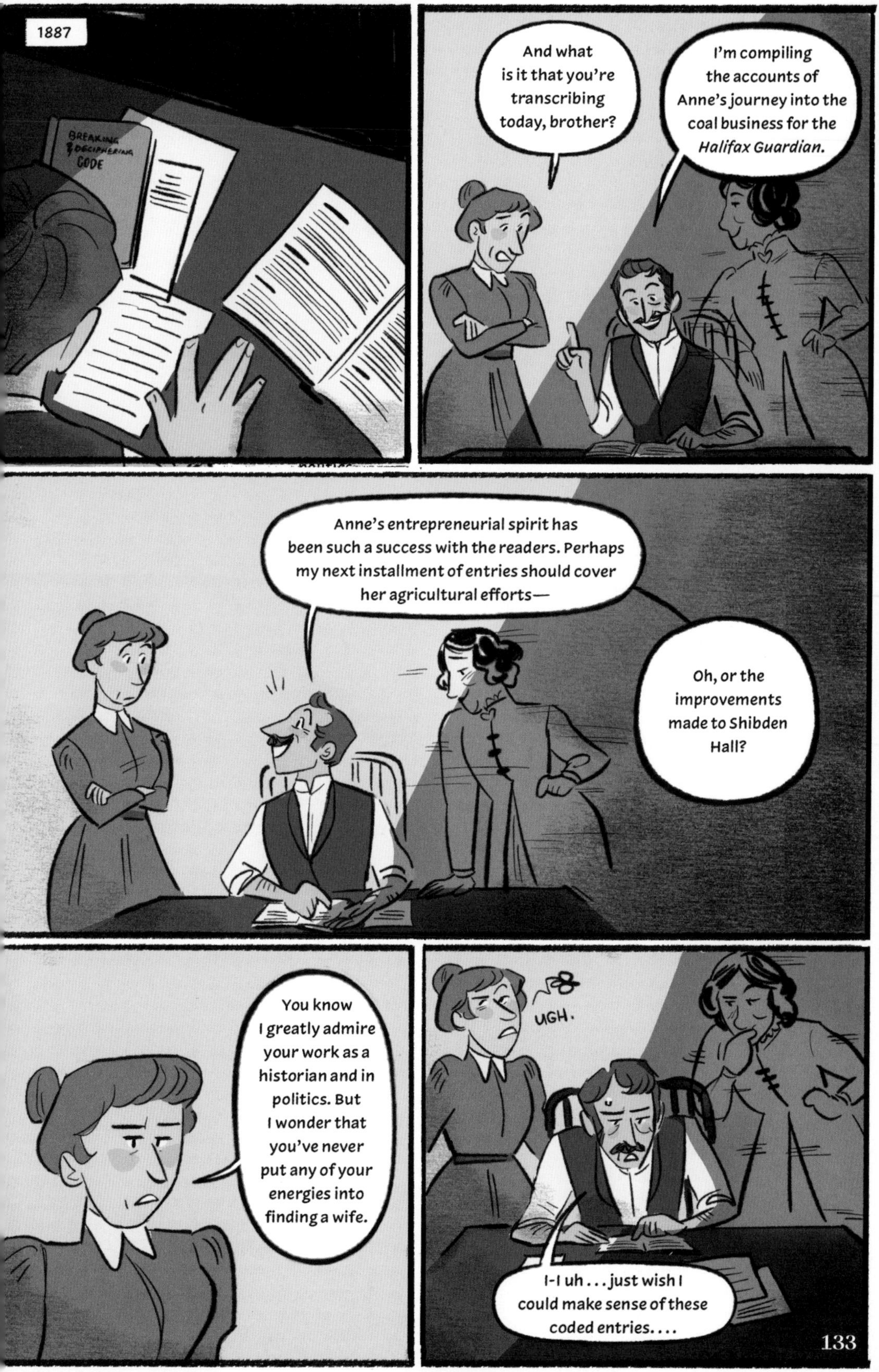
1887
BREAKING & DECIPHERING CODE
And what is it that you're transcribing today, brother?
I'm compiling the accounts of Anne's journey into the coal business for the *Halifax Guardian*.
Anne's entrepreneurial spirit has been such a success with the readers. Perhaps my next installment of entries should cover her agricultural efforts—
Oh, or the improvements made to Shibden Hall?
You know I greatly admire your work as a historian and in politics. But I wonder that you've never put any of your energies into finding a wife.
UGH.
I-I uh . . . just wish I could make sense of these coded entries. . . .

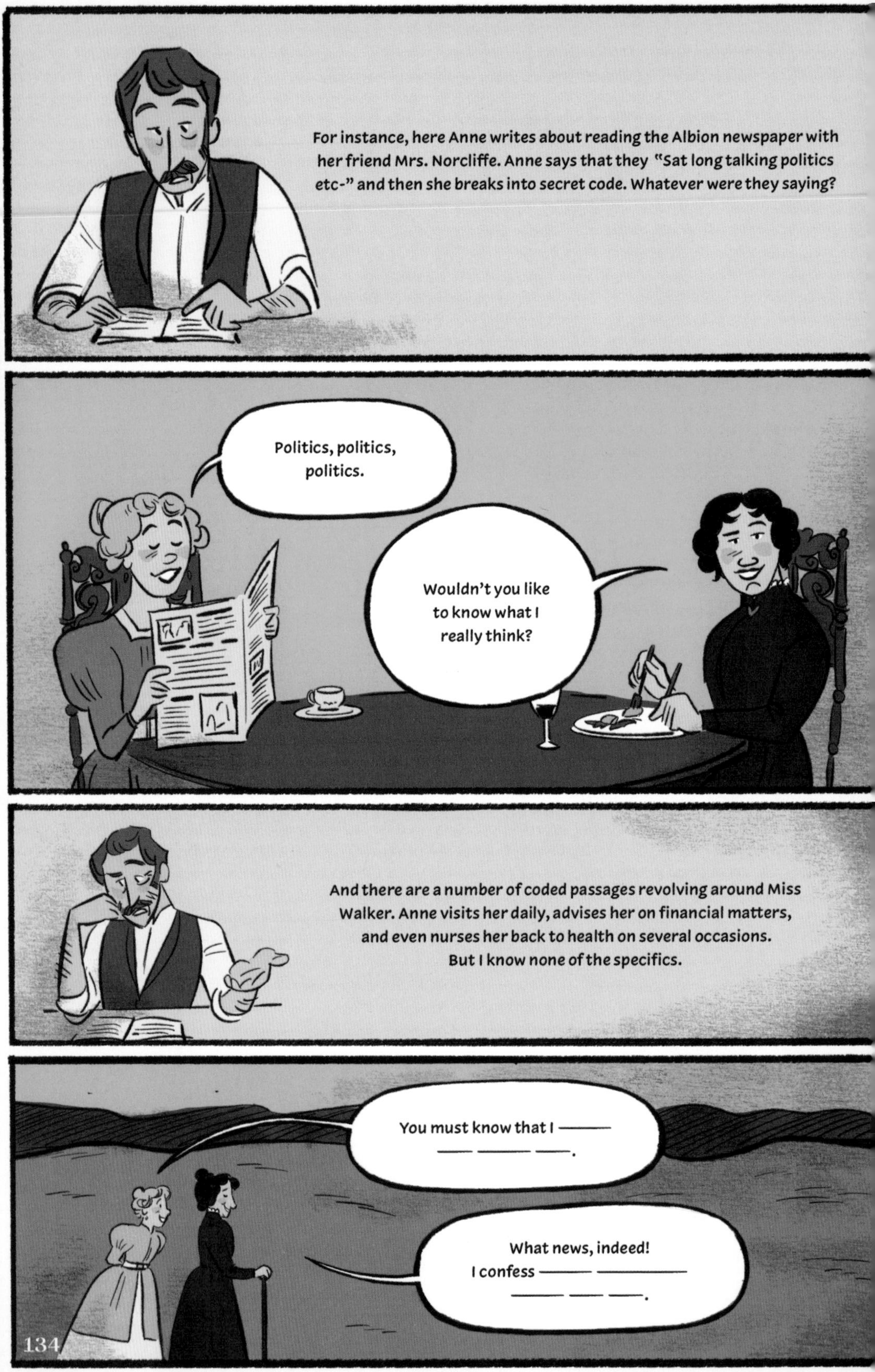

For instance, here Anne writes about reading the Albion newspaper with her friend Mrs. Norcliffe. Anne says that they "Sat long talking politics etc-" and then she breaks into secret code. Whatever were they saying?
Politics, politics, politics.
Wouldn't you like to know what I really think?
And there are a number of coded passages revolving around Miss Walker. Anne visits her daily, advises her on financial matters, and even nurses her back to health on several occasions. But I know none of the specifics.
You must know that I ——— —— ——— ——.
What news, indeed! I confess ——— ———— ——— —— ——.

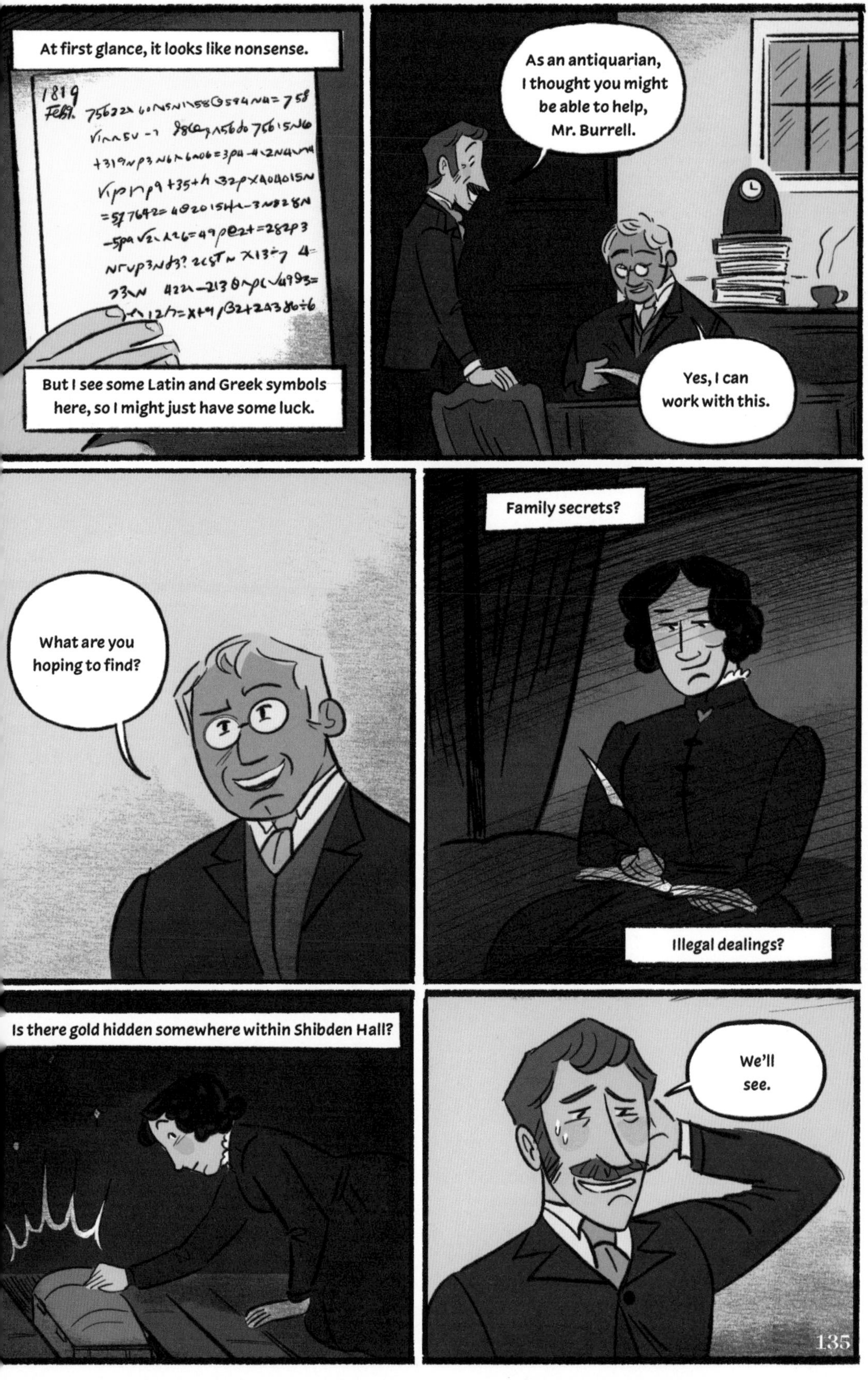
At first glance, it looks like nonsense.
But I see some Latin and Greek symbols here, so I might just have some luck.
As an antiquarian, I thought you might be able to help, Mr. Burrell.
Yes, I can work with this.
What are you hoping to find?
Family secrets?
Illegal dealings?
Is there gold hidden somewhere within Shibden Hall?
We'll see.

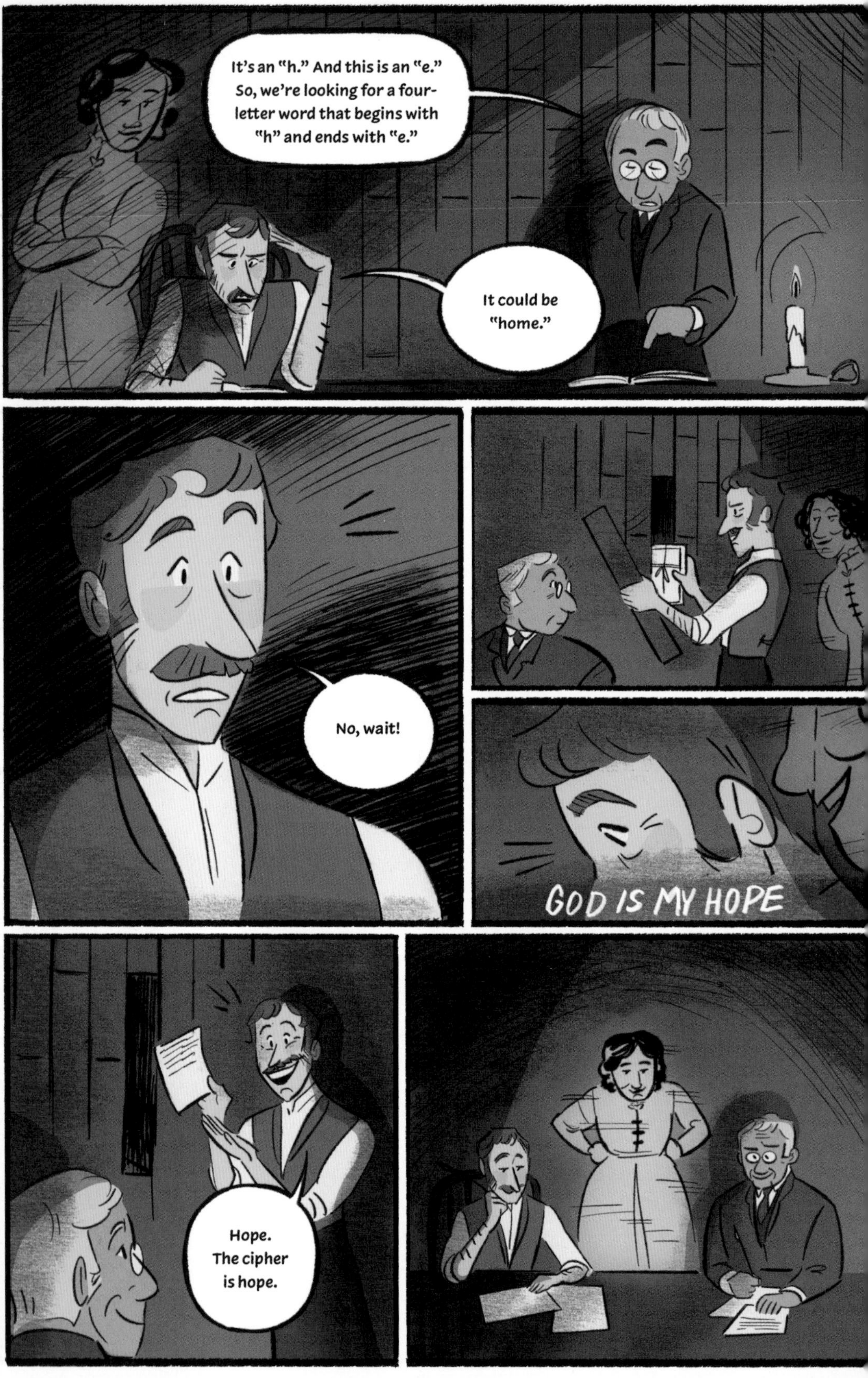
It's an "h." And this is an "e." So, we're looking for a four-letter word that begins with "h" and ends with "e."
It could be "home."
No, wait!
GOD IS MY HOPE
Hope. The cipher is hope.

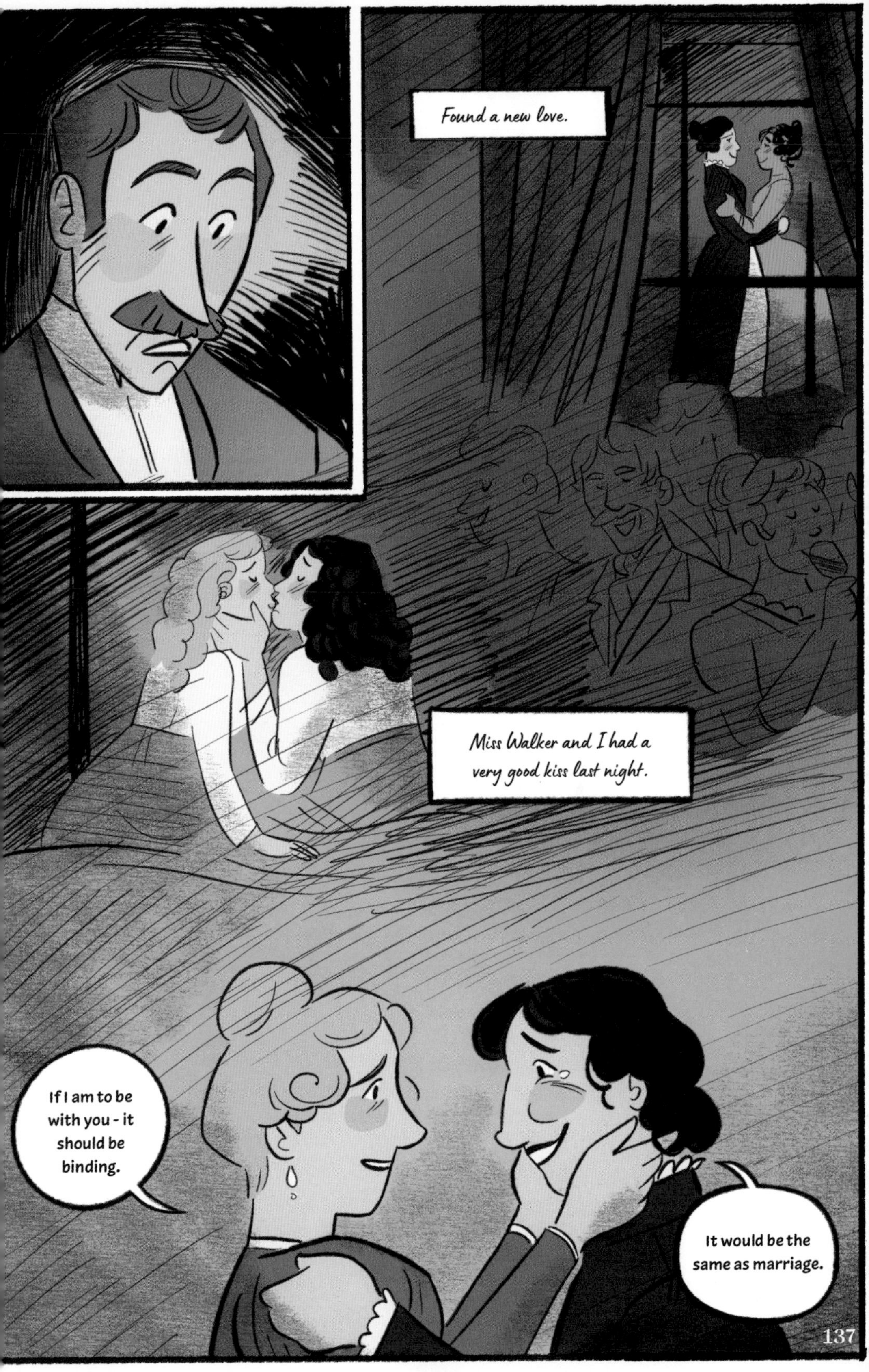
Found a new love.
Miss Walker and I had a very good kiss last night.
If I am to be with you - it should be binding.
It would be the same as marriage.

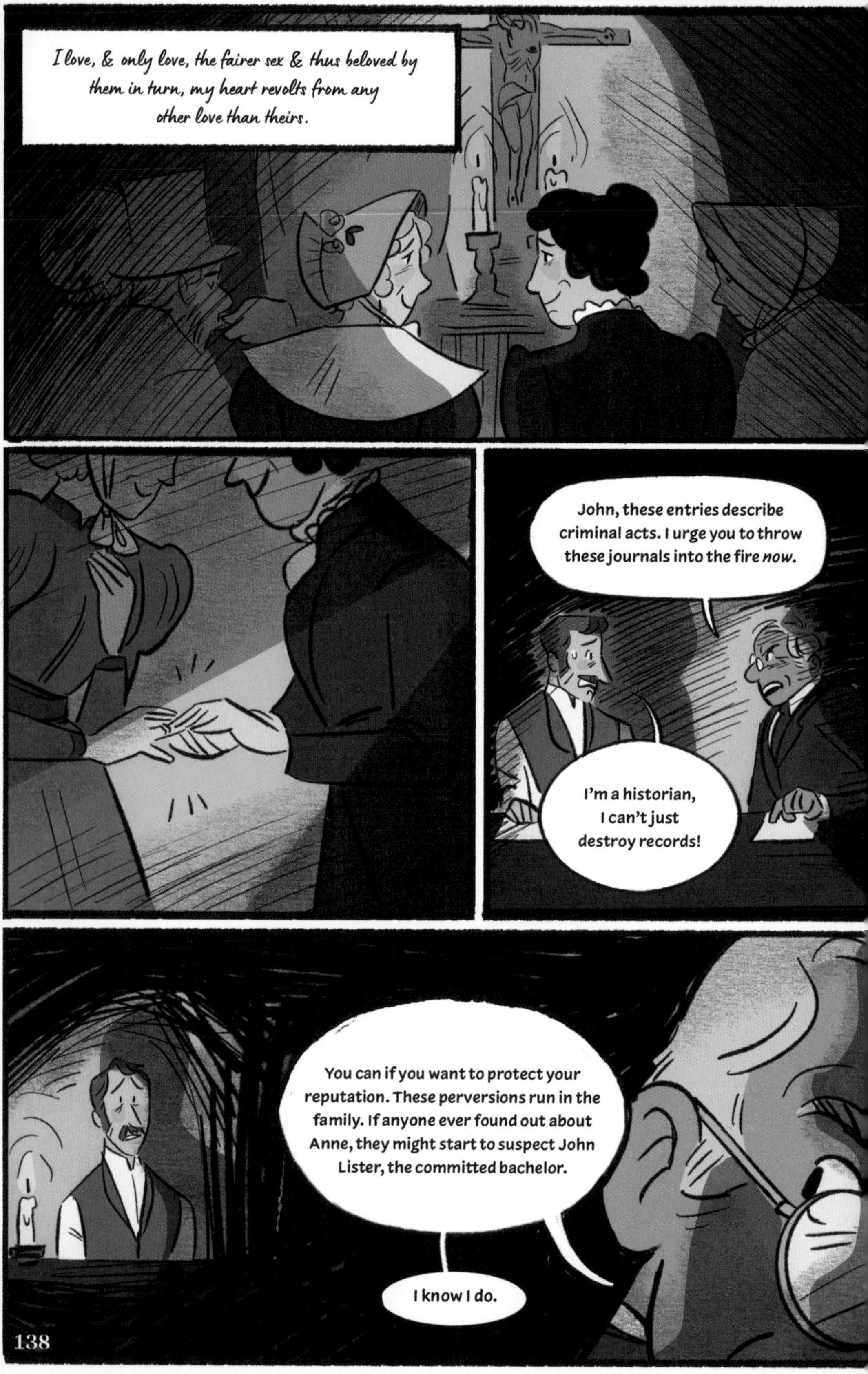
I love, & only love, the fairer sex & thus beloved by them in turn, my heart revolts from any other love than theirs.
John, these entries describe criminal acts. I urge you to throw these journals into the fire *now*.
I'm a historian, I can't just destroy records!
You can if you want to protect your reputation. These perversions run in the family. If anyone ever found out about Anne, they might start to suspect John Lister, the committed bachelor.
I know I do.

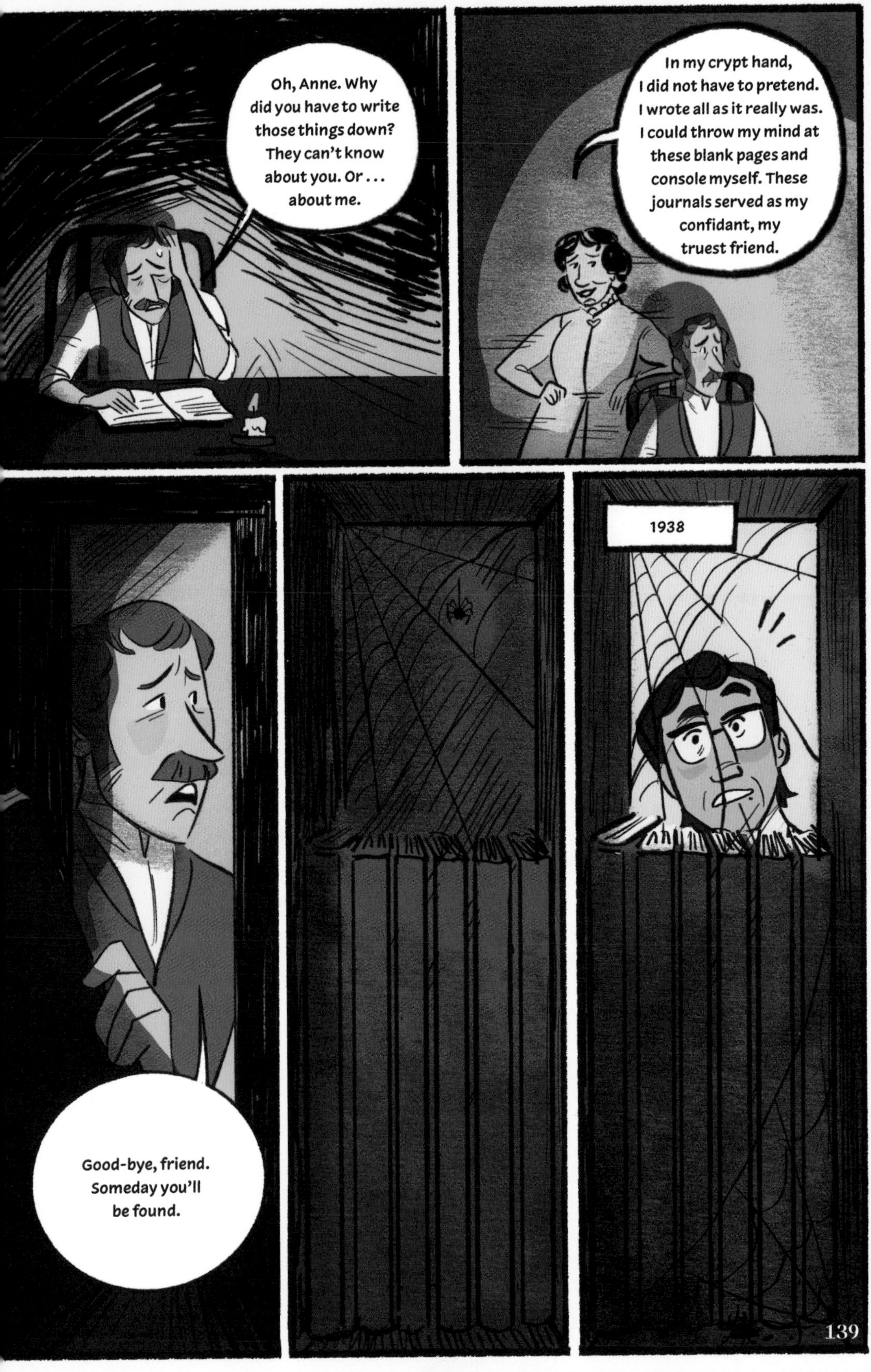

Oh, Anne. Why did you have to write those things down? They can't know about you. Or . . . about me.
In my crypt hand, I did not have to pretend. I wrote all as it really was. I could throw my mind at these blank pages and console myself. These journals served as my confidant, my truest friend.
Good-bye, friend. Someday you'll be found.
1938

Anne Lister wrote an astonishing nearly eight thousand pages and five million words in her diaries between 1806 and 1840. Nearly one-fifth of the entries are in her special code comprised of Greek letters, numbers, punctuation, and mathematical symbols. She called this code her "crypt hand."

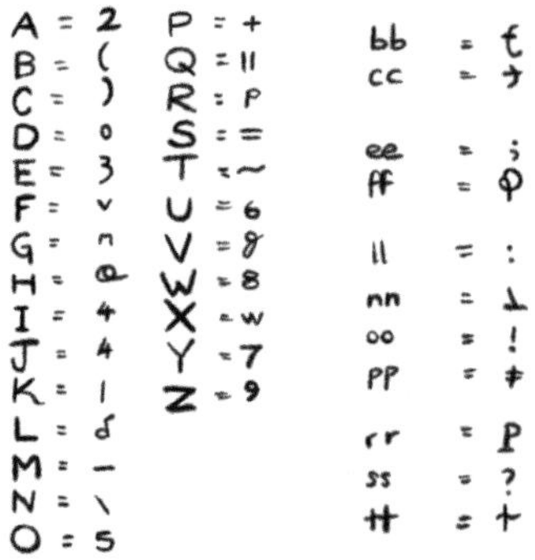

A = 2	P = +	bb = t
B = (	Q = 11	cc = ⅂
C =)	R = P	
D = o	S = =	ee = ;
E = 3	T = ~	ff = φ
F = v	U = 6	
G = n	V = 8	ll = :
H = @	W = 8	nn = ⅃
I = 4	X = w	oo = !
J = 4	Y = 7	pp = ‡
K = 1	Z = 9	
L = δ		rr = P
M = -		ss = ?
N = \		tt = †
O = 5		

In 1988, Halifax-born historian Helena Whitbread published *I Know My Own Heart: The Diaries of Anne Lister 1791–1840* after six years of deciphering Lister's coded entries. To some critics, the decoded diaries read like fiction, as they revealed Anne's most intimate thoughts and explicit accounts of her sex life. A few even (wrongly) declared the book an elaborate hoax.

Although Anne was not published during her lifetime, she may have wanted to become a travel writer. In addition to her personal diaries, Anne Lister wrote fourteen travel journals detailing her trips to France, Denmark, Belgium, Germany, Norway, Holland, and Russia. Just before her death, she made an unusual number of edits to these journals, which suggests that she was pre-paring them for publication.

In 1838, Emily Brontë was employed as a teacher at Law Hill School in Halifax, just a stone's throw away from Shibden Hall. The Patchett sisters, owners and operators of Law Hill, were well acquainted with Miss Lister. Thus, it is possible that the two writers may have crossed paths.

It is also possible that Shibden Hall itself may have served as a model for Thrushcross Grange in Brontë's novel *Wuthering Heights*. In fact, the 1992 film adaptation of the novel used Shibden Hall as a filming location.

Although in recent years, Anne Lister has been the subject of many television movies, documentaries, and the series *Gentleman Jack*, the very first dramatization of the life of Anne Lister dates back to 1872. After a stay at Shibden Hall, the novelist Rosa Mackenzie Kettle published *The Mistress of Langdale Hall: A Romance of West Riding*. Her headstrong protagonist, Maud Langdale, was crafted in Anne Lister's image.

Emily Brontë

1818–1848

"I'll walk where my own nature would be leading:
It vexes me to choose another guide."

— "Often Rebuked," 1850

Emily Brontë, also known as Ellis Bell, is the most elusive of the Brontë sisters. A poet by nature, she penned two hundred poems and one divisive novel—*Wuthering Heights*, the violent tale of love, revenge, and family drama on the moors, is as reviled as it is beloved. "Read *Jane Eyre*," advised *Patterson's Magazine* in 1848, "but burn *Wuthering Heights*."

In 1916, Virginia Woolf theorized that "*Wuthering Heights* is a more difficult book to understand than *Jane Eyre* because Emily was a greater poet." One might add that Emily herself is much more difficult to understand than her sisters because less is known about her. There are no diaries, but just a handful of letters, school essays, and notes. As a result, Emily's life is relayed to us by the people who knew her, claim to have known her, or heard about her secondhand. Following her death, her sister Charlotte served as her chief biographer.

The preface of the 1850 edition of *Wuthering Heights* contains a brief biographical sketch of Emily's life and times written by Charlotte, after Emily's death two years prior. It revealed Ellis Bell's true identity for the first time and paints a frustrating and somewhat contradictory picture of the author as a troubled, but simple, genius. This image served as the seed for Emily Brontë biographers in the decades since, and however controversial, Charlotte's preface does reveal several important details about Emily's life.

It is known for a fact that Emily Brontë was born in 1818 and died thirty years later of tuberculosis. She was briefly educated at Cowan Bridge and Roe Head before attending boarding school in Brussels, and she had a very short career working as a teacher at Law Hill School in Halifax.

More importantly, it is known that Emily wrote. As a child, she joined forces with her sister Anne to write an epic saga about a fictional world called Gondal. Ruled by a ruthless queen called A.G.A. or, Augusta Geraldine Almeda, Gondal was an island nation with a distinct Yorkshire landscape. Emily worked on the adventures of A.G.A. from the time she was twelve until she died. In 1845, Charlotte stumbled across one of Emily's Gondal notebooks and was struck by the genius of her poetry. Inspired by her sister's work, she then formed a plan to publish.

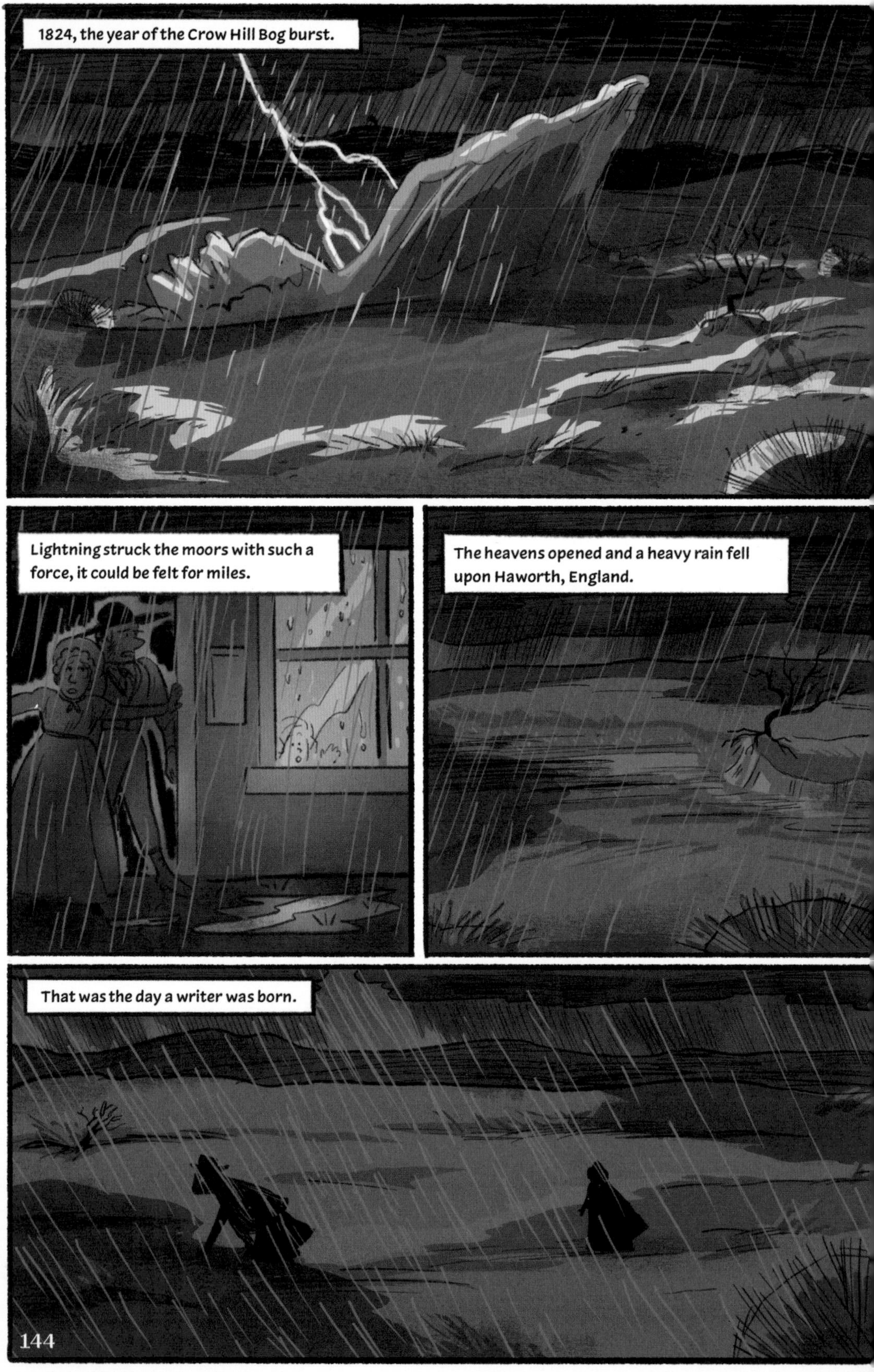
1824, the year of the Crow Hill Bog burst.
Lightning struck the moors with such a force, it could be felt for miles.
The heavens opened and a heavy rain fell upon Haworth, England.
That was the day a writer was born.

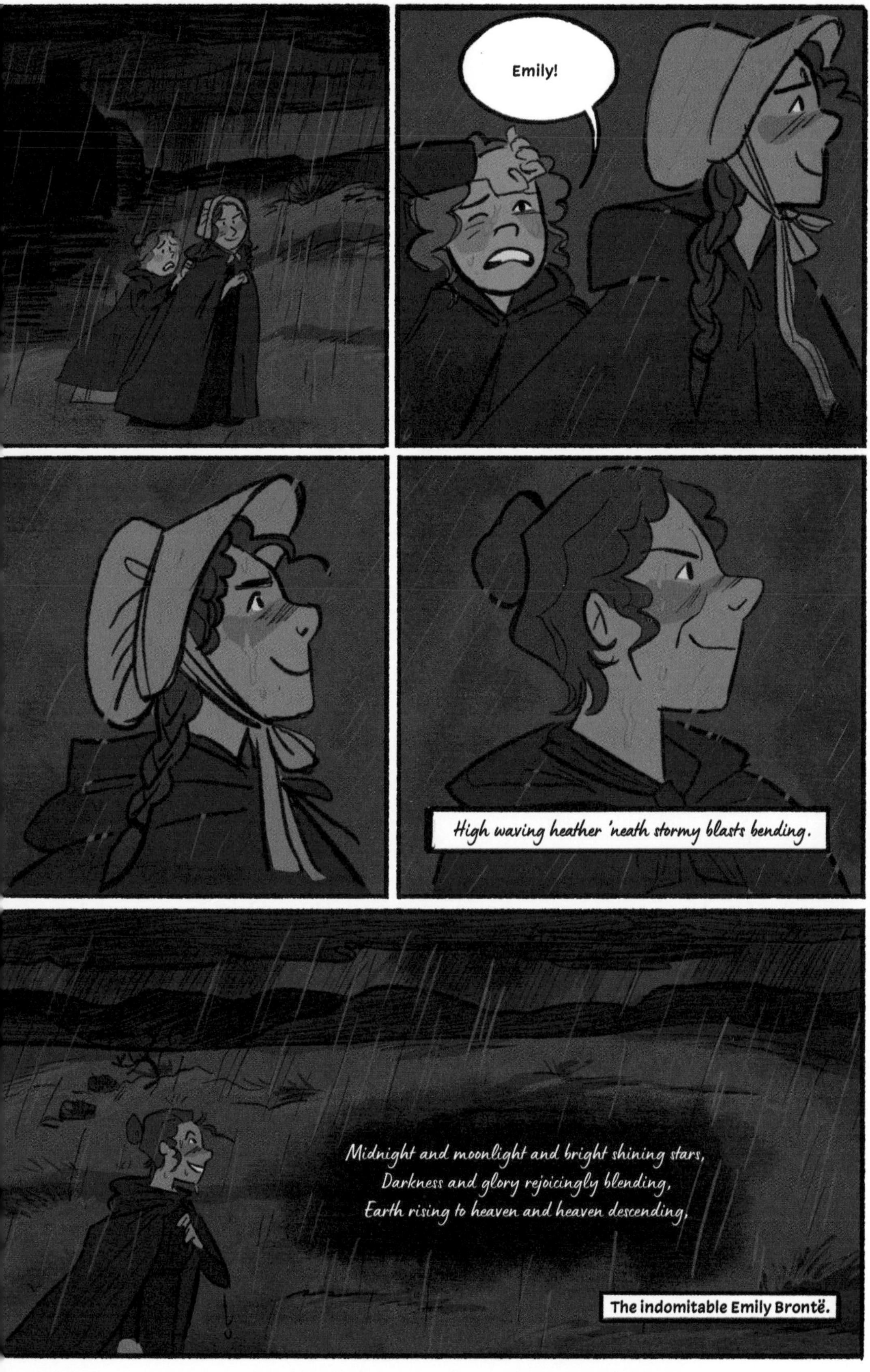
Emily!
High waving heather 'neath stormy blasts bending.
Midnight and moonlight and bright shining stars,
Darkness and glory rejoicingly blending,
Earth rising to heaven and heaven descending,
The indomitable Emily Brontë.

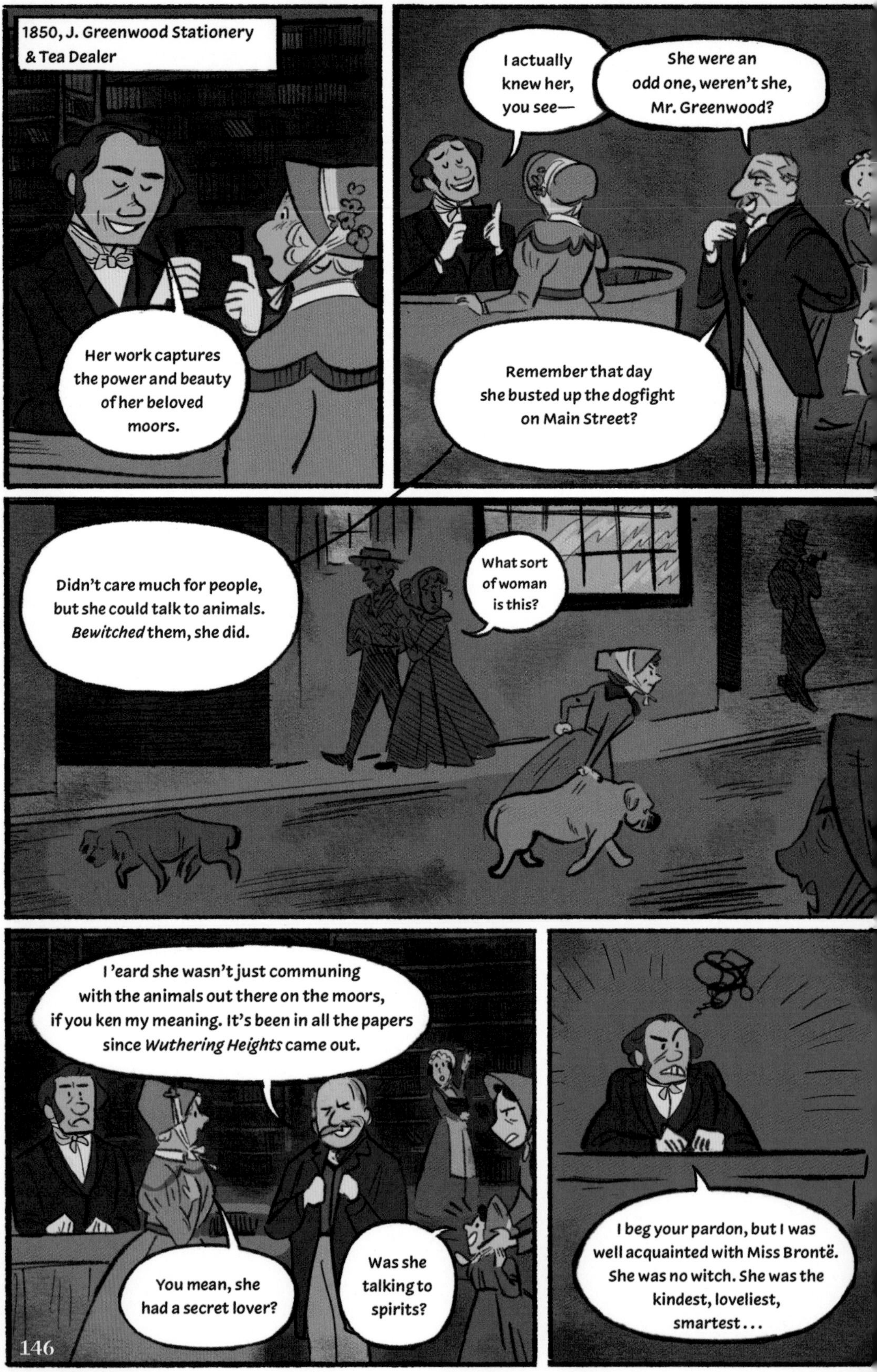
1850, J. Greenwood Stationery & Tea Dealer
Her work captures the power and beauty of her beloved moors.
I actually knew her, you see—
She were an odd one, weren't she, Mr. Greenwood?
Remember that day she busted up the dogfight on Main Street?
Didn't care much for people, but she could talk to animals. *Bewitched* them, she did.
What sort of woman is this?
I 'eard she wasn't just communing with the animals out there on the moors, if you ken my meaning. It's been in all the papers since *Wuthering Heights* came out.
You mean, she had a secret lover?
Was she talking to spirits?
I beg your pardon, but I was well acquainted with Miss Brontë. She was no witch. She was the kindest, loveliest, smartest...

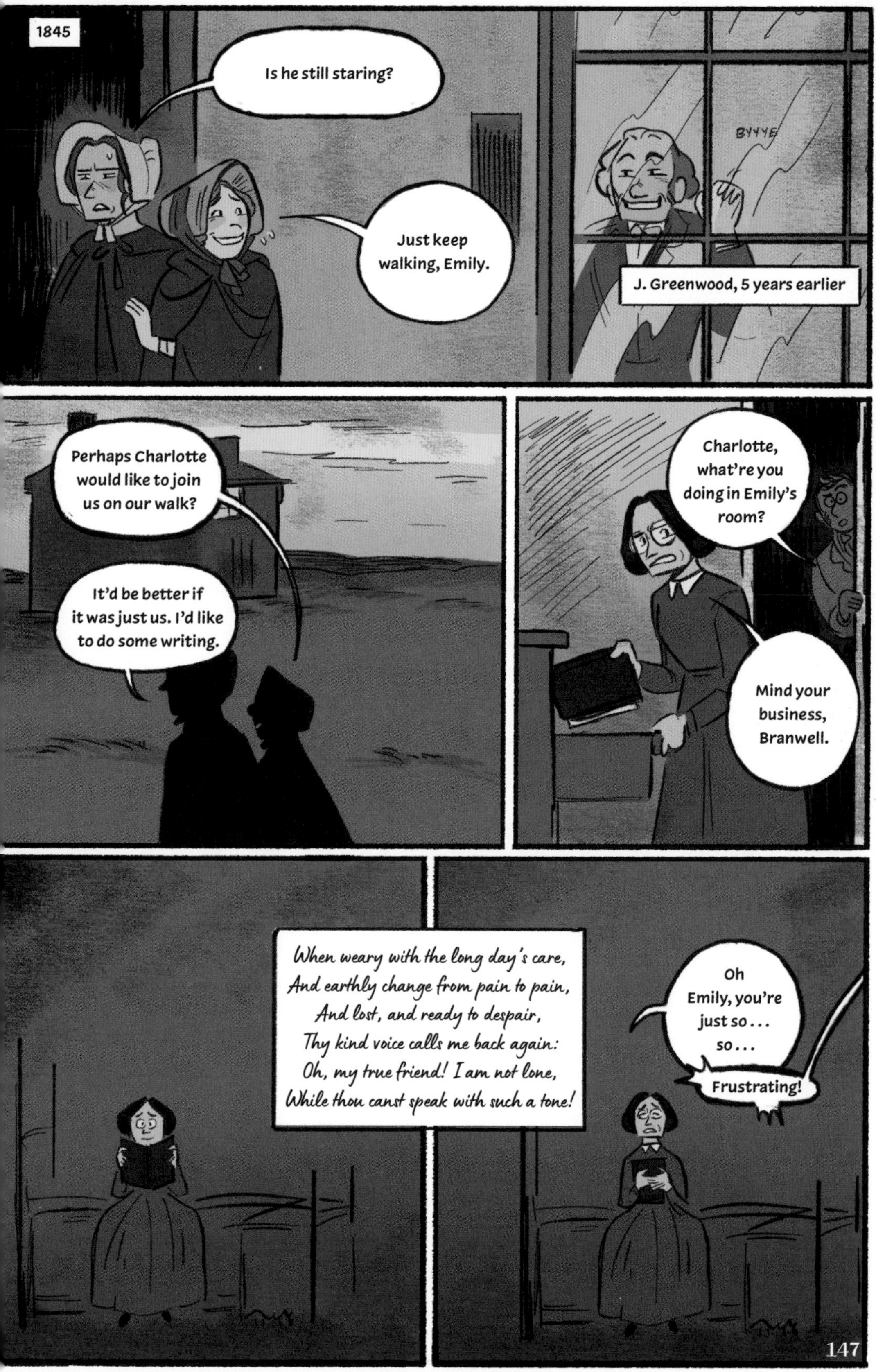
1845
Is he still staring?
Just keep walking, Emily.
BYYYE
J. Greenwood, 5 years earlier
Perhaps Charlotte would like to join us on our walk?
It'd be better if it was just us. I'd like to do some writing.
Charlotte, what're you doing in Emily's room?
Mind your business, Branwell.
When weary with the long day's care,
And earthly change from pain to pain,
And lost, and ready to despair,
Thy kind voice calls me back again:
Oh, my true friend! I am not lone,
While thou canst speak with such a tone!
Oh Emily, you're just so . . . so . . .
Frustrating!

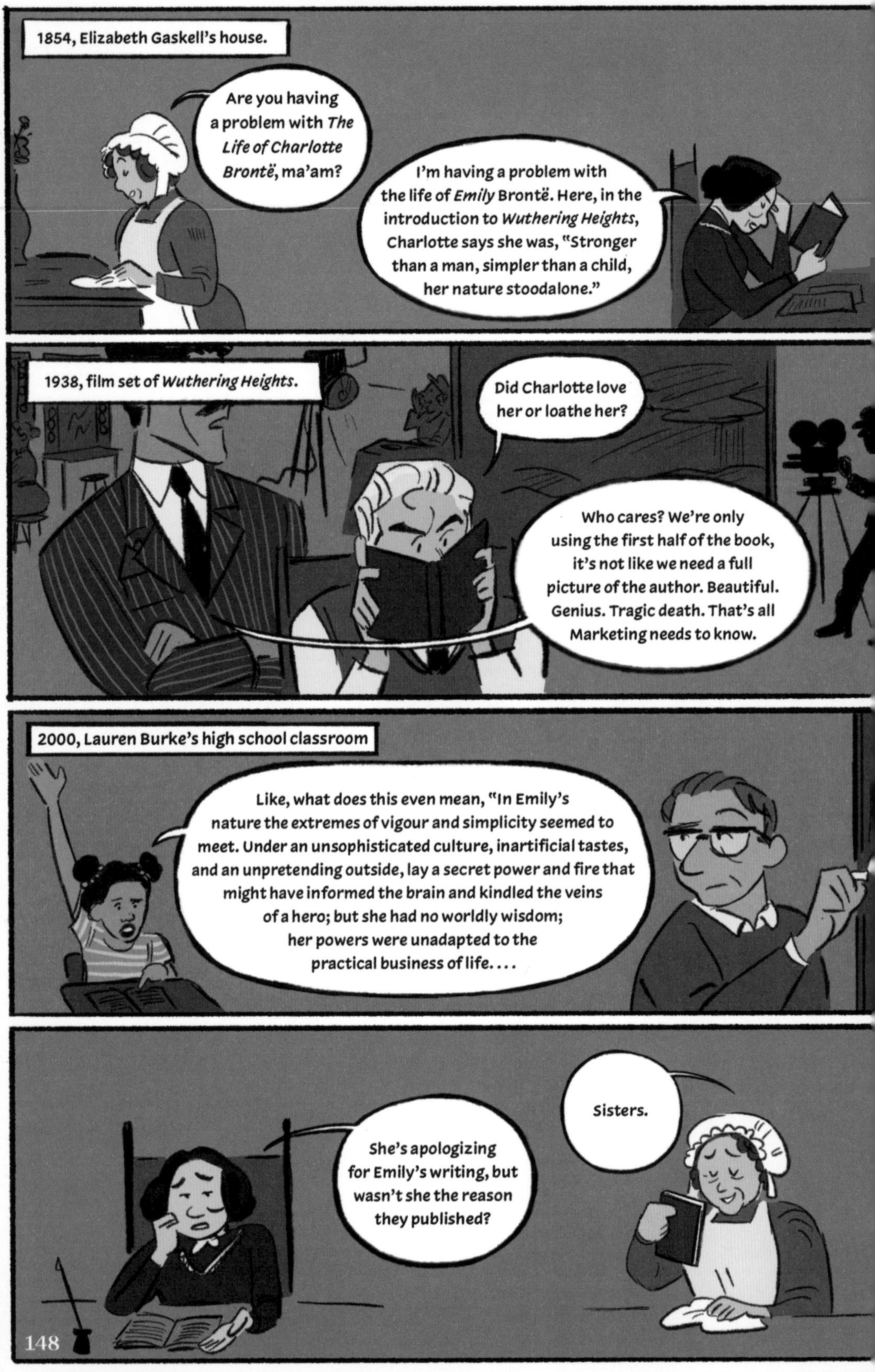
1854, Elizabeth Gaskell's house.
Are you having a problem with *The Life of Charlotte Brontë*, ma'am?
I'm having a problem with the life of *Emily* Brontë. Here, in the introduction to *Wuthering Heights*, Charlotte says she was, "Stronger than a man, simpler than a child, her nature stoodalone."
1938, film set of *Wuthering Heights*.
Did Charlotte love her or loathe her?
Who cares? We're only using the first half of the book, it's not like we need a full picture of the author. Beautiful. Genius. Tragic death. That's all Marketing needs to know.
2000, Lauren Burke's high school classroom
Like, what does this even mean, "In Emily's nature the extremes of vigour and simplicity seemed to meet. Under an unsophisticated culture, inartificial tastes, and an unpretending outside, lay a secret power and fire that might have informed the brain and kindled the veins of a hero; but she had no worldly wisdom; her powers were unadapted to the practical business of life. . . .
She's apologizing for Emily's writing, but wasn't she the reason they published?
Sisters.

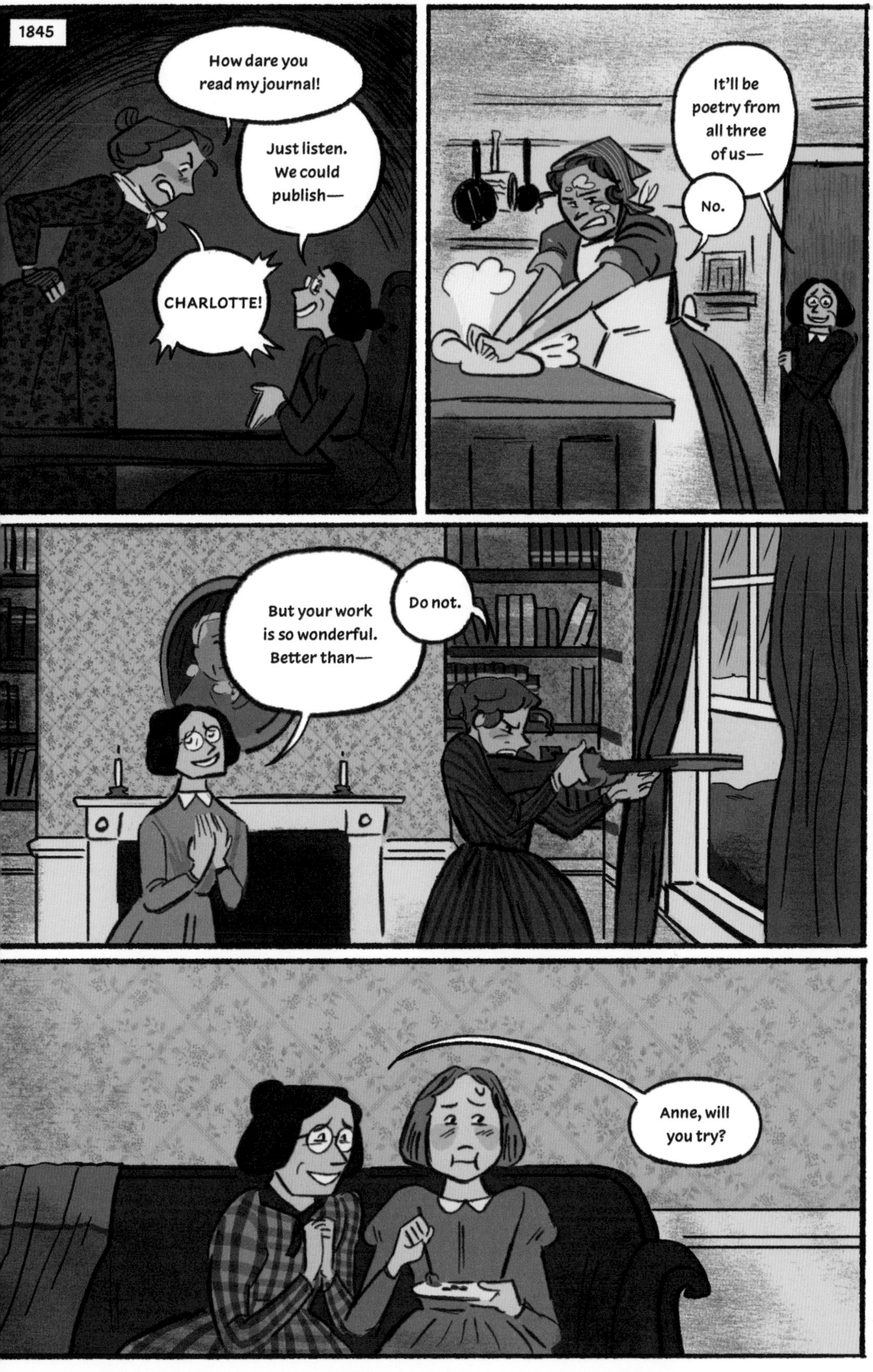
1845
How dare you read my journal!
Just listen. We could publish—
CHARLOTTE!
It'll be poetry from all three of us—
No.
But your work is so wonderful. Better than—
Do not.
Anne, will you try?

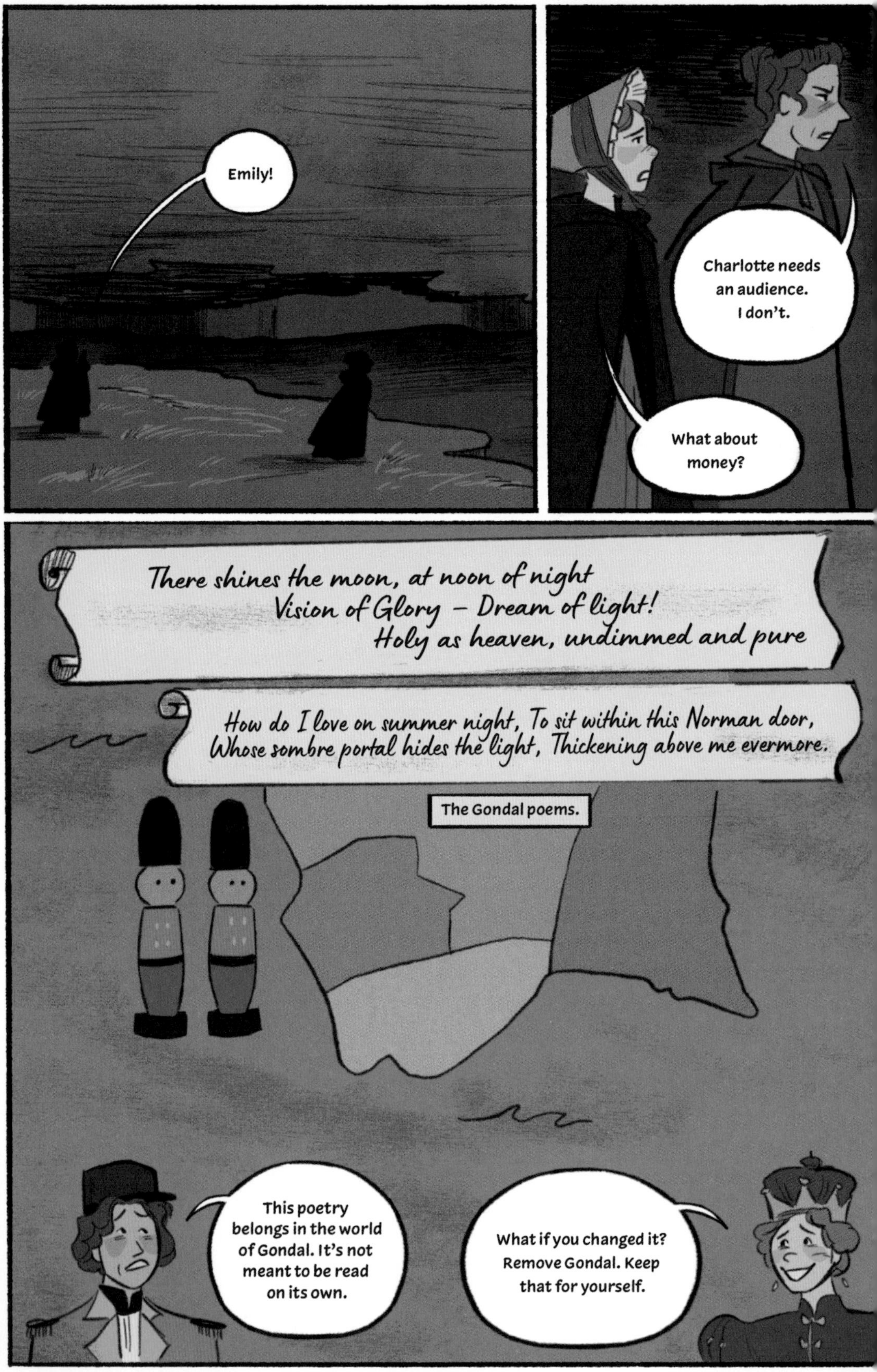
Emily!
Charlotte needs an audience. I don't.
What about money?
There shines the moon, at noon of night
Vision of Glory – Dream of light!
Holy as heaven, undimmed and pure
How do I love on summer night, To sit within this Norman door,
Whose sombre portal hides the light, Thickening above me evermore.
The Gondal poems.
This poetry belongs in the world of Gondal. It's not meant to be read on its own.
What if you changed it? Remove Gondal. Keep that for yourself.

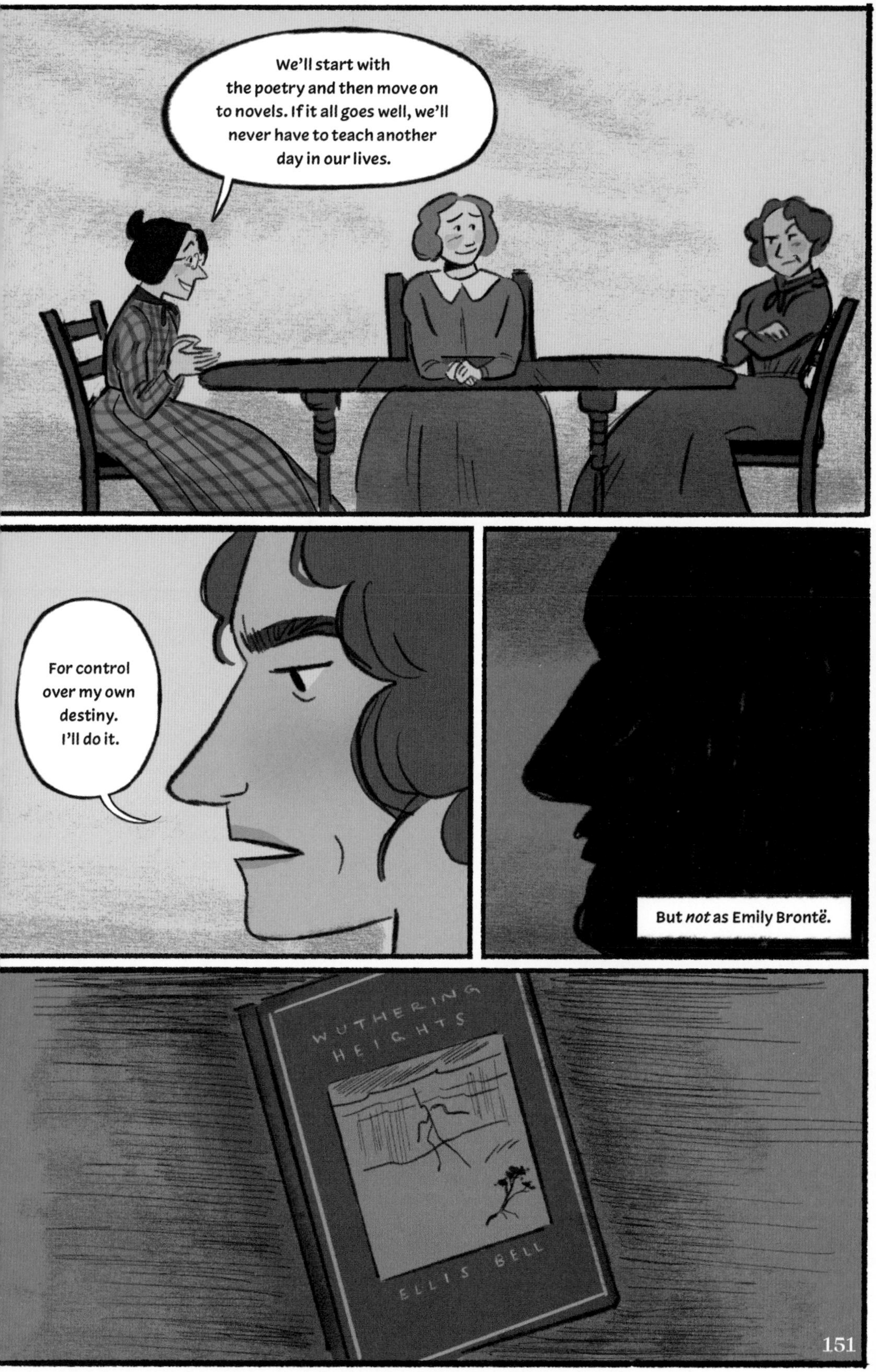
We'll start with the poetry and then move on to novels. If it all goes well, we'll never have to teach another day in our lives.
For control over my own destiny. I'll do it.
But *not* as Emily Brontë.
WUTHERING HEIGHTS
ELLIS BELL

In addition to writing, Emily was a talented artist, musician, and baker. She could often be found in the family kitchen, reading and writing while she baked her famous bread.

In 1955, a Texas librarian named Fannie Ratchford sequenced together eighty-four of Emily's poems to re-create a Gondal narrative. To date, *Gondal's Queen: A Novel in Verse* is the most comprehensive attempt at reconstructing Anne and Emily's fantasy world.

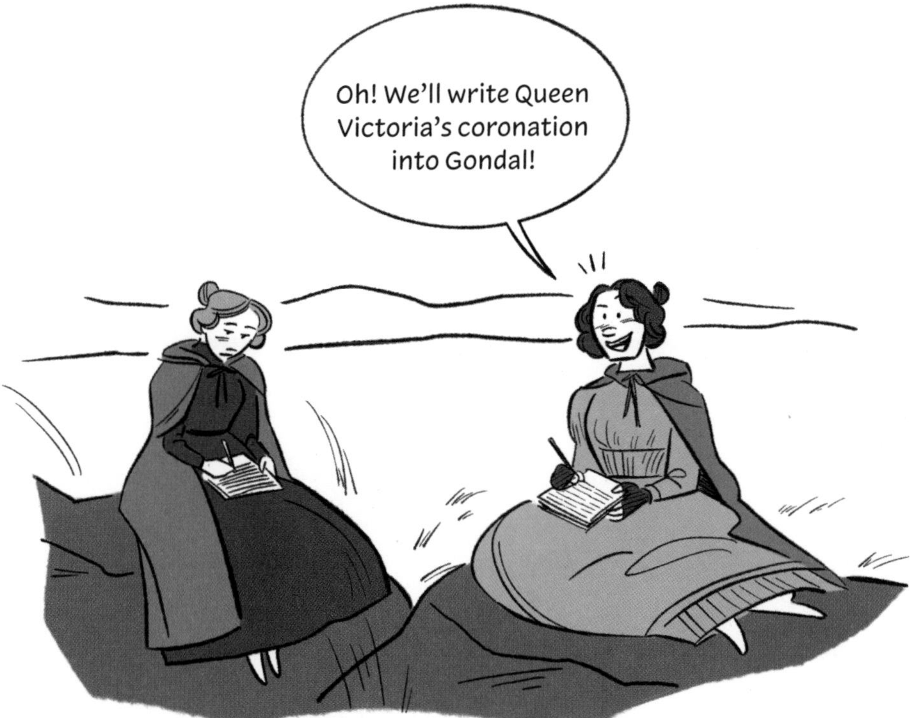
Oh! We'll write Queen Victoria's coronation into Gondal!

SELECTED WORKS

POETRY

1846: *Poems by Currer, Ellis, and Acton Bell*

NOVELS

1847: *Wuthering Heights*

Elizabeth Barrett Browning

1806–1861

"O Art, my Art, thou'rt much, but Love is more!"

—*Aurora Leigh*, 1856

One of the most celebrated poets of the Victorian era, Elizabeth Barrett Browning was a bona fide literary celebrity. It was *Aurora Leigh* (1856) that catapulted her to lasting fame, but the hybrid poem-novel was not without controversy; its challenging content and style split the opinions of Victorian critics down the middle. Heavily influenced by Browning's idol Mary Wollstonecraft, *Aurora Leigh* tackles issues including women's education, industrialization, and the "fallen woman," and was labeled "coarse" and "unfeminine" by detractors. To George Eliot it was "the greatest poem by a woman of genius."

Born in 1806, Elizabeth was the eldest of twelve children. Her parents were the wealthy plantation owner Edward Barrett Moulton Barrett and his wife, Mary Graham Clarke. The family lived on a lavish country estate in County Durham, England called Hope End, where Elizabeth was privately educated and began writing poetry at the age of four. An ardent supporter of her work, Elizabeth's father privately published an epic poem Elizabeth had written as a child entitled *The Battle of Marathon*. He referred to his daughter as the Poet Laureate of Hope End.

At fifteen, Elizabeth developed a mysterious and debilitating illness following a fall from a horse, which prompted doctors to prescribe morphine for her pain. Eventually, her condition worsened due to a weakness in her lungs, and she was confined to her bedroom on Wimpole Street in London. Isolated from the outside world for many years, Elizabeth devoted her life to her work. She produced and published a prolific number of essays and poems that established her reputation as writer who wasn't afraid to tackle the political and social issues of her day. Notably, her 1842 poem "The Cry of The Children," which condemned child labor, inspired child labor law reforms in Parliament.

That same year, a lesser known writer named Robert Browning published a book of poetry entitled *Dramatic Lyrics*. It was very poorly reviewed, but Elizabeth thought the book had some merit, and publicly defended it. In turn, she received a letter of thanks from Browning with a shocking declaration of love. Elizabeth was flattered, but unsure how to handle the attention. She was thirty-six at the time and confined to her bedroom. To further complicate matters, for reasons unknown, her father had strictly forbidden his children from ever marrying. Elizabeth did not want to risk losing her family but, still, she responded.

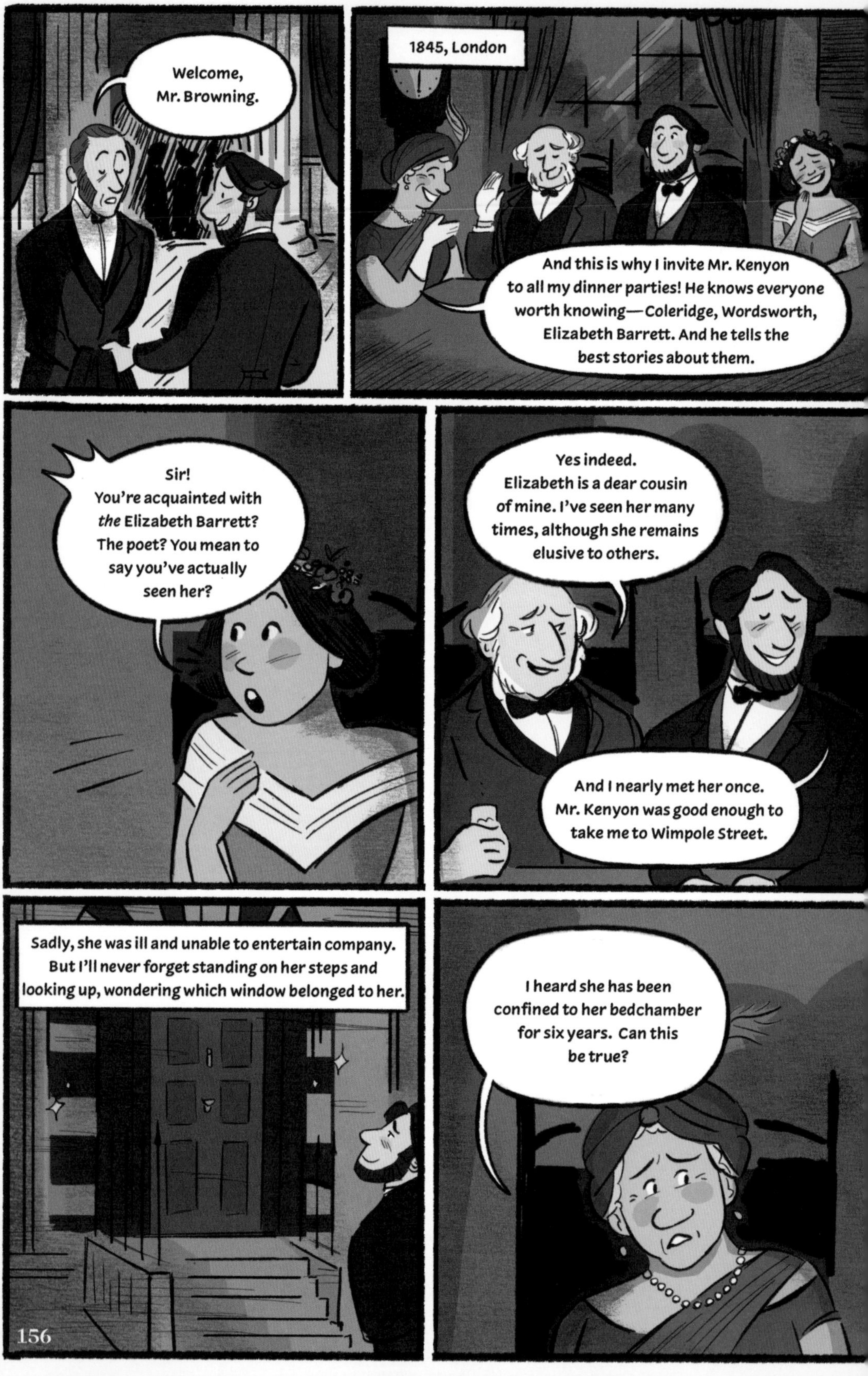
Welcome, Mr. Browning.
1845, London
And this is why I invite Mr. Kenyon to all my dinner parties! He knows everyone worth knowing—Coleridge, Wordsworth, Elizabeth Barrett. And he tells the best stories about them.
Sir! You're acquainted with *the* Elizabeth Barrett? The poet? You mean to say you've actually seen her?
Yes indeed. Elizabeth is a dear cousin of mine. I've seen her many times, although she remains elusive to others.
And I nearly met her once. Mr. Kenyon was good enough to take me to Wimpole Street.
Sadly, she was ill and unable to entertain company. But I'll never forget standing on her steps and looking up, wondering which window belonged to her.
I heard she has been confined to her bedchamber for six years. Can this be true?

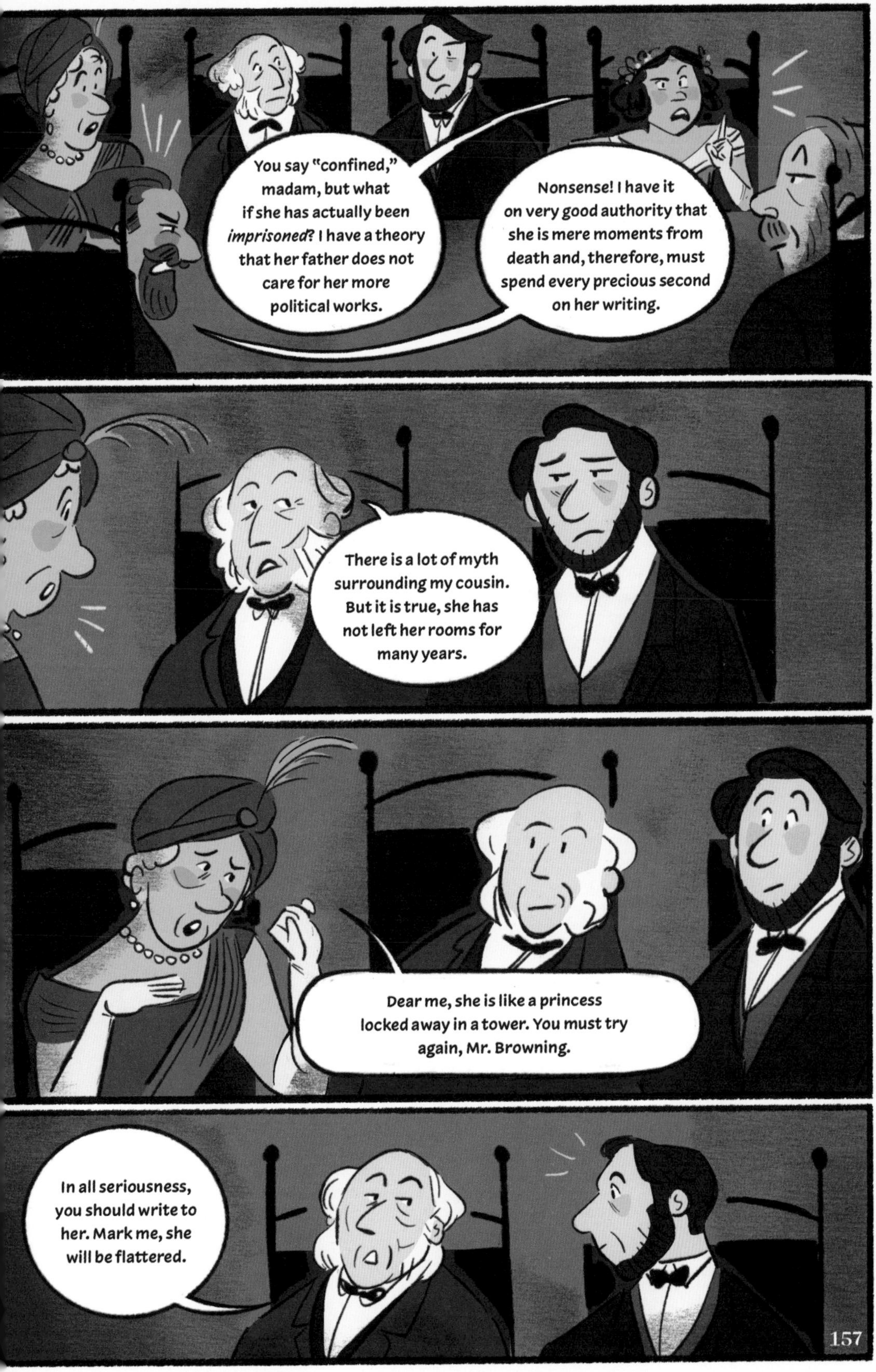

You say "confined," madam, but what if she has actually been *imprisoned*? I have a theory that her father does not care for her more political works.
Nonsense! I have it on very good authority that she is mere moments from death and, therefore, must spend every precious second on her writing.
There is a lot of myth surrounding my cousin. But it is true, she has not left her rooms for many years.
Dear me, she is like a princess locked away in a tower. You must try again, Mr. Browning.
In all seriousness, you should write to her. Mark me, she will be flattered.

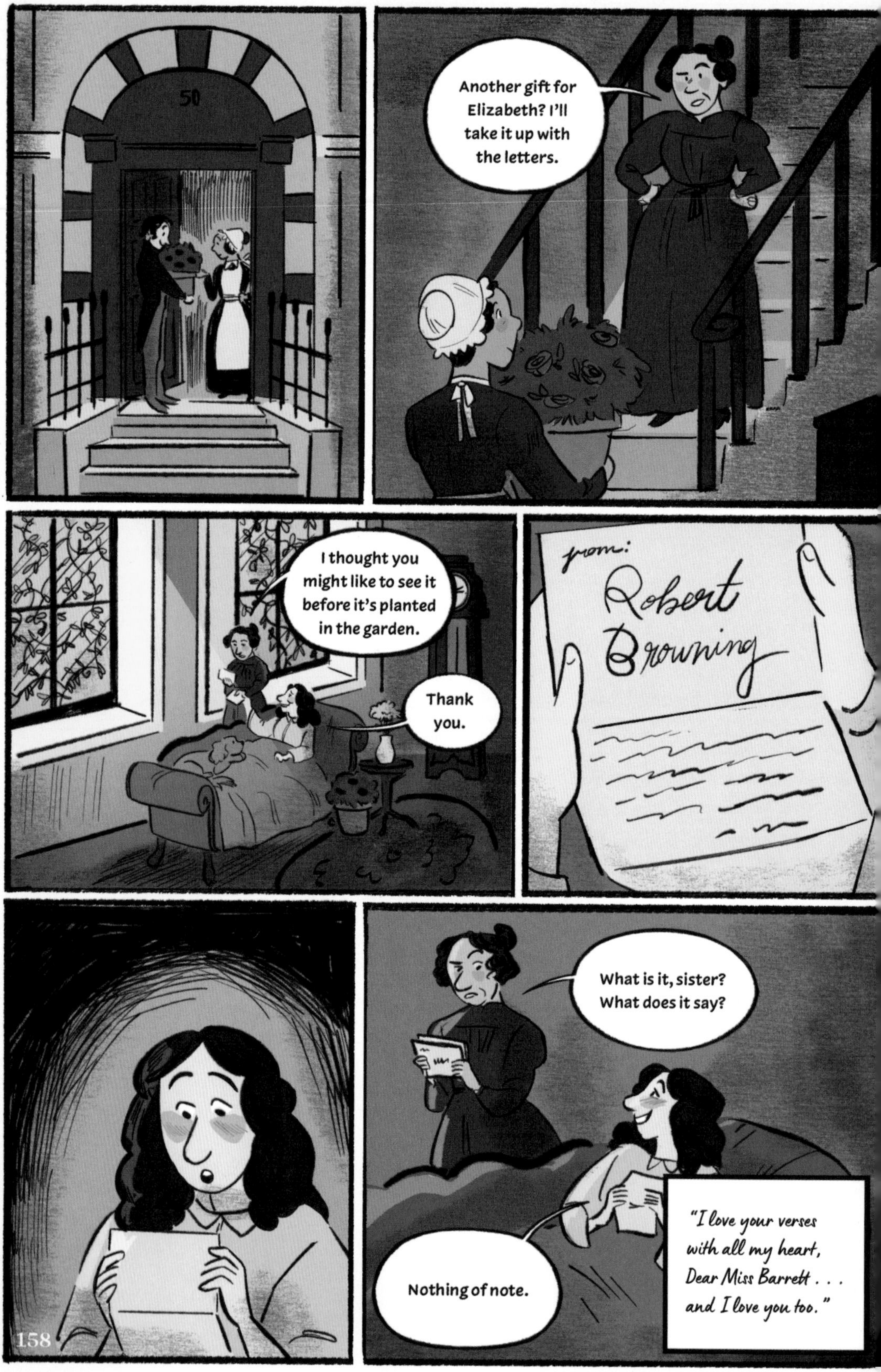
50
Another gift for Elizabeth? I'll take it up with the letters.
I thought you might like to see it before it's planted in the garden.
Thank you.
from:
Robert Browning
What is it, sister? What does it say?
Nothing of note.
"I love your verses with all my heart, Dear Miss Barrett . . . and I love you too."

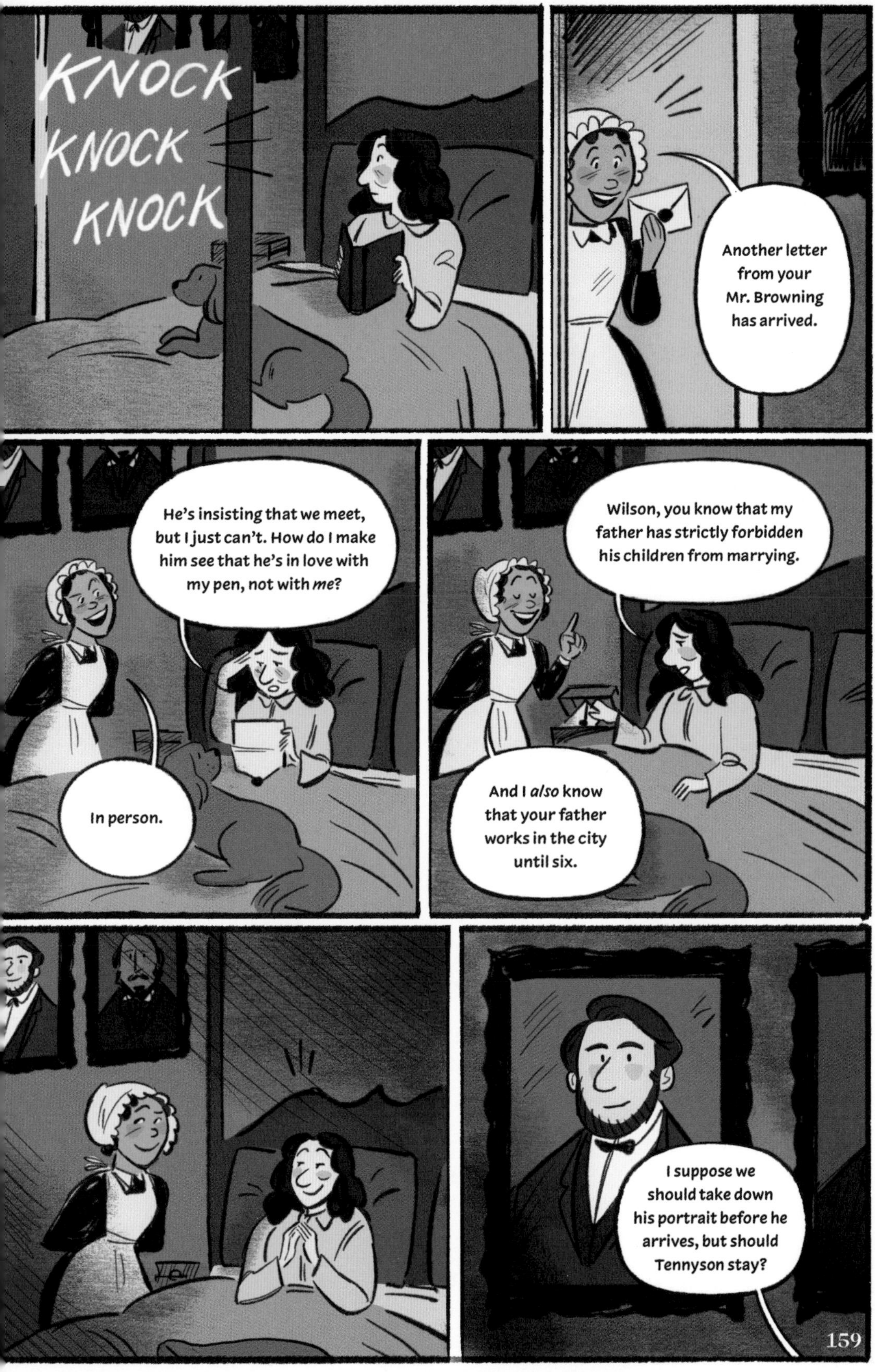
KNOCK
KNOCK
KNOCK
Another letter from your Mr. Browning has arrived.
He's insisting that we meet, but I just can't. How do I make him see that he's in love with my pen, not with *me*?
In person.
Wilson, you know that my father has strictly forbidden his children from marrying.
And I *also* know that your father works in the city until six.
I suppose we should take down his portrait before he arrives, but should Tennyson stay?

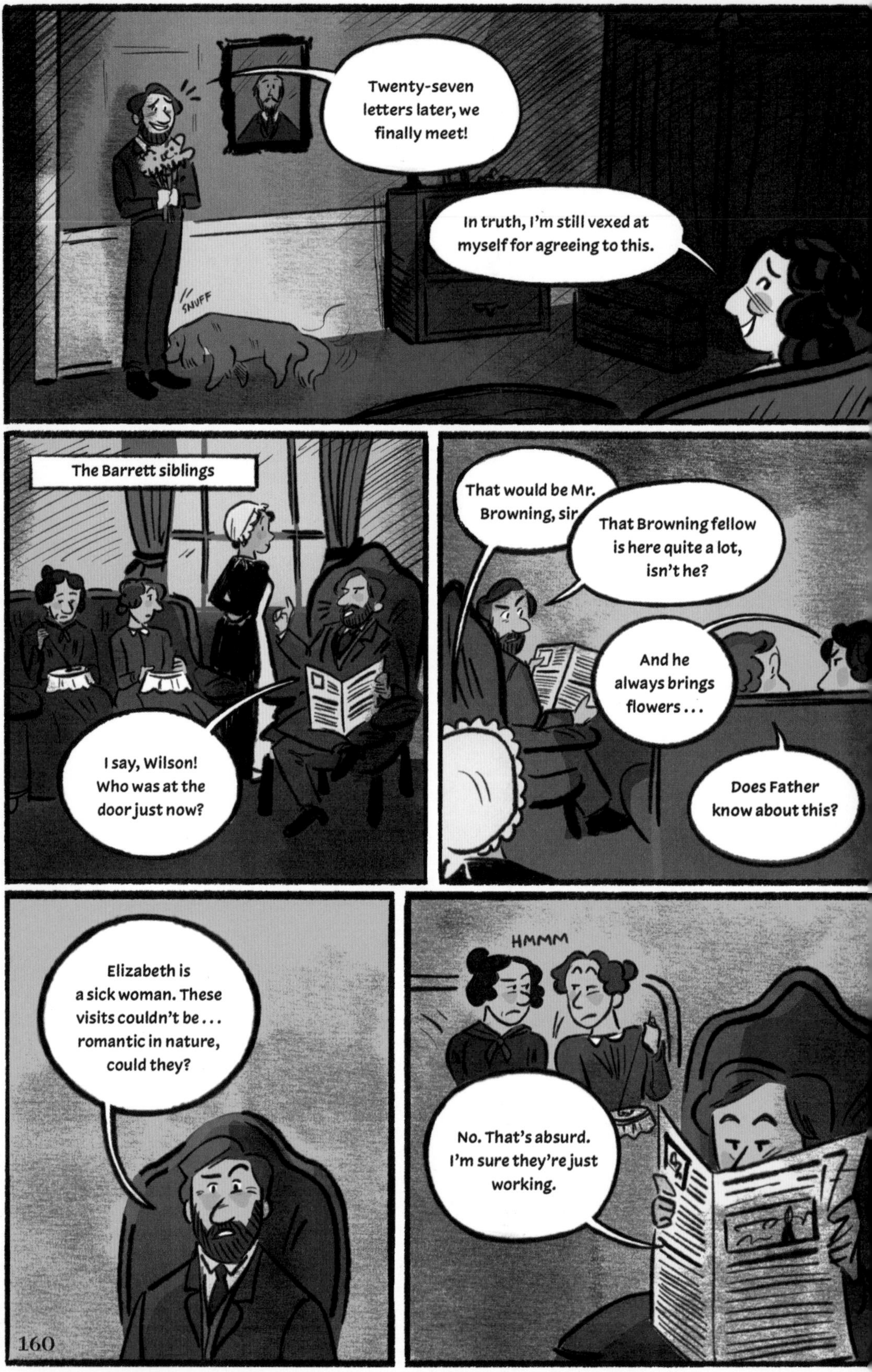
Twenty-seven letters later, we finally meet!
SNUFF
In truth, I'm still vexed at myself for agreeing to this.
The Barrett siblings
I say, Wilson! Who was at the door just now?
That would be Mr. Browning, sir.
That Browning fellow is here quite a lot, isn't he?
And he always brings flowers . . .
Does Father know about this?
Elizabeth is a sick woman. These visits couldn't be . . . romantic in nature, could they?
HMMM
No. That's absurd. I'm sure they're just working.

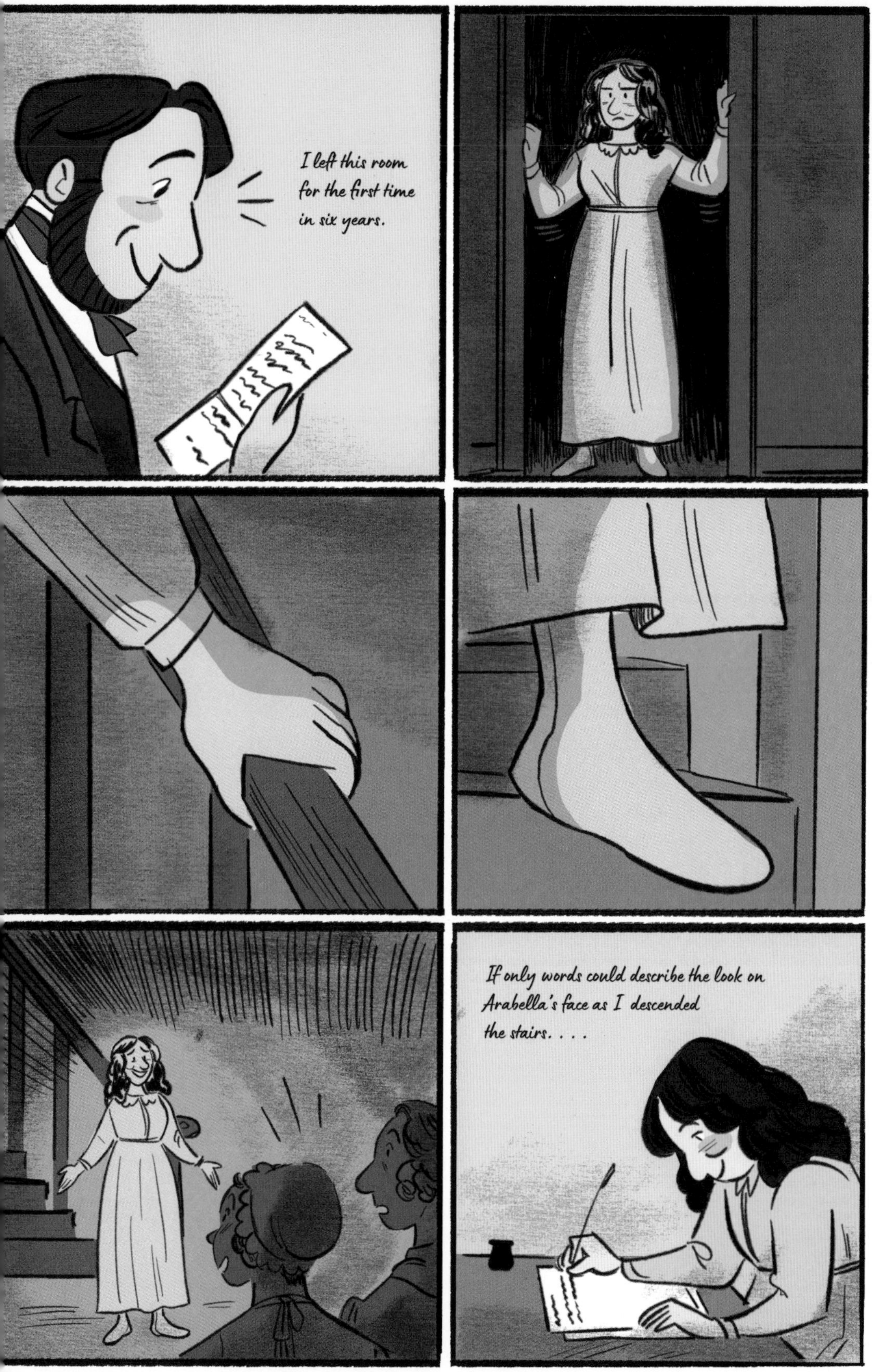
I left this room for the first time in six years.
If only words could describe the look on Arabella's face as I descended the stairs. . . .

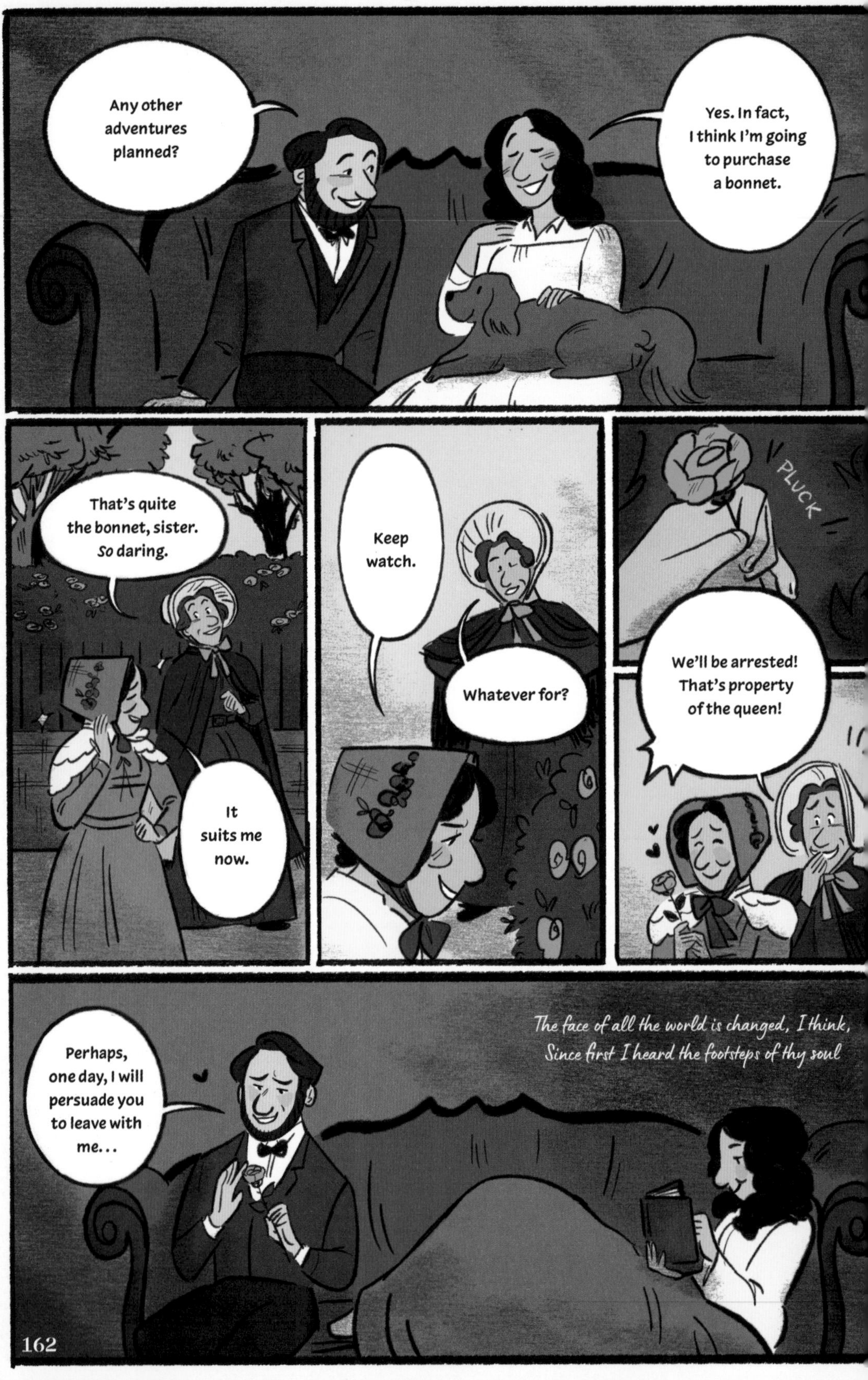
Any other adventures planned?
Yes. In fact, I think I'm going to purchase a bonnet.
That's quite the bonnet, sister. *So* daring.
It suits me now.
Keep watch.
Whatever for?
PLUCK
We'll be arrested! That's property of the queen!
The face of all the world is changed, I think,
Since first I heard the footsteps of thy soul
Perhaps, one day, I will persuade you to leave with me...

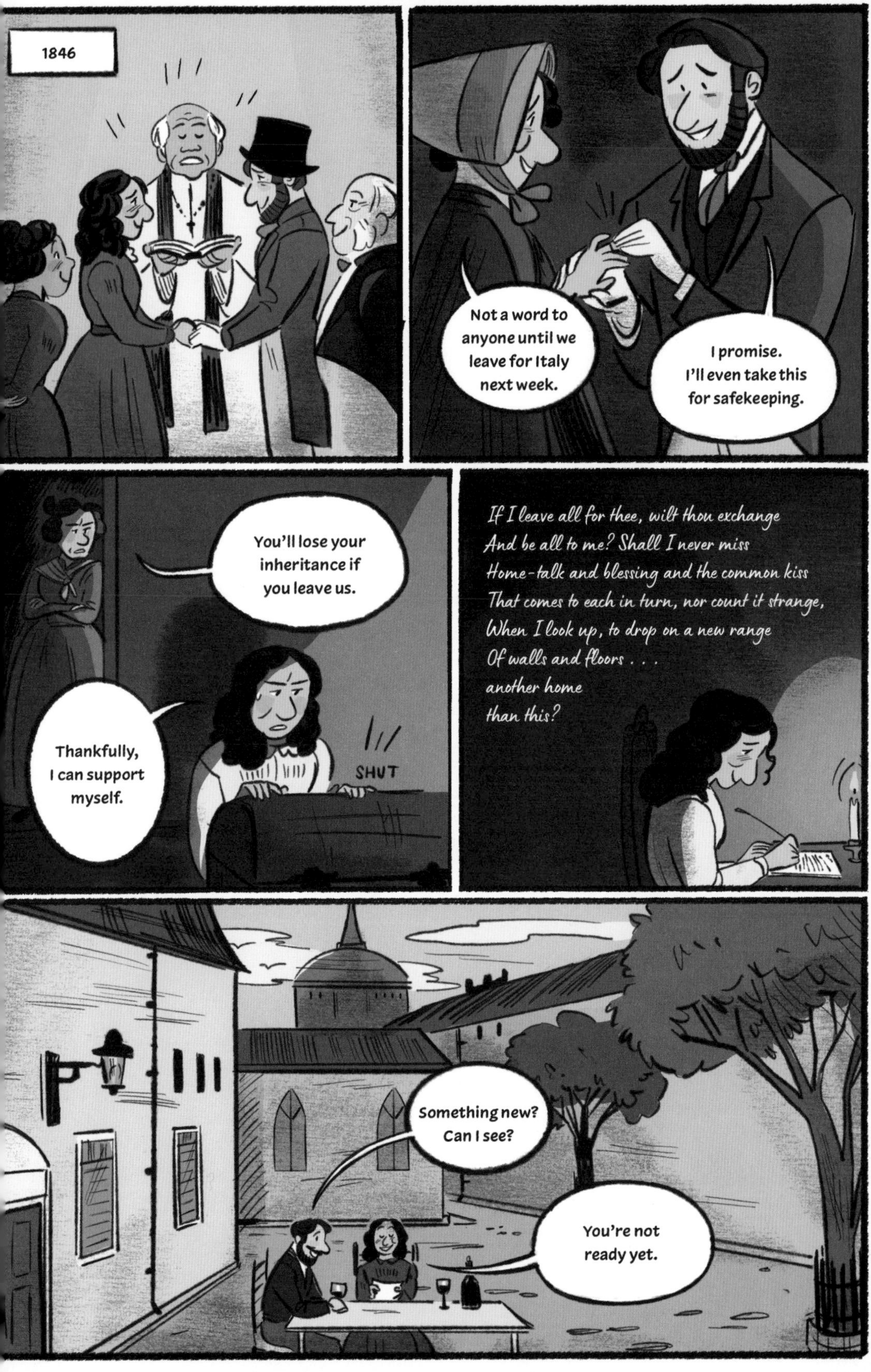
1846
Not a word to anyone until we leave for Italy next week.
I promise. I'll even take this for safekeeping.
You'll lose your inheritance if you leave us.
Thankfully, I can support myself.
SHUT
If I leave all for thee, wilt thou exchange
And be all to me? Shall I never miss
Home-talk and blessing and the common kiss
That comes to each in turn, nor count it strange,
When I look up, to drop on a new range
Of walls and floors . . .
another home
than this?
Something new? Can I see?
You're not ready yet.

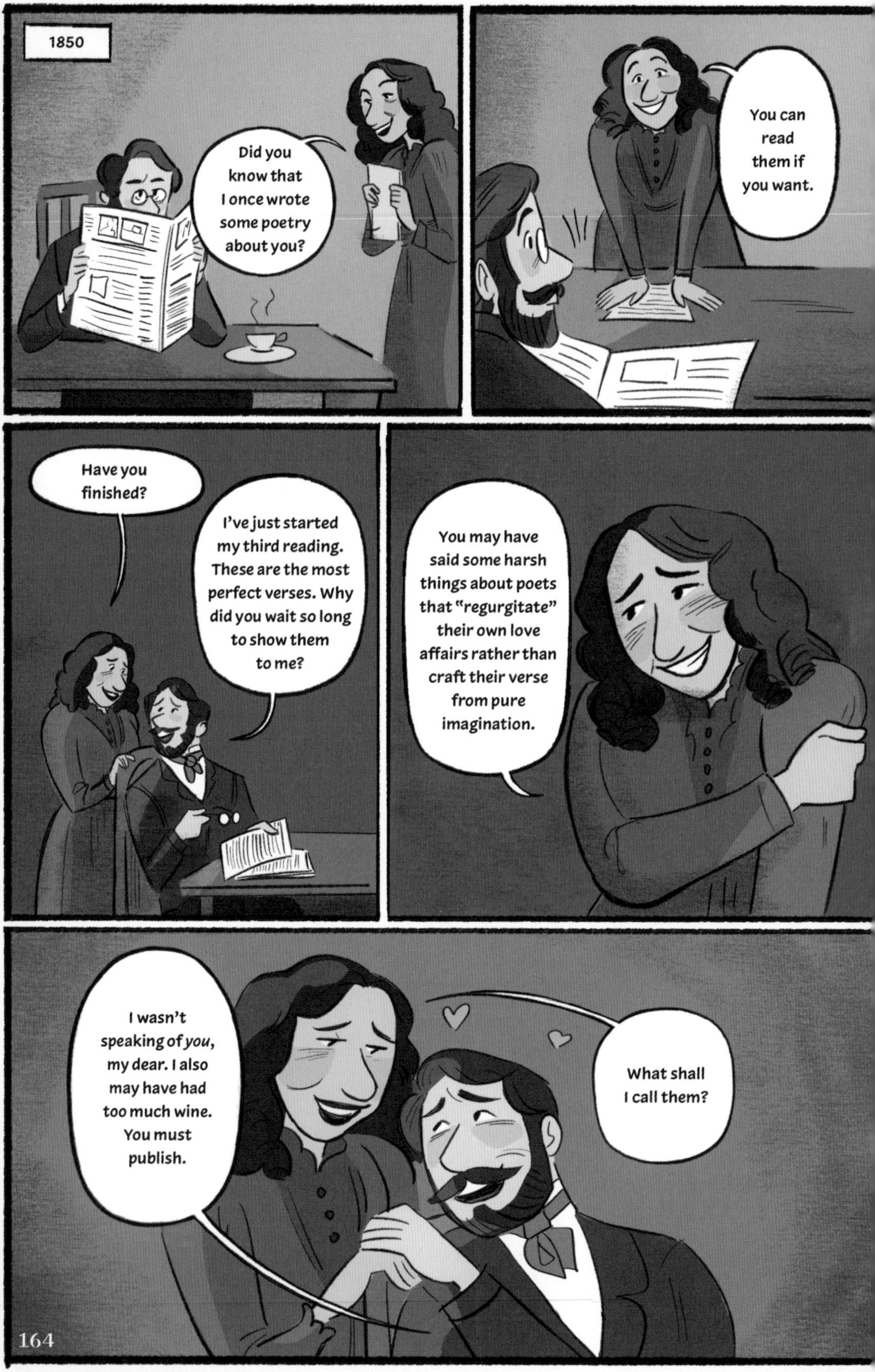
1850
Did you know that I once wrote some poetry about you?
You can read them if you want.
Have you finished?
I've just started my third reading. These are the most perfect verses. Why did you wait so long to show them to me?
You may have said some harsh things about poets that "regurgitate" their own love affairs rather than craft their verse from pure imagination.
I wasn't speaking of *you*, my dear. I also may have had too much wine. You must publish.
What shall I call them?

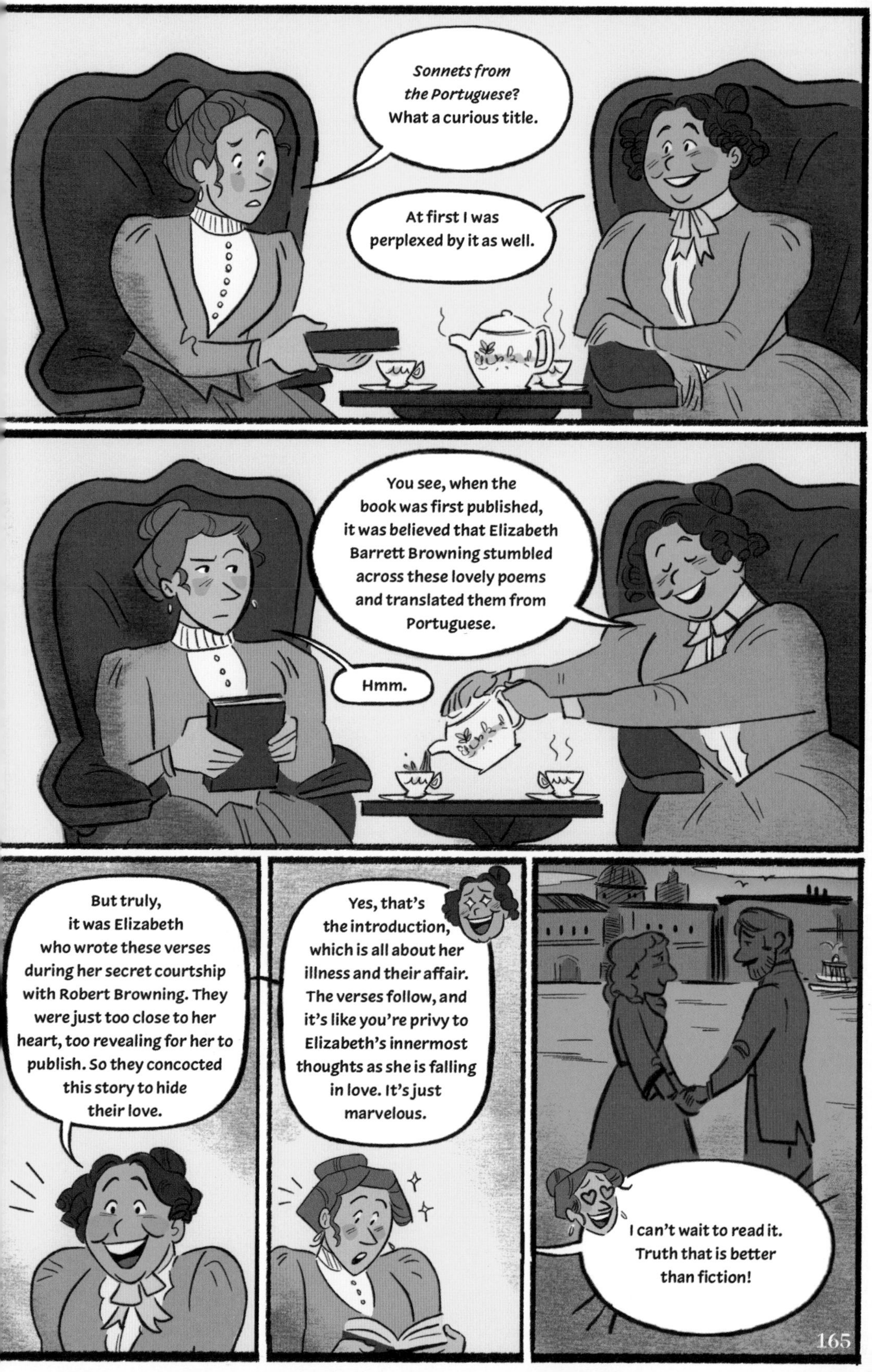
Sonnets from the Portuguese? What a curious title.
At first I was perplexed by it as well.
You see, when the book was first published, it was believed that Elizabeth Barrett Browning stumbled across these lovely poems and translated them from Portuguese.
Hmm.
But truly, it was Elizabeth who wrote these verses during her secret courtship with Robert Browning. They were just too close to her heart, too revealing for her to publish. So they concocted this story to hide their love.
Yes, that's the introduction, which is all about her illness and their affair. The verses follow, and it's like you're privy to Elizabeth's innermost thoughts as she is falling in love. It's just marvelous.
I can't wait to read it. Truth that is better than fiction!

Elizabeth Barrett Browning was a particular favorite of many women writers. Elizabeth Gaskell often quoted her poetry in her work. Notably, the epitaph for Gaskell's *The Life of Charlotte Brontë* was pulled from *Aurora Leigh*. Virginia Woolf wrote a biography of the poet told through the perspective of her cocker spaniel, Flush. And Emily Dickinson loved Elizabeth Barrett Browning so much that she hung a framed portrait of her idol in her bedroom.

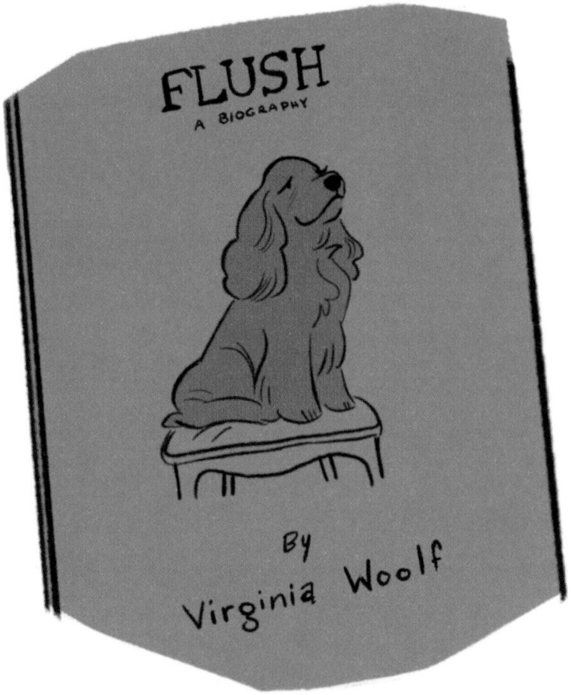
FLUSH
A BIOGRAPHY
By
Virginia Woolf

Writing for the *Westminster Review*, Marian Evans, also known as George Eliot, said in her review of *Aurora Leigh*, "Mrs. Browning has added one more to the imitations of the catastrophe in *Jane Eyre* by smiting her hero with blindness."

SELECTED WORKS

POETRY COLLECTIONS

1820: *The Battle of Marathon: A Poem*
1826: *An Essay on Mind, with Other Poems*
1833: *Prometheus Bound, Translated from the Greek of Aeschylus, and Miscellaneous Poems*
1838: *The Seraphim, and Other Poems*
1844: *Poems*
1850: *Poems* (revision of 1844 edition with the addition of *Sonnets from the Portuguese* and others)
1851: *Casa Guidi Windows*
1856: *Aurora Leigh*
1860: *Poems Before Congress*
1862: *Last Poems*

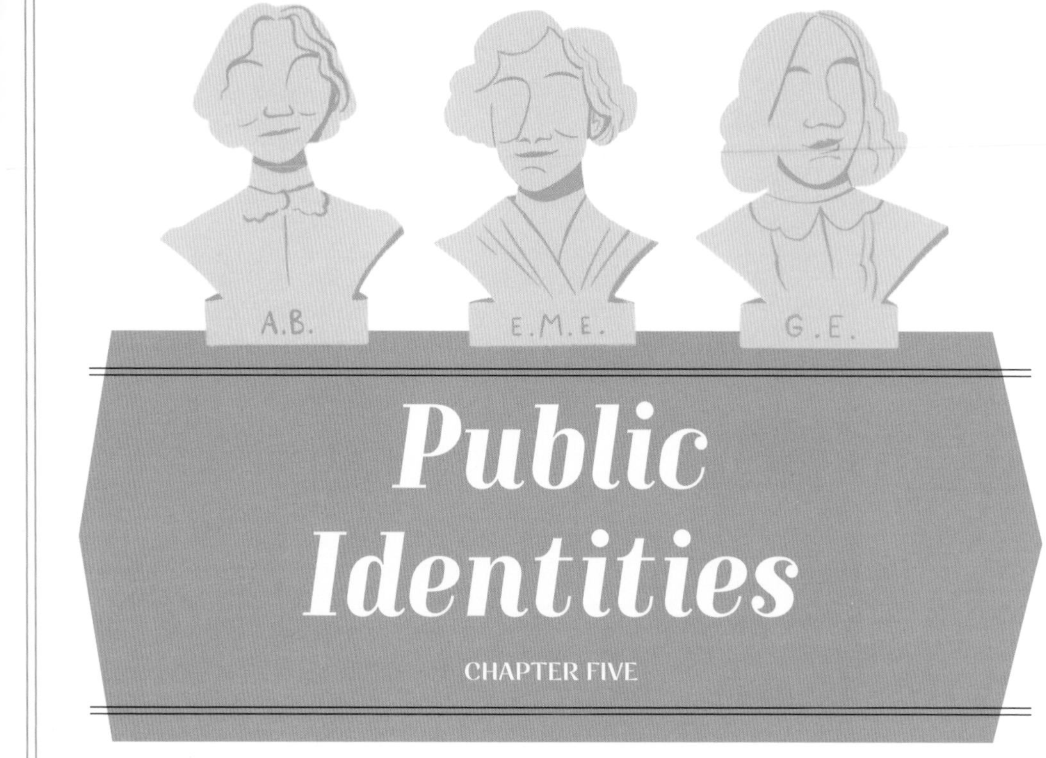
A.B.
E.M.E.
G.E.

Public Identities

CHAPTER FIVE

Though we have some sense of why a woman writer might choose to disguise her name, the truth is often more complex than "women weren't allowed to write." Jane Austen's books were attributed to a mysterious and unknown lady; while Mary Wollstonecraft, Elizabeth Gaskell, and Beatrix Potter published under their own names with seemingly little fear of persecution—indicating a complex relationship between women writers and their public identities.

Anne Brontë, Edith Maude Eaton, and Mary Anne Evans all chose to change their identities on their written works, and though their justifications for doing so varied, this choice offered them significant freedom to shape the narrative around their work. As women, their work and their lives were under much closer scrutiny than those of their male counterparts, and their politically charged writings often challenged societal norms and double standards. By removing names, race, and gender from the equation, they protected themselves and those around them from an inevitable backlash.

Though she would later be known by her pseudonym, Sui Sin Far, when Edith Maude Eaton began writing about the Chinese community living in Canada in 1890, she did so anonymously. In a period of growing unease about the flow of migrant workers entering America in search of jobs and opportunity, public opinion was divided. By reporting on the harsh treatment this community faced and referencing her own experiences as a woman of dual heritage, Eaton was taking an unpopular and defiant stance. Anonymity was a means of protection.

When the Brontë sisters chose to publish their first book of poetry under pseudonyms in 1846, it was a group decision, and an important one. In the words of Charlotte Brontë, it allowed the sisters to "walk invisible" and write about subjects that would otherwise have been inaccessible to them as women writers. Described as "coarse," Anne's writing in particular challenged the fundamentals of marriage and women's rights. Publishing under a more masculine name may have spared her from censure; but it also left her open to predatory publishers.

For Mary Anne Evans, assuming a new name was a means of distancing her work from her very public love affair. After falling in love with a married man and finding he was legally unable to divorce, Evans made the bold decision to take his name anyway and became the second Mrs. Lewes. This act of defiance shocked society, and if she were to continue writing, a new name would be needed. As Mrs. Lewes, she was a pariah, but as George Eliot, she could find success.

Though there can be safety in anonymity, it is not guaranteed; the risk of having the truth revealed is always a very real and present danger. However, for these women, having their voices heard without prejudice or censure was more important than staying quiet. By removing their names and identities from the picture, these authors allowed their work to speak for them.

Edith Maude Eaton (Sui Sin Far)

1865–1914

"Individuality is more than nationality."

—"Leaves from the Mental Portfolio of an Eurasian," 1909

Though she is most well-known under the pseudonym Sui Sin Far, the writer Edith Maude Eaton wrote under multiple pennames throughout her career as a journalist and author of short stories. These names included her own initials, Fire Fly, several variations of Sui Sin Far (including Sui Seen Far and Sui Sin Fah), and Wing Sin.

Born in Macclesfield, England, in 1865 to Englishman Edward Eaton and his Chinese wife, Grace Trefusis, Edith was the second of fourteen children. Her parents moved the family across the Atlantic a number of times before settling in Montreal in 1872. Growing up biracial in a predominantly white country was a struggle, and much of Eaton's writing focuses on the lives of Eurasian children and young people, trying to make a life for themselves in a world where neither community accepted them fully. In 1909, Eaton wrote, "I have no nationality and I am not anxious to claim any."

Some of her earliest works, written between 1890 and 1896, were published anonymously. Eaton, then in her mid-twenties, was working as a reporter for the *Montreal Daily Star*. Because of her dual heritage, she had been tasked with reporting on the lives and customs of the migrant Chinese workers living in Montreal. These stories were not just about recording the day-to-day life, cultural norms, and traditions of the workers, but also took a political stance. Anonymity was a means of protecting herself and those she wrote about.

It was not an easy time to be Chinese in North America. The Chinese Exclusion Act, passed in 1882, was the first American law to exclude a community based on their ethnicity from entering the country. Although the Chinese laborers had initially been hired to complete the First Transcontinental Railroad, with the end of the Gold Rush in 1855, public opinion turned, and these same workers were blamed for job scarcity and low wages. In the years that followed, further laws were introduced making it harder not only for laborers but also diplomats, businessmen, and servants of Chinese descent to live and work in America. Husbands were separated from wives, fathers from children, and business owners from their livelihoods. People wishing to enter America resorted to crossing the border from Canada or Mexico until pressure from the United States saw laws and stricter border control passed in those countries as well.

Eaton was no stranger to smuggling. In July 1895, while writing for the *Montreal Daily Star*, Eaton penned "The Thrilling Experience of a Band of Smugglers in the Lachine Rapids." The text reads like a work of fiction, with steadily growing tension as the group undertakes a perilous night-time border crossing. Eaton's bold experiment with narrative style places her in the vessel, and invites her readers to imagine themselves there alongside her. Less than a year after her story was published, her father was arrested for ferrying Chinese workers over the American border. By December 1896, Eaton had moved to Jamaica, leaving both Montreal and her anonymous newspaper articles behind her.

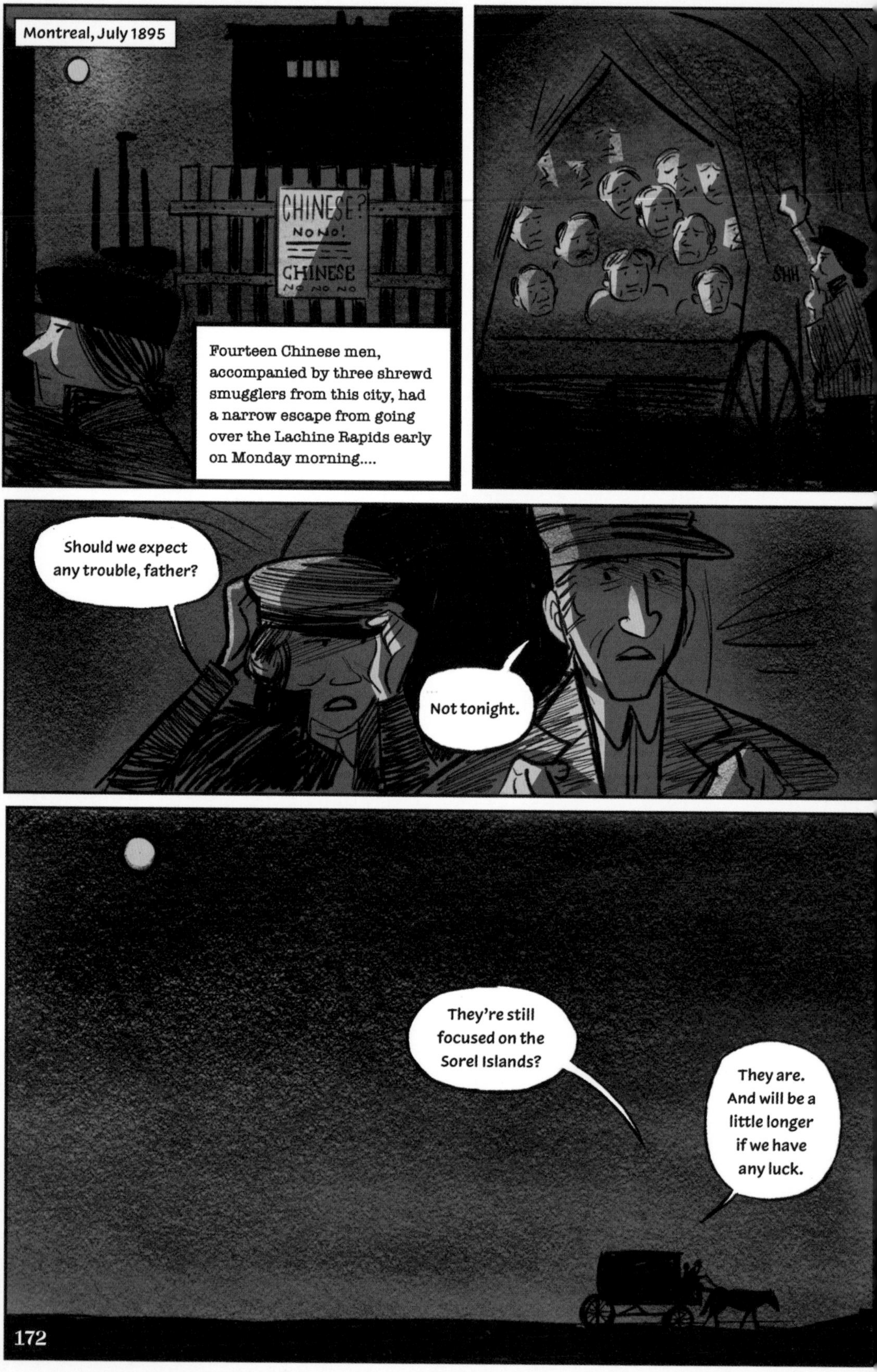
Montreal, July 1895
CHINESE? NO NO!
CHINESE NO NO NO
Fourteen Chinese men, accompanied by three shrewd smugglers from this city, had a narrow escape from going over the Lachine Rapids early on Monday morning....
SHH
Should we expect any trouble, father?
Not tonight.
They're still focused on the Sorel Islands?
They are. And will be a little longer if we have any luck.

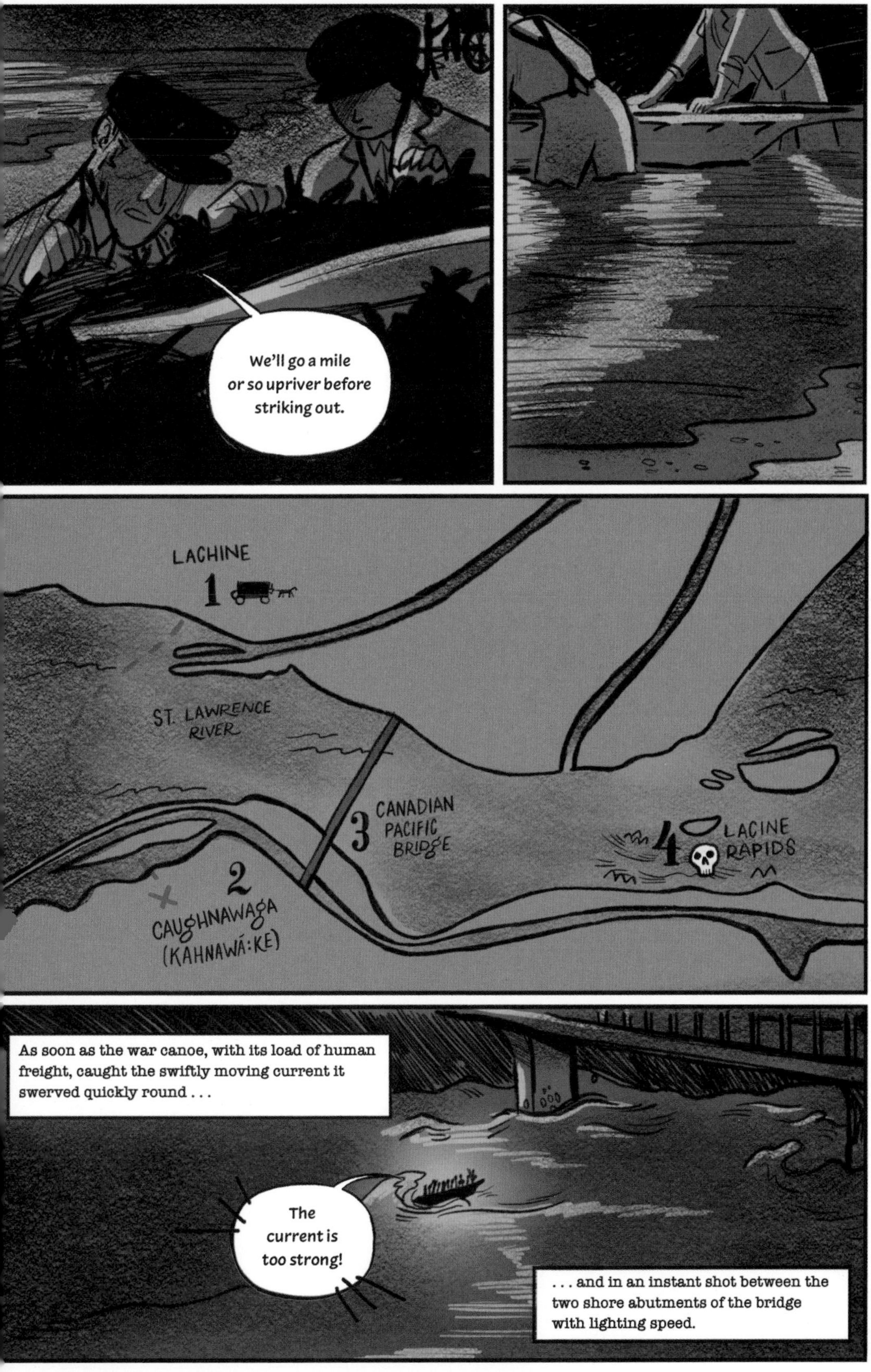

We'll go a mile or so upriver before striking out.
LACHINE
1
ST. LAWRENCE RIVER
2
CAUGHNAWAGA (KAHNAWÁ:KE)
3
CANADIAN PACIFIC BRIDGE
4
LACINE RAPIDS
As soon as the war canoe, with its load of human freight, caught the swiftly moving current it swerved quickly round . . .
The current is too strong!
. . . and in an instant shot between the two shore abutments of the bridge with lighting speed.

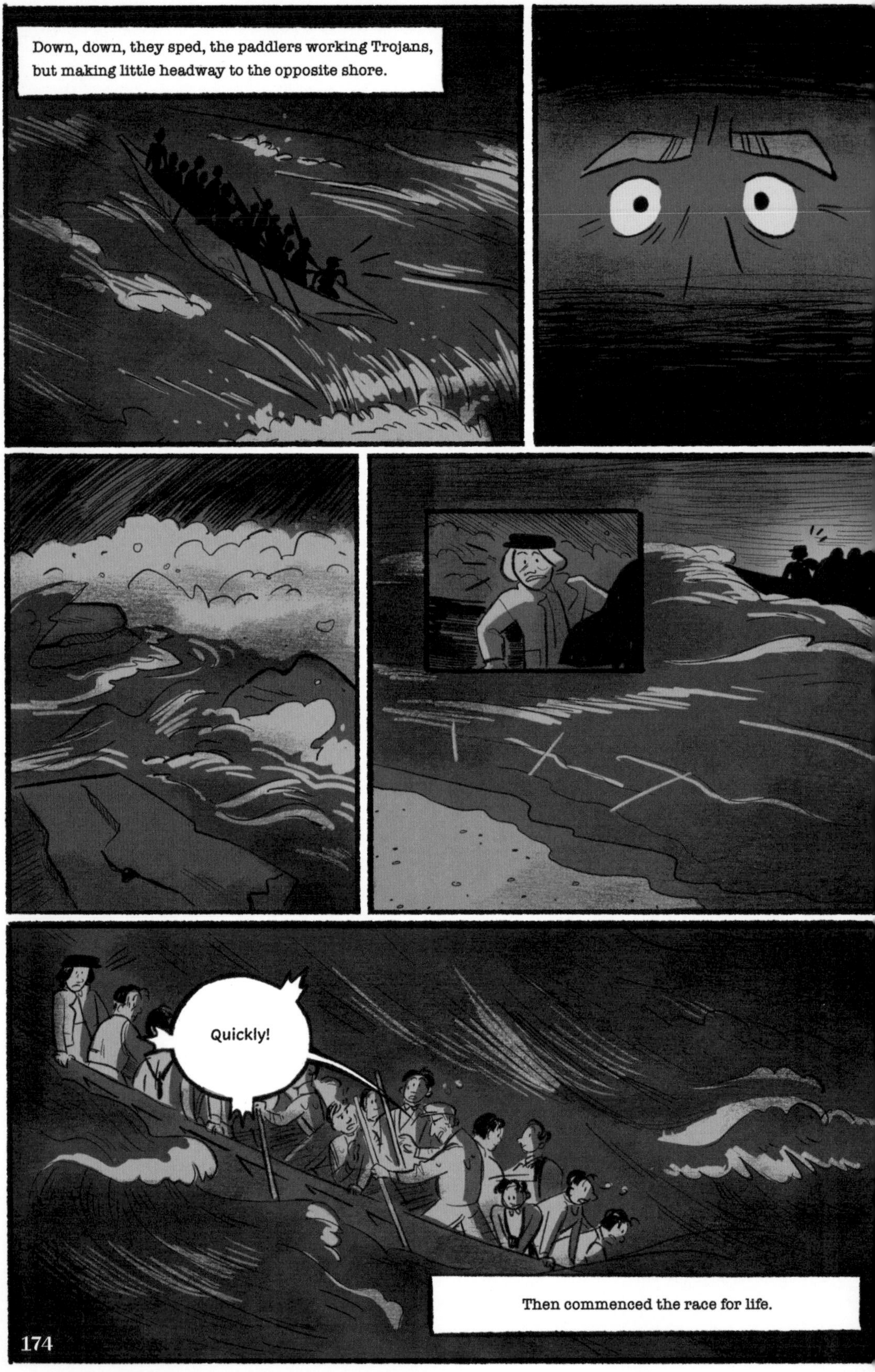
Down, down, they sped, the paddlers working Trojans, but making little headway to the opposite shore.
Quickly!
Then commenced the race for life.

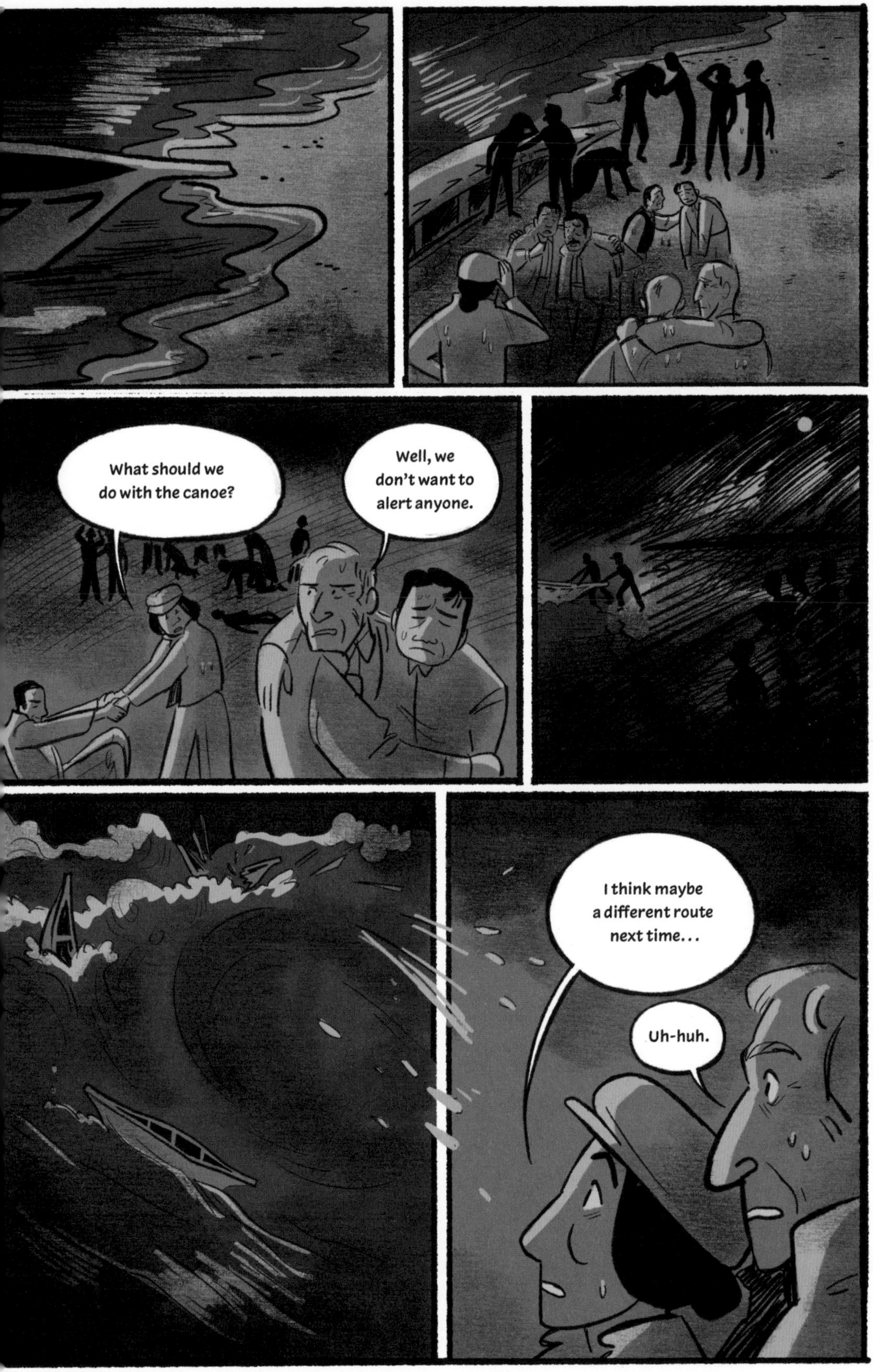
What should we do with the canoe?
Well, we don't want to alert anyone.
I think maybe a different route next time...
Uh-huh.

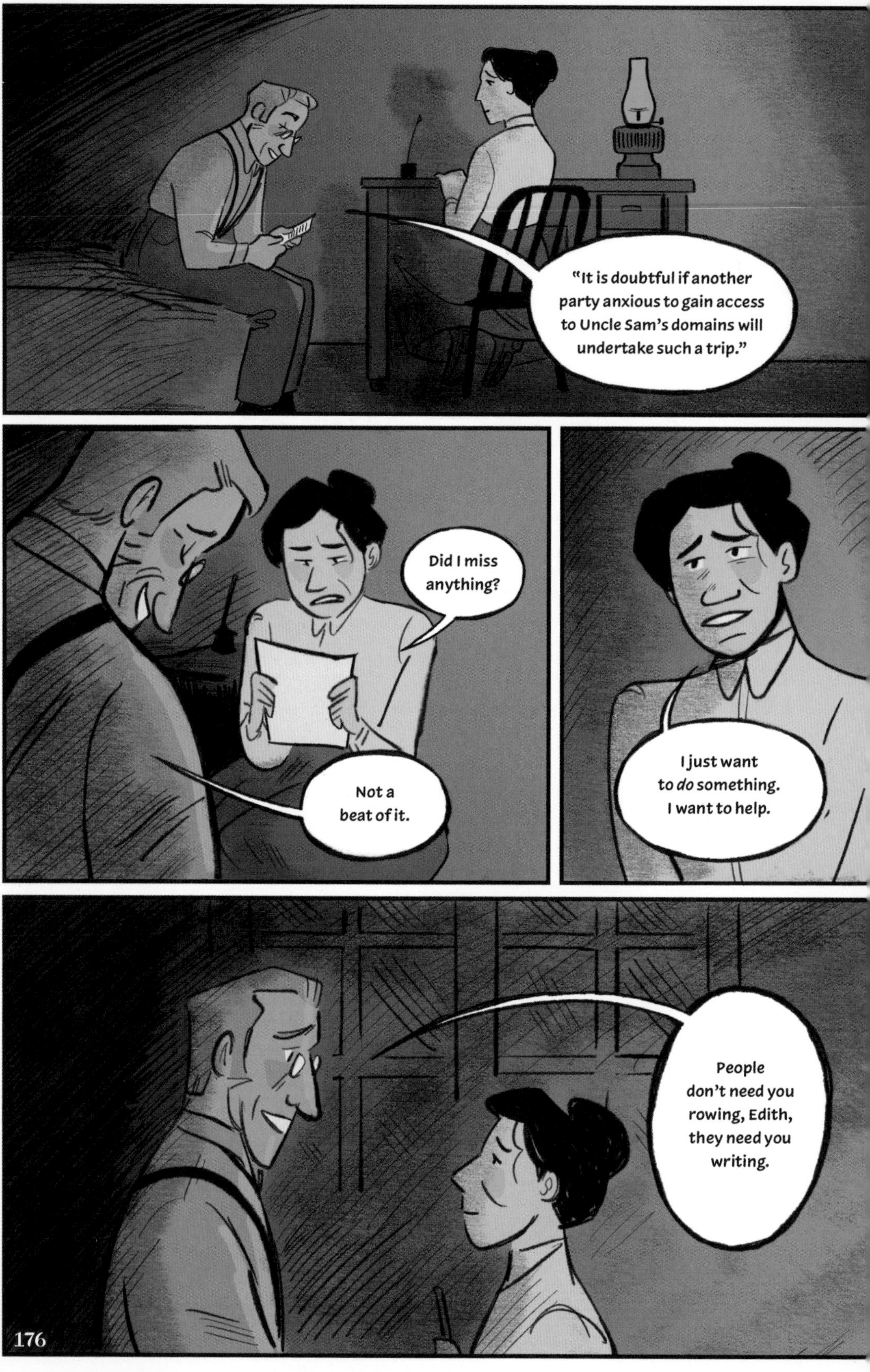
"It is doubtful if another party anxious to gain access to Uncle Sam's domains will undertake such a trip."
Did I miss anything?
Not a beat of it.
I just want to *do* something. I want to help.
People don't need you rowing, Edith, they need you writing.

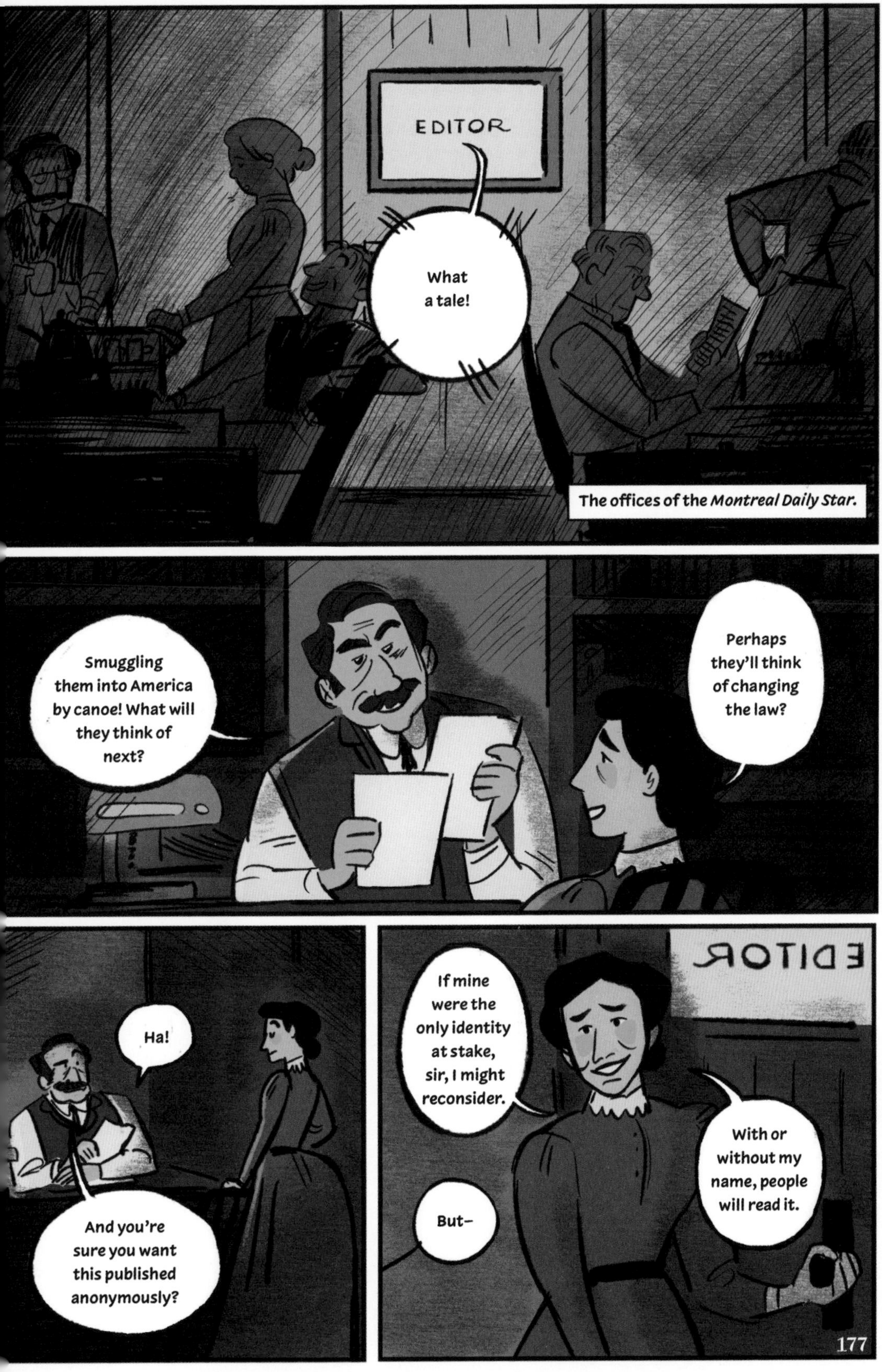
EDITOR
What a tale!
The offices of the *Montreal Daily Star*.
Smuggling them into America by canoe! What will they think of next?
Perhaps they'll think of changing the law?
Ha!
And you're sure you want this published anonymously?
If mine were the only identity at stake, sir, I might reconsider.
With or without my name, people will read it.
But–

In 1904, writing for the *Los Angeles Express,* Eaton took her readers on another journey, this time crossing the American border by train. Though it remains a mystery whether Eaton herself made the journey, the series, titled "Wing Sing of Los Angeles on His Travels," once again shares a perspective and experience her readers may otherwise have overlooked.

Thirteen years after her death, an addition was made to Eaton's grave. The new tombstone read "Erected by her Chinese friends in grateful memory." And above this, in Chinese characters, "It is right and good that we should remember China." It is not known who commissioned the monument.

義不
忘華

ERECTED BY HER
CHINESE FRIENDS
IN GRATEFUL MEMORY
– OF –
EDITH EATON
·SUI SUN FAR·
DEARLY BELOVED
DAUGHTER OF
EDWARD & GRACE
EATON
BORN MAR. 15, 1865
DIED APRIL 7, 1914

EATON

SELECTED WORKS:

ARTICLES

As Sui Sin Far:
1889: "A Chinese Ishmael." *Overland Monthly*, July.
1890: "Leaves from the Mental Portfolio of an Eurasian." *Independent*, 21 January.
1910: "An Autumn Fan." *New England Magazine*, August.
1910: "The Bird of Love." *New England Magazine*, September.
1912: "Chan Hen Yen, Chinese Student." *New England Magazine*, January.
1912: *Mrs. Spring Fragrance and Other Writings*

As Edith Eaton:
1888: "A Trip in a Horse Car." *Dominion Illustrated*, 13 October.
1888: "Misunderstood: The Story of a Young Man." *Dominion Illustrated*, 17 November.
1888: "A Fatal Tug of War." *Dominion Illustrated*, 8 December.
1889: "The Origin of a Broken Nose." *Dominion Illustrated*, 11 May.
1889: "Robin." *Dominion Illustrated*, 22 June.
1889: "Albemarle's Secret." *Dominion Illustrated*, 19 October.
1890: "Lines." *Dominion Illustrated*, 5 April.
1890: "In Fairyland." *Dominion Illustrated*, 18 October.
1891: "A Plea for Sad Songs." *Dominion Illustrated*, 3 October.
1896: "The Chinese Defended. 'E.E.' Replied to Her Critics of Saturday and Is Supported by a Brooklyn Doctor." *Montreal Daily Star*, 29 September.

Selection of anonymous works:
1890: "A Chinese Party." *Montreal Daily Witness*, 7 November.
1894: "Girl Slave in Montreal. Our Chinese Colony Cleverly Described. Only Two Women from the Flowery Land in Town." *Montreal Daily Witness*, 4 May.
1894: "Our Local Chinatown. Little Mystery of a St. Denis Street Laundry." *Montreal Daily Witness*, 19 July.
1894: "No Tickee, No Washee." *Montreal Daily Witness*, 25 July.
1895: "Half-Chinese Children." *Montreal Daily Star*, 20 April.
1895: "Thrilling Experience of a Band of Smugglers in the Lachine Rapids." *Montreal Daily Star*, 9 July.
1895: "They Are Going Back to China: Hundreds of Chinese at the CPR Station." *Montreal Daily Star*, 21 August.
1895: "Chinese Religion Information Given a Lady by Montreal Chinamen." *Montreal Daily Star*, 21 September.
1895: "Chinese Food." *Montreal Daily Star*, 25 November.
1895: "Chinamen with German Wives." *Montreal Daily Star*, 13 December.
1895: "The Chinese and Christmas." *Montreal Daily Star*, 21 December.
1896: "Born a Britisher But Fifty Dollars Is the Tax on Him as a Chinaman." *Montreal Daily Witness*, 27 October.

Mary Anne Evans (George Eliot)

1819–1880

"And, of course, men know best about everything, except what women know better."

—*Middlemarch*, 1872

Despite the fame of *Middlemarch*, there are few readers today who are as familiar with the real name or history of the writer George Eliot. As Mary Anne, she was a nobody; as Marian, an adventurous young professional; as Mrs. Lewes, a laughingstock; and as George Eliot? A literary sensation.

Born Mary Anne Evans to Robert Evans and his wife, Christiana, she was not considered conventionally attractive and would need to rely on something other than marriage to secure her future. Therefore, her forward- thinking parents invested heavily in her education. At the age of twenty-one, having lost her mother some years before, Mary Anne was uprooted to nearby Coventry with her father upon his retirement, and here she made friends with the radical thinking philanthropist Charles Bray and his wife, Cara. Her introduction to their circle of liberal-minded free-thinkers challenged her previously narrow world view and shook her beliefs to the core. Encouraged by her new friends, she sold some of her earliest pieces to Bray's *Coventry Herald and Observer*, and began to go by a shortened version of her name: Marian Evans.

In 1851, Marian, now in her early thirties, was living and working in London as the co-editor of *The Westminster Review*. It was in London that Marian met George Henry Lewes—philosopher, critic, and the man who would change her life forever. The pair were kindred spirits, and within a few short years they were devoted to one another. There was just one problem: Lewes was already married. Though he and his wife, Agnes, had agreed to an open marriage, and were together raising children from different fathers, divorce—amicable or other-wise—was not legally an option. If Marian and Lewes were to be together, they would have to live on the edges of polite society. Even Marian's liberal-minded friends in Coventry struggled to make peace with her decision to live with Lewes and, fearful of their censure, Marian shut them out almost completely.

In 1854, Marian and Lewes left London and traveled to Germany. While they were away, they began referring to each other as husband and wife; the trip served as both research for their writing and as a honeymoon, and Marian Evans became Marian Lewes. Lewes began research for what would be his most well-known book, *The Life of Goethe*, a biography of the famous German poet. Meanwhile, at Lewes's urging, Marian began translating the Dutch philosopher Spinoza's *Ethics*.

But when they returned to England, the honeymoon was over. By refusing to live as Lewes's mistress and by publicly claiming his name, Marian was cutting ties with both family and friends; for a long time, she would live in almost complete isolation. On top of this, after fifteen months of working on *Ethics*, a disagree-ment between Lewes and the publisher, H. G. Bohn, left the book unpublished. Disappointed and lonely, Marian would have to find something to fill her days. A fresh start was needed and a new name to go with it.

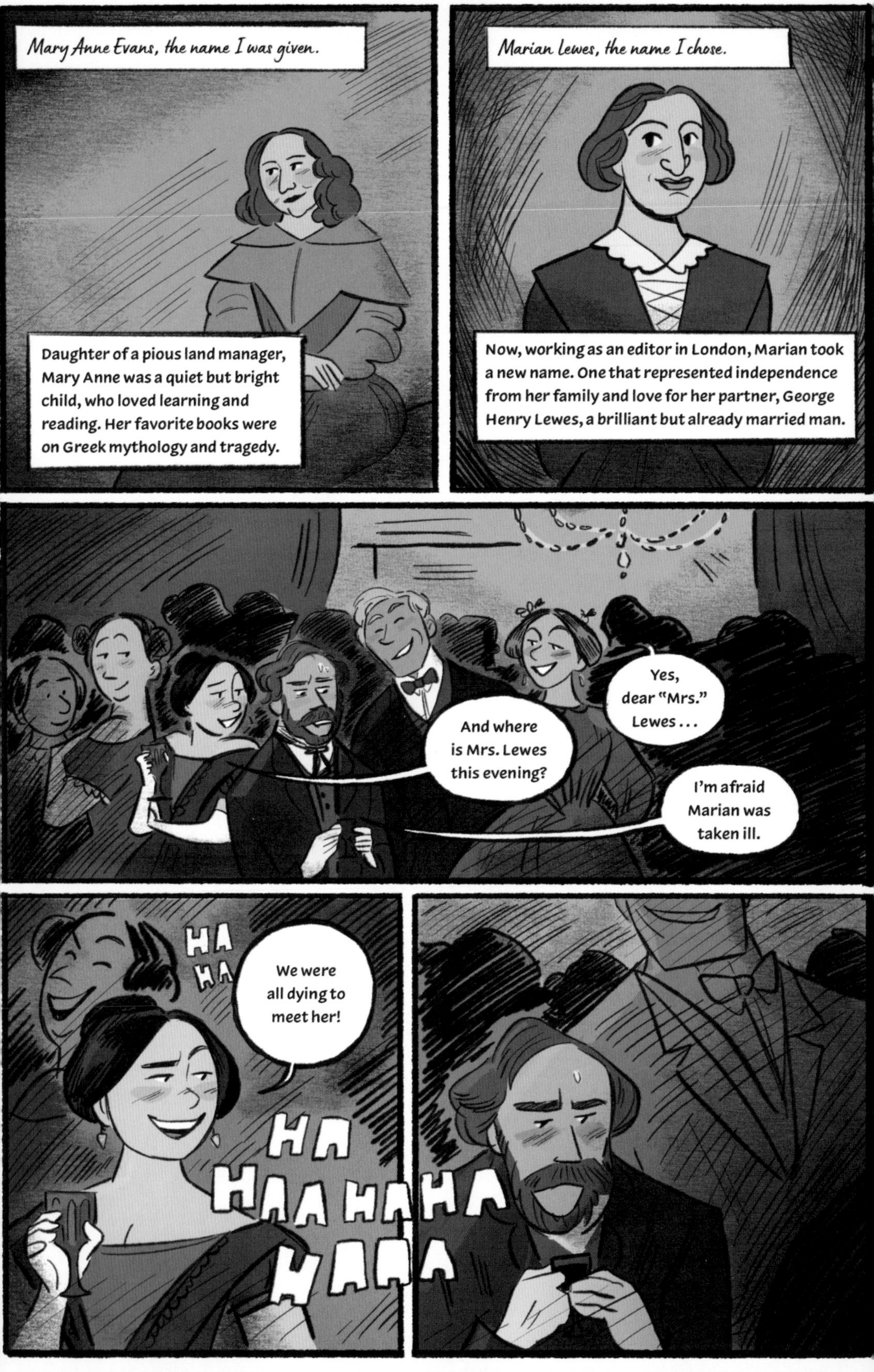
Mary Anne Evans, the name I was given.
Daughter of a pious land manager, Mary Anne was a quiet but bright child, who loved learning and reading. Her favorite books were on Greek mythology and tragedy.
Marian Lewes, the name I chose.
Now, working as an editor in London, Marian took a new name. One that represented independence from her family and love for her partner, George Henry Lewes, a brilliant but already married man.
And where is Mrs. Lewes this evening?
Yes, dear "Mrs." Lewes . . .
I'm afraid Marian was taken ill.
HA HA
We were all dying to meet her!
HA HAAHAHAHA HAAA

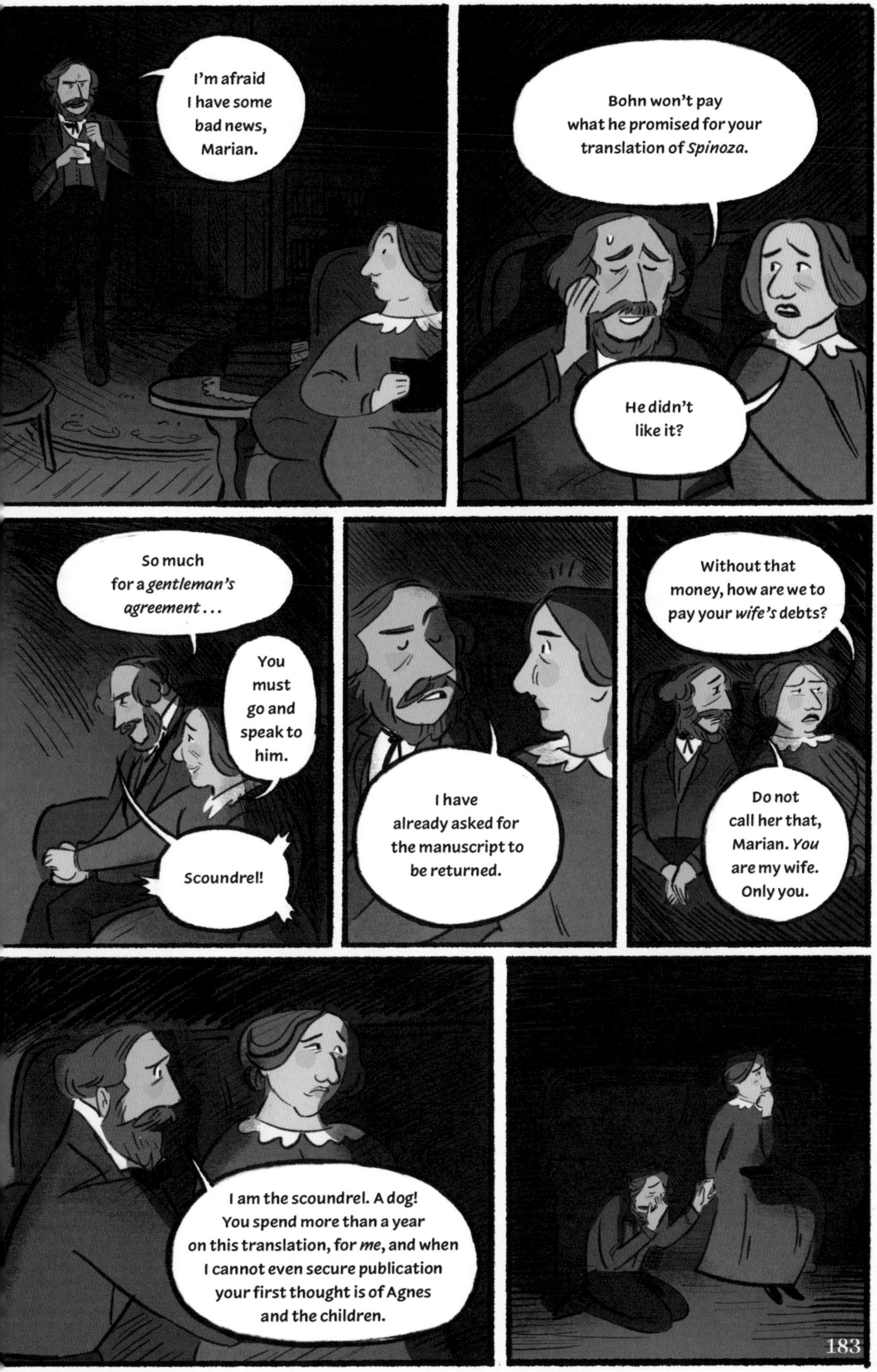
I'm afraid I have some bad news, Marian.
Bohn won't pay what he promised for your translation of *Spinoza*.
He didn't like it?
So much for a *gentleman's agreement* . . .
You must go and speak to him.
Scoundrel!
I have already asked for the manuscript to be returned.
Without that money, how are we to pay your *wife's* debts?
Do not call her that, Marian. *You* are my wife. Only you.
I am the scoundrel. A dog! You spend more than a year on this translation, for *me*, and when I cannot even secure publication your first thought is of Agnes and the children.

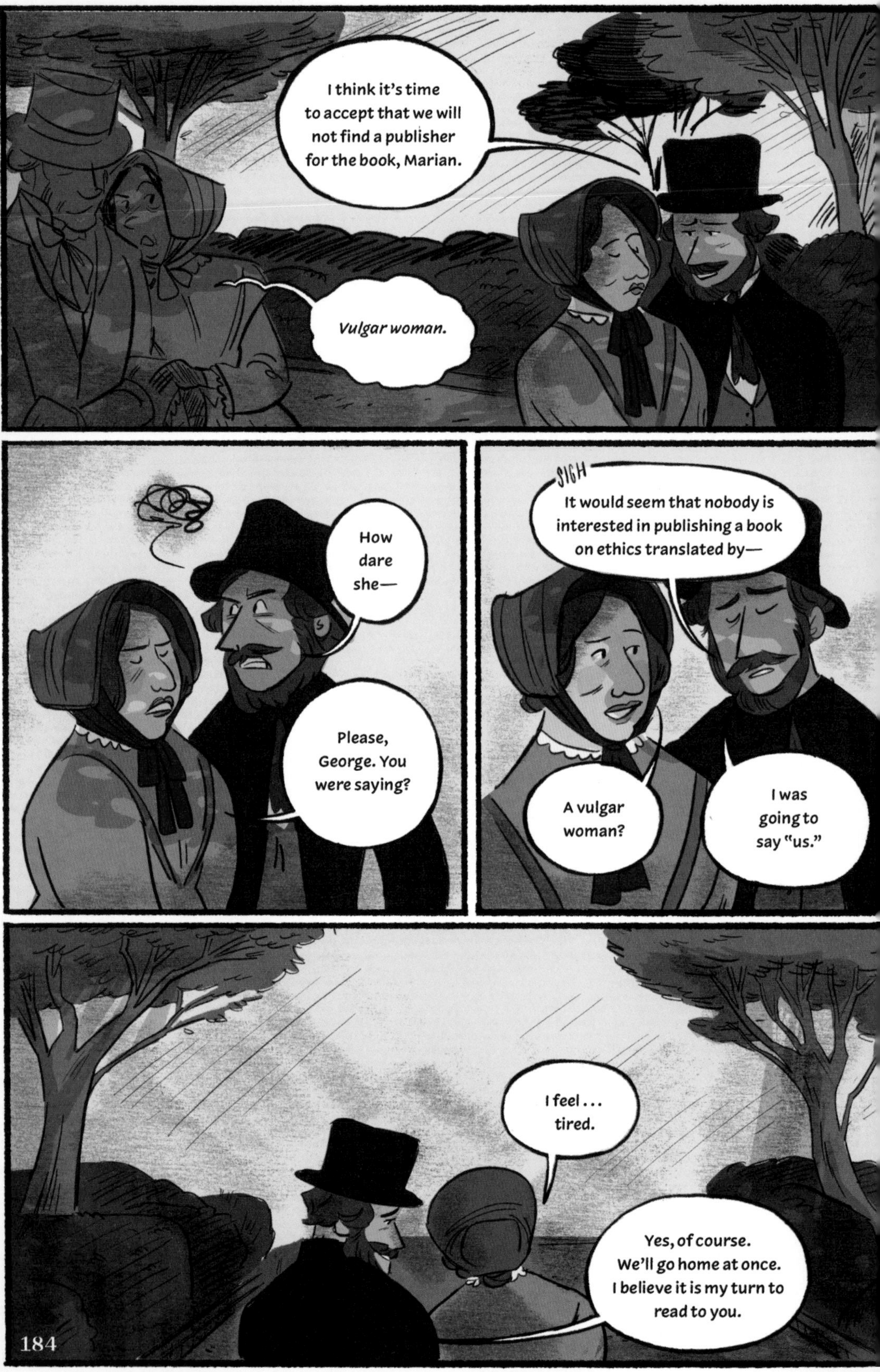
I think it's time to accept that we will not find a publisher for the book, Marian.
Vulgar woman.
How dare she—
Please, George. You were saying?
SIGH
It would seem that nobody is interested in publishing a book on ethics translated by—
A vulgar woman?
I was going to say "us."
I feel . . . tired.
Yes, of course. We'll go home at once. I believe it is my turn to read to you.

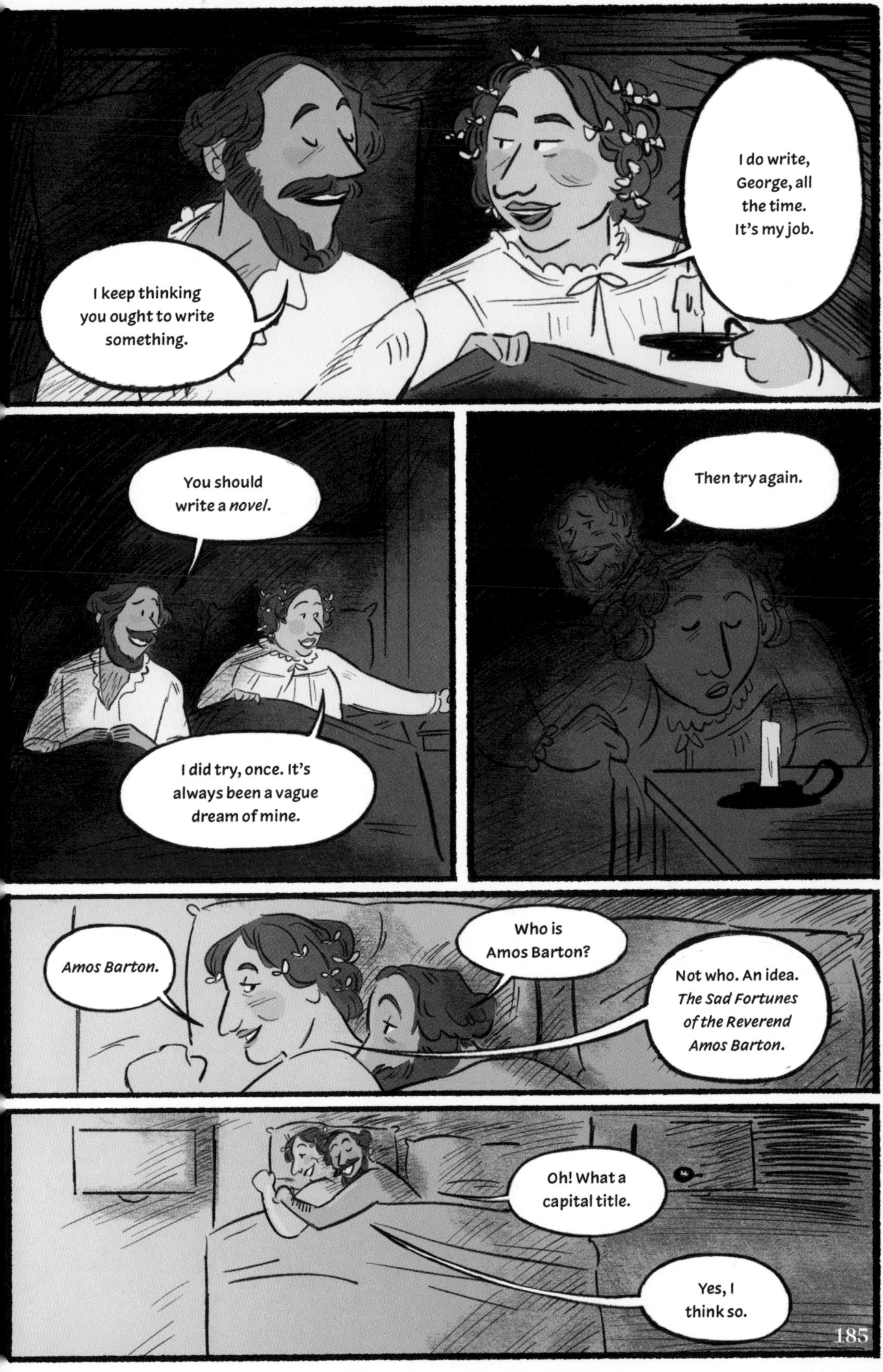
I keep thinking you ought to write something.
I do write, George, all the time. It's my job.
You should write a *novel*.
I did try, once. It's always been a vague dream of mine.
Then try again.
Amos Barton.
Who is Amos Barton?
Not who. An idea. *The Sad Fortunes of the Reverend Amos Barton.*
Oh! What a capital title.
Yes, I think so.

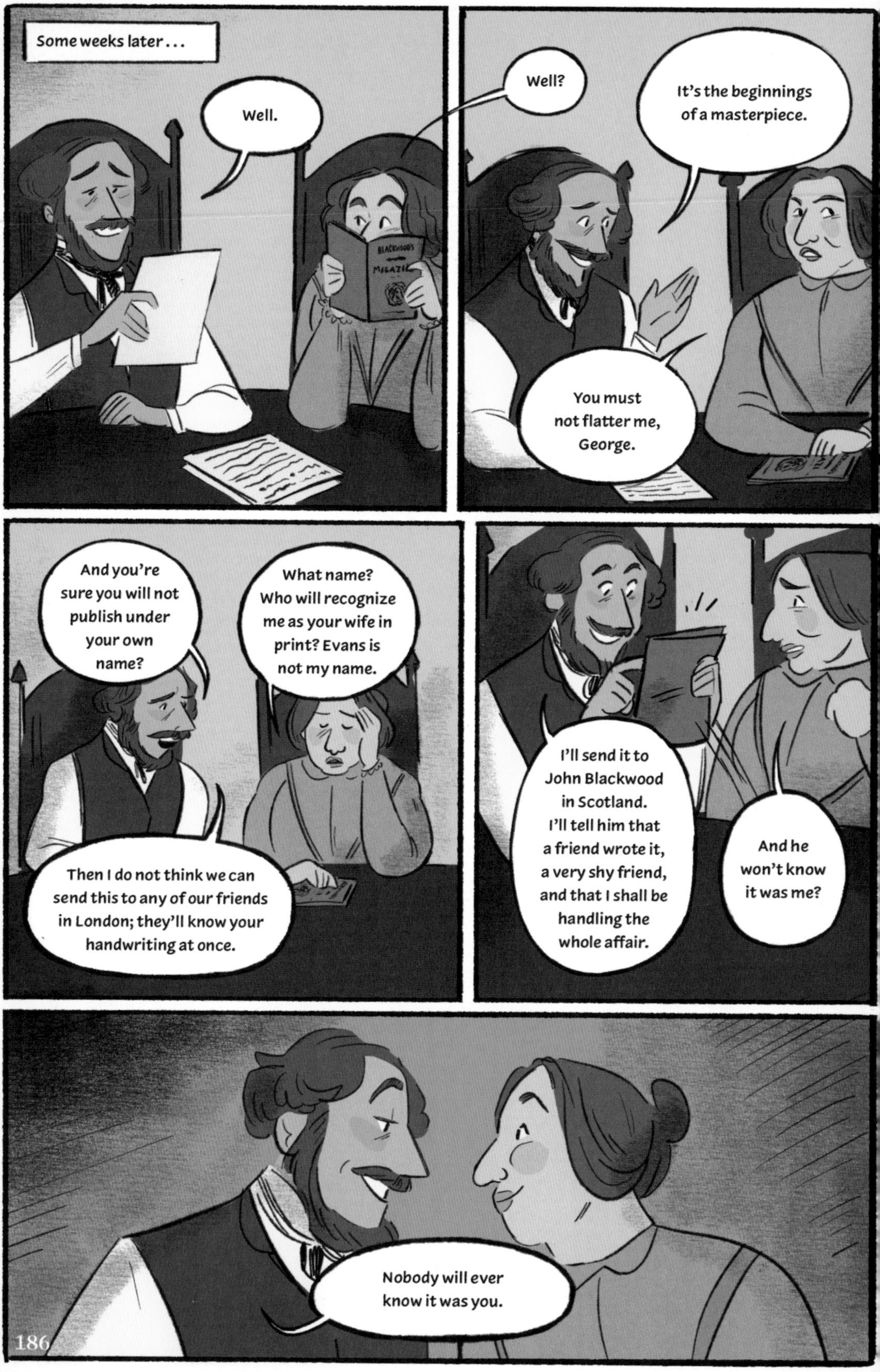

Some weeks later . . .
Well.
Well?
It's the beginnings of a masterpiece.
You must not flatter me, George.
And you're sure you will not publish under your own name?
What name? Who will recognize me as your wife in print? Evans is not my name.
Then I do not think we can send this to any of our friends in London; they'll know your handwriting at once.
I'll send it to John Blackwood in Scotland. I'll tell him that a friend wrote it, a very shy friend, and that I shall be handling the whole affair.
And he won't know it was me?
Nobody will ever know it was you.

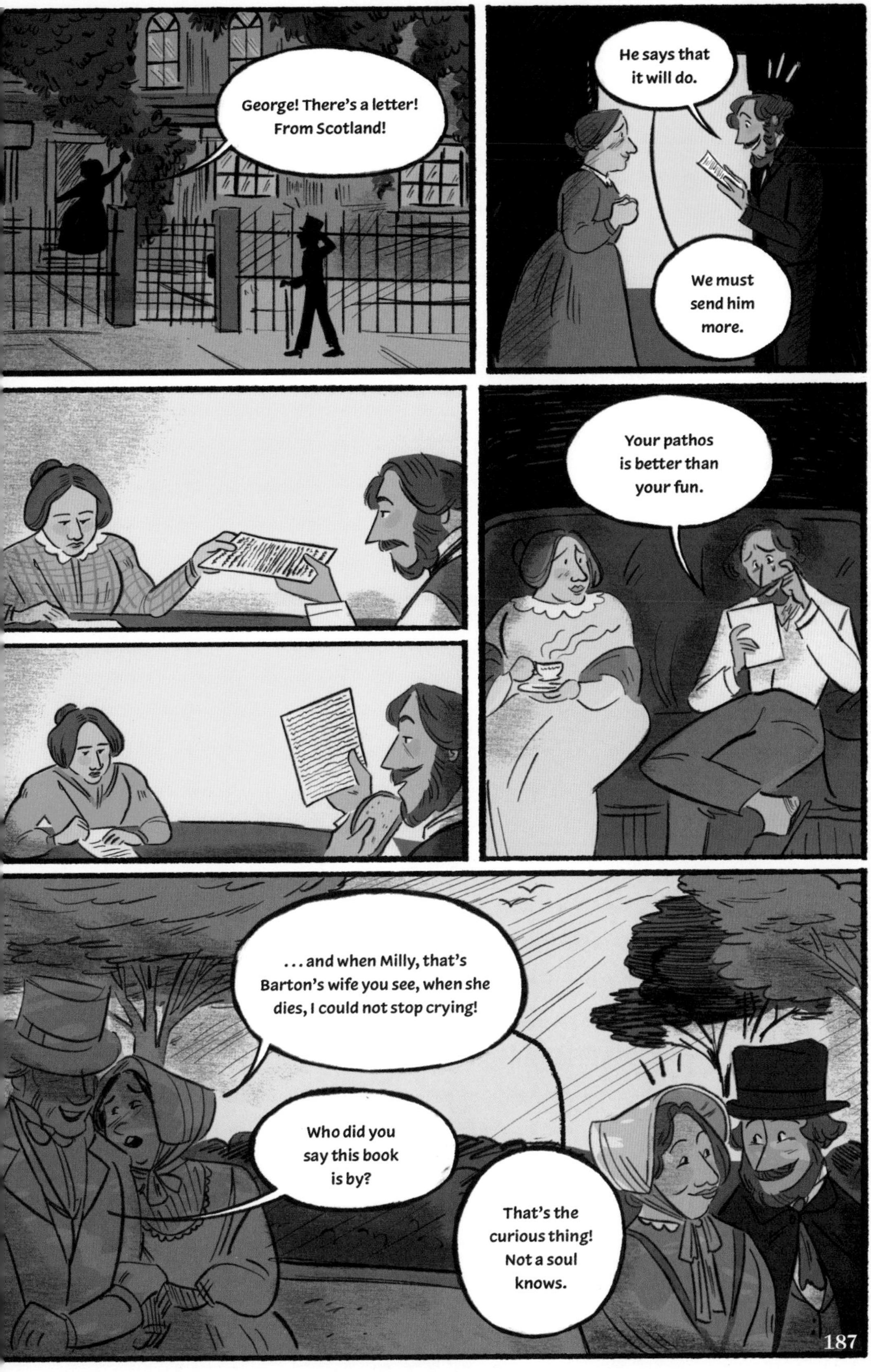
George! There's a letter! From Scotland!
He says that it will do.
We must send him more.
Your pathos is better than your fun.
. . . and when Milly, that's Barton's wife you see, when she dies, I could not stop crying!
Who did you say this book is by?
That's the curious thing! Not a soul knows.

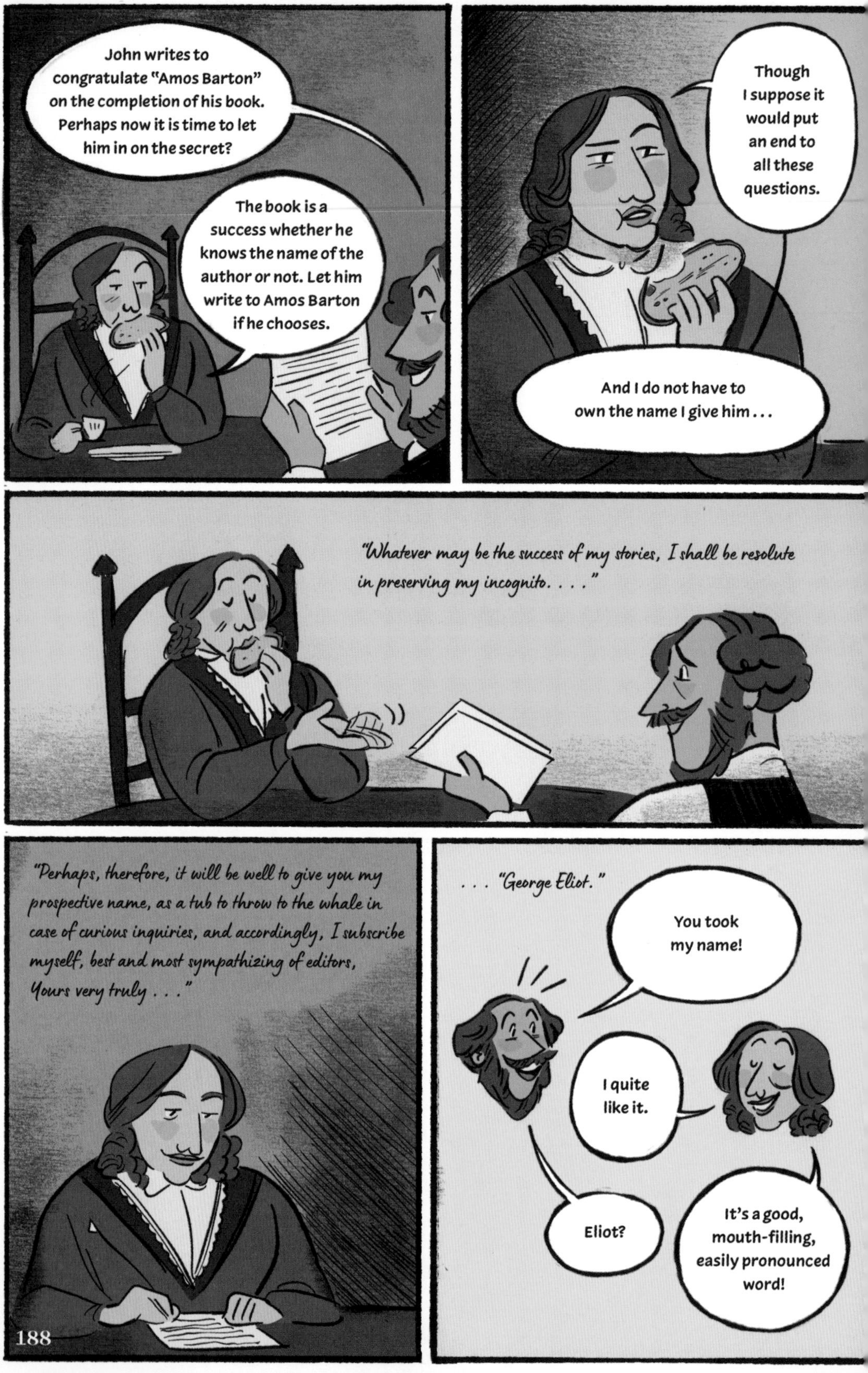
John writes to congratulate "Amos Barton" on the completion of his book. Perhaps now it is time to let him in on the secret?
The book is a success whether he knows the name of the author or not. Let him write to Amos Barton if he chooses.
Though I suppose it would put an end to all these questions.
And I do not have to own the name I give him . . .
"Whatever may be the success of my stories, I shall be resolute in preserving my incognito. . . ."
"Perhaps, therefore, it will be well to give you my prospective name, as a tub to throw to the whale in case of curious inquiries, and accordingly, I subscribe myself, best and most sympathizing of editors, Yours very truly . . ."
. . . "George Eliot."
You took my name!
I quite like it.
Eliot?
It's a good, mouth-filling, easily pronounced word!

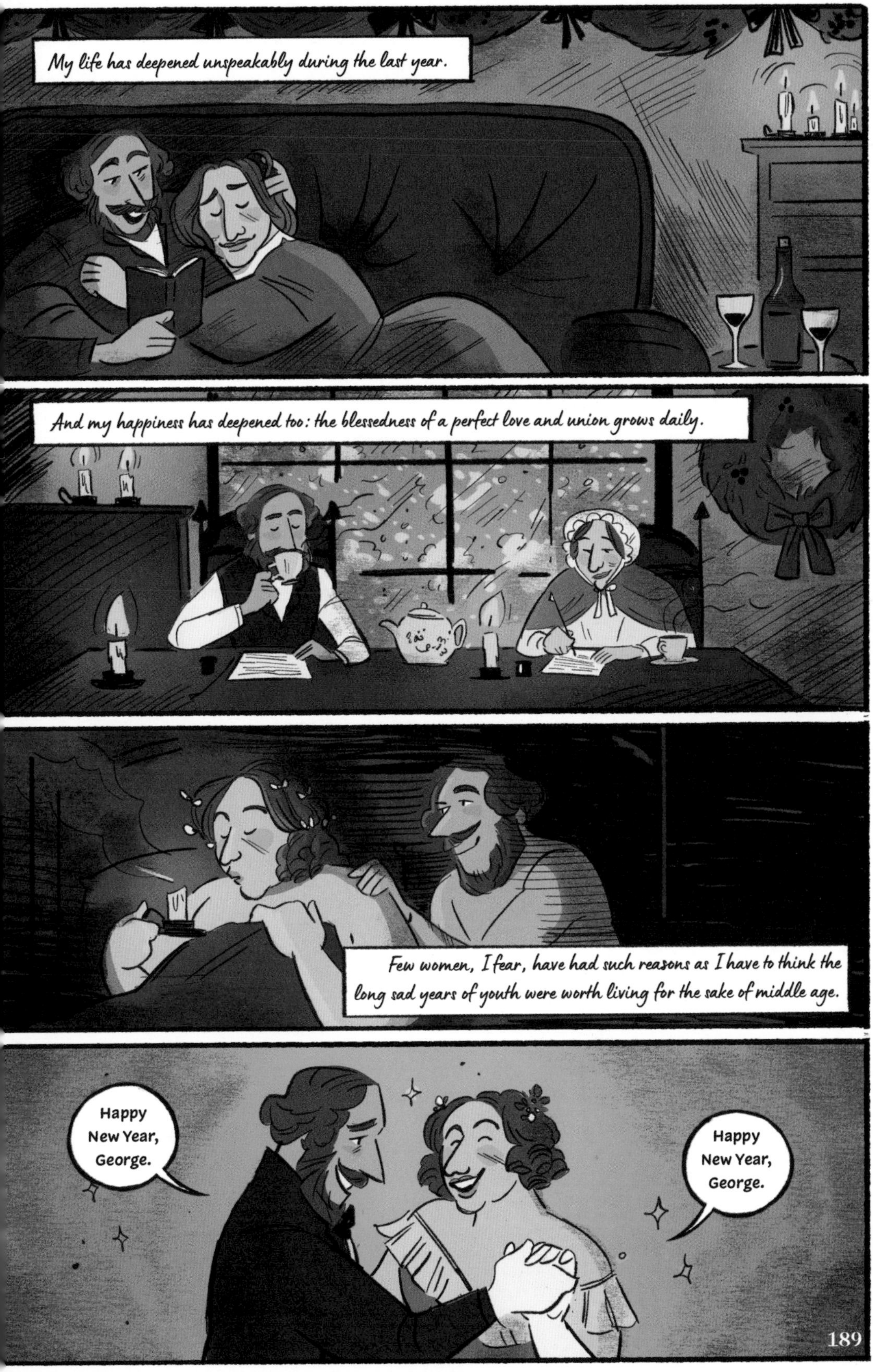
My life has deepened unspeakably during the last year.
And my happiness has deepened too: the blessedness of a perfect love and union grows daily.
Few women, I fear, have had such reasons as I have to think the long sad years of youth were worth living for the sake of middle age.
Happy New Year, George.
Happy New Year, George.

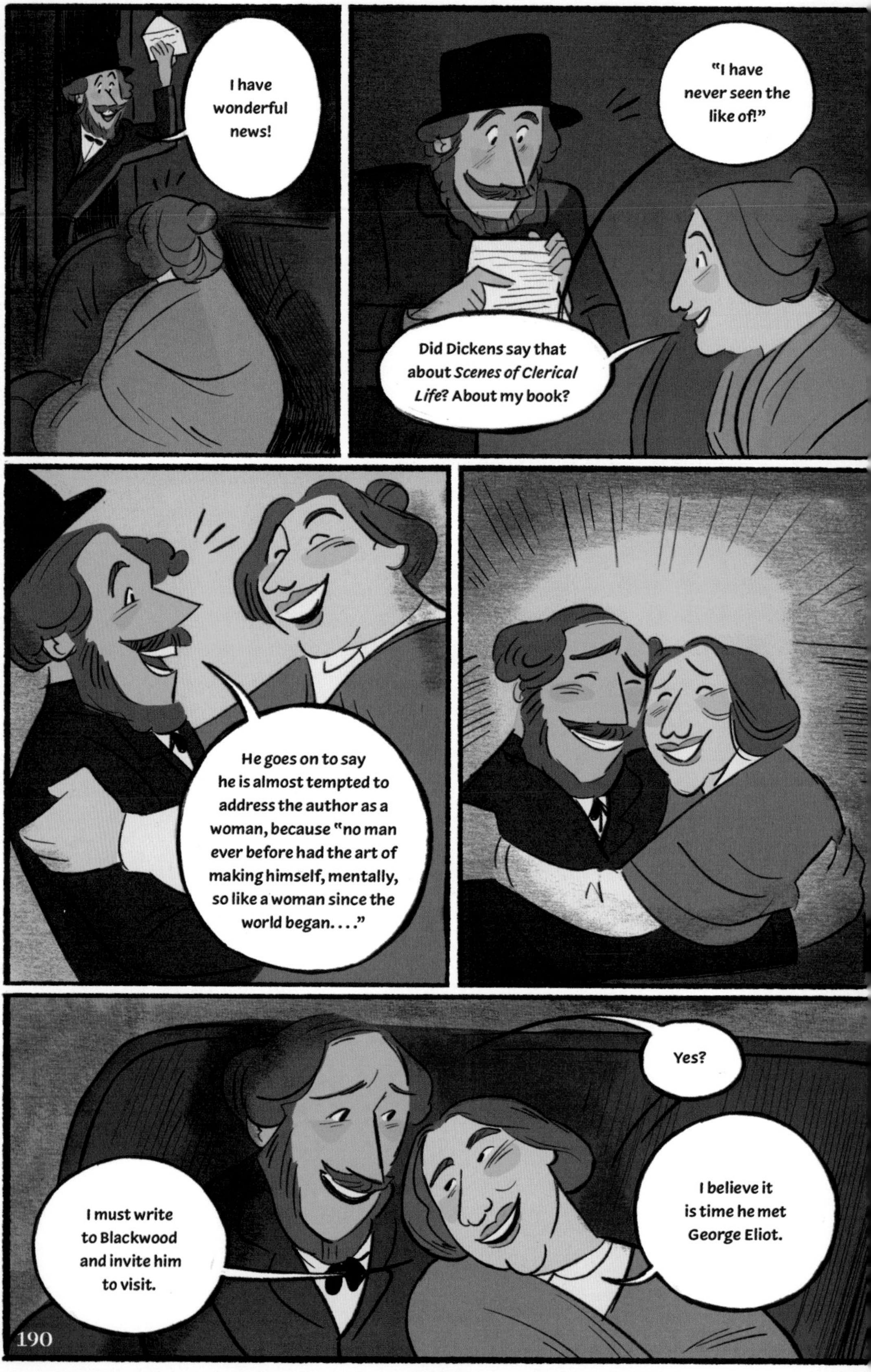
I have wonderful news!
"I have never seen the like of!"
Did Dickens say that about *Scenes of Clerical Life*? About my book?
He goes on to say he is almost tempted to address the author as a woman, because "no man ever before had the art of making himself, mentally, so like a woman since the world began. . . ."
Yes?
I must write to Blackwood and invite him to visit.
I believe it is time he met George Eliot.

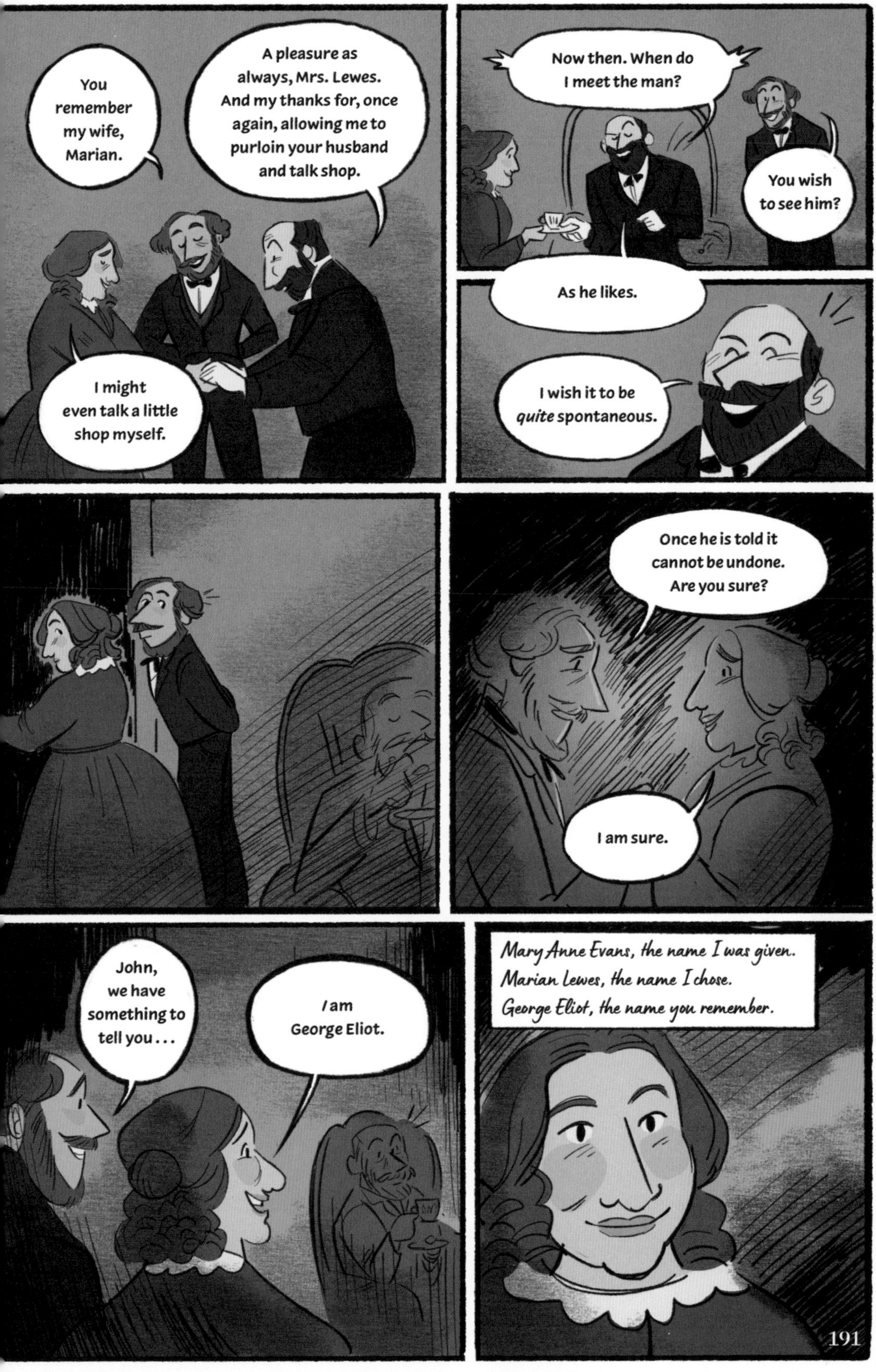

You remember my wife, Marian.
A pleasure as always, Mrs. Lewes. And my thanks for, once again, allowing me to purloin your husband and talk shop.
I might even talk a little shop myself.
Now then. When do I meet the man?
You wish to see him?
As he likes.
I wish it to be *quite* spontaneous.
Once he is told it cannot be undone. Are you sure?
I am sure.
John, we have something to tell you . . .
I am George Eliot.
Mary Anne Evans, the name I was given.
Marian Lewes, the name I chose.
George Eliot, the name you remember.

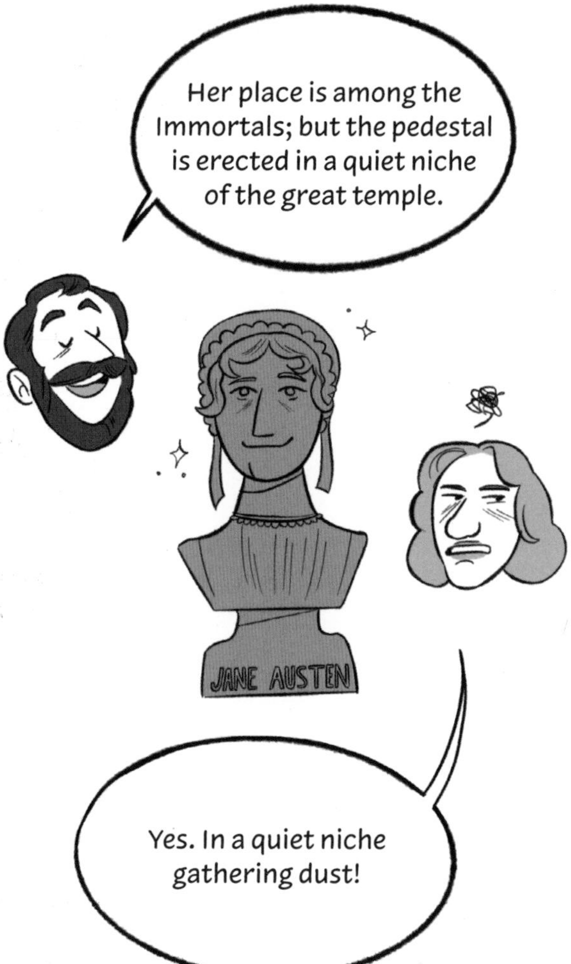
Her place is among the Immortals; but the pedestal is erected in a quiet niche of the great temple.
JANE AUSTEN
Yes. In a quiet niche gathering dust!

Though Marian and Lewes had a lot in common, they were not able to agree on Jane Austen. In an anonymous article later credited to Marian, Austen's work is described as: "Without brilliancy of any kind—without imagination, depth of thought, or wide experience."

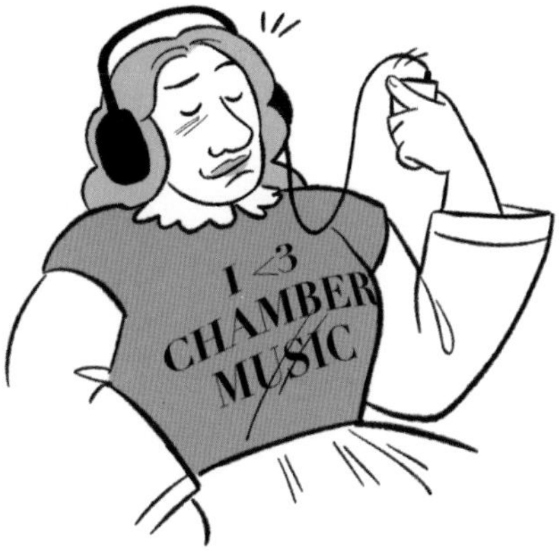
I <3
CHAMBER
MUSIC

Marian gave us the first recorded usage of the word "pop" to describe music in a letter written in 1862. Though her definition might be a little different from the current understanding of the term. . .

SELECTED WORKS:

FICTION

1858: *Scenes of Clerical Life*
1859: *The Lifted Veil*
1859: *Adam Bede*
1860: *The Mill on the Floss*
1861: *Silas Marner*
1863: *Romola*
1866: *Felix Holt, the Radical*
1872: *Middlemarch*
1876: *Daniel Deronda*
1879: *Impressions of Theophrastus Such*

TRANSLATIONS

1846: Translation of *Das Leben Jesu, kritisch bearbeitet* (The Life of Jesus, Critically Examined) by David Strauss
1854: Translation of *Das Wesen des Christentums* (The Essence of Christianity) by Ludwig Feuerbach
1856: Translation of *Ethica, ordine geometrico demonstrata* (Ethics, Demonstrated in Geometrical Order) by Benedict de Spinoza [published posthumously in 1981]

ESSAYS

1856: "Silly Novels by Lady Novelists." *Westminster Review*, October.

Anne Brontë (Acton Bell)

1820–1849

"I am satisfied that if a book is a good one, it is so whatever the sex of the author may be."

—Preface from the second edition of *The Tenant of Wildfell Hall*, 1848

Born in 1820, Anne Brontë's earliest years were shrouded in death. Her mother, Maria, died of cancer when Anne was just a year old and her two oldest sisters, Maria and Elizabeth, died of consumption when she was five. Of the three siblings that remained, Charlotte, Emily, and Branwell, it was Emily that Anne was closest to. She spent her days tramping across the moors after Emily, confiding in her, and writing tales of their fictional world Gondal. But despite her closeness with Emily, it was Charlotte who would define, and limit, Anne's legacy.

Like Charlotte, Anne had spent many years working as a governess. Her first novel, *Agnes Grey*, exposed the often shocking treatment endured by many young women in service. Anne's second novel, *The Tenant of Wildfell Hall*, was no less sensational, with its vivid depictions of abuse, adultery, and alcoholism. In many ways, it was their brother, Branwell's, own struggles that Anne was publicizing; and Charlotte wanted nothing to do with it. She claimed the subject matter a mistake and suppressed further editions of the novel after Anne's death.

When the sisters first pursued publication, they did so under the pseudonyms Currer, Ellis, and Acton Bell. The unknown authors, and the free-minded, three-dimensional women they wrote about, took the London literary scene completely by storm. Everybody wanted to, or claimed to, know the identity of the mysterious Bells.

In 1848 Anne's publisher, Thomas Newby, took advantage of the Brontë pseudonyms and claimed that *The Tenant of Wildfell Hall* was written by Currer, not Acton Bell. Charlotte's *Jane Eyre* had been published the year before to wild success, and Newby wanted to cash in on the book's popularity. This claim raised questions with Charlotte's own publisher, George Smith of Smith, Elder, & Co. When Charlotte received a letter demanding an explanation as to *why* Currer Bell saw fit to give his new novel to Newby and not to them, she knew what had to be done. The sisters would have to travel to London to reveal once and for all that Acton and Currer (and Ellis) were not one man, but three women.

Though the Brontë sisters' decision to publish under pseudonyms had been reached collectively, the decision of how and when to reveal their true identities was not. For Emily, it was out of the question entirely; anonymity had been the one reason she'd agreed to publication in the first place. For Charlotte, publicly claiming Currer Bell for herself was the only way to correct their reputations and avoid speculation about the authorship of their novels. But for Anne, in danger of being erased by her older sisters' success, this was a moment of action—a chance to defend the voice she had risked so much to claim.

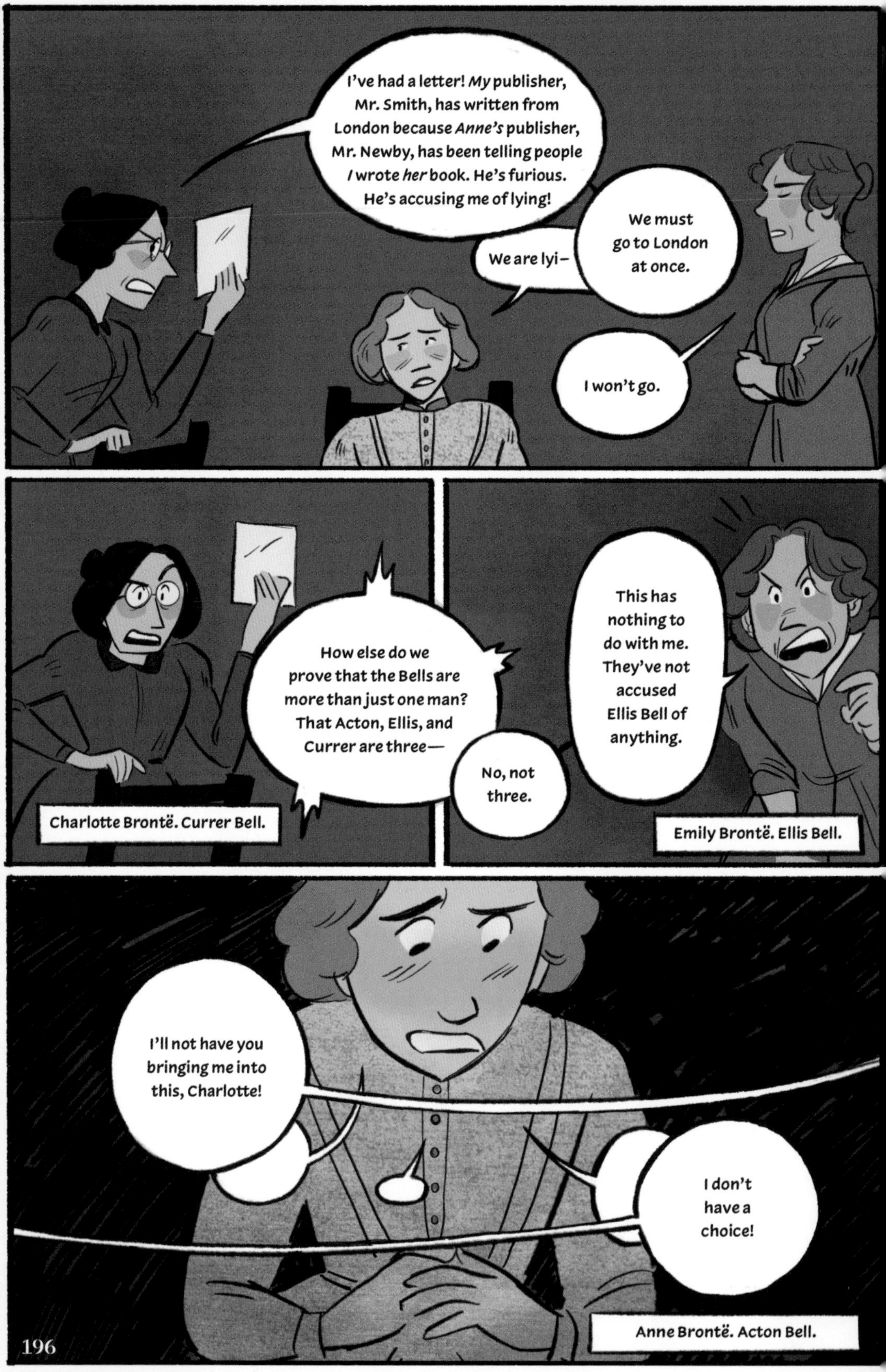
I've had a letter! *My* publisher, Mr. Smith, has written from London because *Anne's* publisher, Mr. Newby, has been telling people *I* wrote *her* book. He's furious. He's accusing me of lying!
We are lyi–
We must go to London at once.
I won't go.
Charlotte Brontë. Currer Bell.
How else do we prove that the Bells are more than just one man? That Acton, Ellis, and Currer are three—
No, not three.
This has nothing to do with me. They've not accused Ellis Bell of anything.
Emily Brontë. Ellis Bell.
I'll not have you bringing me into this, Charlotte!
I don't have a choice!
Anne Brontë. Acton Bell.

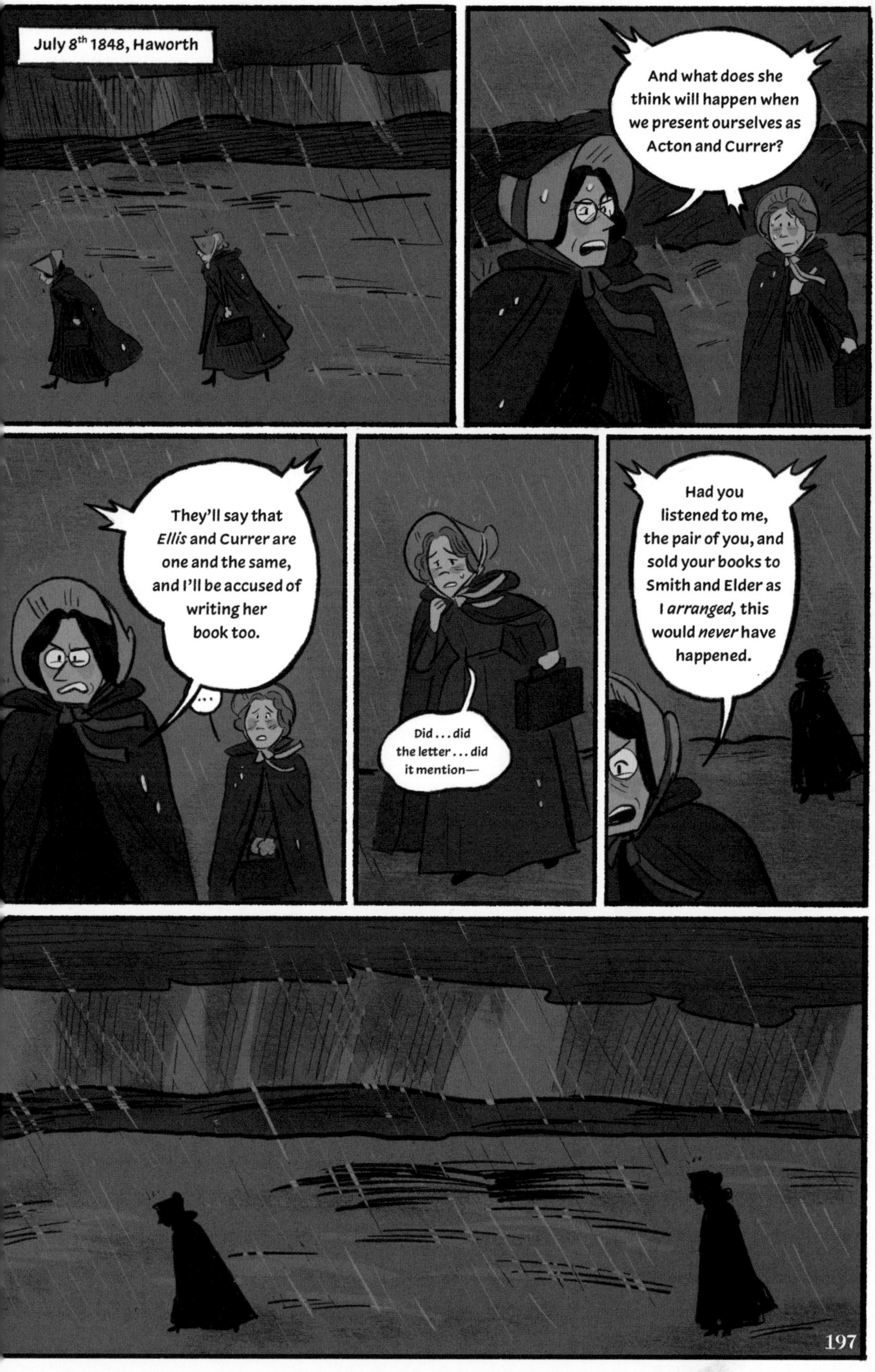
July 8th 1848, Haworth
And what does she think will happen when we present ourselves as Acton and Currer?
They'll say that *Ellis* and Currer are one and the same, and I'll be accused of writing her book too.
...
Did . . . did the letter . . . did it mention—
Had you listened to me, the pair of you, and sold your books to Smith and Elder as I *arranged*, this would *never* have happened.

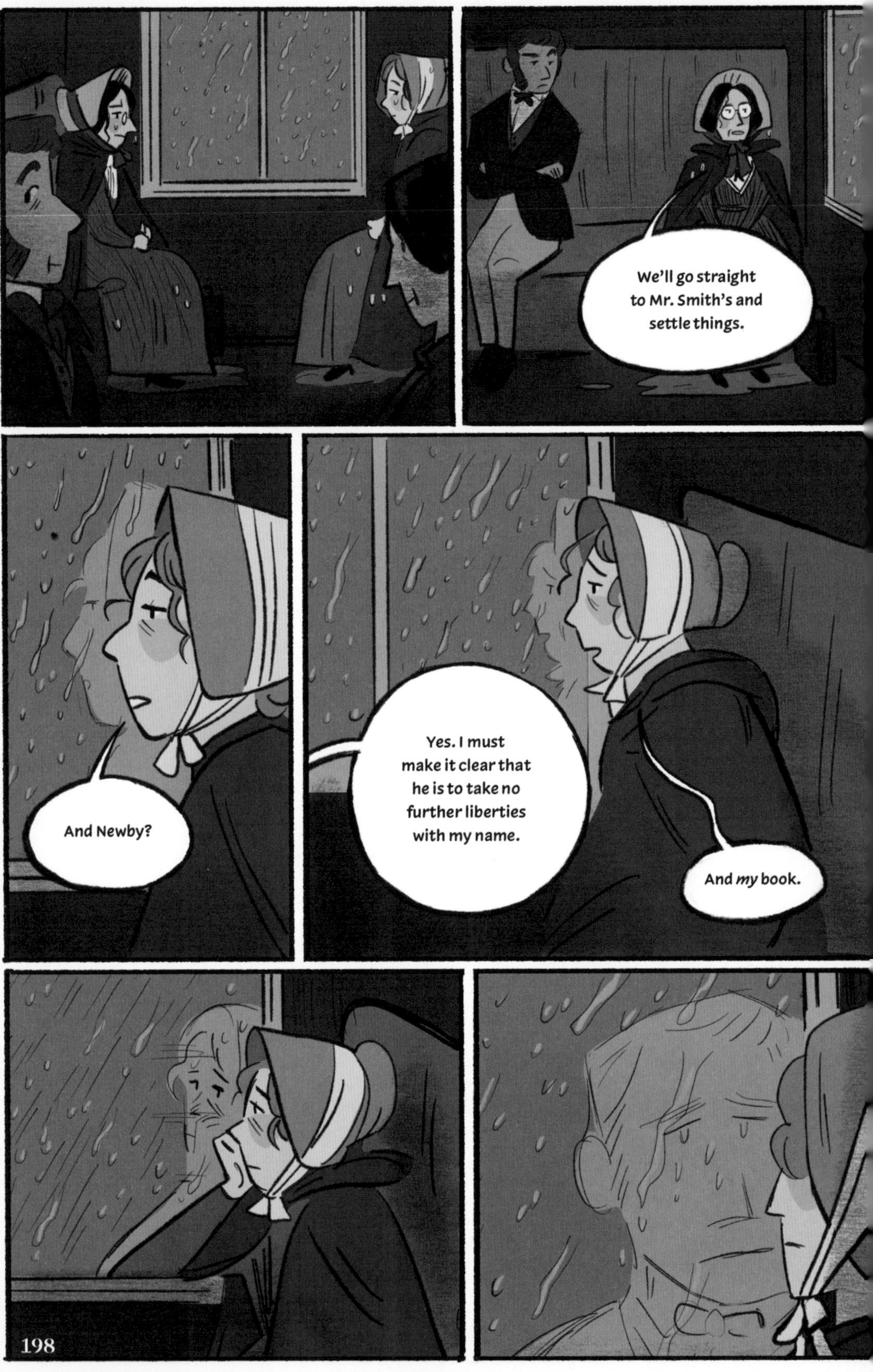
We'll go straight to Mr. Smith's and settle things.
And Newby?
Yes. I must make it clear that he is to take no further liberties with my name.
And *my* book.

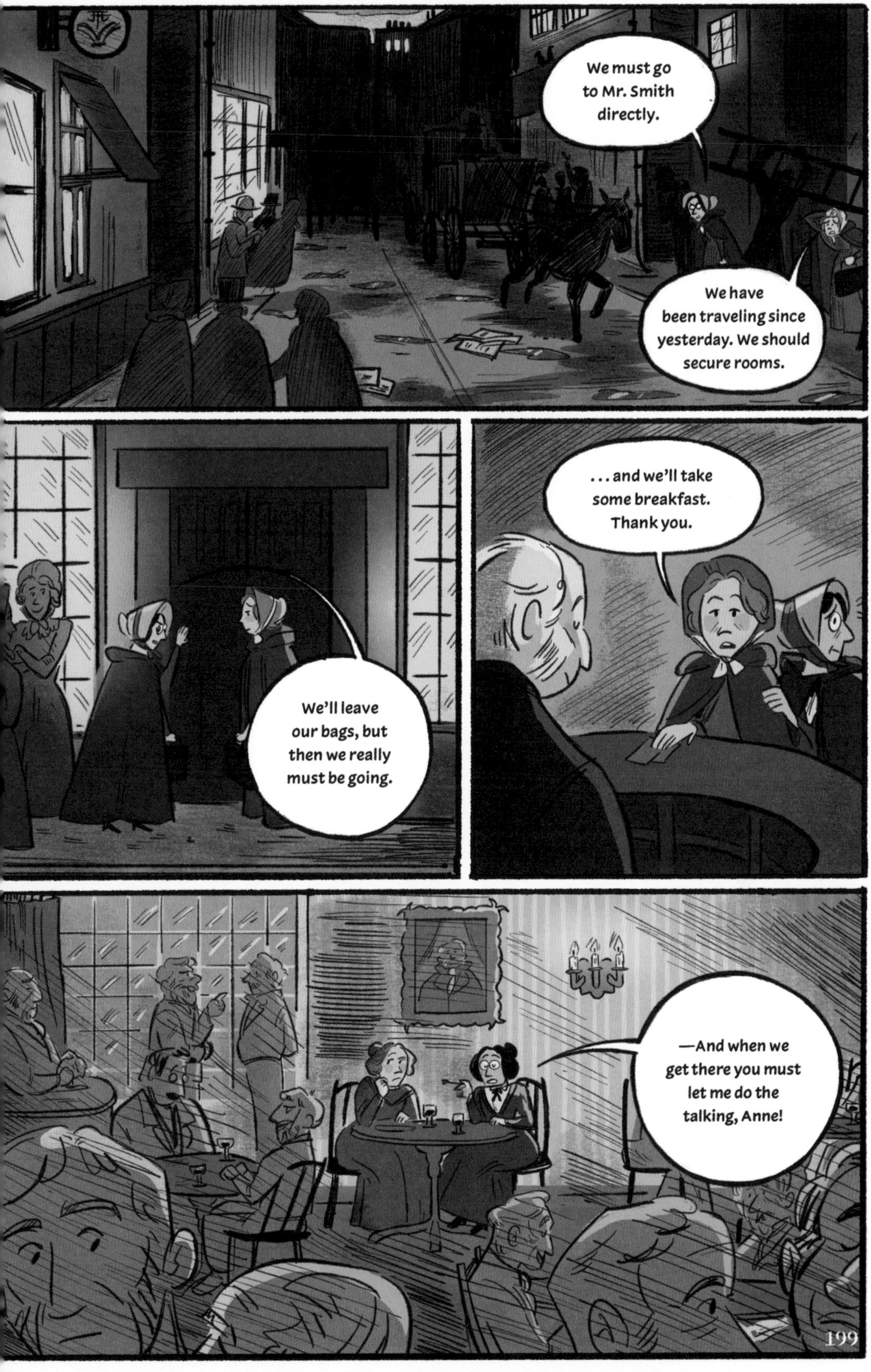
We must go to Mr. Smith directly.
We have been traveling since yesterday. We should secure rooms.
We'll leave our bags, but then we really must be going.
. . . and we'll take some breakfast. Thank you.
—And when we get there you must let me do the talking, Anne!

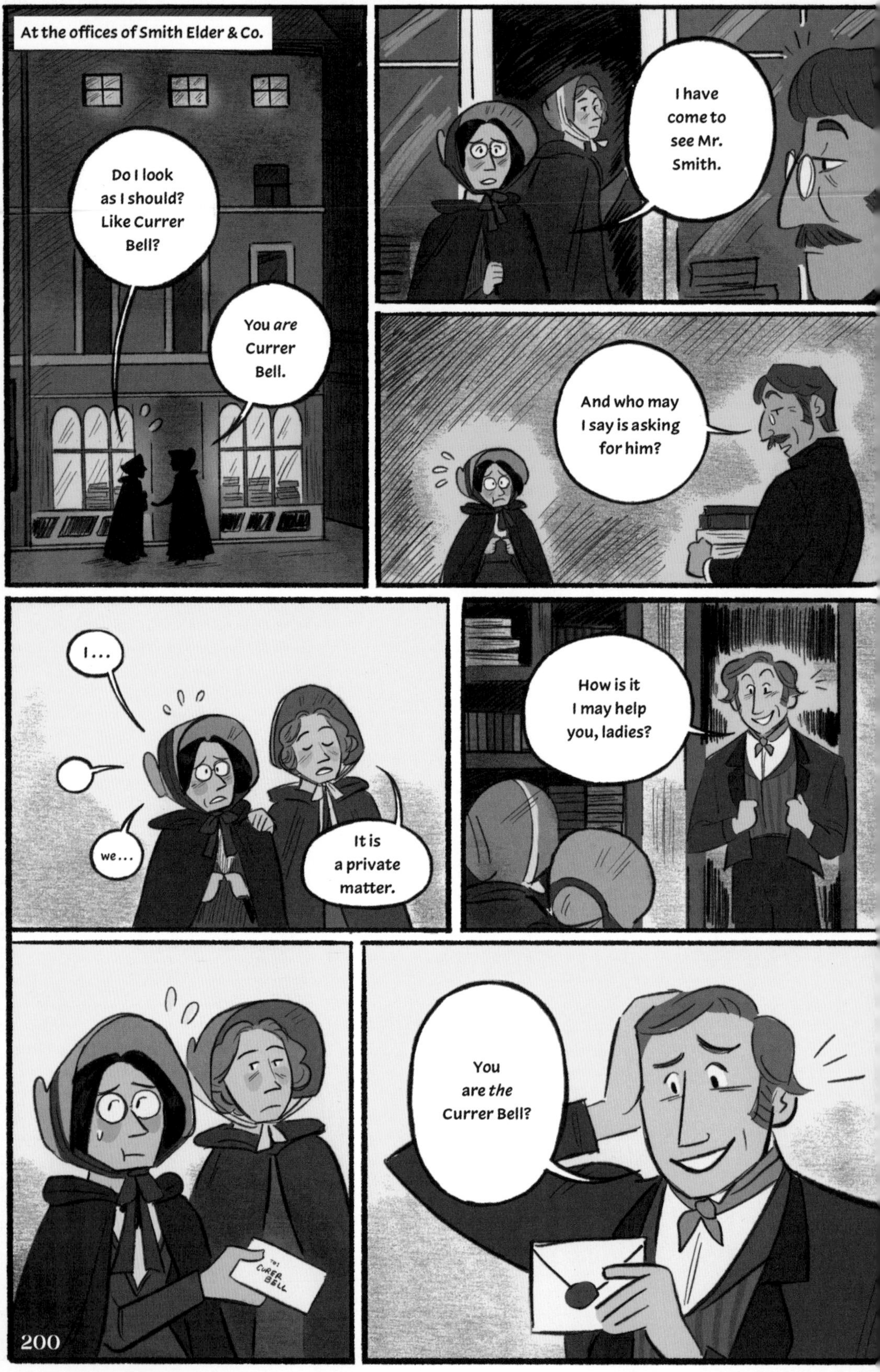
At the offices of Smith Elder & Co.
Do I look as I should? Like Currer Bell?
You *are* Currer Bell.
I have come to see Mr. Smith.
And who may I say is asking for him?
I...
we...
It is a private matter.
How is it I may help you, ladies?
You are *the* Currer Bell?

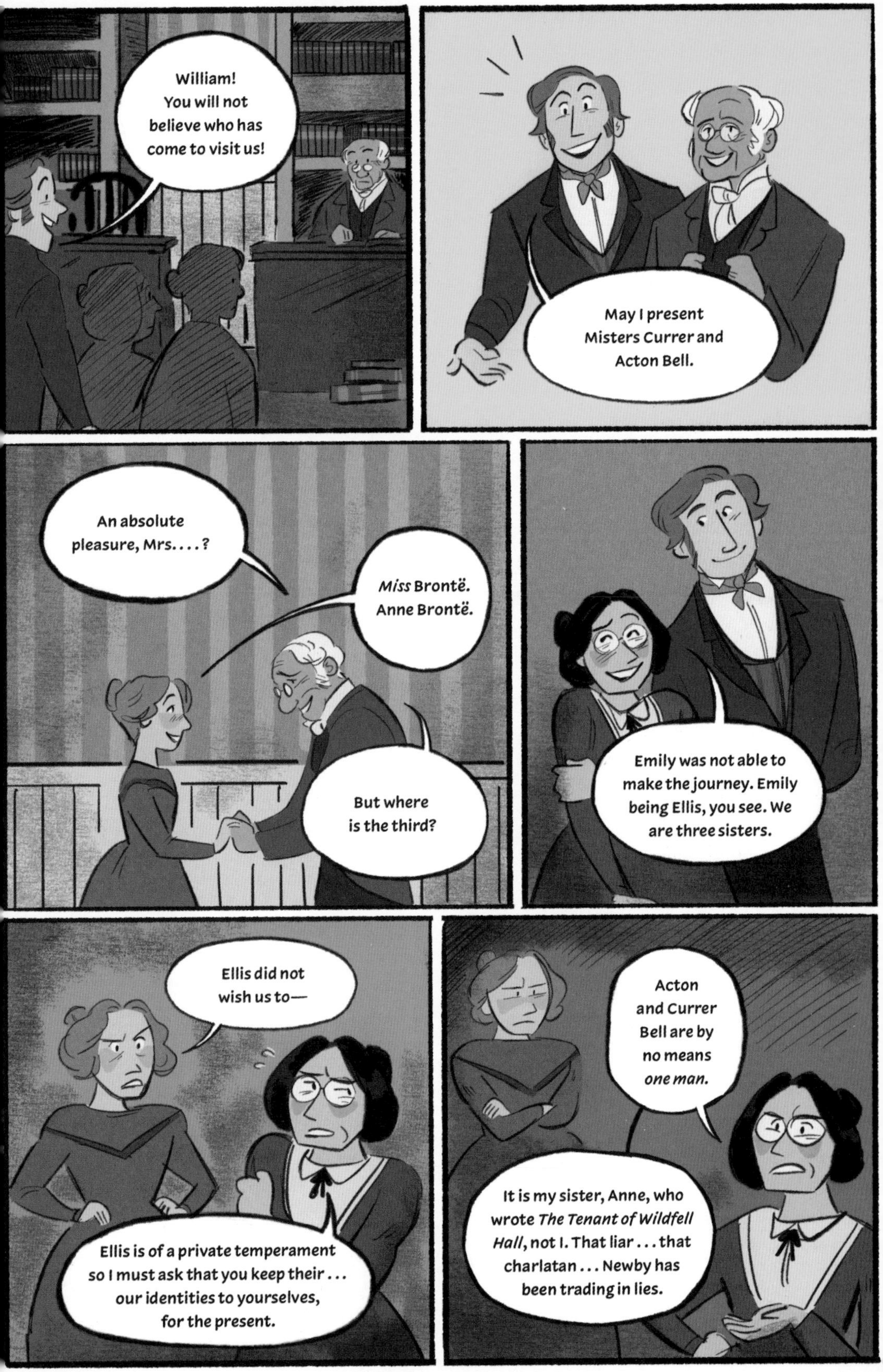
William! You will not believe who has come to visit us!
May I present Misters Currer and Acton Bell.
An absolute pleasure, Mrs. . . . ?
Miss Brontë. Anne Brontë.
But where is the third?
Emily was not able to make the journey. Emily being Ellis, you see. We are three sisters.
Ellis did not wish us to—
Ellis is of a private temperament so I must ask that you keep their . . . our identities to yourselves, for the present.
Acton and Currer Bell are by no means *one man.*
It is my sister, Anne, who wrote *The Tenant of Wildfell Hall*, not I. That liar . . . that charlatan . . . Newby has been trading in lies.

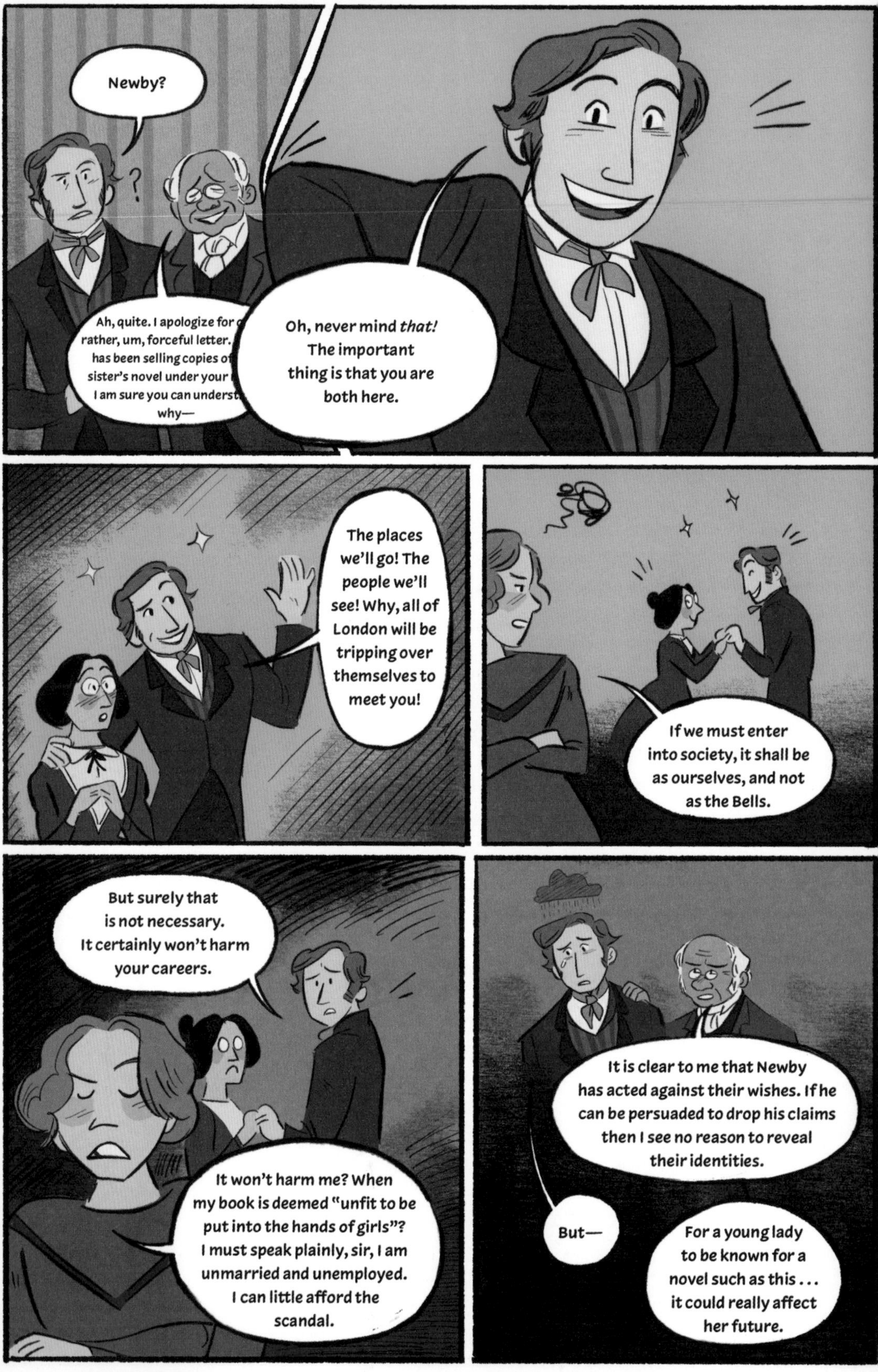

Newby?
Ah, quite. I apologize for rather, um, forceful letter. has been selling copies of sister's novel under your I am sure you can why—
Oh, never mind *that!* The important thing is that you are both here.
The places we'll go! The people we'll see! Why, all of London will be tripping over themselves to meet you!
If we must enter into society, it shall be as ourselves, and not as the Bells.
But surely that is not necessary. It certainly won't harm your careers.
It won't harm me? When my book is deemed "unfit to be put into the hands of girls"? I must speak plainly, sir, I am unmarried and unemployed. I can little afford the scandal.
It is clear to me that Newby has acted against their wishes. If he can be persuaded to drop his claims then I see no reason to reveal their identities.
But—
For a young lady to be known for a novel such as this . . . it could really affect her future.

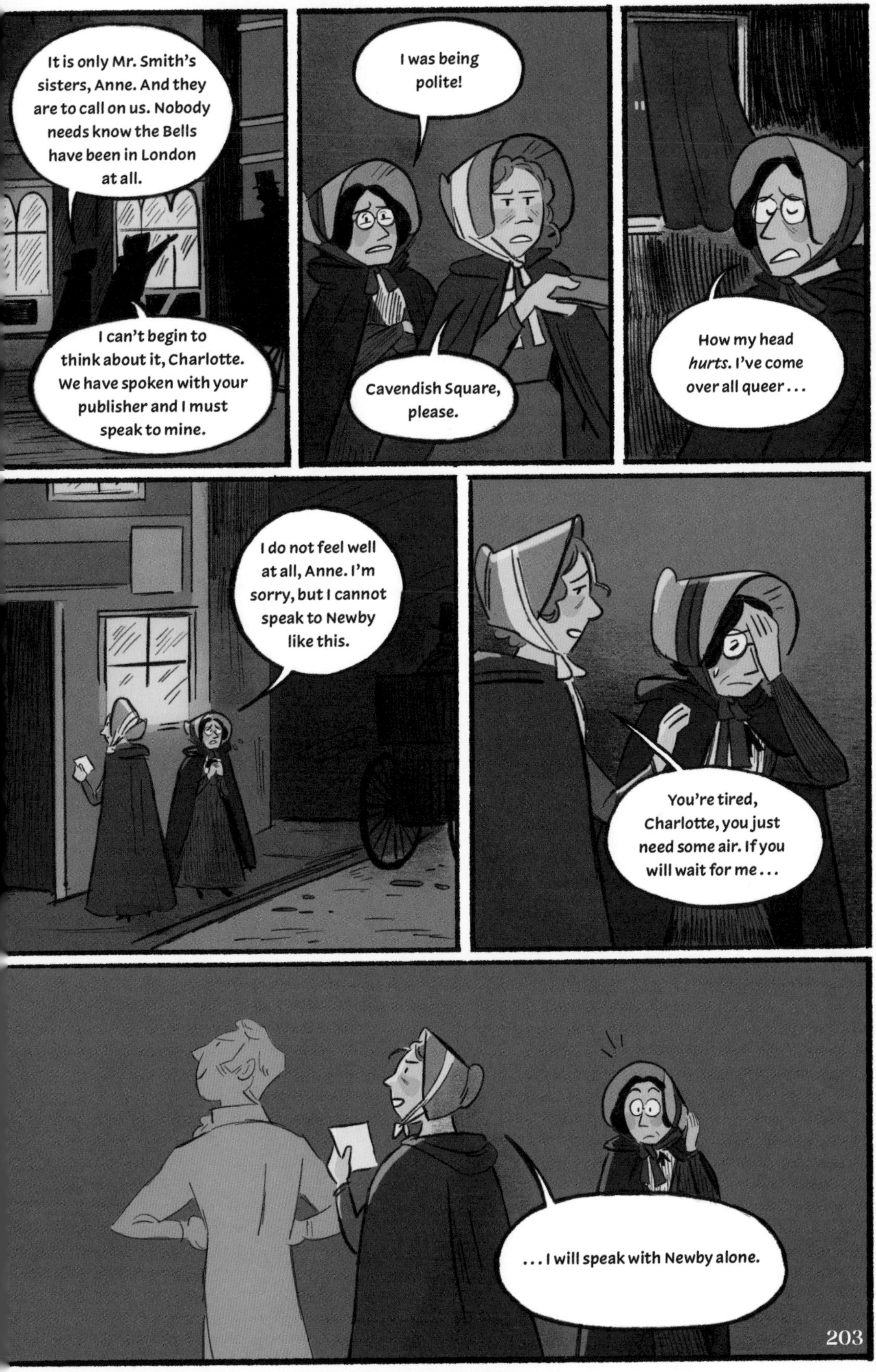
It is only Mr. Smith's sisters, Anne. And they are to call on us. Nobody needs know the Bells have been in London at all.
I can't begin to think about it, Charlotte. We have spoken with your publisher and I must speak to mine.
I was being polite!
Cavendish Square, please.
How my head *hurts*. I've come over all queer . . .
I do not feel well at all, Anne. I'm sorry, but I cannot speak to Newby like this.
You're tired, Charlotte, you just need some air. If you will wait for me . . .
. . . I will speak with Newby alone.

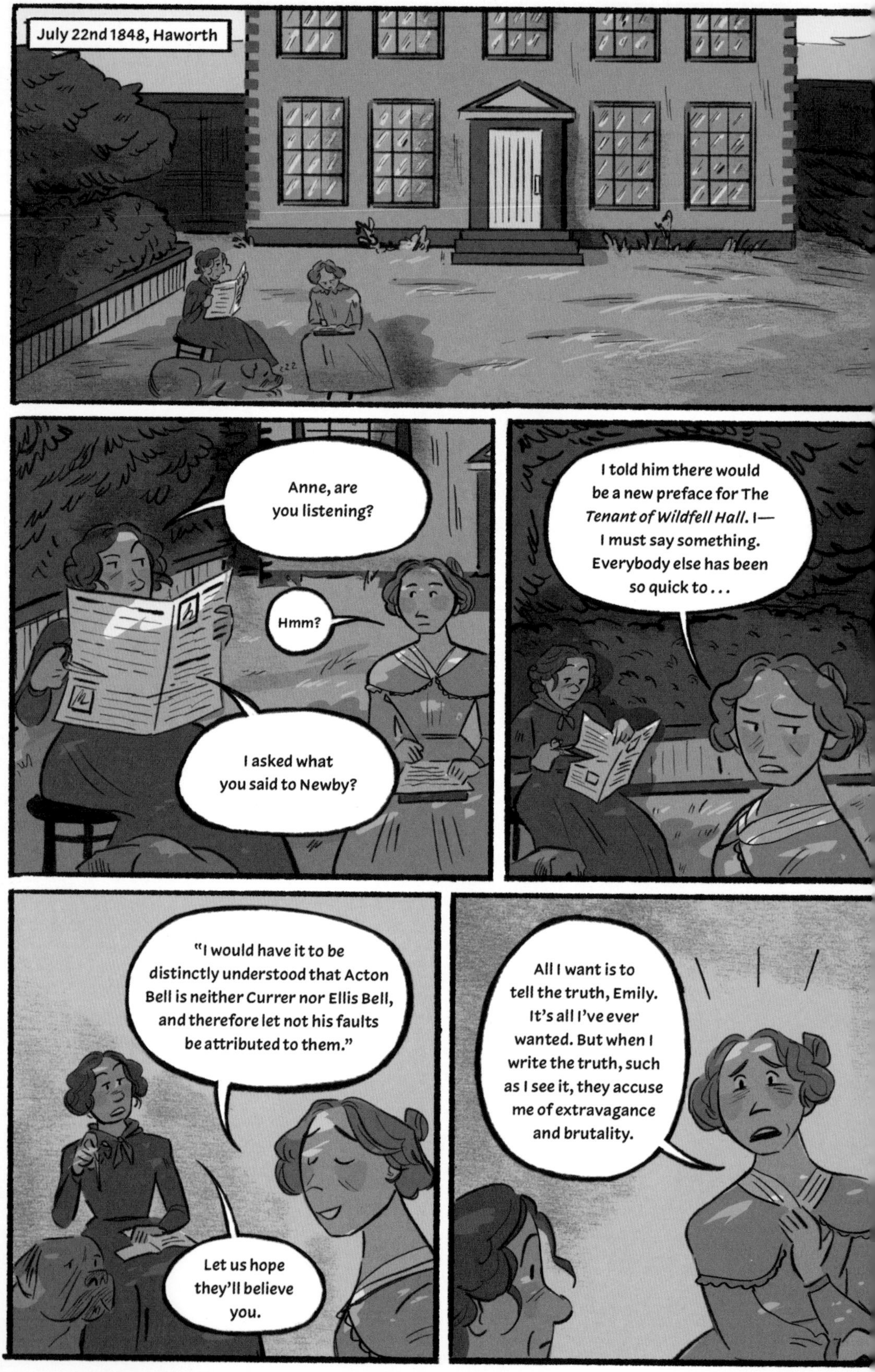
July 22nd 1848, Haworth
Anne, are you listening?
Hmm?
I asked what you said to Newby?
I told him there would be a new preface for The *Tenant of Wildfell Hall*. I— I must say something. Everybody else has been so quick to . . .
"I would have it to be distinctly understood that Acton Bell is neither Currer nor Ellis Bell, and therefore let not his faults be attributed to them."
Let us hope they'll believe you.
All I want is to tell the truth, Emily. It's all I've ever wanted. But when I write the truth, such as I see it, they accuse me of extravagance and brutality.

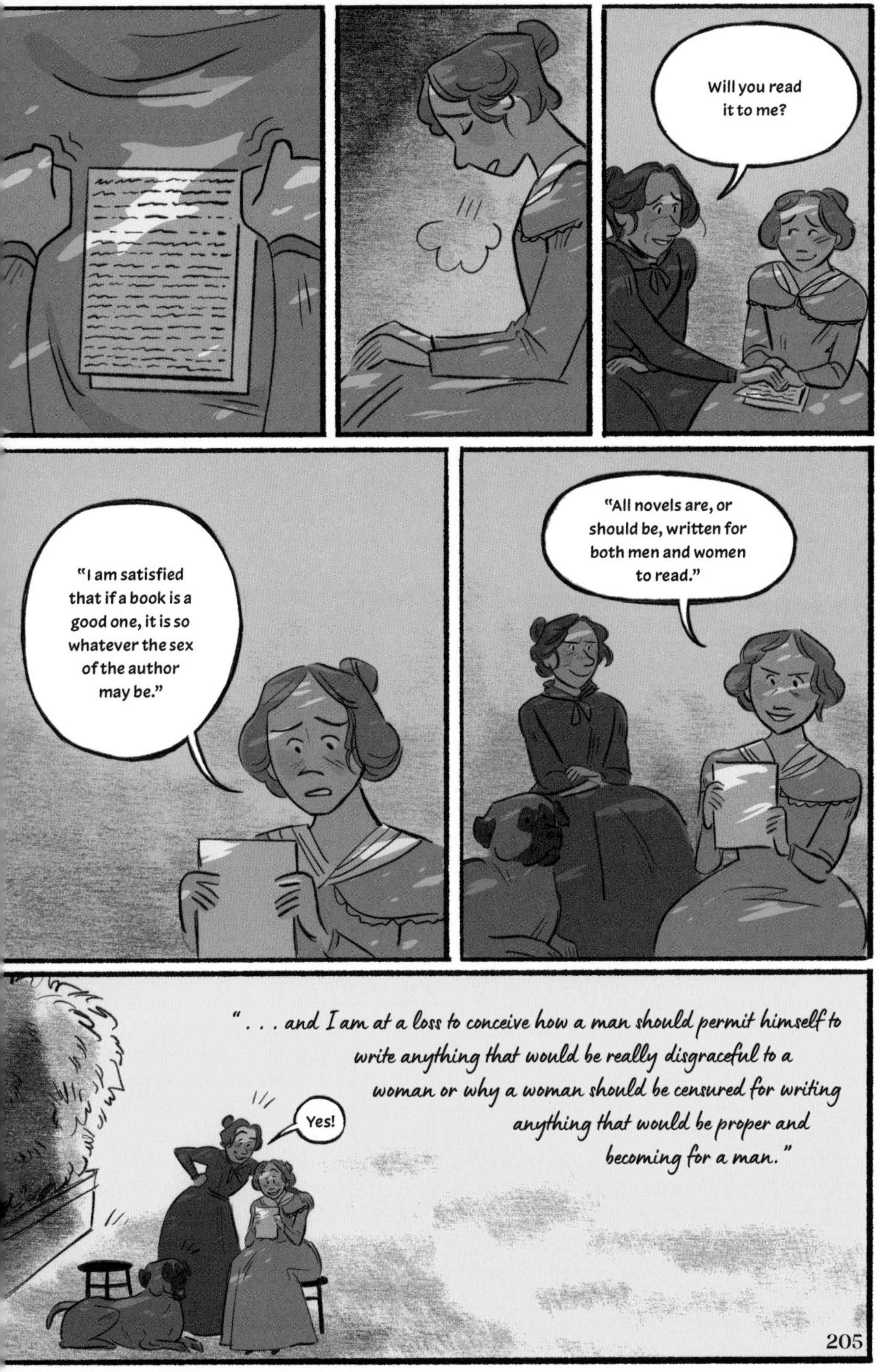
Will you read it to me?
"I am satisfied that if a book is a good one, it is so whatever the sex of the author may be."
"All novels are, or should be, written for both men and women to read."
". . . and I am at a loss to conceive how a man should permit himself to write anything that would be really disgraceful to a woman or why a woman should be censured for writing anything that would be proper and becoming for a man."
Yes!

Despite being a runaway success, *The Tenant of Wildfell Hall* was not reprinted in Great Britain, at Charlotte's request, for six years. When it was finally re-released, it was heavily edited by the publisher Thomas Hodgson, with some chapters disappearing almost entirely.

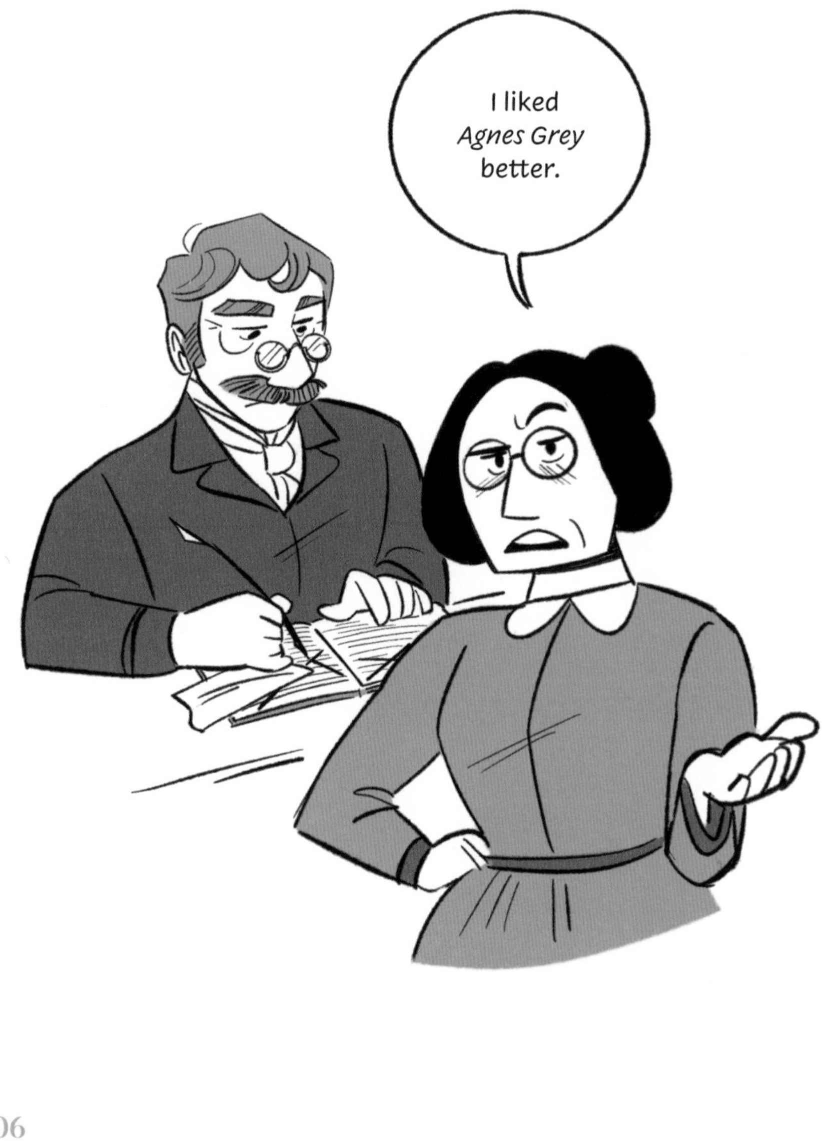
I liked *Agnes Grey* better.

Anne Brontë is a woman of few remaining words; only five of her letters have survived. Many speculate that in life, too, she was the quietest of the Brontë siblings and possibly suffered from a stutter. In a letter to family friend Ellen Nussey, Anne apologized for her shyness, saying: "You must know there is a lamentable deficiency in my organ of language which makes me almost as bad a hand at writing as talking unless I have something particular to say."

SELECTED WORKS:

POETRY

1846: *Poems by Currer, Acton, and Ellis Bell*

NOVELS

1847: *Agnes Grey*
1848: *The Tenant of Wildfell Hall*

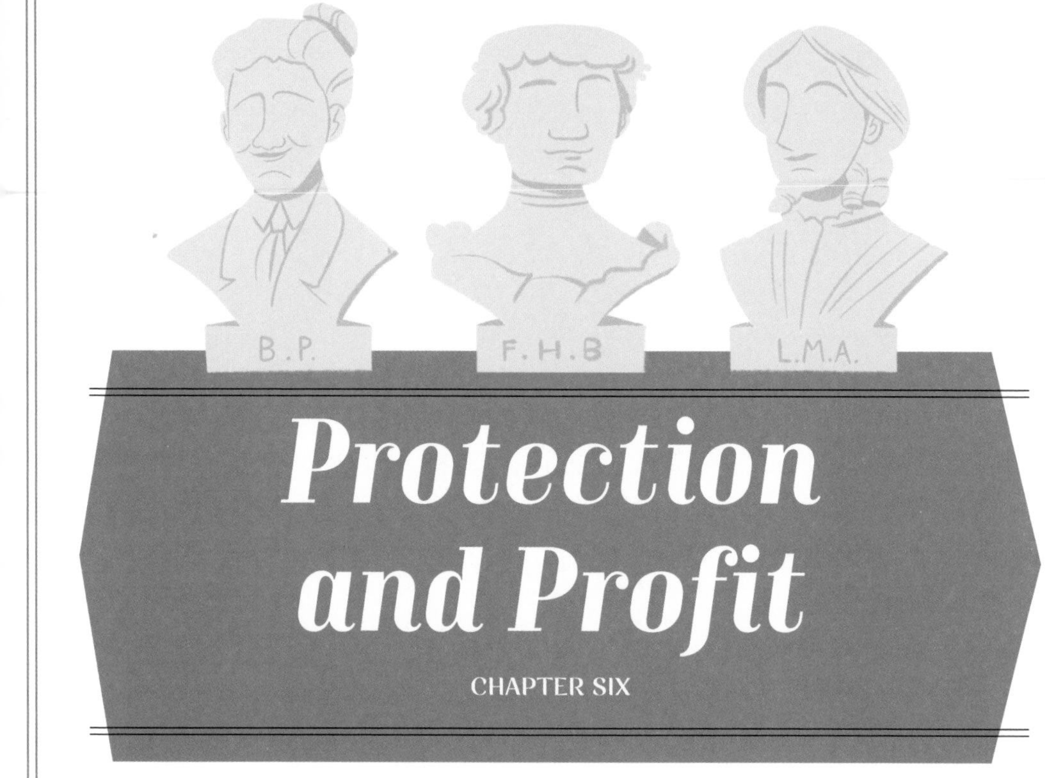
B.P.
F.H.B
L.M.A.

Protection and Profit

CHAPTER SIX

Though the names of Beatrix Potter, Louisa May Alcott, and Frances Hodgson Burnett might bring to mind wholesome, nurturing stories for children, the legacy of these authors is much greater. By recognizing their brand, tapping into new markets, and challenging unfair copyright laws, all three authors changed the landscape of publishing forever.

But they didn't set out to change the world—they only sought financial security and the freedom it affords. For each of these authors, writing was an opportunity to change their lives and the lives of those around them. For Potter, independent wealth was the only way out of London and an oppressive family home; for Burnett, it was giving her own children a life she had never known; and for Alcott, that meant supporting an extended family.

For Beatrix Potter, success brought its own set of problems, with a market glutted with poor reproductions of her own creations. Like Burnett, her only recourse was to forge a new legal path to protecting her copyright. When she patented an official Peter Rabbit doll in 1903, the first patent of its kind, Potter defended her ability to earn, and she invested the profits back into her books.

In the case of Frances Hodgson Burnett, it was seeing people profit from her hard work time and time again due to poor legal precedent that drove her to take matters into her own hands. Just because something *had* happened didn't mean it *should*, and in taking legal action against one man in 1888, Burnett won the right to protect her work from unauthorized theatrical adaptation, a right that authors had been fighting for for years.

All business is a gamble; and Louisa May Alcott knew when to play and when to hold her cards. *Little Women* was the book she never wanted to write, and it seemed unlikely to succeed, but the risk paid off tenfold. Though she was offered a fair one-time payment for her efforts by her publisher in 1868, she knew that gambling on the book's success by retaining ownership of the copyright was a choice between short-term comfort and long-term security.

All three women were driven to protect their rights and their work—and to ensure their own financial security and legacy in the process. *Century Illustrated Magazine*, with authors from around the world (including Louisa May Alcott), published an open letter in 1886 by Frances Hodgson Burnett that argued that "a right to the control and the protection of the products of one's brain . . . cannot be in question."

Beatrix Potter

1866–1943

"If it were done at all it *ought* to be done by me."

—Beatrix Potter in a letter to Norman Warne, October 23, 1904

For almost thirty years, Beatrix Potter delighted young readers with stories about her animal friends, including Peter Rabbit, Tom Kitten, Jemima Puddle-Duck, and Squirrel Nutkin. Potter was a staunch believer in keeping her books small enough for children's hands and cheap enough for their pockets. More than one hundred years later, the twenty-three original tales are still printed in much the same size and format.

Born on the 28th of July 1866 to Rupert and Helen Potter, Beatrix's childhood was a lonely one. Her younger brother, Walter Bertram, was sent to school, while she was educated at home by a series of governesses, and though the family lived in an affluent borough of London, they were rarely seen in society. The Potter fortune came from trade; calico printers on her father's side and cotton merchants and ship builders on her mother's. Self-conscious of their roots, the Potters kept mostly to themselves.

They were also an artistic family, and both children were encouraged to paint. Long family holidays to Scotland, and later the Lake District, proved a stark contrast to Potter's restrictive life in London, allowing her the freedom to explore and paint as she liked. A keen observer of the natural world, Potter also kept a variety of pets throughout her life, including rabbits, mice, lizards, and even a bat. She drew endless inspiration and comfort from her animal companions, and in them found hope for future independence.

After first tasting commercial success by selling paintings of rabbits for use on Christmas cards in 1890, Potter began writing picture books. Her first, *The Tale of Peter Rabbit*, was inspired by her earlier illustrated letter written in 1893 to a young friend who was recovering from an illness. Potter approached several publishers with the story, including Warne & Co, but after receiving multiple rejections for *Peter Rabbit*, she made the decision to print 250 copies of the book herself. By the time she received these books, however, Warne & Co. had changed their mind. While the formalities of this agreement were finalized, the 250 original copies distributed to friends and family proved a runaway success.

Finally, the chance to live for and by herself was in reach. But success also meant competition and copycats. In America, where it was harder for British authors to protect and secure their rights, bootleg copies of *Peter Rabbit* sold by the thousands. Closer to home, in department stores and toy stores all over London, stuffed animals bearing the name and characteristics of her characters began to appear on shelves. Potter took these matters into her own hands and set out to protect what would become a globally recognized brand.

Potter's stories were born from a desire to comfort and enrich the lives of children around the world, and their success meant financial independence and the freedom she'd always hoped for. But publishing these books was just the start of her journey. Protecting them would be where the real work began.

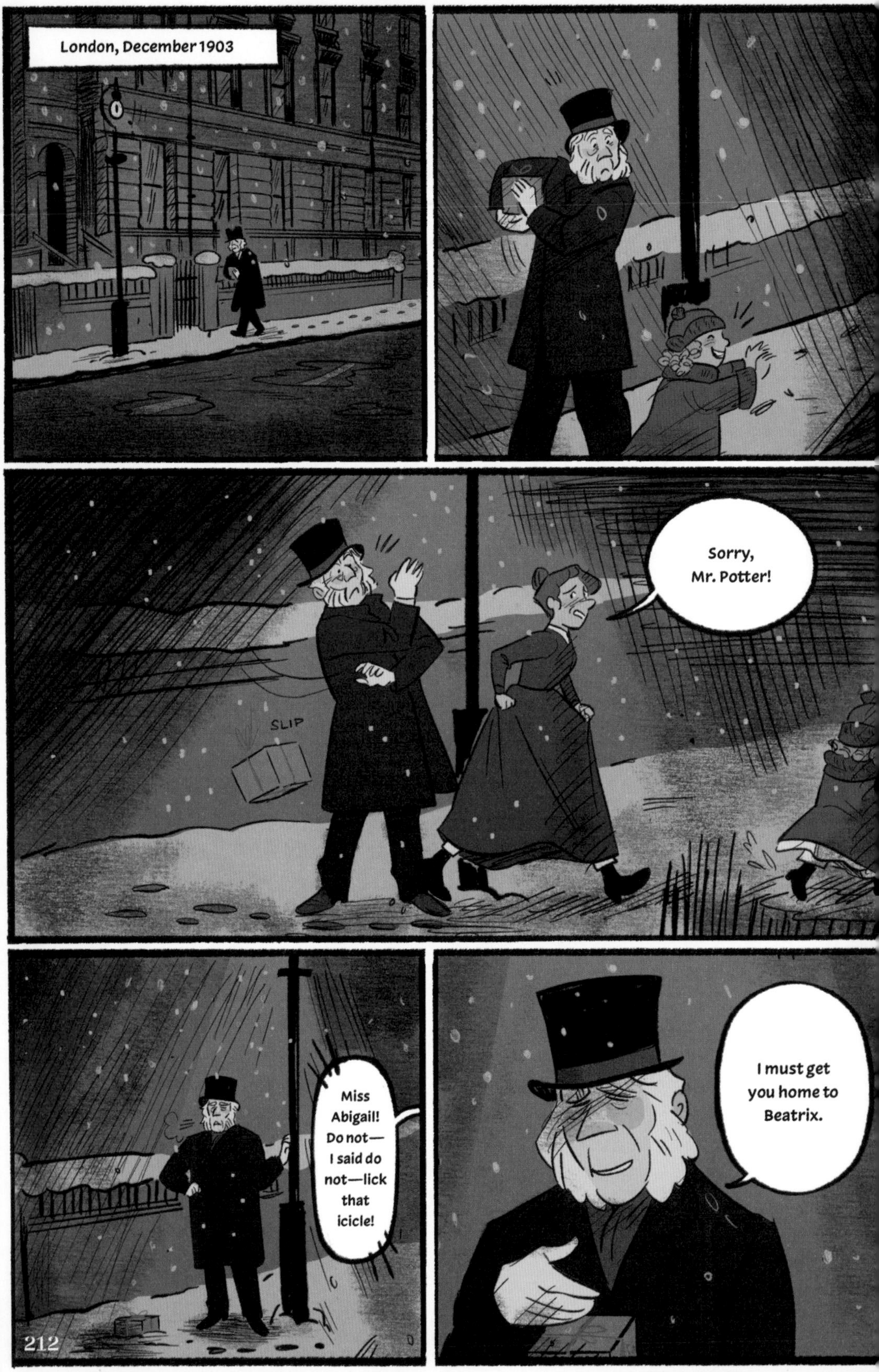
London, December 1903
SLIP
Sorry, Mr. Potter!
Miss Abigail! Do not— I said do not—lick that icicle!
I must get you home to Beatrix.

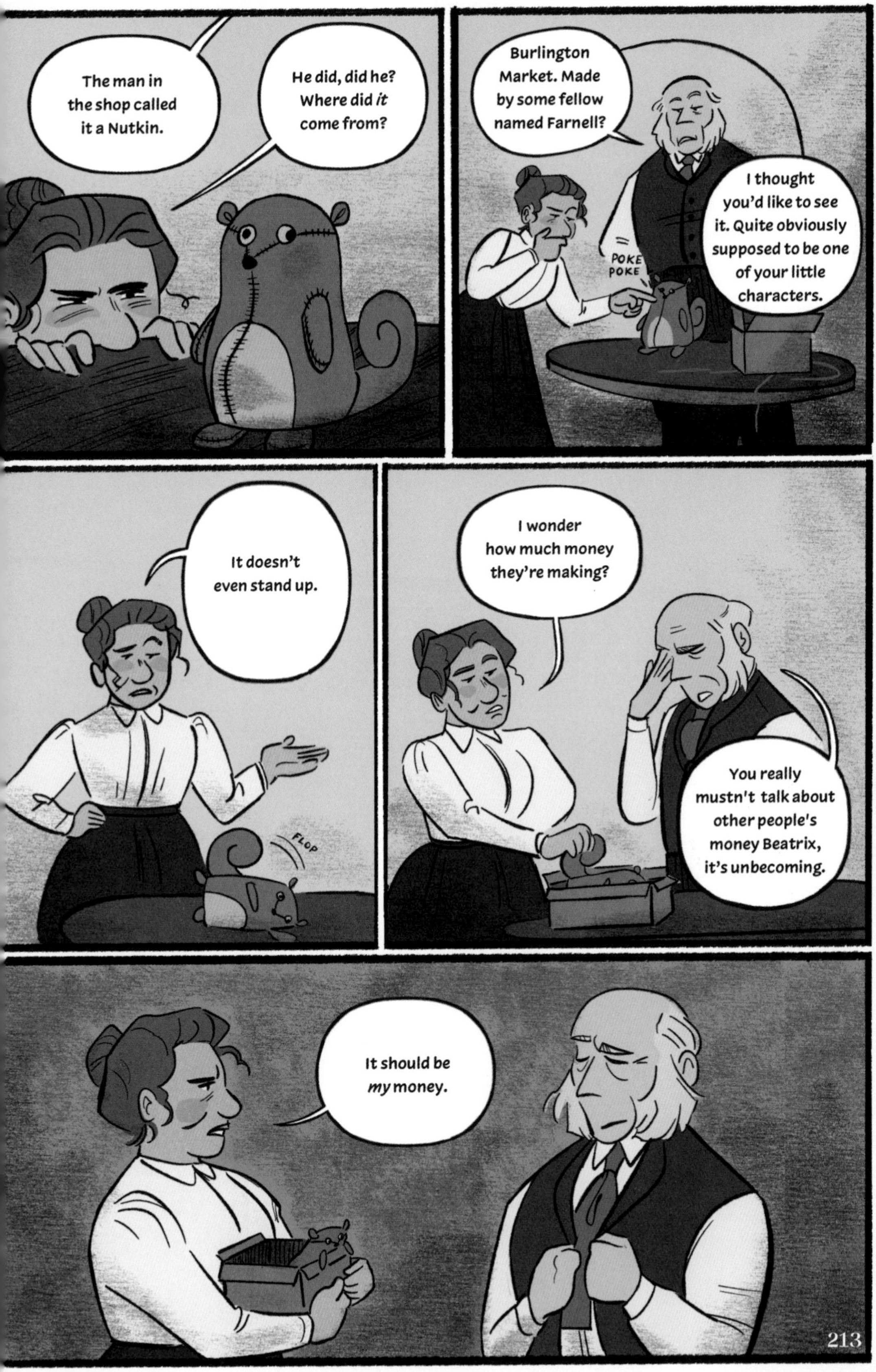
The man in the shop called it a Nutkin.
He did, did he? Where did *it* come from?
Burlington Market. Made by some fellow named Farnell?
POKE POKE
I thought you'd like to see it. Quite obviously supposed to be one of your little characters.
It doesn't even stand up.
FLOP
I wonder how much money they're making?
You really mustn't talk about other people's money Beatrix, it's unbecoming.
It should be *my* money.

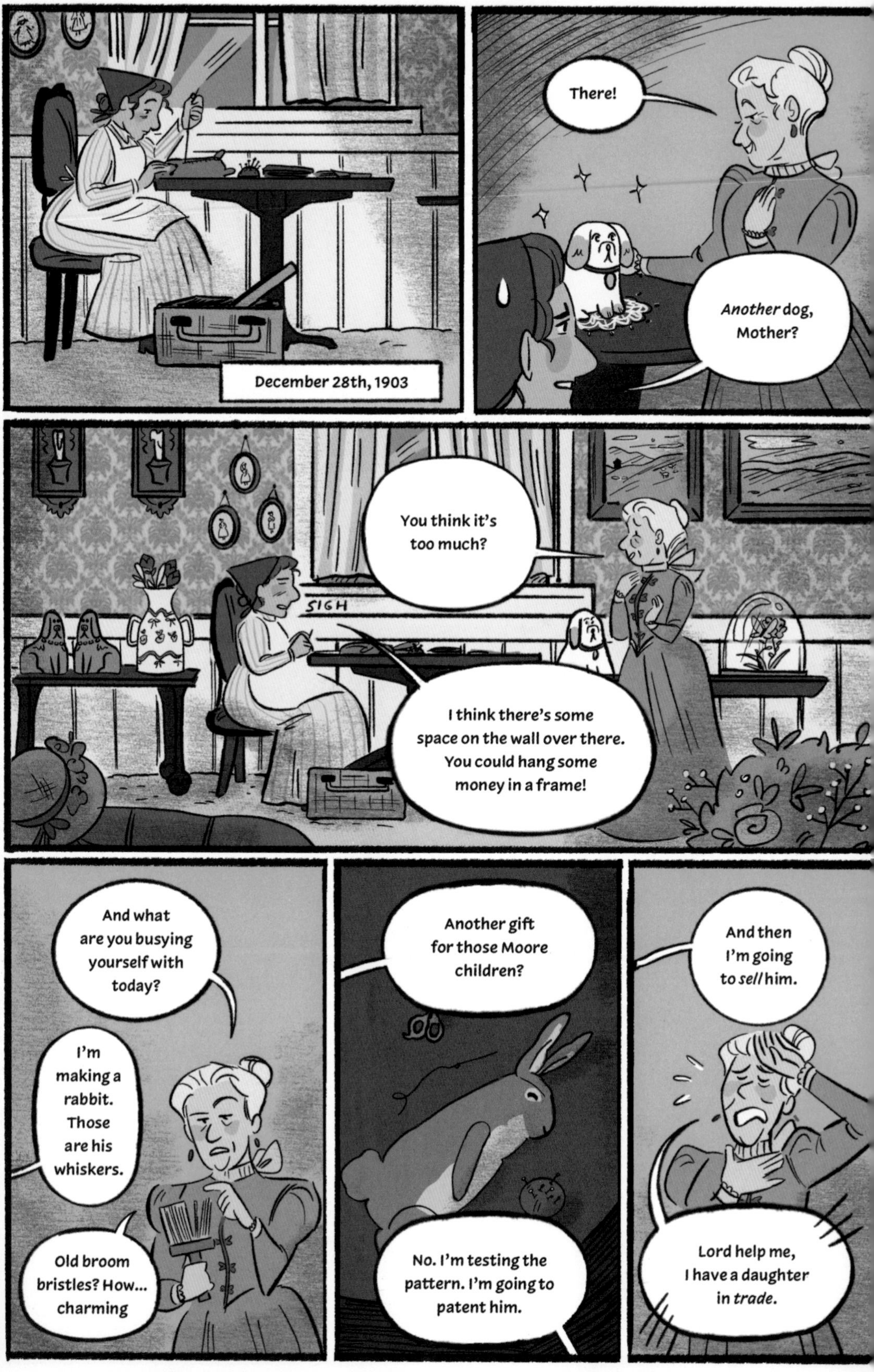
December 28th, 1903
There!
Another dog, Mother?
You think it's too much?
SIGH
I think there's some space on the wall over there. You could hang some money in a frame!
And what are you busying yourself with today?
I'm making a rabbit. Those are his whiskers.
Old broom bristles? How... charming
Another gift for those Moore children?
No. I'm testing the pattern. I'm going to patent him.
And then I'm going to *sell* him.
Lord help me, I have a daughter in *trade*.

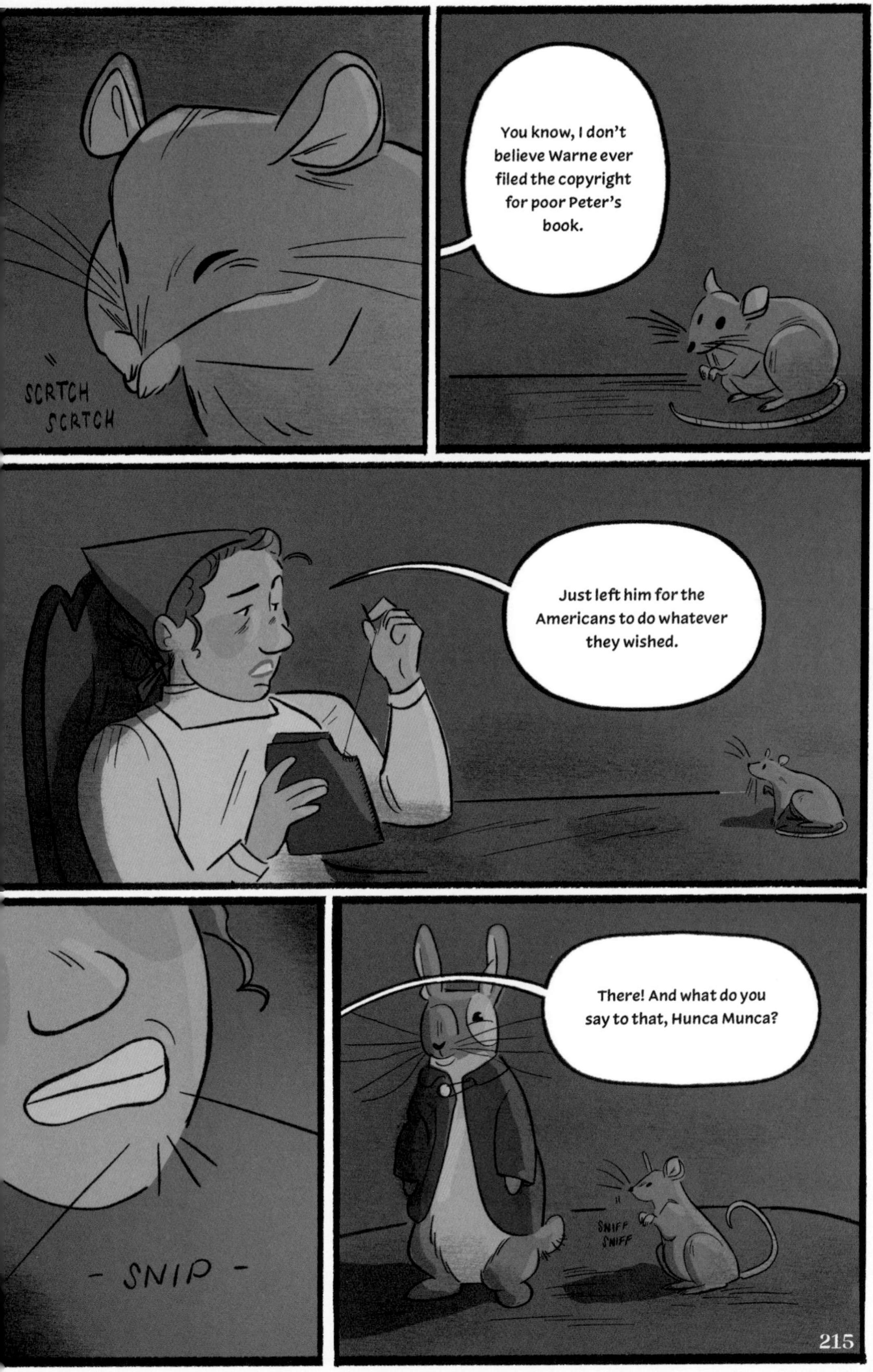
SCRTCH SCRTCH
You know, I don't believe Warne ever filed the copyright for poor Peter's book.
Just left him for the Americans to do whatever they wished.
- SNIP -
There! And what do you say to that, Hunca Munca?
SNIFF SNIFF

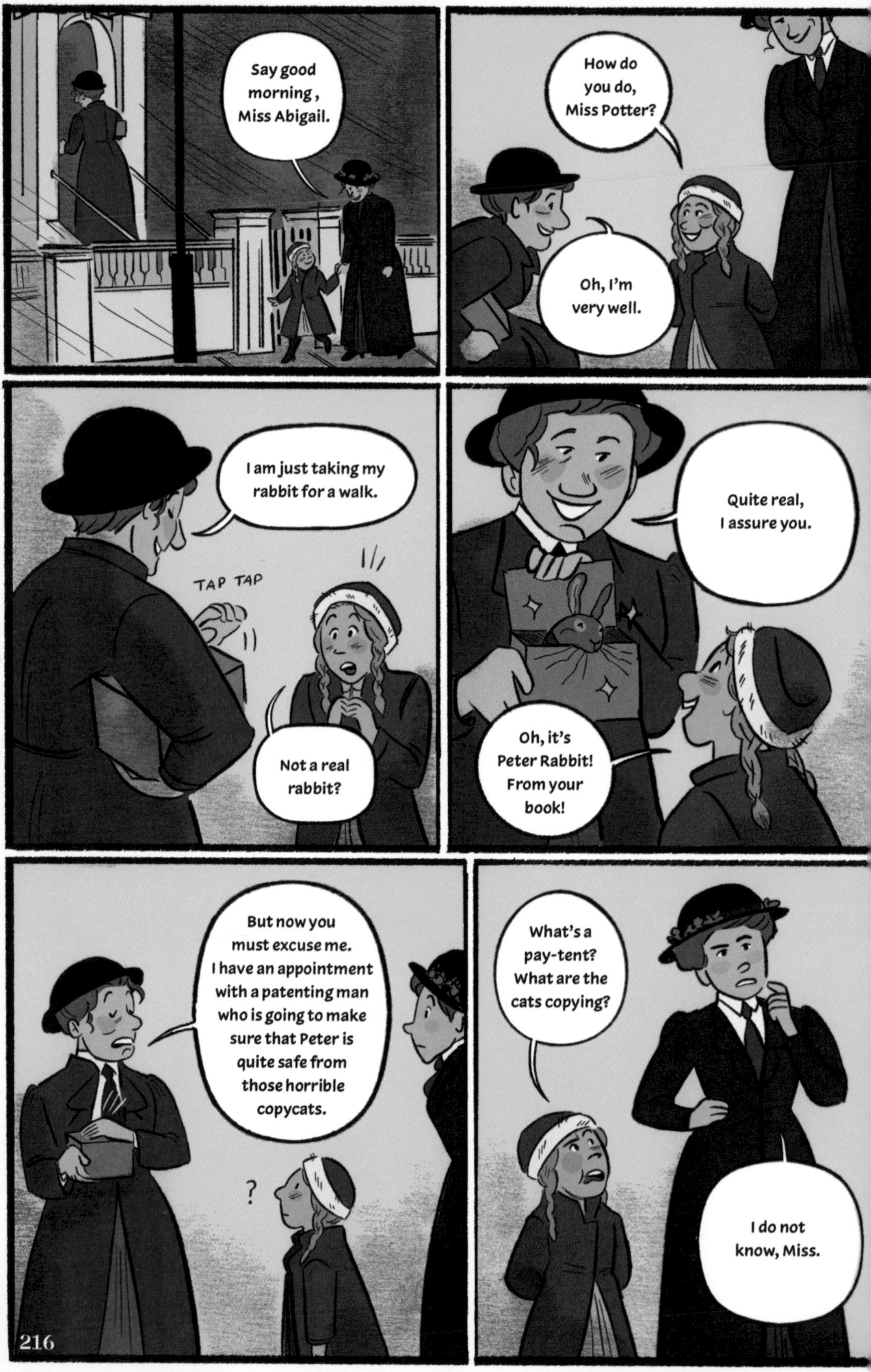

Say good morning, Miss Abigail.
How do you do, Miss Potter?
Oh, I'm very well.
I am just taking my rabbit for a walk.
TAP TAP
Not a real rabbit?
Quite real, I assure you.
Oh, it's Peter Rabbit! From your book!
But now you must excuse me. I have an appointment with a patenting man who is going to make sure that Peter is quite safe from those horrible copycats.
?
What's a pay-tent? What are the cats copying?
I do not know, Miss.

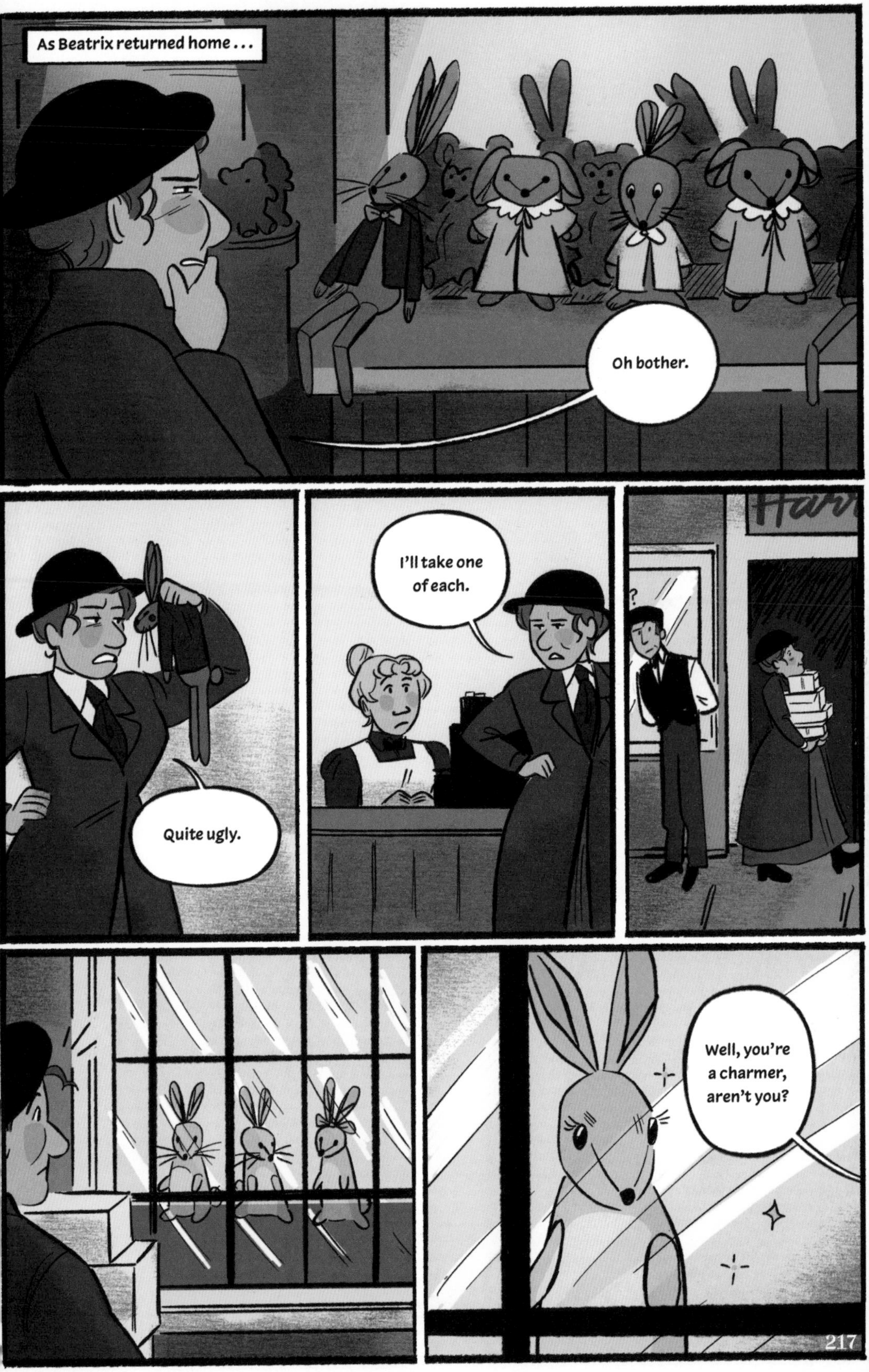
As Beatrix returned home . . .
Oh bother.
Quite ugly.
I'll take one of each.
?
Well, you're a charmer, aren't you?

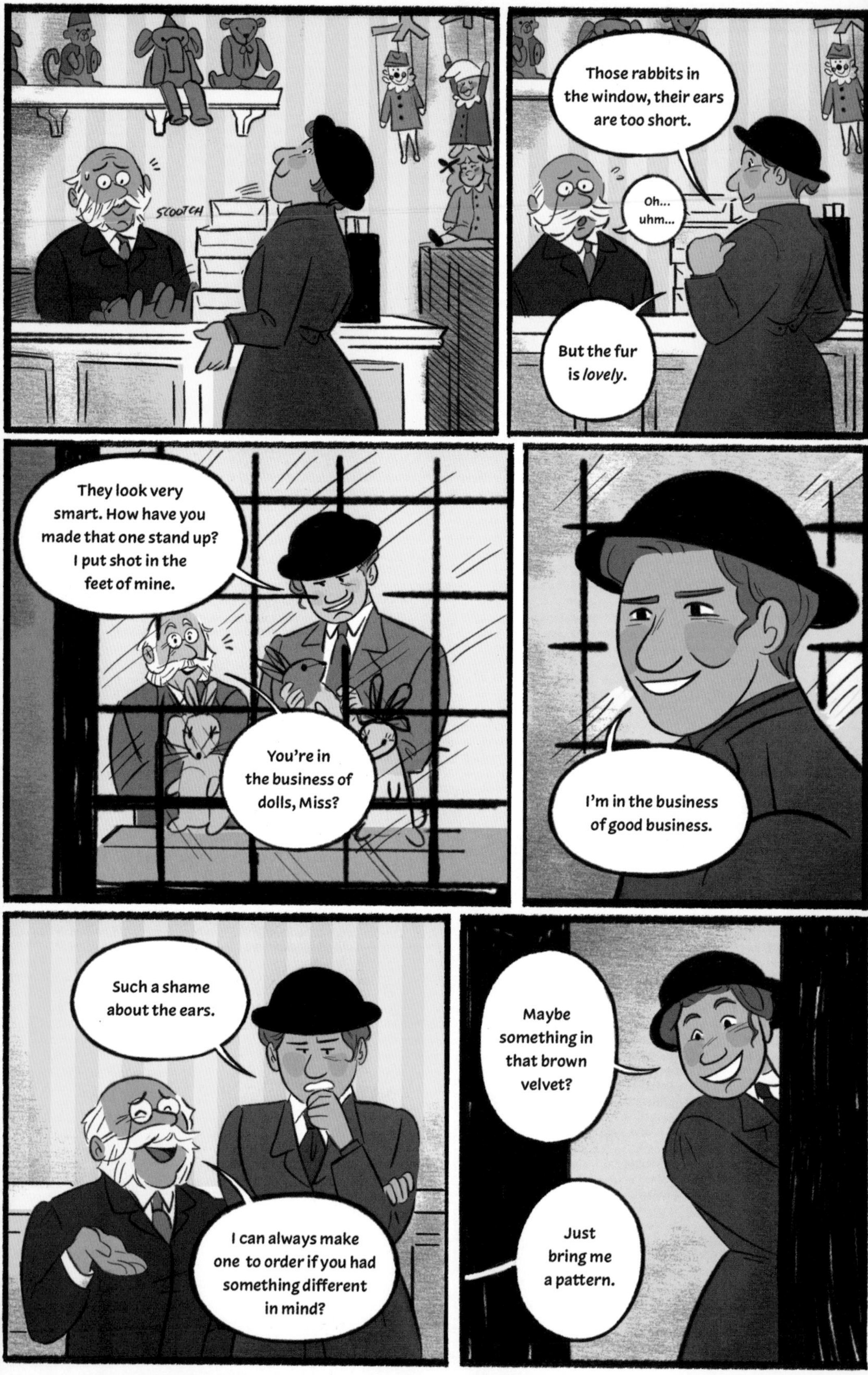
SCOOTCH
Those rabbits in the window, their ears are too short.
Oh... uhm...
But the fur is *lovely*.
They look very smart. How have you made that one stand up? I put shot in the feet of mine.
You're in the business of dolls, Miss?
I'm in the business of good business.
Such a shame about the ears.
I can always make one to order if you had something different in mind?
Maybe something in that brown velvet?
Just bring me a pattern.

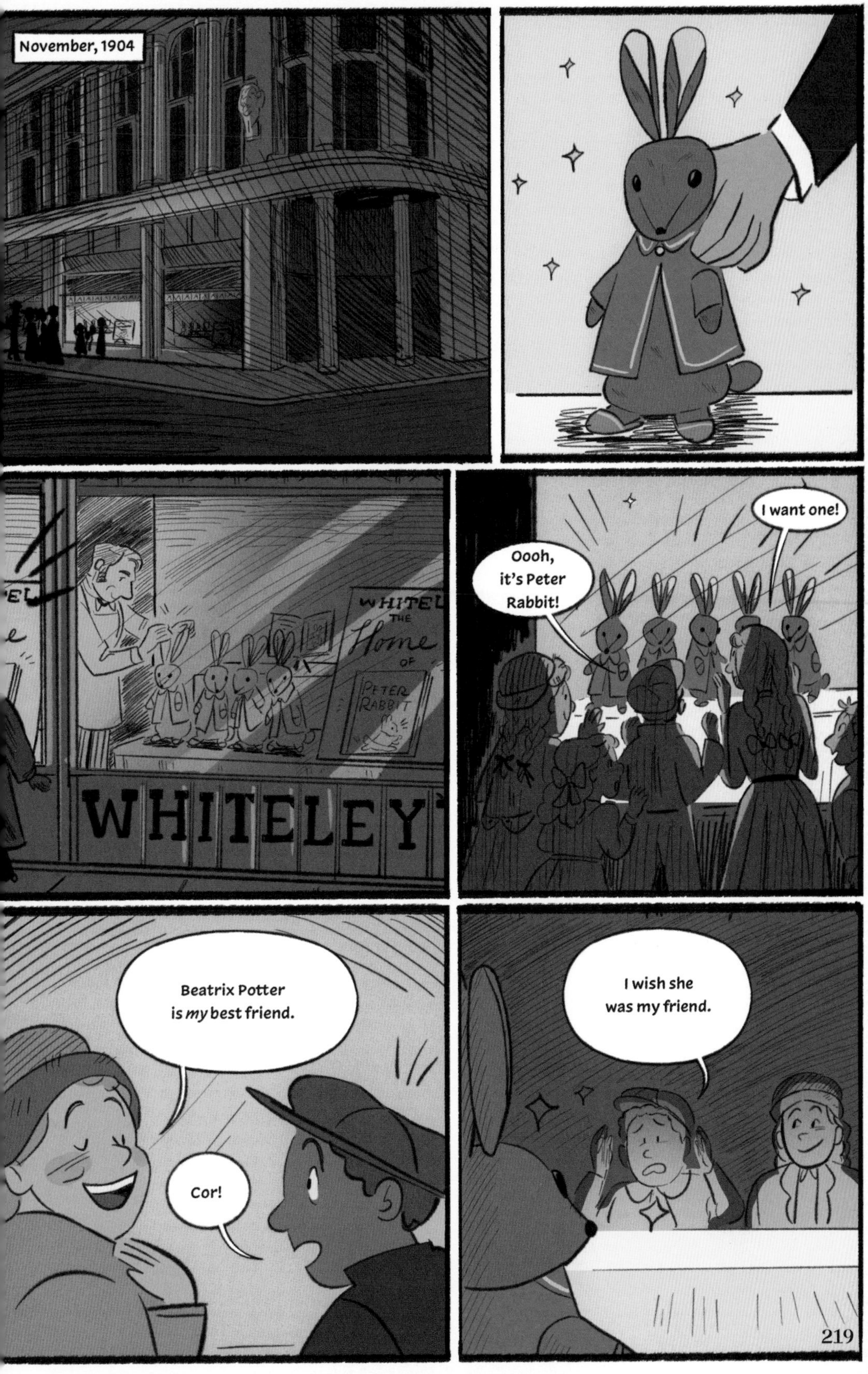
November, 1904
Oooh, it's Peter Rabbit!
I want one!
WHITELEY'S
THE Home OF PETER RABBIT
Beatrix Potter is *my* best friend.
Cor!
I wish she was my friend.

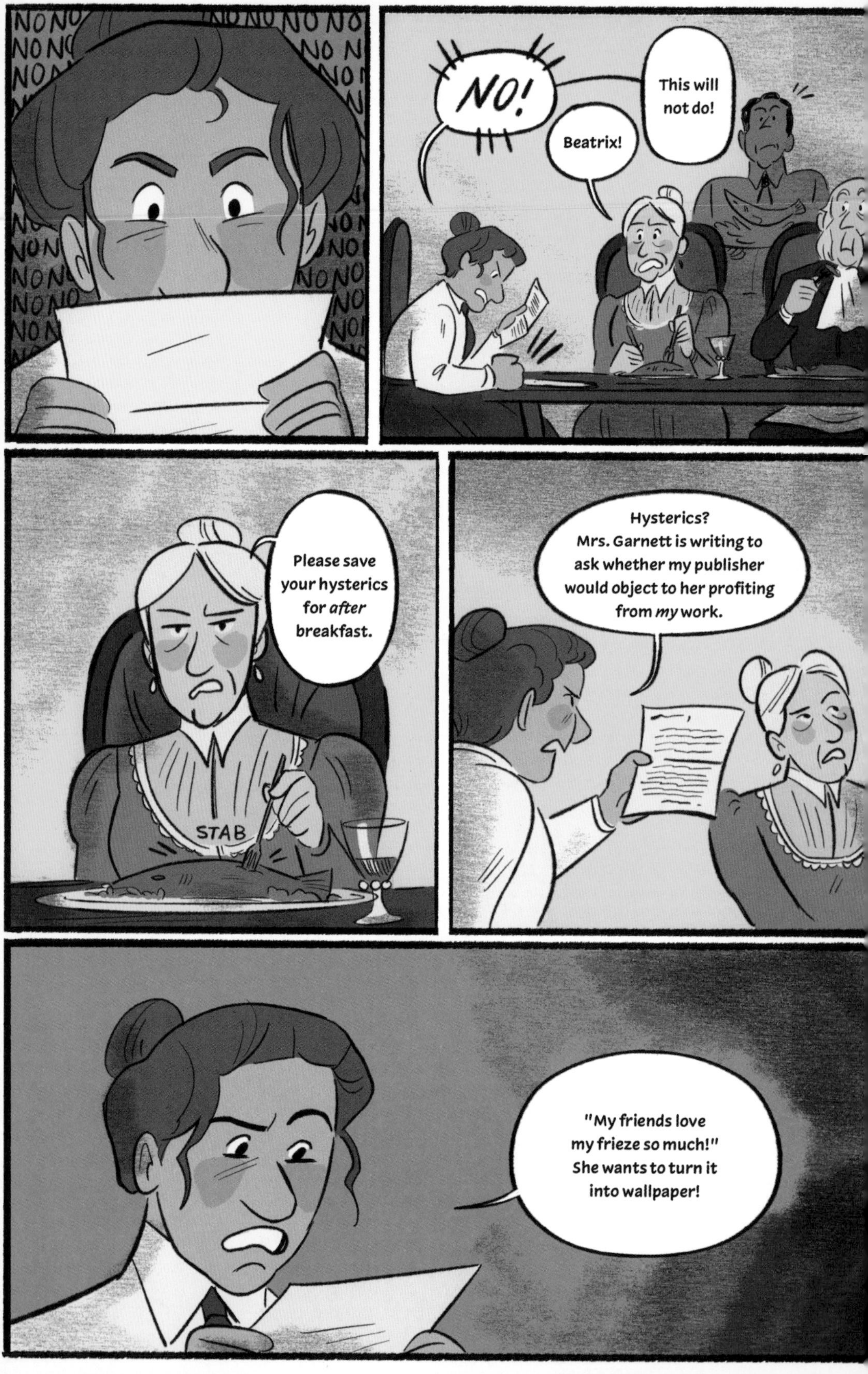
NO NO NO NO NO NO
NO!
Beatrix!
This will not do!
Please save your hysterics for *after* breakfast.
STAB
Hysterics? Mrs. Garnett is writing to ask whether my publisher would object to her profiting from *my* work.
"My friends love my frieze so much!" She wants to turn it into wallpaper!

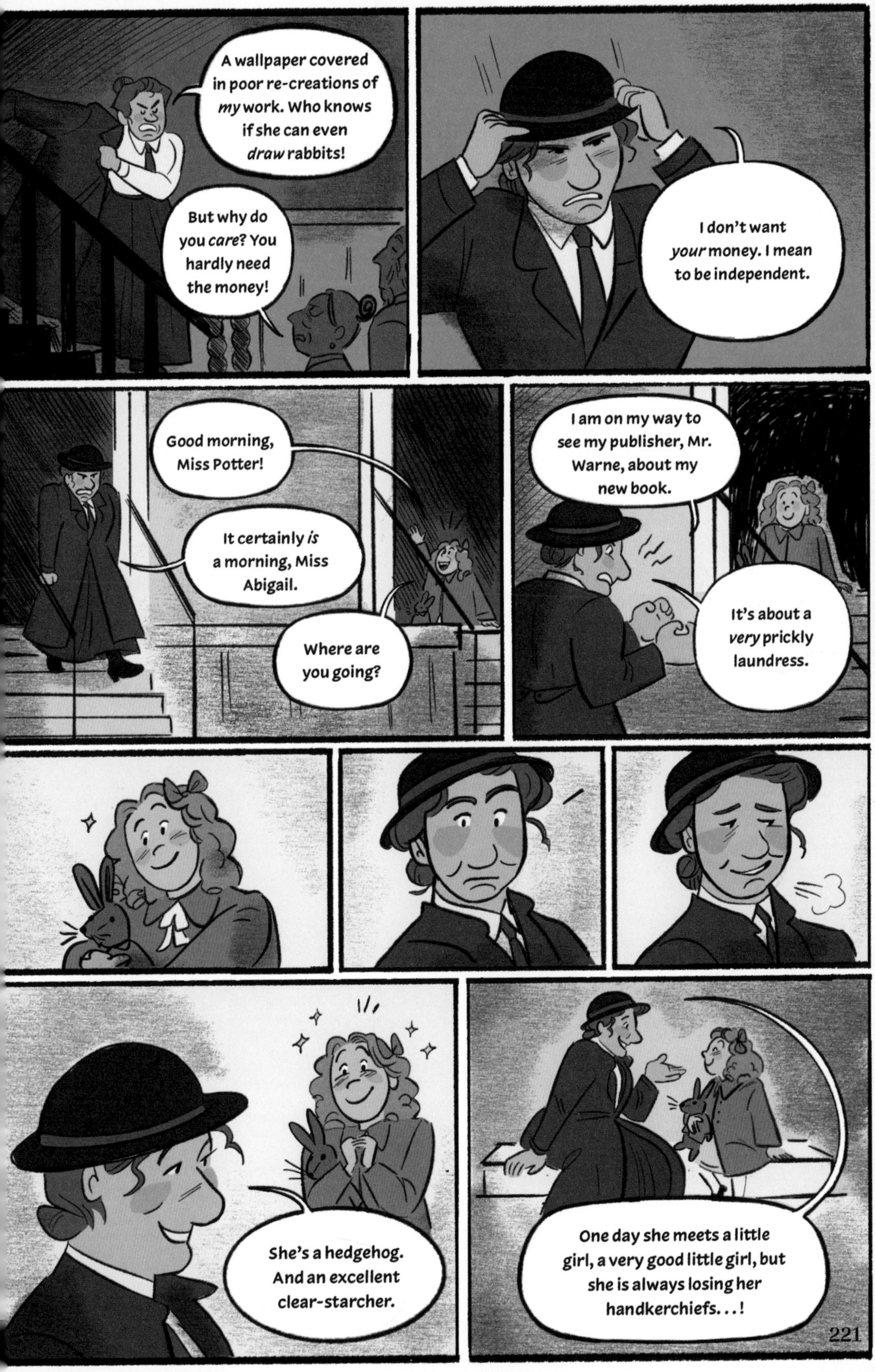
A wallpaper covered in poor re-creations of *my* work. Who knows if she can even *draw* rabbits!
But why do you *care*? You hardly need the money!
I don't want *your* money. I mean to be independent.
Good morning, Miss Potter!
It certainly *is* a morning, Miss Abigail.
Where are you going?
I am on my way to see my publisher, Mr. Warne, about my new book.
It's about a *very* prickly laundress.
She's a hedgehog. And an excellent clear-starcher.
One day she meets a little girl, a very good little girl, but she is always losing her handkerchiefs...!

Like Anne Lister before her, Beatrix Potter kept a journal written in code, for over fifteen years. The journal gave Potter a place to explore her interests, ideas, and emotions in a way she never could with her parents.

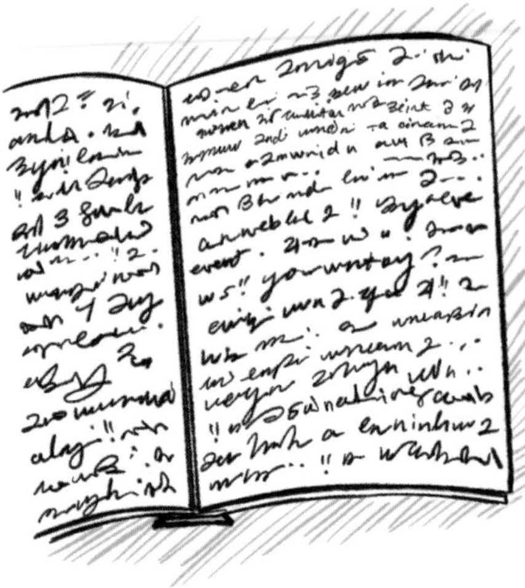

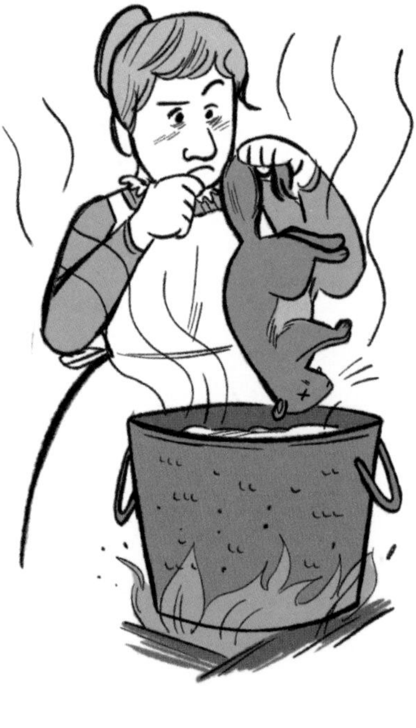

As a child, Potter would boil the carcasses of small animals in order to extract the skeleton and better understand their anatomy. It was this scientific attention to detail that would bring her animal drawings to life.

SELECTED WORKS:

THE 23 ORIGINAL TALES

1902: *The Tale of Peter Rabbit*
1903: *The Tale of Squirrel Nutkin*
1903: *The Tailor of Gloucester*
1904: *The Tale of Benjamin Bunny*
1904: *The Tale of Two Bad Mice*
1905: *The Tale of Mrs. Tiggy-Winkle*
1905: *The Tale of the Pie and the Patty-Pan*
1906: *The Tale of Mr. Jeremy Fisher*
1906: *The Story of a Fierce Bad Rabbit*
1906: *The Story of Miss Moppet*
1907: *The Tale of Tom Kitten*
1908: *The Tale of Jemima Puddle-Duck*
1908: *The Tale of Samuel Whiskers or, The Roly-Poly Pudding*
1909: *The Tale of the Flopsy Bunnies*
1909: *The Tale of Ginger and Pickles*
1910: *The Tale of Mrs. Tittlemouse*
1911: *The Tale of Timmy Tiptoes*
1912: *The Tale of Mr. Tod*
1913: *The Tale of Pigling Bland*
1917: *Appley Dapply's Nursery Rhymes*
1918: *The Tale of Johnny Town-Mouse*
1922: *Cecily Parsley's Nursery Rhymes*
1930: *The Tale of Little Pig Robinson*

OTHER:

1911: *Peter Rabbit's Painting Book*
1917: *Tom Kitten's Painting Book*
1925: *Jemima Puddle-Duck's Painting Book*
1928: *Peter Rabbit's Almanac for 1929*
1929: *The Fairy Caravan*

Frances Hodgson Burnett

1849–1924

"There's nothing so strong as rage, except what
makes you hold it in—that's stronger. It's a good thing
not to answer your enemies. I scarcely ever do."

—*A Little Princess*, 1905

Today, Frances Hodgson Burnett's most well-known novels are *The Secret Garden* and *The Little Princess*; but in her lifetime, her most popular work was Little Lord Fauntleroy, the tale of young American boy who inherits an estate in England and charms all that meet him. *Little Lord Fauntleroy* was also a deeply personal novel, whose titular character was modeled after Burnette's own son Vivian, and the legal battle over its dramatization would change copyright law forever.

Burnett was not born into poverty but came to it slowly. Born in Manchester, England, in 1849, Frances was raised by a single mother, Eliza Boond Hodgson, after her father, Edwin, died suddenly in 1852, and though Eliza did her best to provide for their five children, money was always in short supply. Her limited earnings went to her children's education, and it was during these years that Frances developed a love of writing and reading stories. After years of struggling financially, in 1865, the family finally accepted the invitation of Eliza's brother, William Boond, to live with him in Knoxville, Tennessee.

William had promised to find jobs for Eliza's boys, but the Hodgsons arrived in an America decimated by civil war, so they were forced to make do with what little they had, poorer than ever before. Fortunately, their new neighbors welcomed the Hodgsons. One boy, Swan Burnett, became the particular friend of Frances and the pair would spend hours discussing books and poetry.

In 1868, at the age of nineteen, Frances sold her first story. She was good at writing, and she needed to be to support her family, especially after her mother died just two years later. And soon Frances had a family of her own to consider: she and Swan married in 1873, and their first son, Lionel, was born within a year, quickly followed by a younger brother, Vivian. While Swan studied to be a doctor, Frances wrote, knowing that each story she sold would afford her sons a childhood she herself had never known.

By 1887, aged thirty-nine, Frances Hodgson Burnett was a huge success, and although her marriage to Swan was struggling, she was able to comfortably support her family with her writing. It was at this time, while traveling in Florence, Italy, with her sons and her companion, Miss Chiellini, that Frances began receiving letters from a young British man named E. V. Seebohm, who was seeking her blessing for his stage adaptation of her hit novel, *Little Lord Fauntleroy*. Burnett, a playwright herself, had previously suffered two unauthorized stage adaptations of her books, and she took action at once to prevent Seebohm, settling her sons with a friend and traveling to London. En route, she began work on an adaptation of her own: *The Real Little Lord Fauntleroy*.

While traveling, she encountered E. V. Seebohm himself, who caught up with her at a train station in Turin and tried to convince her in person that she should accept his offer.

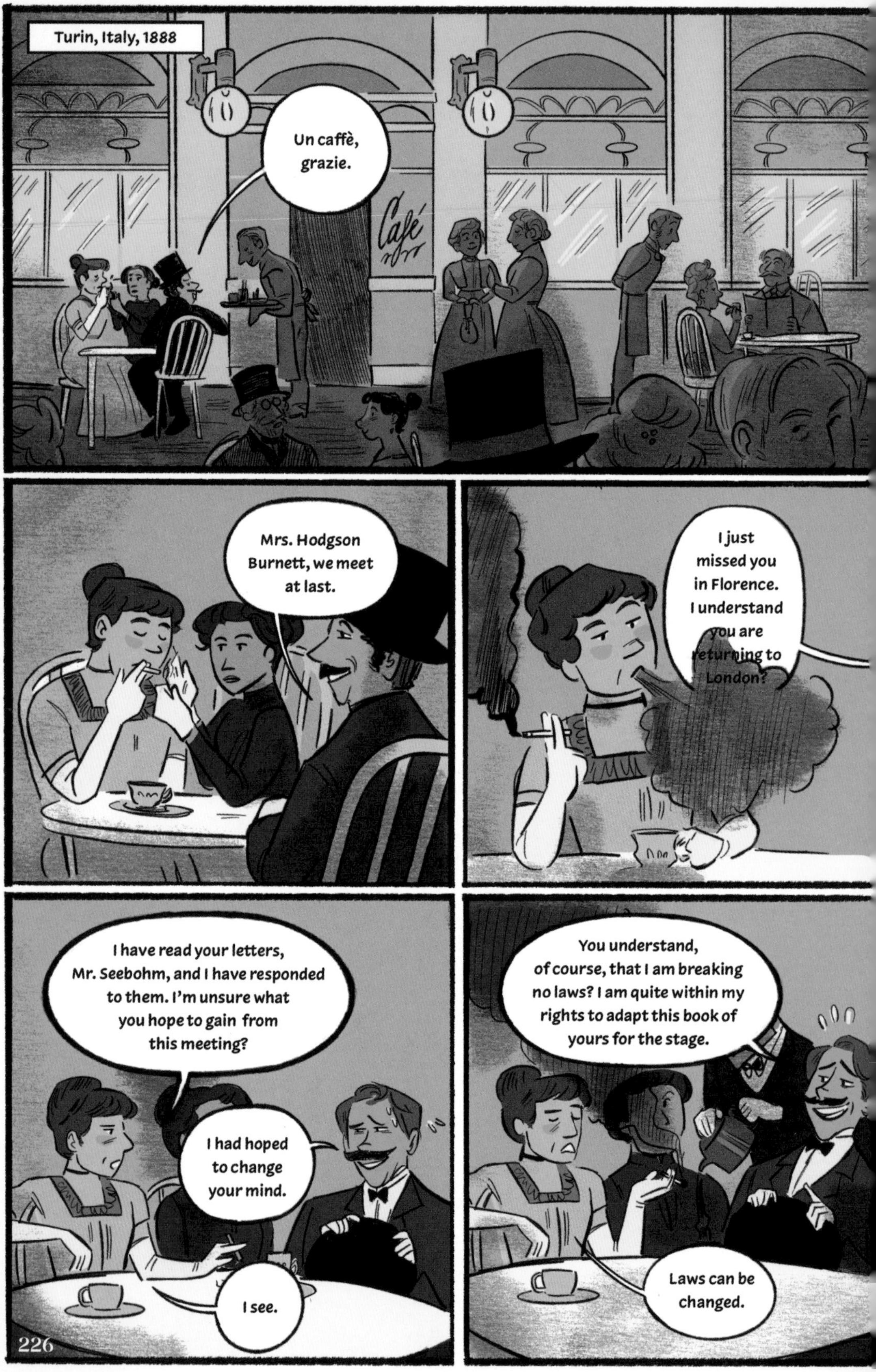
Turin, Italy, 1888
Un caffè, grazie.
Café
Mrs. Hodgson Burnett, we meet at last.
I just missed you in Florence. I understand you are returning to London?
I have read your letters, Mr. Seebohm, and I have responded to them. I'm unsure what you hope to gain from this meeting?
I had hoped to change your mind.
I see.
You understand, of course, that I am breaking no laws? I am quite within my rights to adapt this book of yours for the stage.
Laws can be changed.

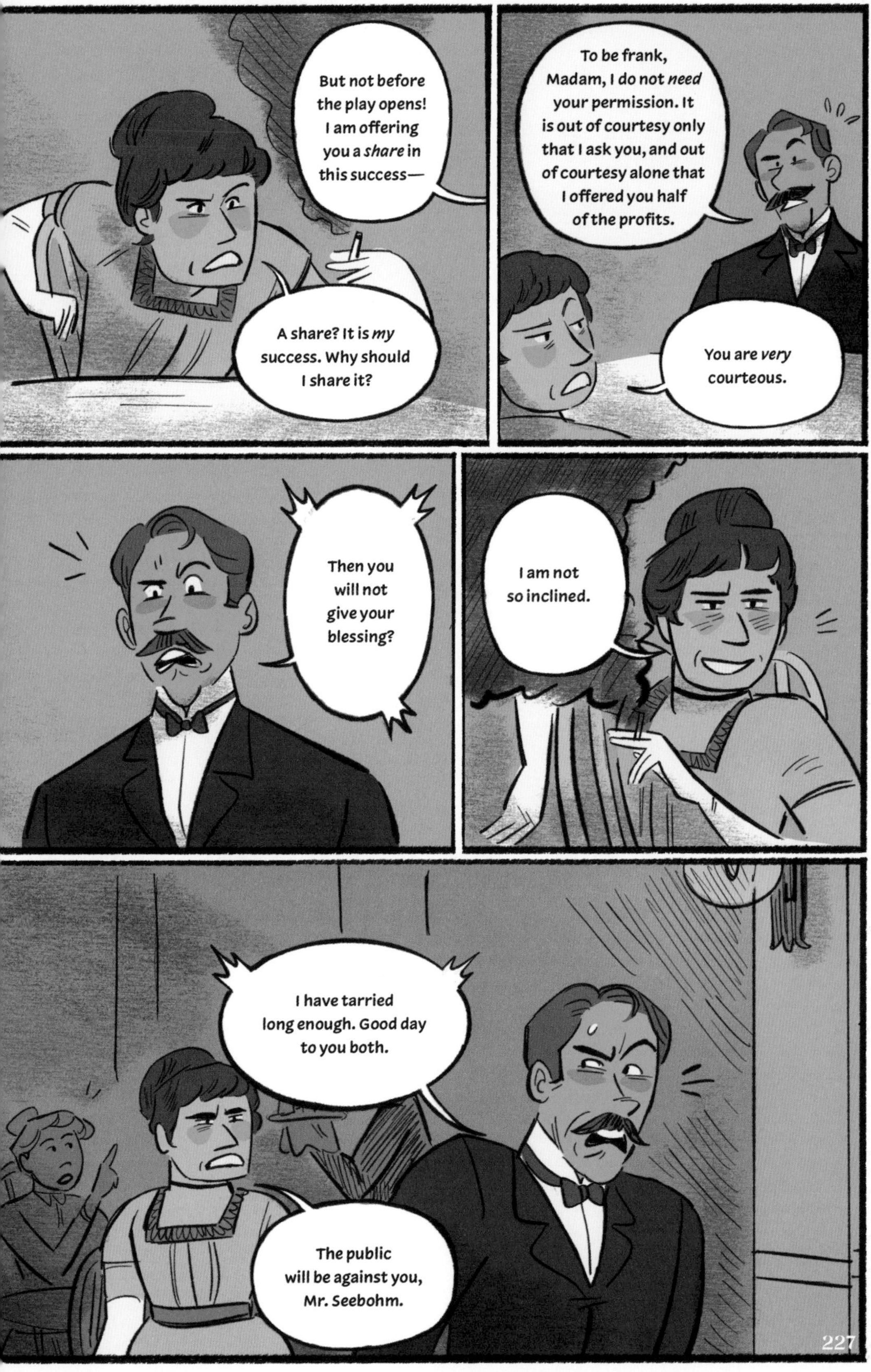
But not before the play opens! I am offering you a *share* in this success—
A share? It is *my* success. Why should I share it?
To be frank, Madam, I do not *need* your permission. It is out of courtesy only that I ask you, and out of courtesy alone that I offered you half of the profits.
You are *very* courteous.
Then you will not give your blessing?
I am not so inclined.
I have tarried long enough. Good day to you both.
The public will be against you, Mr. Seebohm.

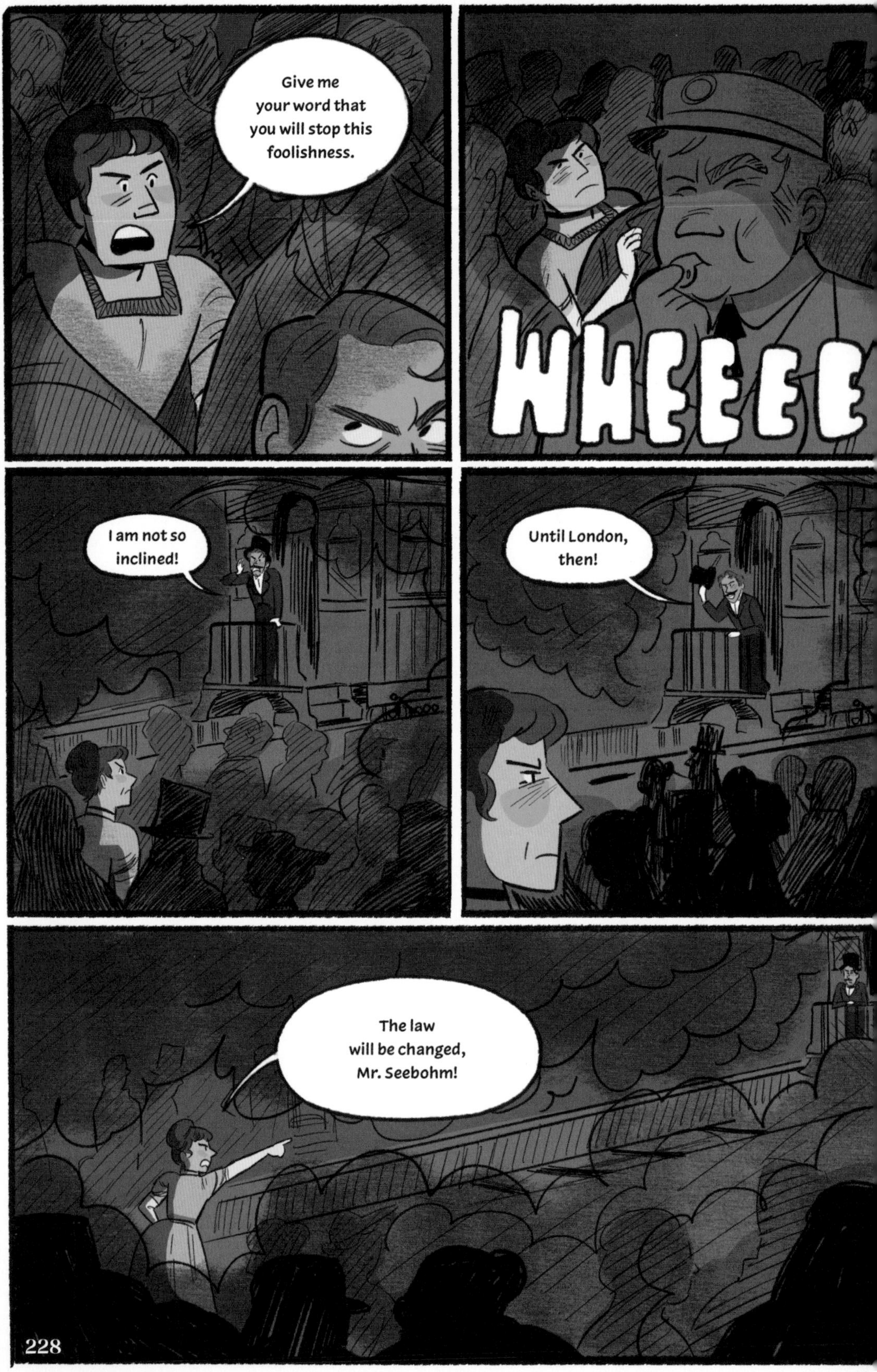
Give me your word that you will stop this foolishness.
WHEEEE
I am not so inclined!
Until London, then!
The law will be changed, Mr. Seebohm!

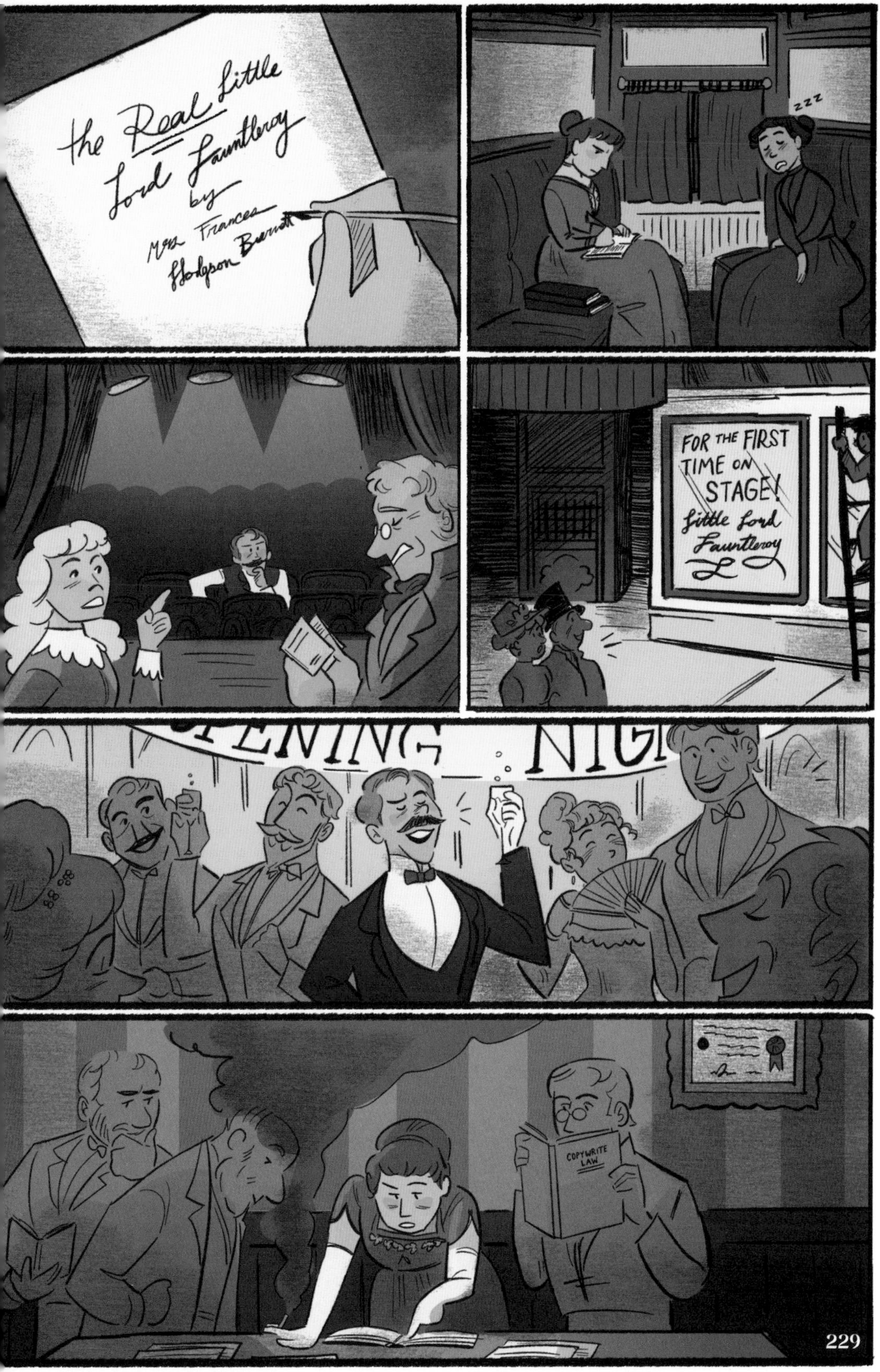

the Real Little Lord Fauntleroy by Mrs Frances Hodgson Burnett
ZZZ
FOR THE FIRST TIME ON STAGE! Little Lord Fauntleroy
NIG
COPYWRITE LAW

The Chancery Division of the High Court of Justice

Why, if presenting the novel on stage is of such value to Mrs. Hodgson Burnett, would she not make reasonable effort to protect her work?

Why, if Mrs. Hodgson Burnett is so successful, would she balk at paying the trifling sum of £30 to secure the performance copyright?

I really did think I was protected by the "All rights reserved" on the title page.

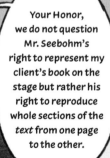

Your Honor, we do not question Mr. Seebohm's right to represent my client's book on the stage but rather his right to reproduce whole sections of the *text* from one page to the other.

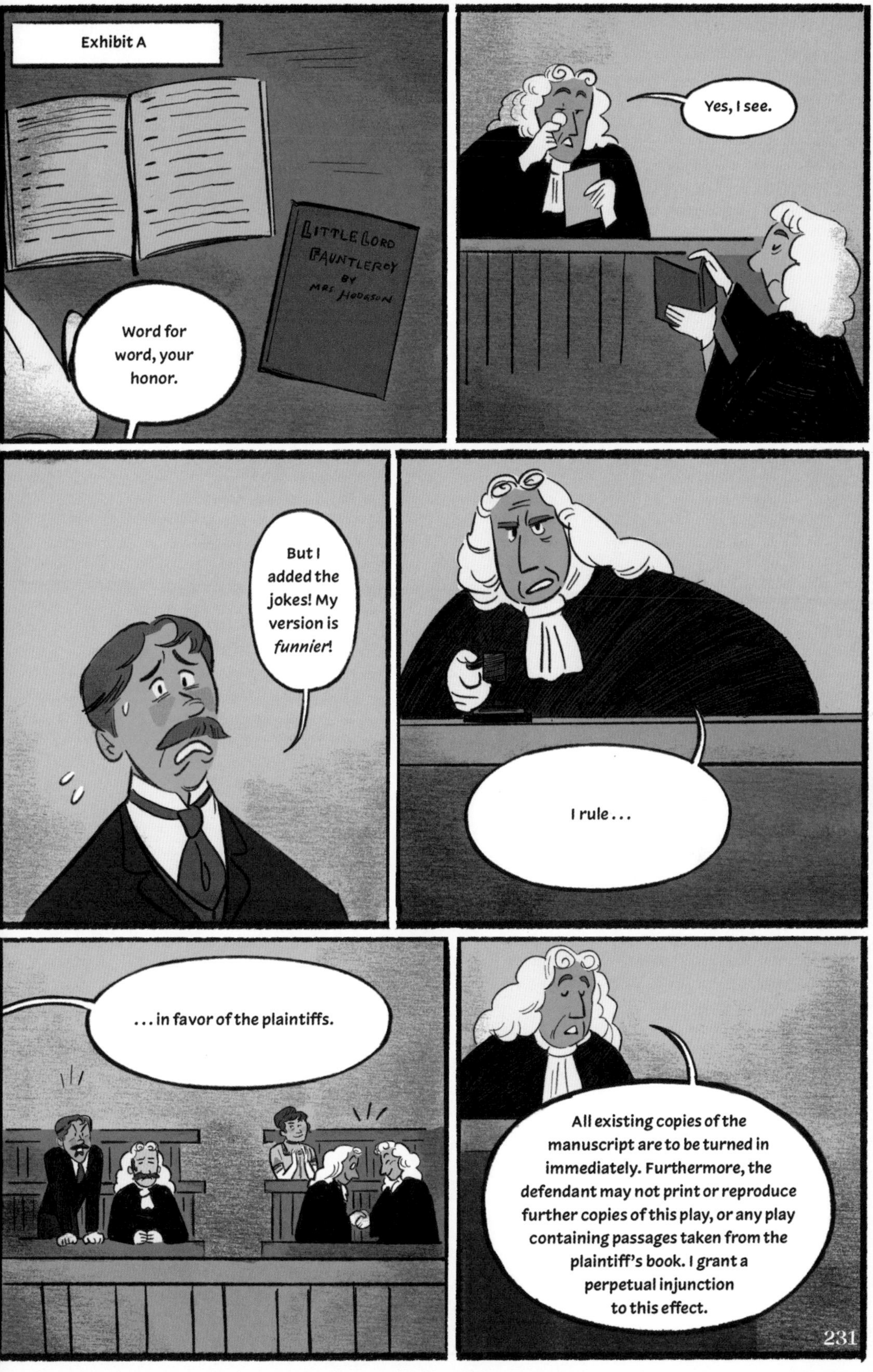
Exhibit A
LITTLE LORD FAUNTLEROY BY MRS HODGSON
Word for word, your honor.
Yes, I see.
But I added the jokes! My version is *funnier*!
I rule . . .
. . . in favor of the plaintiffs.
All existing copies of the manuscript are to be turned in immediately. Furthermore, the defendant may not print or reproduce further copies of this play, or any play containing passages taken from the plaintiff's book. I grant a perpetual injunction to this effect.

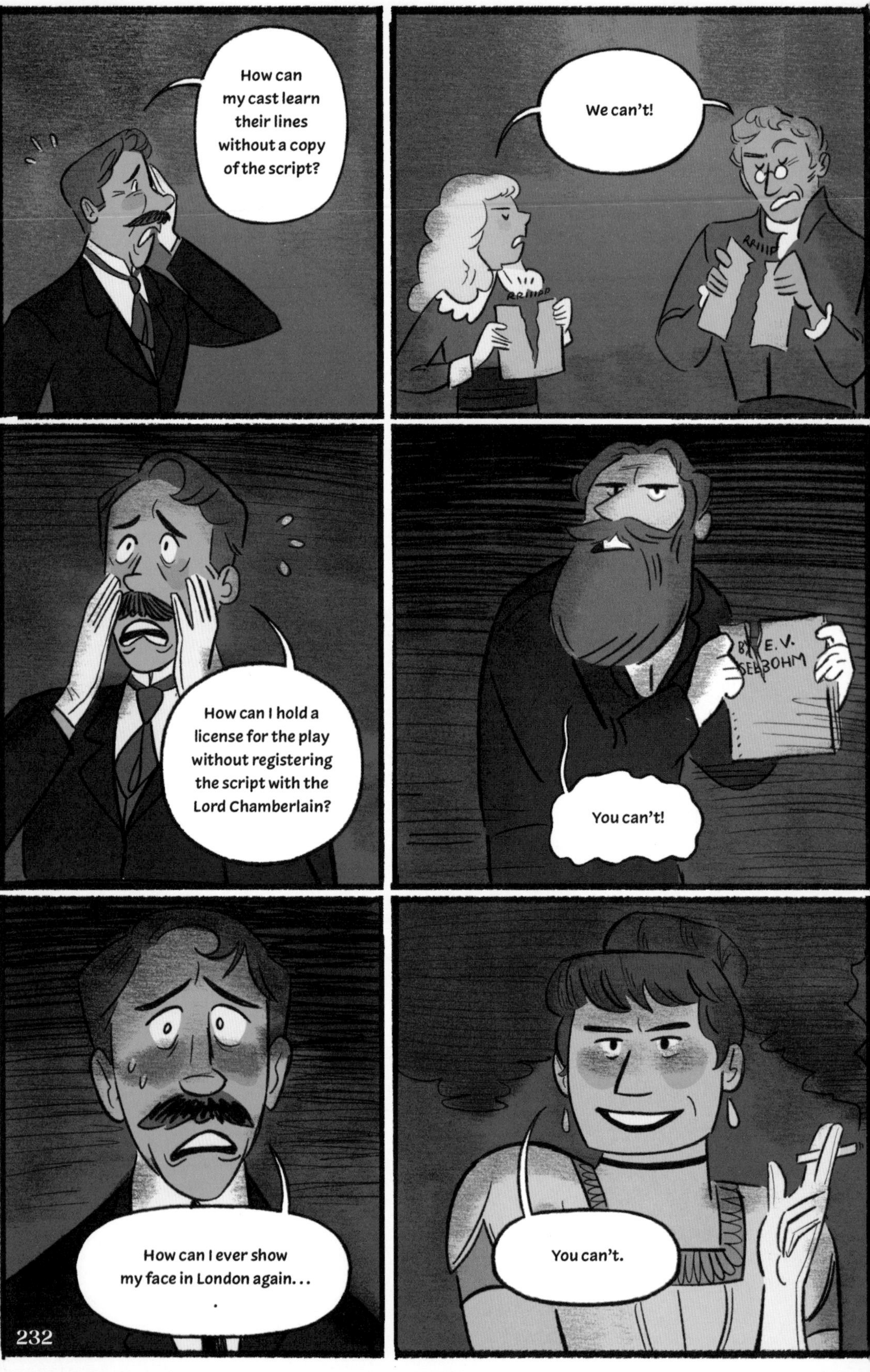
How can my cast learn their lines without a copy of the script?
We can't!
RRIIIPP
RRIIIPP
How can I hold a license for the play without registering the script with the Lord Chamberlain?
BY E.V. SELBOHM
You can't!
How can I ever show my face in London again. . . .
You can't.

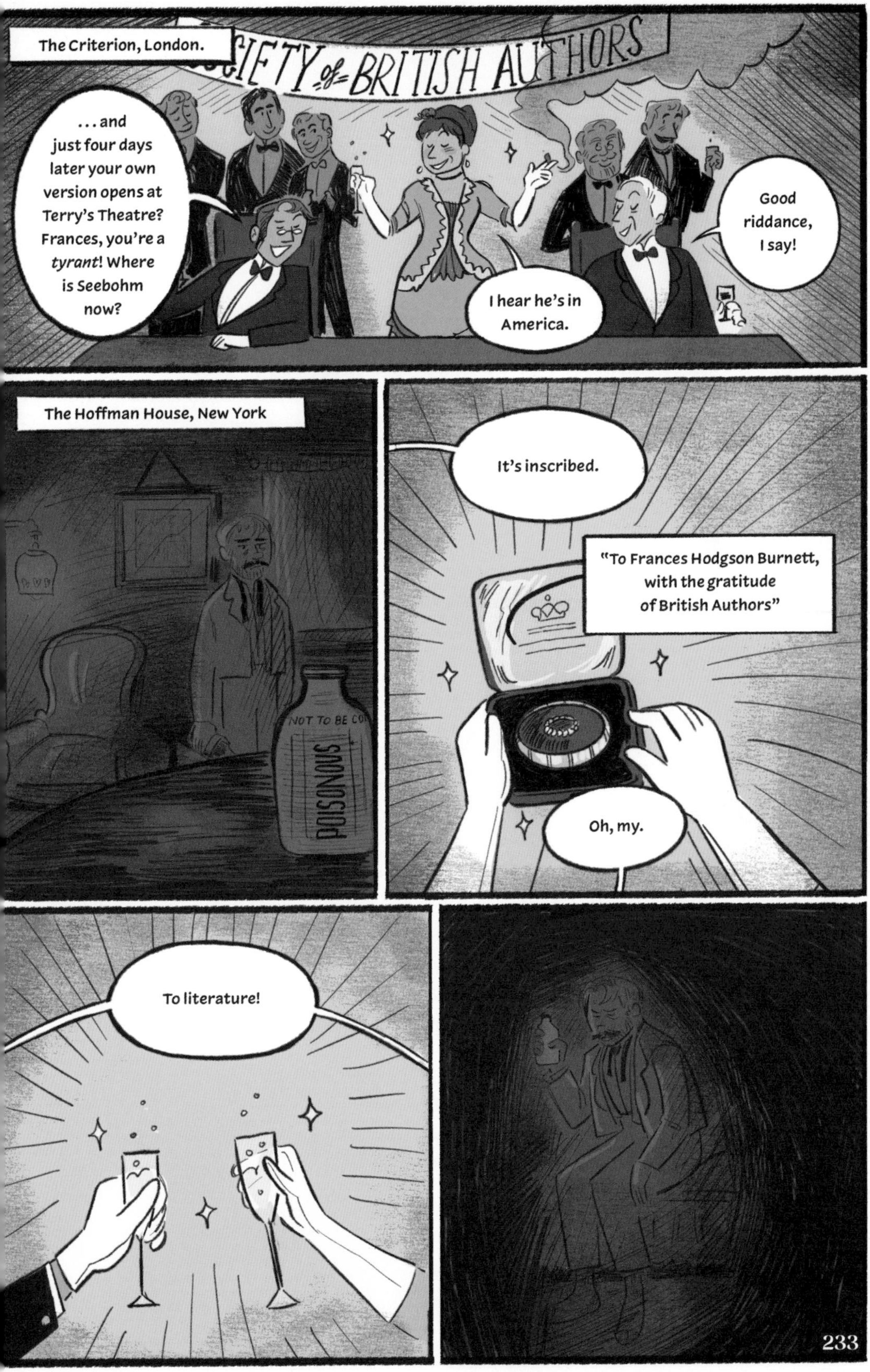
The Criterion, London.
SOCIETY of BRITISH AUTHORS
. . . and just four days later your own version opens at Terry's Theatre? Frances, you're a *tyrant*! Where is Seebohm now?
I hear he's in America.
Good riddance, I say!
The Hoffman House, New York
NOT TO BE
POISONOUS
It's inscribed.
"To Frances Hodgson Burnett, with the gratitude of British Authors"
Oh, my.
To literature!

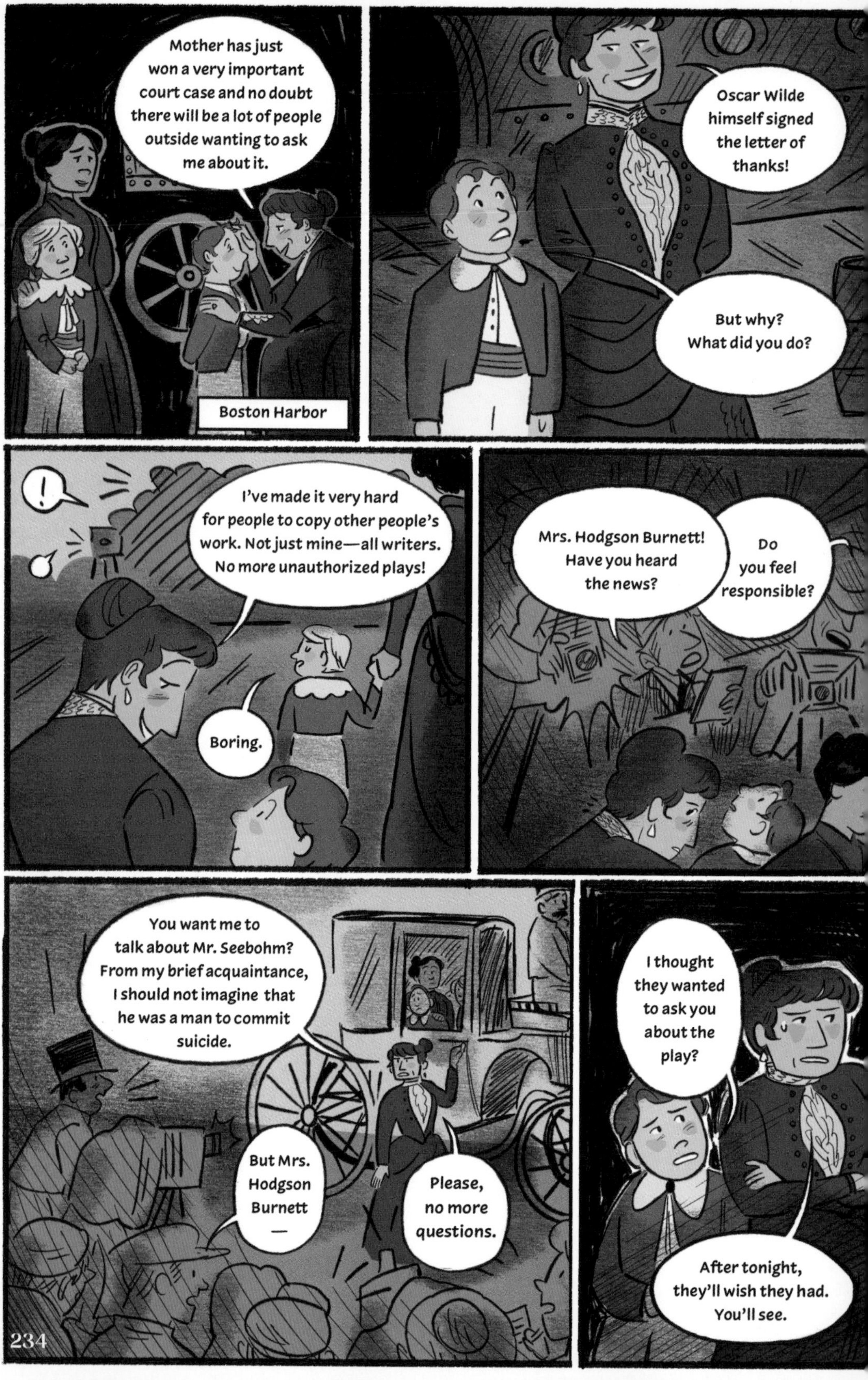
Mother has just won a very important court case and no doubt there will be a lot of people outside wanting to ask me about it.
Boston Harbor
Oscar Wilde himself signed the letter of thanks!
But why? What did you do?
!
I've made it very hard for people to copy other people's work. Not just mine—all writers. No more unauthorized plays!
Boring.
Mrs. Hodgson Burnett! Have you heard the news?
Do you feel responsible?
You want me to talk about Mr. Seebohm? From my brief acquaintance, I should not imagine that he was a man to commit suicide.
But Mrs. Hodgson Burnett —
Please, no more questions.
I thought they wanted to ask you about the play?
After tonight, they'll wish they had. You'll see.

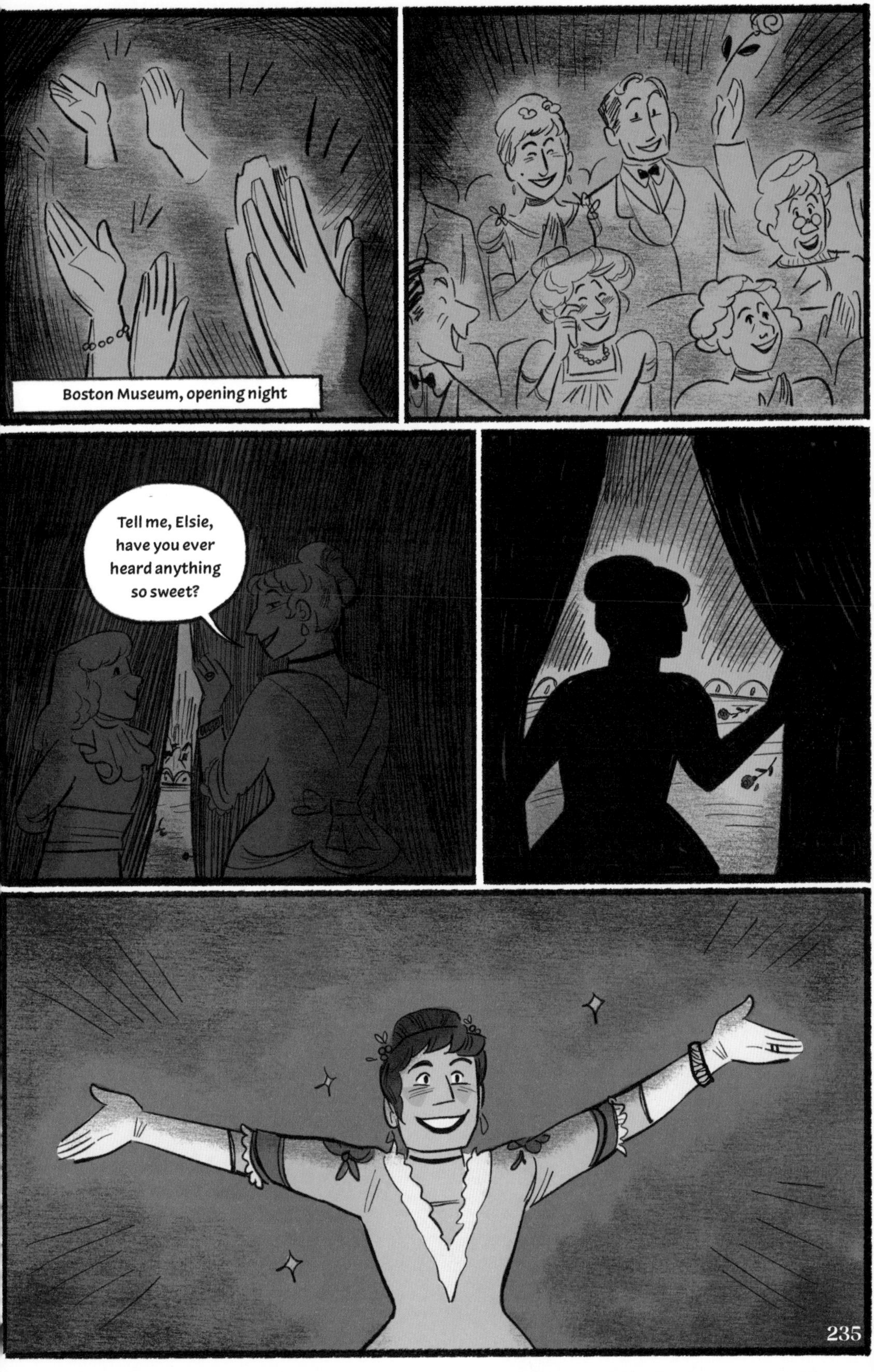
Boston Museum, opening night
Tell me, Elsie, have you ever heard anything so sweet?

In 1879, while visiting Boston, Frances Hodgson Burnett met Louisa May Alcott for the first time. For the next five years the pair would share a publisher, Mary Mapes Dodge, and write for the same children's magazine, *The St. Nicholas.*

Little Lord Fauntleroy wasn't responsible only for legal reform. From the 1880s to the early 1900s, middle class families across Europe and America rushed to dress their sons in full Fauntleroy finery. For these little lords, more was definitely more, as the pricy materials used to complete their ensembles were a sign of affluence.

SELECTED WORKS:

NOVELS

1877: *That Lass o' Lowrie's*
1886: *Little Lord Fauntleroy*
1888: *Editha's Burglar: A Story for Children*
1888: *The Fortunes of Philippa Fairfax*
1889: *The Pretty Sister of José*
1896: *A Lady of Quality*
1899: *In Connection with the De Willoughby Claim*
1901: *The Making of a Marchioness*
1905: *A Little Princess: Being the Whole Story of Sara Crewe Now Told for the First Time*
1906: *Racketty-Packetty House*
1907: *The Shuttle*
1911: *The Secret Garden*
1922: *The Head of the House of Coombe*
1922: *Robin*

PLAYS

1878: *That Lass o' Lowrie's*
1881: *Esmerelda*
1888: *The Real Little Lord Fauntleroy*
1889: *Phyllis*
1890: *Nixie*
1892: *The Showman's Daughter*
1897: *The First Gentleman of Europe*
1897: *A Lady of Quality*
1902: *A Little Princess*
1903: *The Pretty Sister of José*
1904: *That Man and I*
1909: *Dawn of Tomorrow*
1912: *Racketty Packetty House*

Louisa May Alcott

1832–1888

"Nothing is impossible to a determined woman."

—*The Abbot's Ghost or Maurice Treherne's Temptation,* 1867

Little Women is a deeply impactful text for many readers. An intimate look into the lives of four sisters, it is the story of overcoming poverty, self-doubt, and the expectations that society places on young women. A fictionalized account of her own upbringing in Concord, Massachusetts, it is the honesty of Alcott's book that makes is timeless; and this honesty opened wide the doors of Alcott's childhood home to an audience that was always hungry for just a little bit more.

Alcott began writing *Little Women* in 1868, setting the novel just a few years earlier during the American Civil War. In Alcott's novel, Mr. March has left his recently impoverished family to work as a pastor and join the war effort, and his wife and four daughters settle into their new, fatherless home as best they can. Alcott herself was no stranger to hardship, as her own father was distant in a different way. Amos Bronson Alcott was a major figure in the transcendentalist movement, an abolitionist, and a women's rights activist—but his ideals did not guarantee financial stability. When his experiments in teaching and communal living continued to fail, it was his family who felt it deepest.

The year before *Little Women* changed her life forever, Alcott was at home, nursing their sick mother by day and writing by night. Despite the care and worry, Alcott produced twenty-five stories, earned one thousand dollars, and paid off her debts. When her mother's health finally improved, Alcott was able to devote her full efforts to writing, and in October 1867 she took a small room of her own in Boston. It proved a brief respite. By February 28, 1868, Alcott was preparing to return home once more; her family needed her. In her journal she described her sadness at leaving her quiet room in Boston, but she did not begrudge her mother a moment of care. Knowing "Marmee" was comfortable was "better than any amount of fame." *Little Women* was completed within six months of her return.

Honesty, the root of *Little Women*'s success, also became the root of Alcott's unhappiness. Her readers saw so much of themselves in her quiet story that they wanted to see more of *her* too. As the money flooded in, so did letters, and as more copies sold, more and more fans flocked to Concord to meet the real-life March family. Alcott secured her finances and the future of her family by retaining the copyright and royalties for her novel, but in doing so, she gave something away too. Orchard House would never again be the secluded family home it once was, and the now-famous Alcott would spend the rest of her life running as far and as hard as she could to escape the public eye.

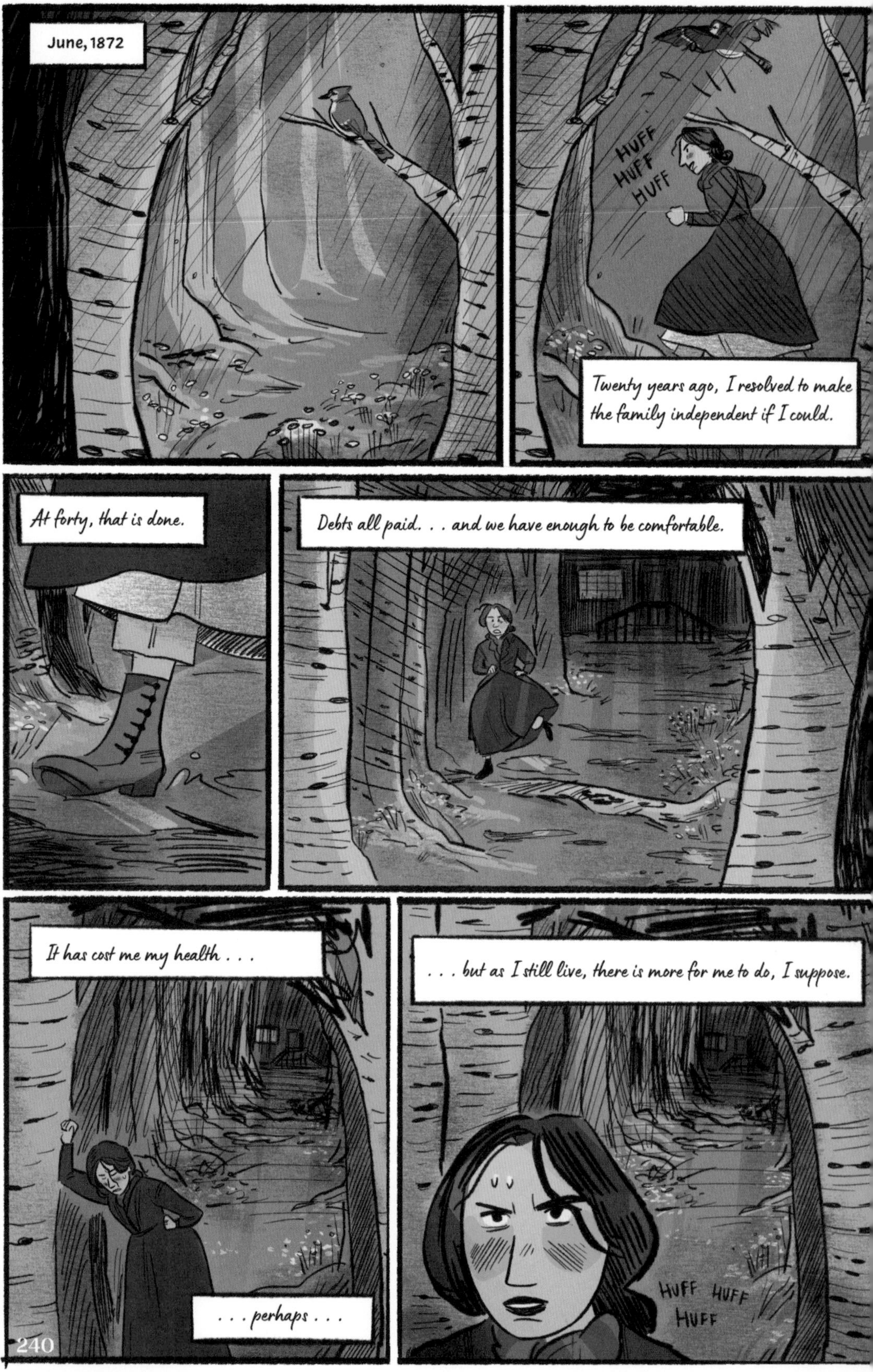
June, 1872
HUFF HUFF HUFF
Twenty years ago, I resolved to make the family independent if I could.
At forty, that is done.
Debts all paid. . . and we have enough to be comfortable.
It has cost me my health . . .
. . . perhaps . . .
. . . but as I still live, there is more for me to do, I suppose.
HUFF HUFF HUFF

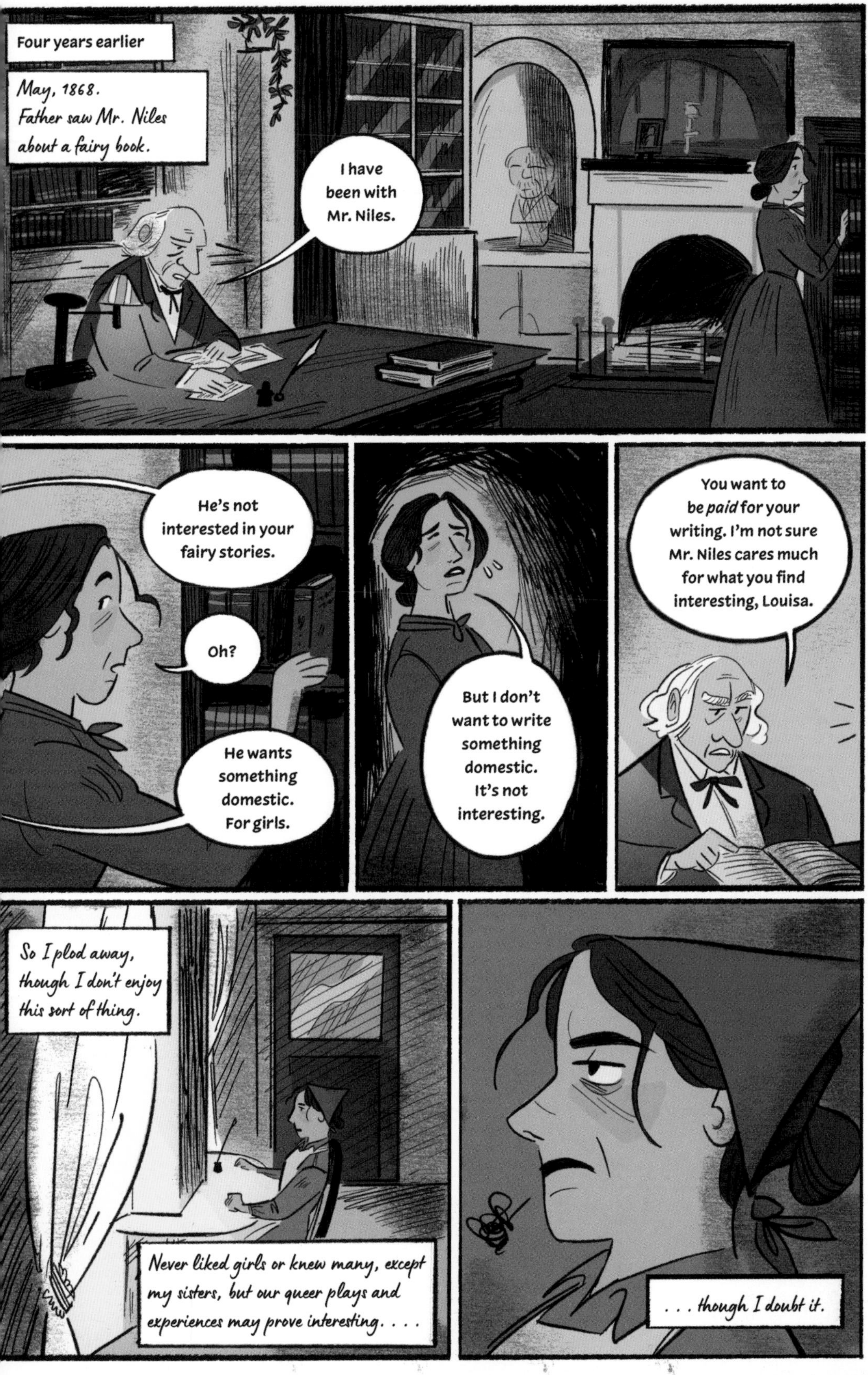

Four years earlier
May, 1868.
Father saw Mr. Niles about a fairy book.
I have been with Mr. Niles.
He's not interested in your fairy stories.
Oh?
He wants something domestic. For girls.
But I don't want to write something domestic. It's not interesting.
You want to be *paid* for your writing. I'm not sure Mr. Niles cares much for what you find interesting, Louisa.
So I plod away, though I don't enjoy this sort of thing.
Never liked girls or knew many, except my sisters, but our queer plays and experiences may prove interesting. . . .
. . . though I doubt it.

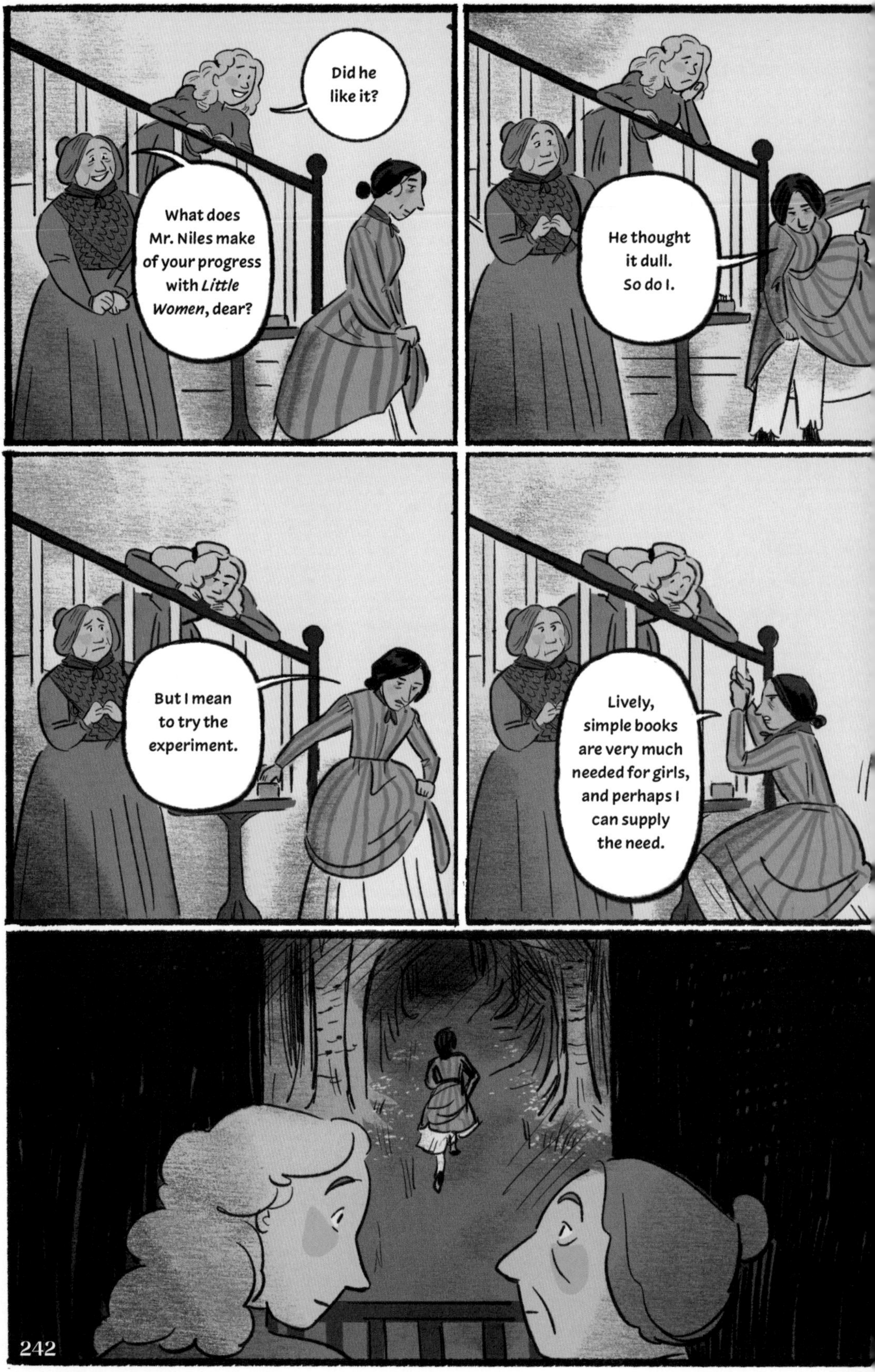

What does Mr. Niles make of your progress with *Little Women*, dear?
Did he like it?
He thought it dull. So do I.
But I mean to try the experiment.
Lively, simple books are very much needed for girls, and perhaps I can supply the need.

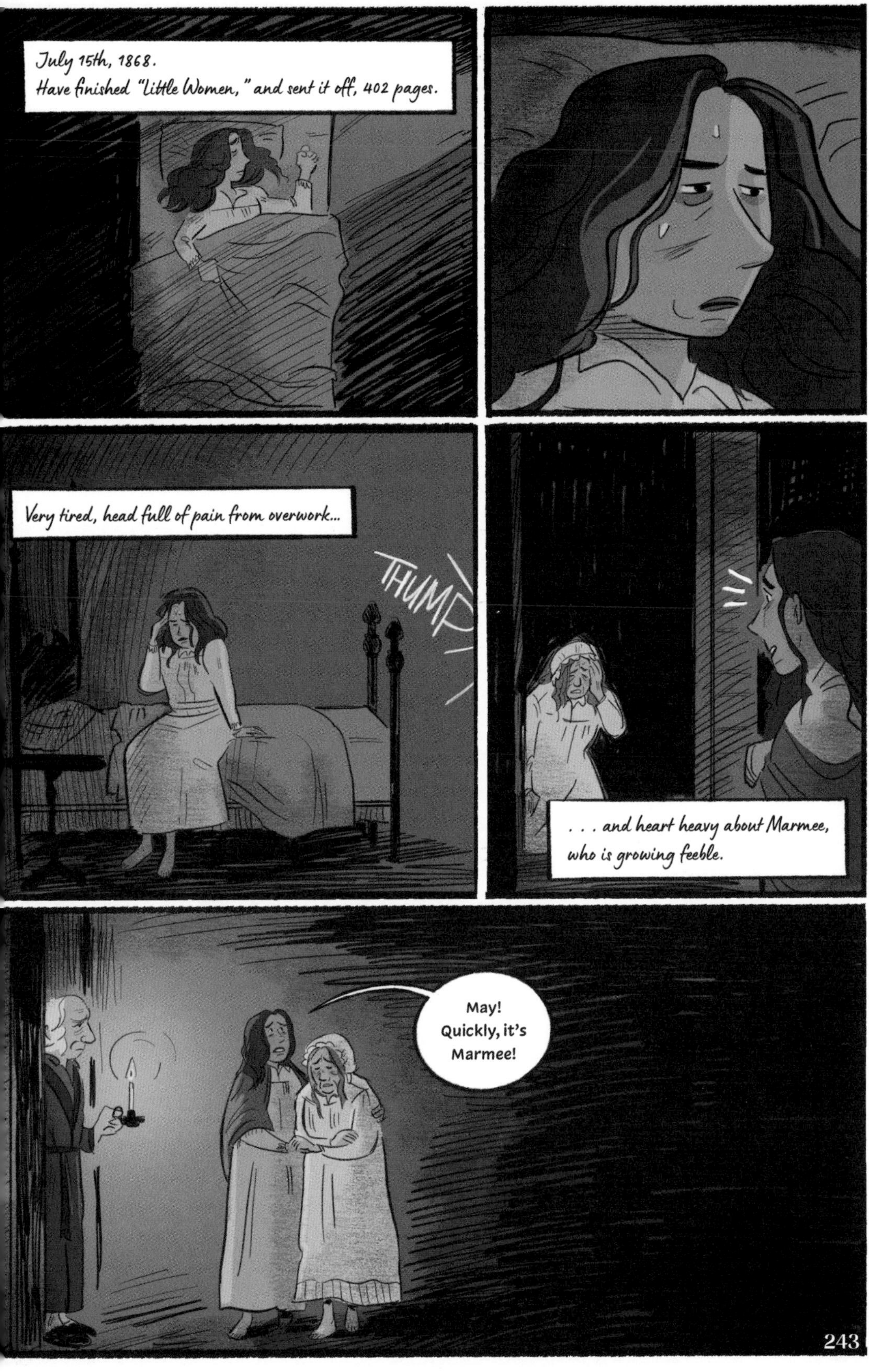
July 15th, 1868.
Have finished "Little Women," and sent it off, 402 pages.
Very tired, head full of pain from overwork...
THUMP
. . . and heart heavy about Marmee, who is growing feeble.
May! Quickly, it's Marmee!

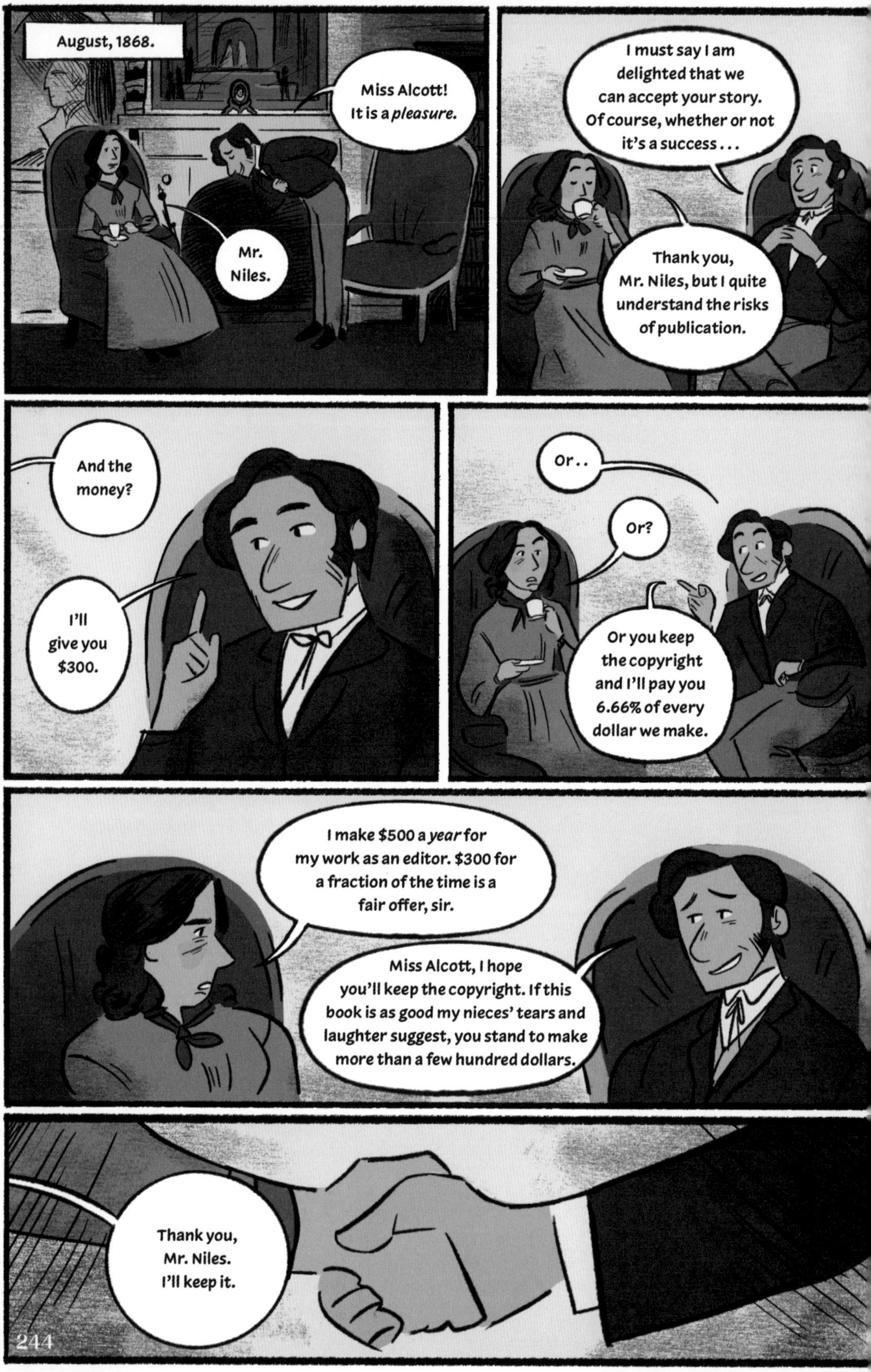
August, 1868.
Miss Alcott! It is a *pleasure.*
Mr. Niles.
I must say I am delighted that we can accept your story. Of course, whether or not it's a success . . .
Thank you, Mr. Niles, but I quite understand the risks of publication.
And the money?
I'll give you $300.
Or . .
Or?
Or you keep the copyright and I'll pay you 6.66% of every dollar we make.
I make $500 a *year* for my work as an editor. $300 for a fraction of the time is a fair offer, sir.
Miss Alcott, I hope you'll keep the copyright. If this book is as good my nieces' tears and laughter suggest, you stand to make more than a few hundred dollars.
Thank you, Mr. Niles. I'll keep it.

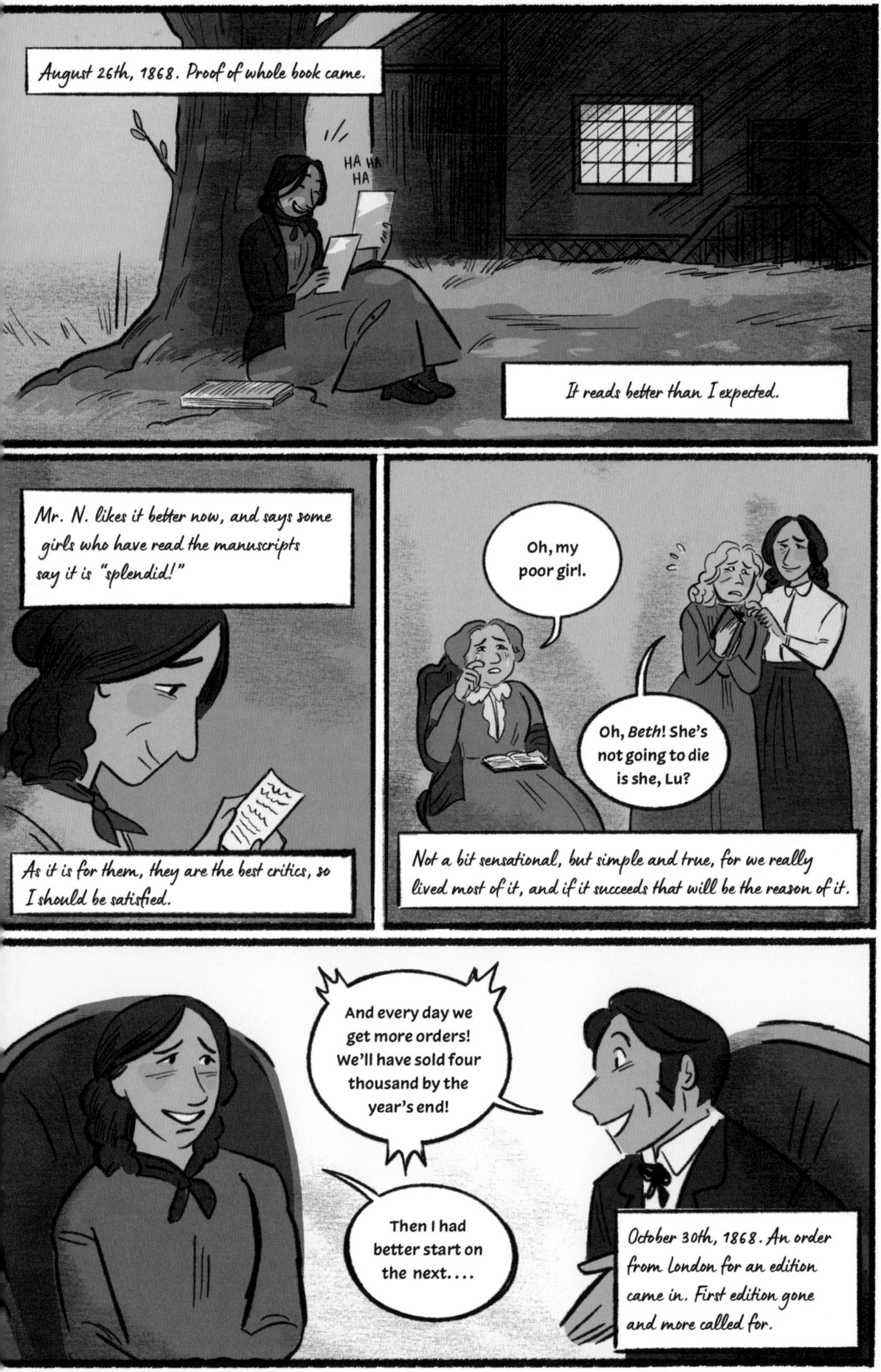
August 26th, 1868. Proof of whole book came.
HA HA HA
It reads better than I expected.
Mr. N. likes it better now, and says some girls who have read the manuscripts say it is "splendid!"
As it is for them, they are the best critics, so I should be satisfied.
Oh, my poor girl.
Oh, Beth! She's not going to die is she, Lu?
Not a bit sensational, but simple and true, for we really lived most of it, and if it succeeds that will be the reason of it.
And every day we get more orders! We'll have sold four thousand by the year's end!
Then I had better start on the next....
October 30th, 1868. An order from London for an edition came in. First edition gone and more called for.

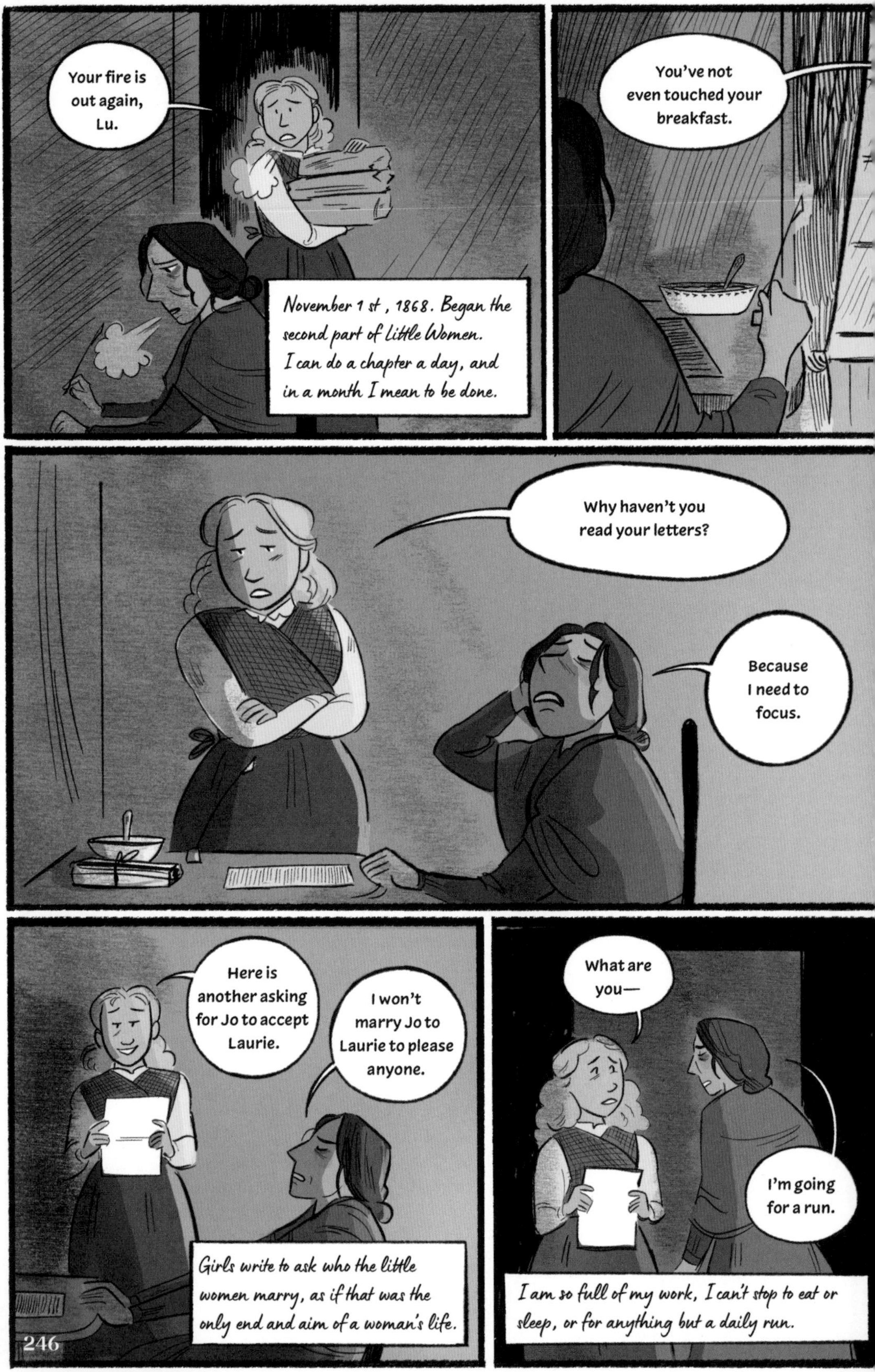

Your fire is out again, Lu.
November 1st, 1868. Began the second part of Little Women. I can do a chapter a day, and in a month I mean to be done.
You've not even touched your breakfast.
Why haven't you read your letters?
Because I need to focus.
Here is another asking for Jo to accept Laurie.
I won't marry Jo to Laurie to please anyone.
Girls write to ask who the little women marry, as if that was the only end and aim of a woman's life.
What are you—
I'm going for a run.
I am so full of my work, I can't stop to eat or sleep, or for anything but a daily run.

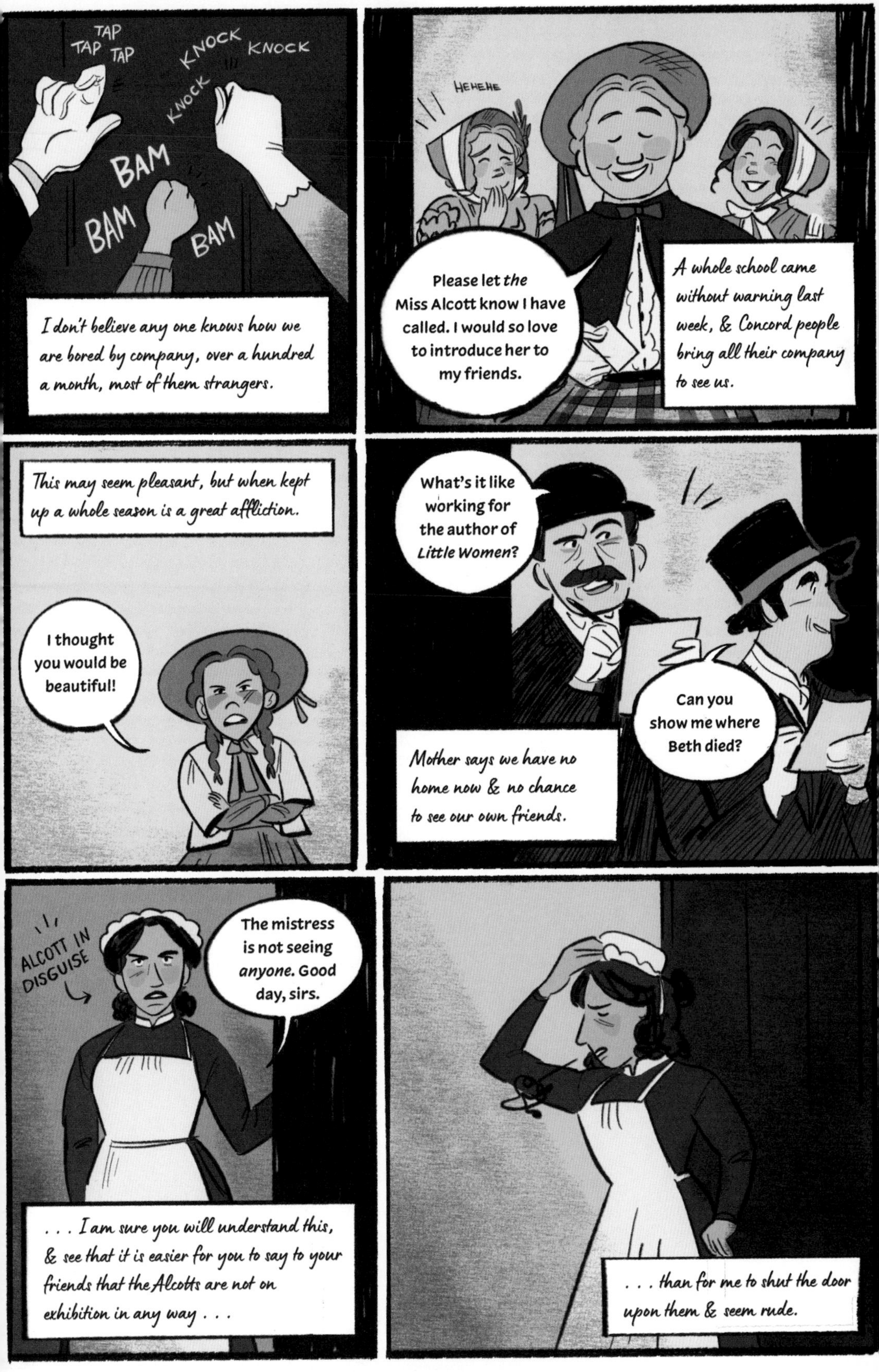
TAP TAP TAP
KNOCK KNOCK KNOCK
BAM BAM BAM
I don't believe any one knows how we are bored by company, over a hundred a month, most of them strangers.
HEHEHE
Please let *the* Miss Alcott know I have called. I would so love to introduce her to my friends.
A whole school came without warning last week, & Concord people bring all their company to see us.
This may seem pleasant, but when kept up a whole season is a great affliction.
I thought you would be beautiful!
What's it like working for the author of *Little Women*?
Can you show me where Beth died?
Mother says we have no home now & no chance to see our own friends.
ALCOTT IN DISGUISE
The mistress is not seeing *anyone*. Good day, sirs.
. . . I am sure you will understand this, & see that it is easier for you to say to your friends that the Alcotts are not on exhibition in any way . . .
. . . than for me to shut the door upon them & seem rude.

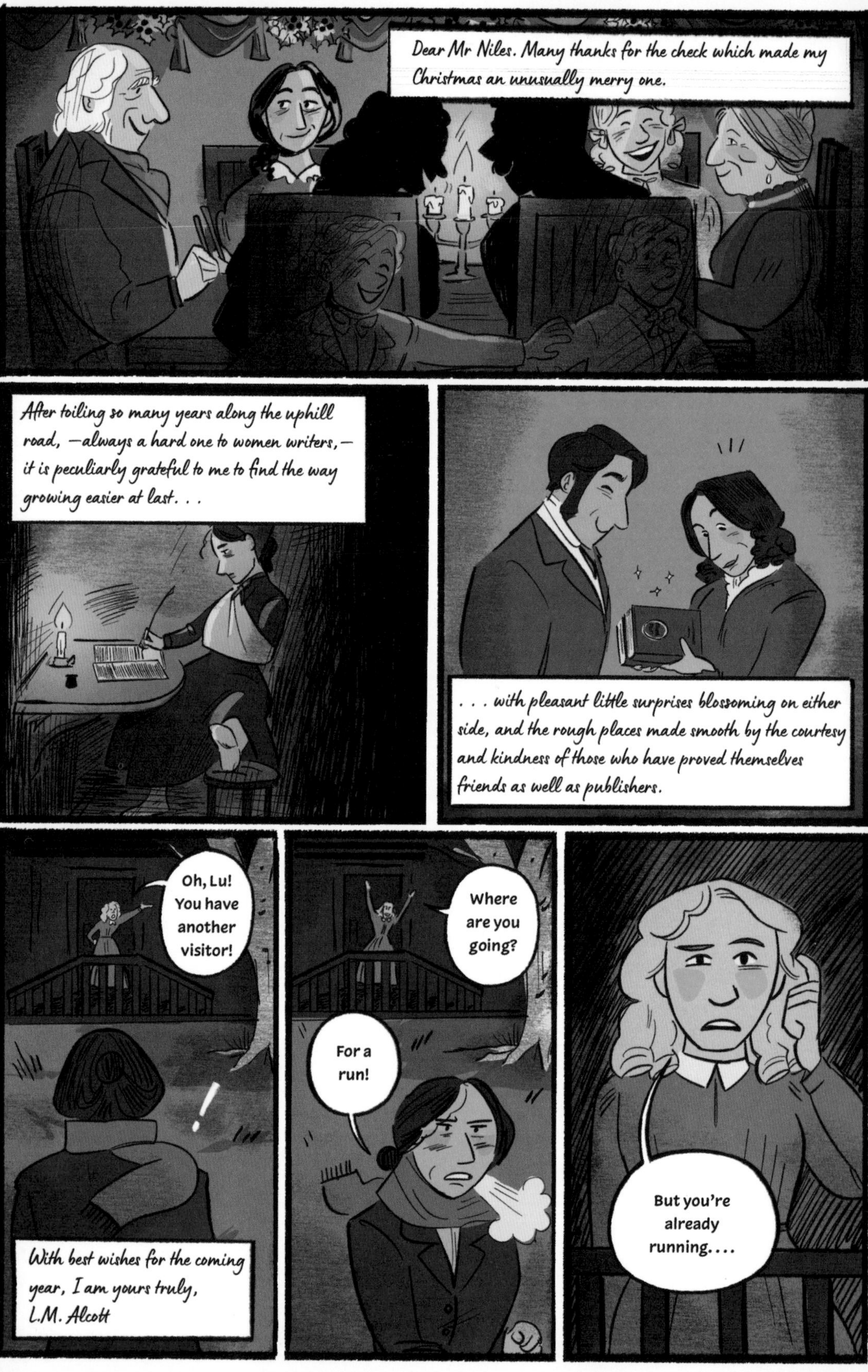

Dear Mr Niles. Many thanks for the check which made my Christmas an unusually merry one.
After toiling so many years along the uphill road, —always a hard one to women writers,— it is peculiarly grateful to me to find the way growing easier at last. . .
. . . with pleasant little surprises blossoming on either side, and the rough places made smooth by the courtesy and kindness of those who have proved themselves friends as well as publishers.
Oh, Lu! You have another visitor!
With best wishes for the coming year, I am yours truly, L.M. Alcott
Where are you going?
For a run!
But you're already running. . . .

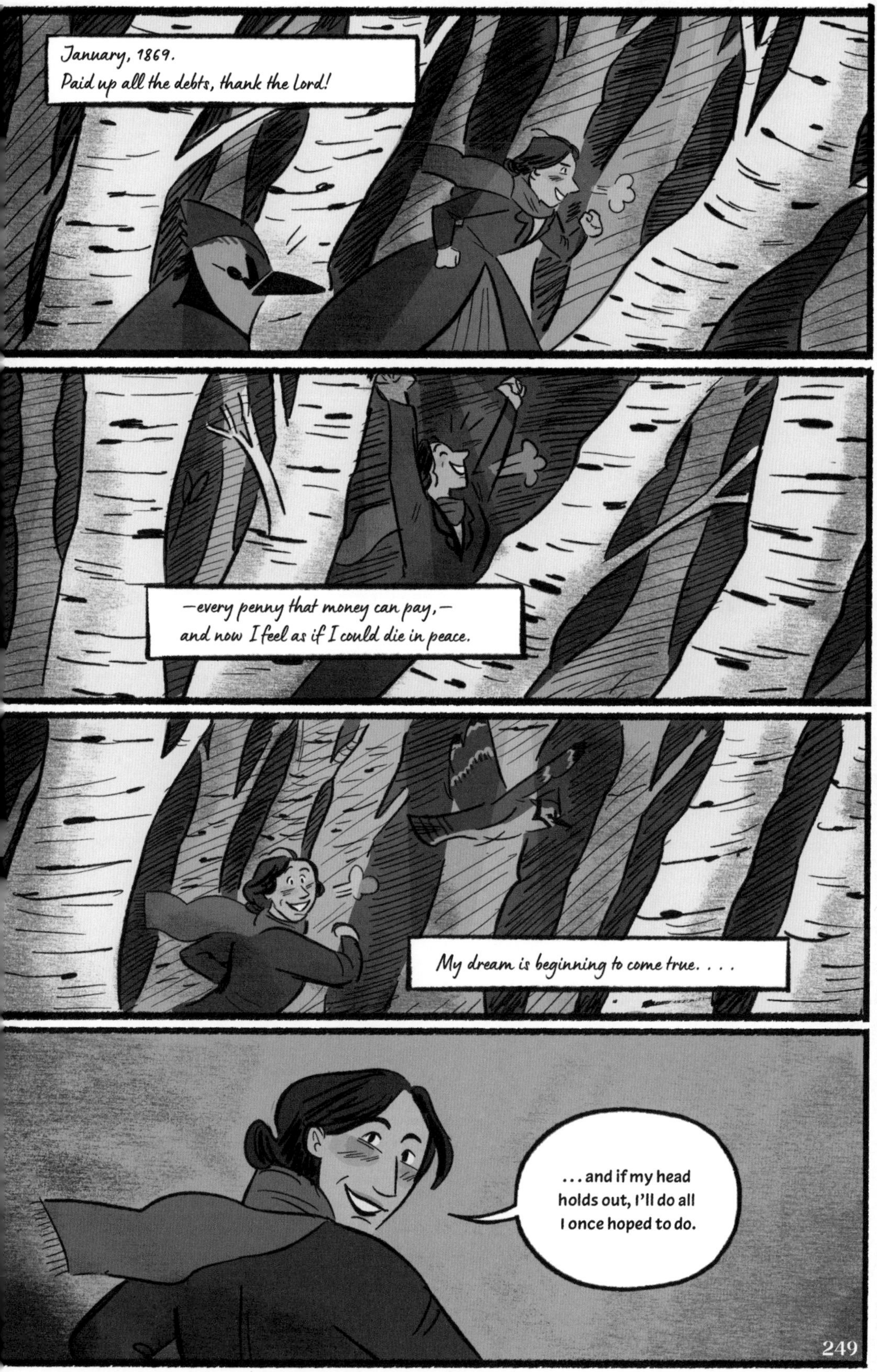
January, 1869.
Paid up all the debts, thank the Lord!
—every penny that money can pay,—
and now I feel as if I could die in peace.
My dream is beginning to come true. . . .
. . . and if my head holds out, I'll do all I once hoped to do.

In 1862, publisher and editor J. T. Fields gave Alcott the sum of forty dollars and some well-meant advice: stop writing and open a school. Years later, after the runaway success of *Little Women*, Alcott returned the money with a note that read: “Once upon a time you lent me forty dollars, kindly saying that I might return them when I made ‘a pot of gold.’ As the miracle has been unexpectedly wrought I wish to fulfill my part of the bargain, & herewith repay my debt with many thanks.”

Stick to your teaching; you can’t write.

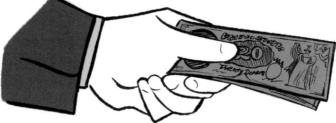

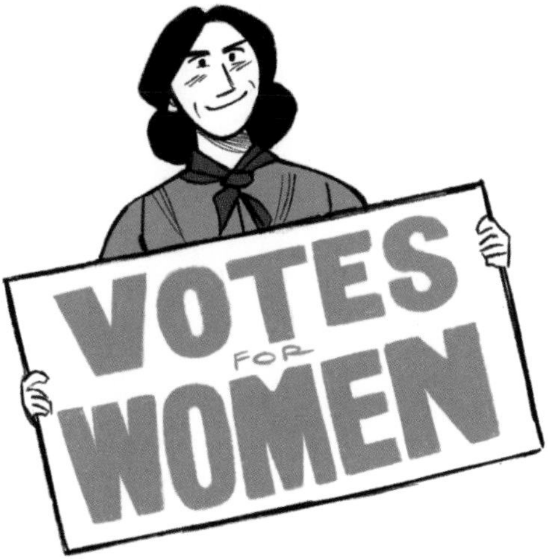
VOTES
FOR
WOMEN

Alcott's mother once declared: "I am seventy-three, but I mean to go to the polls before I die, even if my daughters have to carry me." But she never got the chance, dying just two years before Alcott became the first woman in Concord, Massachusetts, to register to vote in 1879.

SELECTED WORKS:

NOVELS

1865: *Moods*
1867: *The Mysterious Key and What It Opened*
1868: *Little Women or Meg, Jo, Beth and Amy*
1869: *Good Wives* [later published together with *Little Women*]
1870: *An Old Fashioned Girl*
1870: *Will's Wonder Book*
1871: *Little Men: Life at Plumfield with Jo's Boys*
1873: *Work: A Story of Experience*
1875: *Beginning Again, Being a Continuation of Work*
1875: *Eight Cousins or The Aunt-Hill*
1876: *Rose in Bloom: A Sequel to Eight Cousins*
1878: *Under the Lilacs*
1880: *Jack and Jill: A Village Story*
1882: *Proverb Stories*
1886: *Jo's Boys and How They Turned Out: A Sequel to "Little Men"*

CONCLUSION

It's impossible to capture a life in a few short pages. There are facts, of course, but without context, they are simply numbers and dates. What happens between the bullet points is life—the blank spaces, days not described in diaries and barely traced in letters. This book invites you into both worlds: the known and unknowable. It is an introduction, a study of a specific moment in each of our eighteen authors' lives, and an exploration of their motivations, inspirations, and the ties that bind them. There were so many stories we wanted to share, and so many authors we wanted to include, but we decided to focus on those with shared connections. The connections between these women tell us so much—the similarities between their careers; the way they explored the same themes; how they inspired one another; and the overlap with our modern-day experiences of writer's block, financial insecurity, and fights for equality.

Examining why she wrote not only gave us a focal point for these stories, but it also gave us new insights into their writing. Exploring Louisa May Alcott's relationship with money, for example, helped us come to terms with the ending of *Little Women*. Researching Mary Shelley's turbulent teens and experience with motherhood made us reconsider Frankenstein's monster. And by digging into the motivations behind Edith Maude Eaton's earliest works we understand how, by publishing anonymously, she was better able to serve the community she was writing about.

These women led full, rich, and complicated lives, which contained many more stories than we could fit between these pages: tales of love, loss, and financial distress; overseas adventures; and bad decisions. Unlike Mrs. Gaskell, we wish we had space to explore Charlotte Brontë's time in Brussels, and her unrequited love for her tutor. We're fascinated by the years Frances Burney spent living in the court of King George III as second keeper of the robes, or Louisa May Alcott's work as a Civil War nurse and the effect it had on her writing, but we fully realize that each of these could be books of their own. We hope that this is only the start of your journey with them and their writing.

ACKNOWLEDGMENTS

Just as Louisa May Alcott was inspired by *The Life of Charlotte Brontë*, we were inspired by the many scholars and biographers who have come before us. They keep the memories of our favorite authors alive, and we urge you to seek out the intelligent, thoughtful, highly researched work of Anne Boyd Rioux, Devoney Looser, Tara T. Green, Ruth Livesey, Joanna Ortner, Karen Skinazi, Amber Pouliot, Angela Clare, Marlowe Daly, Fiona Sampson, Roberta Wedge, Claire O'Callaghan, Jenny Uglow, Mary Chapman, Claire Harman, Claire Tomalin, Helena Kelley, Melba Boyd, Gloria T. Hull, Jill Liddington, Brenda Maddox, Samantha Ellis, Marlowe Daly, Ann Thwaite, Jan Turnquist, Linda Lear, and Jennie Batchelor.

We also want to thank the literary homes and societies that have helped us along the way: Sally Jastrzebski-Lloyd and all the volunteers at Elizabeth Gaskell's House, the Beatrix Potter Society, the Brontë Parsonage, Chawton House, the British Library, Orchard House, and the George Eliot Fellowship.

Special thanks to Edward A. Wilson, Georges Beauville, and Beth and Joe Krush for their artistic inspiration.

And of course our family and friends for supporting as we follow the footsteps of these great authors. Thanks to John Craig, Sam Pounsberry, Maureen Chapman, Amy Rowbottom, Isabel Greenberg, Sophie Nuttall, Beverly Newman Adams, Audrey Louise Craig, the Bonnets at Dawn Community, and our amazing team at Chronicle Books: Julia Patrick, Juliette Capra, Maggie Edelman, Morgan Guttierez, and Alison Petersen.

SOURCES AND FURTHER READING

CITATIONS

Pages 52–59: Mastectomy letter © Henry W. and Albert A. Berg Collection of English and American Literature, The New York Public Library, Astor, Lenox and Tilden Foundations.

Page 82: Bessie Parks to Elizabeth Parkes, June 10, 1857. Letter provided courtesy of The Mistress and Fellows, Girton College, Cambridge. GCPP Parkes 2/10.

Page 82: Charles Kingsley to ECG, August 4, 1857. Letter provided courtesy of The University of Manchester, John Rylands, MS 730/584, transcribed in SHB, IV, 222–3.

Page 82: Anna Jameson to Bessie Parkes, May 20, 1857. Letter provided courtesy of The Mistress and Fellows, Girton College, Cambridge. GCPP Parkes 6/20.

Page 82: George Henry Lewes to ECG, April 15, 1857. Letter provided courtesy of The University of Manchester, John Rylands MS 731/61, in The George Eliot Letters, ed. G.S Haight (London and New Haven, 1954), II, 316.

Page 247: Louisa May Alcott to Mrs. Woods, July 20, 1875. Letter provided courtesy of Alcott Family Papers, Archives & Research Center, The Trustees of Reservations.

BOOKS

Barker, Juliet. *The Brontës*. Abacus 2010.

Boyd, Melba Joyce. *Discarded Legacy: Politics and Poetics in the Life of Frances E. W. Harper, 1825–1911*. Wayne State University Press, 1994.

Byrne, Paula. *The Real Jane Austen: A Life in Small Things*. HarperPress 2013.

Carpenter, Angelica Shirley. *In the Garden: Essays in Honor of Frances Hodgson Burnett*. Scarecrow Press, 2006.

Chapman, Mary. *Becoming Sui Sin Far: Early Fiction, Journalism, and Travel Writing by Edith Maude Eaton*. McGill-Queen's University Press, 2016.

Cheney, Ednah D., ed. *Louisa May Alcott: Her Life, Letters, and Journals*. Little, Brown, and Company, 1898.

Choma, Anne. *Gentleman Jack: the Real Anne Lister*. Penguin Books, 2019.

Cook, D., and A. Culley. *Women's Life Writing, 1700–1850: Gender, Genre and Authorship*. Palgrave 2012.

Cross, John Walter, ed. *George Eliot's Life, as Related in Her Letters and Journals. Vol. 1–3*, George Eliot. Cambridge University Press, 2010.

Culley, Amy, and Anna M. Fitzer. *Editing Women's Writing (Chawton Studies in Scholarly Editing), 1670–1840*. Routledge 2017.

Davis, Philip. *The Transferred Life of George Eliot*. Oxford University Press, 2017.

Ellis, Samantha. *Take Courage: Anne Brontë and the Art of Life*. Vintage 2018.

Gaskell, Elizabeth Cleghorn. *The Letters of Mrs. Gaskell*. Manchester University Press, 1966.

Gordon, Charlotte. *Romantic Outlaws: the Extraordinary Lives of Mary Wollstonecraft & Mary Shelley*. Random House, 2016.

Gordon, Lyndall. *Outsiders: Five Women Writers Who Changed the World*. Virago 2017.

Harman, Claire. *Fanny Burney: A Biography*. Flamingo 2001.

Hughes, Kathryn. *George Eliot: The Last Victorian*. Fourth Estate, 1999.

Hull, Gloria T., and Alice Dunbar Nelson. *Give Us Each Day: the Diary of Alice Dunbar-Nelson*. W.W. Norton, 1986.

Kelly, Helena. *Jane Austen the Secret Radical*. Icon 2016.

Lear, Linda. *Beatrix Potter: A Life in Nature*. Penguin 2008.

Leigh, William Austen. *Jane Austen: Her Life and Letters, A Family Record*. Symonds Press, 2007.

Liddington, Jill. *Nature's Domain: Anne Lister and the Landscape of Desire*. Pennine Pens, 2003

Maddox, Brenda. *George Elliot in Love*. Palgrave Macmillan, 2011.

Marcus, Julia. *Dared and Done: the Marriage of Elizabeth Barrett and Robert Browning*. Ohio University Press, 1998.

Midorikawa, Emily, and Emma Claire. *A Secret Sisterhood: The Hidden Friendships of Austen, Brontë, Eliot, and Woolf*. Aurum Press 2017.

Moers, Ellen. *Literary Women*. Doubleday & Co., 1972.

O'Callaghan, Claire. *Emily Brontë Reappraised: a View from the Twenty-First Century*. Saraband, 2018.

Powell, Kerry. *Women and Victorian Theatre*. Cambridge University Press, 1997.

Russ, Joanna. *How to Suppress Women's Writing*. University of Texas Press 2018.

Sampson, Fiona. *In Search of Mary Shelley*. Pegasus Books, 2019.

Showalter, Elaine. *A Literature of Their Own: British Women Writers, from Charlotte Brontë to Doris Lessing*. Princeton University Press 1977.

Spencer, Jane. *The Rise of the Woman Novelist: from Aphra Behn to Jane Austen*. Blackwell, 1993.

Stern, Madeleine. *Louisa May Alcott: A Biography*. Random House 1996.

Stevens, Nell. *Mrs Gaskell and Me: Two Women, Two Love Stories, Two Centuries Apart*. Picador 2018.

Taylor, Judy. *Beatrix Potter's Letters: A selection by Judy Taylor*. Penguin 1989.

Thwaite, Ann. *Beyond the Secret Garden: The Life of Frances Hodgson Burnett*. Bello 2014.

Tomalin, Claire. *The Life and Death of Mary Wollstonecraft*. Penguin Books, 1992.

Uglow, Jenny. *Elizabeth Gaskell*. Faber and Faber Limited 1993.

ACADEMIC ARTICLES

Chapman, Mary. "Finding Edith Eaton." *Legacy*, 29, no. 2 (2012): 263–69. JSTOR, www.jstor.org/stable/10.5250/legacy.29.2.0263.

Diana, Vanessa Holford. "Biracial/Bicultural Identity in the Writings of Sui Sin Far." *MELUS*, 26, no. 2 (2001): 159–86. JSTOR, www.jstor.org/stable/3185523.

Epstein, Julia L. "Writing the Unspeakable: Fanny Burney's Mastectomy and the Fictive Body." *Representations*, no. 16 (1986): 131–66. JSTOR, www.jstor.org/stable/2928516.

Fergus, Jan. "'The Whinnying of Harpies?': Humor in Jane Austen's Letters." *Persuasions*, http://www.jasna.org/persuasions/printed/number27/fergus.pdf

Greenwood, John. "'Our Happy Days in Rome': The Gaskell-Norton Correspondence." *The Gaskell Journal*, 28 (2014).

Liddington, Jill. "Anne Lister of Shibden Hall, Halifax (1791–1840): Her Diaries and the Historians." *History Workshop* 35 (1993): 45–77. www.jstor.org/stable/4289206.

Maibor, Carolyn R. "Upstairs, Downstairs, and In-Between: Louisa May Alcott on Domestic Service." *The New England Quarterly*, 79, no. 1 (2006): 65–91. JSTOR, www.jstor.org/stable/20474412.

Messer, Persis B. "A Bibliographic Essay: Beatrix Potter: Classic Novelist of the Nursery." *Elementary English*, 45, no. 3 (1968): 325–33. JSTOR, www.jstor.org/stable/41386316

Mitchell, Barbara. "The Biographical Process: Writing the Lives of Charlotte Brontë" Phd thesis, 1994.

Rivas, Sarah. Defining Nineteenth-Century Womanhood: The Cult of Marmee and Little Women. *Scientia et Humanitas*, [S.l.], 4 (June 2016): 53-64. ISSN 2470-8178. Available at: https://libjournals.mtsu.edu/index.php/scientia/article/view/626.

Solberg, S. E. "Sui Sin Far/Edith Eaton: First Chinese-American Fictionist." *MELUS*, 8, no. 1 (1981): 27–39. JSTOR, www.jstor.org/stable/467366.

Thomson, Keith Stewart. "Marginalia: Beatrix Potter, Conservationist." *American Scientist*, 95, no. 3 (2007): 210–12. JSTOR, www.jstor.org/stable/27858956.

Twain, Mark, and S. L. Clemens (Mark Twain). "Concerning Copyright. An Open Letter to the Register of Copyrights." *The North American Review*, 180, no. 578 (1905): 1–8. JSTOR, www.jstor.org/stable/25105337.

Wangensteen, Owen H. *Bulletin of the History of Medicine*, 51, no. 4 (1977): pp. 632–635. JSTOR, www.jstor.org/stable/44450476.

Yellin, Jean Fagan. "From Success to Experience: Louisa May Alcott's Work." *The Massachusetts Review*, 21, no. 3 (1980): 527–39. JSTOR, www.jstor.org/stable/25089071.

AUTHOR BIOS

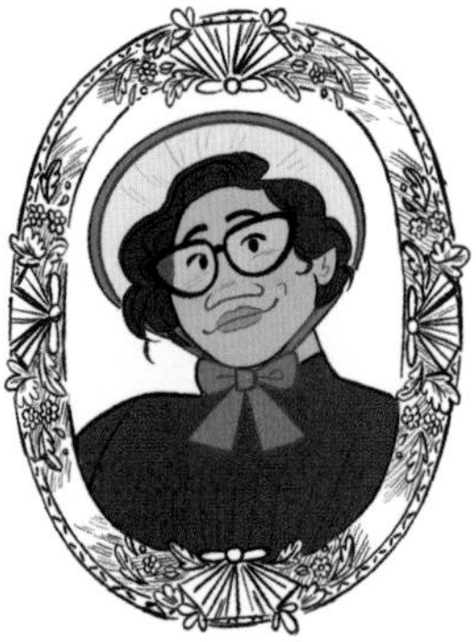

Lauren Burke is a writer of comics and children's books from Chicago, Illinois. As a young girl, she fell in love with storytelling after reading *The Secret Garden*, by Frances Hodgson Burnett, and then again after reading *Little Women*, by Louisa May Alcott, and yet again after reading *Jane Eyre*, by Charlotte Brontë. When she is not co-hosting the podcast Bonnets at Dawn, she can be found in her garden or at a literary home, asking questions.

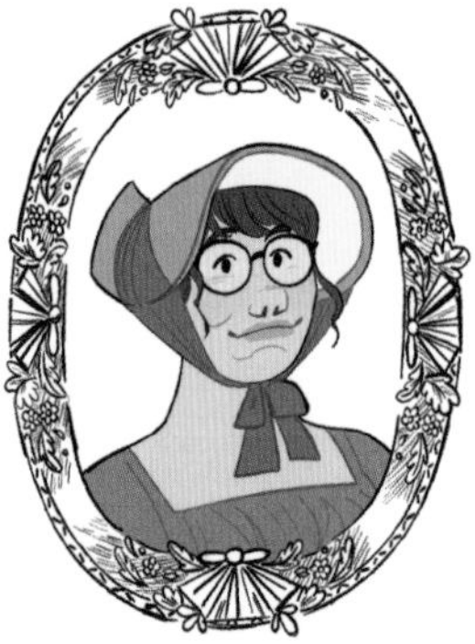

Hannah K. Chapman is a writer and podcaster living in Bristol, England. She is one half of Bonnets at Dawn and is the creator of the award-nominated anthology series *Comic Book Slumber Party*. She holds a master's degree in transnational writing, once worked at the Jane Austen Centre, and her two favorite things are sausage rolls and castles.

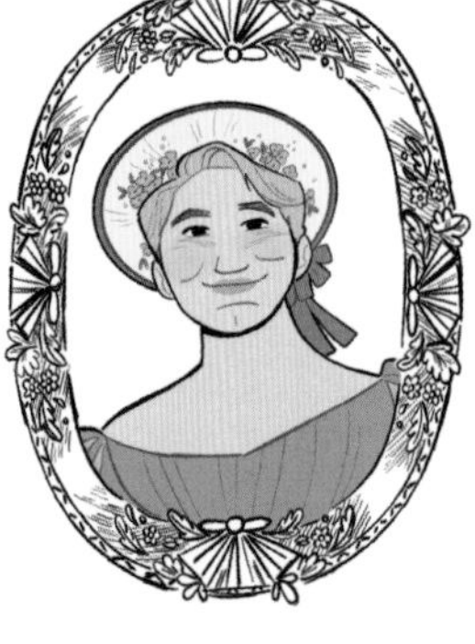

Kaley Bales is a freelance illustrator and storyteller from California. She became enamored with *Jane Eyre* at a young age, and has been hooked on gothic horror and female writers ever since. Kaley hopes to one day visit North Lees Hall in Hathersage, thought to be Charlotte Brontë's inspiration for Thornfield Hall, and maybe even spot a ghost or two while there!